The History of Anglo-Japanese Relations, 1600–2000

The History of Anglo-Japanese Relations, 1600–2000

General Editors: **Chihiro Hosoya** and **Ian Nish**

The five volumes which make up the series *The History of Anglo-Japanese Relations, 1600–2000*, cover the relationship between these two island communities from the first contacts at the start of the seventeenth century through to the end of the second millennium. While the studies cover the Anglo-Japanese relationship over the past four centuries, they tend to concentrate on features of the past 150 years. The volumes have been prepared independently over the past five years by Japanese and non-Japanese scholars who have met to debate and discuss their papers. These studies analyse the rise and fall of these relations in four dimensions: political and diplomatic; economic and business; military and naval; and social and cultural.

Titles in the series:

Volume 1:   THE POLITICAL-DIPLOMATIC DIMENSION, 1600–1930
Ian Nish and Yoichi Kibata (*editors*)

Volume 2:   THE POLITICAL-DIPLOMATIC DIMENSION, 1931–2000
Ian Nish and Yoichi Kibata (*editors*)

Volume 3:   THE MILITARY-NAVAL DIMENSION
Ian Gow and Yoichi Hirama (*editors*)

Volume 4:   ECONOMIC AND BUSINESS RELATIONS
Janet Hunter and Shinya Sugiyama (*editors*)

Volume 5:   SOCIAL AND CULTURAL PERSPECTIVES
Gordon Daniels and Chushichi Tsuzuki (*editors*)

The History of Anglo-Japanese Relations, 1600–2000
Series Standing Order ISBN 0-333-79224-6
(*outside North America only*)

The titles in this series can be ordered through your bookseller or, in case of difficulty, by writing to us at the address below with your name and address, the title of the series, the title(s) you wish to order and the ISBN quoted above.

Customer Services Department, Macmillan Distribution Ltd, Houndmills, Basingstoke, Hampshire RG21 6XS, England

The History of Anglo-Japanese Relations 1600–2000

Volume 5
Social and Cultural Perspectives

Edited by

Gordon Daniels and Chushichi Tsuzuki

First published 2002 by
PALGRAVE MACMILLAN
Houndmills, Basingstoke, Hampshire RG21 6XS and
175 Fifth Avenue, New York, N.Y. 10010
Companies and representatives throughout the world

PALGRAVE MACMILLAN is the global academic imprint of the Palgrave
Macmillan division of St. Martin's Press, LLC and of Palgrave Macmillan Ltd.
Macmillan® is a registered trademark in the United States, United Kingdom
and other countries. Palgrave is a registered trademark in the European Union
and other countries.

ISBN 0–333–79195–9

This book is printed on paper suitable for recycling and made from fully
managed and sustained forest sources.

A catalogue record for this book is available from the British Library.

A catalog record for this book is available from the Library of Congress.

10   9   8   7   6   5   4   3   2   1
11   10   09   08   07   06   05   04   03   02

Printed and bound in Great Britain by
Antony Rowe Ltd, Chippenham and Eastbourne

Contents

List of Table and Figures

Table

Figures

List of Plates

1 Illustration of the Emperor's reception of the Dutch Minister at the Shishinden, Kyoto, 26 March 1868, by Hiroshima Koho, 1931 (*reproduced with kind permission of the Seitoku kinen kaigakan, Tokyo, Japan*)
2 A foldout reception of Hiroshige, *Yodogawa* (c. 1834), Francis Hawks, *Narrative of an Expedition of an American Squadron to the China Seas and Japan*, Washington DC, 1856 (*reproduced with the kind permission of the British Library*)
3 A reproduction of Hiroshige, *Hoki* from his series *Rokjuyoshu meisho zue* (Famous places from more than 60 provinces) (1853–56), Sherard Osborn, *Japanese Fragments*, London, 1861 (*reproduced with the kind permission of the British Library*)
4 J. B. Waring (ed.), *Masterpieces of Industrial Art & Sculpture at the International Exhibition*, London, 1862 (*reproduced by permission of Roy W. Norman of Timeframe LSC International*)
5 Walter Crane, *One, Two, Buckle My Shoe* from the *Sixpenny Toy Series*, London: George Routledge & Sons, 1869 (*reproduced with the kind permission of Routledge, London*)
6 *The Geisha*, 1896, sheet music cover, John Culme Collection (*reproduced with the kind permission of the British Library*)
7 Theodore Roussel, *A Girl Reading*, 1886–87, oil painting (*reproduced with the kind permission of Tate, London, 2000*)
8 Front cover of the exhibition catalogue, *Art Treasures of Japan*, The Victoria and Albert Museum, London: Arts Council, 1958 (*reproduced with the kind permission of the Arts Council of England*)
9 Yusaka Kamekura, poster for the Tokyo Olympics, 1964 (*reproduced with the kind permission of the IOC/Olympic Museum Collections, Lausanne, Switzerland*)

List of Contributors and their Affiliations

Christopher Aldous (*King Alfred's College, Winchester*)
James Babb (*University of Newcastle*)
John Breen (*School of Oriental and African Studies, University of London*)
Philip Charrier (*University of Regina, Canada*)
Andrew Cobbing (*Kyushu University, Fukuoka*)
Gordon Daniels (*University of Sheffield*)
Kei Imai (*Daito Bunka University, Tokyo*)
A. Hamish Ion (*Royal Military College of Canada, Kingston, Ontario*)
Yuko Kikuchi (*The Chelsea College of Art and Design, The London Institute*)
Kazuhiko Kondo (*Tokyo University*)
Toshio Kusamitsu (*Tokyo University*)
Takao Matsumura (*Keio University, Tokyo*)
Kevin McCormick (*University of Sussex*)
Tamotsu Nishizawa (*Hitotsubashi University, Tokyo*)
Jon Pardoe (*formerly University of Newcastle*)
Brian W. F. Powell (*Keble College, Oxford*)
David Rycroft (*Konan University, Kobe*)
Susan C. Townsend (*University of Nottingham*)
Chushichi Tsuzuki (*formerly of Hitotsubashi University, Tokyo*)
Toshio Watanabe (*The Chelsea College of Art and Design, The London Institute*)
Mark Williams (*University of Leeds*)

Foreword

We write as chief co-ordinators of the Anglo-Japanese History Project, a Project for studying the history of the relationship of these two countries from 1600 to 2000. The Project originated in the statement of 31 August 1994 by Mr Murayama Tomiichi, on behalf of the coalition cabinet which he led. In this he announced the setting up of the Peace, Friendship and Exchange Initiative which would begin in 1995, the fiftieth anniversary of the end of the Asia-Pacific War. One part of the Initiative consisted of support for researchers in order 'to enable everyone to face squarely the facts of history'. The relationship between Japan and Britain was deemed to be one of the areas which came within the Initiative.

In order to implement this policy decision, the Japanese government announced that it would 'support the compilation of a series of volumes forming a comprehensive history of the UK–Japanese Relationship (Nichi-Ei kankeishi)'. The Project was to be conducted by researchers from both Japan and the United Kingdom and to be funded over five years by a sub-vention administered by the Japan Society, London. Project offices were opened in London and Tokyo.

After preliminary discussions in London and Tokyo in 1995, it was agreed that the Project would aim at conducting academic research and publishing volumes covering four central fields in Anglo-Japanese historical relations. Co-ordinators from the Japanese and British sides were appointed as follows:

The Political-Diplomatic Dimension (2 volumes)
[Yoichi Kibata and Ian Nish]
The Military-Naval Dimension (1 volume)
[Yoichi Hirama and Ian Gow]
The Economic-Business Dimension (1 volume)
[Shinya Sugiyama and Janet Hunter]
The Social-Cultural Dimension (1 volume)
[Chushichi Tsuzuki and Gordon Daniels]

These co-ordinators, in turn, selected experts in these fields and commissioned them to conduct research and write chapters for publication.

The first fruits of this research were discussed by both sides at workshops held at the Civil Service College, Sunningdale, UK (July 1996), Shonan Village Centre, Hayama, Japan (September 1997) and Stephenson Hall, Sheffield University (August 1998). The Social-Cultural section held its own workshop aat International House, Tokyo (April 1999). On these occasions draft chapters were presented by the contributors; and the discussion which ensued led to the revision of manuscripts.

Discussion at the workshops pointed out the positive aspects of the relationship between the two countries which has been strong enough to survive setbacks and even disasters. Just as Britain's naval actions at Shimonoseki and Kagoshima in the 1860s were followed by the years of the Anglo-Japanese Alliance (1902–23), so the dark years culminating in the Asia-Pacific war have been followed by the broadly favourable development of bilateral relations over the last fifty years, strengthened by wider common interests and deeper and more extensive exchanges in every field of activity. We recognize that there are problems outstanding between the two countries and hope that this series will make some contribution to their solution by clarifying some of the issues and will help to promote better understanding.

We as chief co-ordinators would like to thank the contributors who devoted much time and effort to the Project. Thanks are due to the Japan Society (and the Tokyo office of the Project) for arranging its financial and administrative aspects. Finally, we are grateful for the co-operation of the officials of the Japanese Embassy, London, and the Japanese Ministry of Foreign Affairs. They have made it clear from the start that they would not take any part in the publication programme itself. What appears in these volumes is the work of independent scholars.

In conclusion, we should say that the joint Project, which has been administered by a Steering Committee in London, presided over by Sir Sydney Giffard, and an Advisory Committee in Japan, has, since its inauguration in 1995, been conducted most harmoniously.

CHIHIRO HOSOYA and IAN NISH
2002

Preface: International History – From Diplomacy to Culture

Gordon Daniels and Chushichi Tsuzuki

For much of the twentieth century international history was viewed as little more than the history of relations between national governments. These restrictive academic boundaries were perhaps appropriate in a century when issues of war and peace, Cold War and coexistence dominated the inter-relationships of most major states. Yet, with the ending of the Cold War, and the reappearance of economic and technological change as major determinants of social development, broader definitions of international relations have become accepted. The roles of national and multinational corporations, voluntary groupings, international organizations and communications networks have been increasingly incorporated into the study of inter-state and inter-national relations. Furthermore, a new appreciation of the importance of culture and imagination in human conduct has further widened perceptions of international links and frictions. Mass transport, new information streams and pluralistic politics have added further layers of sophistication to the scholarly study of international relations.

The Japanese, British and Canadian essays which follow adopt a series of thematic approaches to the exploration of the history of social and cultural relations between Japan and Britain. Together they provide a series of samplers of current research; and explore beyond earlier definitions of Anglo-Japanese relations. It is hoped that these new approaches to relations between *whole societies* rather than between *governments* will provide signposts for further research, and contribute to a fuller understanding of the history of Anglo-Japanese frictions, interactions and mutual co-operation.

Acknowledgements

The editors wish to thank the Japan Society and Professor Tim Wright of the School of East Asian Studies in the University of Sheffield for their help and support in the preparation of this volume. They are particularly grateful to Dr Philip Charrier for his work in the initial stages of the project, and to Mrs Susie Tranter for her devoted efforts as editorial and research assistant. Without her support the work could not have been completed.

Note on Japanese Names

The names of all Japanese contributors and Japanese authors of works in English are given in the Western form – with personal names preceding family names. Japanese authors of books and articles in Japanese are cited in the Japanese form with family names first.

Part I
Introduction

1
Elites, Governments and Citizens: Some British Perceptions of Japan, 1850–2000

Gordon Daniels

In the nineteenth and twentieth centuries British perceptions of Japan have been moulded and remoulded by complex and rapidly changing circumstances. The transformation of Japan and the transformation of Britain have shaped both realities and perceptions, while government cultural policies, developments in communications, and the spread of popular education have all been potent influences on British ideas. This essay will outline some major shifts in British perceptions of nineteenth- and twentieth-century Japan, and suggest the many forces which have created and modified elite and popular attitudes.

In the years preceding the American opening of Japan in 1854 British commentators, writing for the aristocracy and rising middle class, already demonstrated a significant interest in Japan's condition. In London and Edinburgh news of the American naval expedition stimulated much writing on Japanese history and society. At this time no significant Victorian writer had visited Japan or studied its language; consequently all authors relied upon earlier European accounts as their major sources of information. Virtually all eighteenth- and early-nineteenth-century European writing had described Japan's relatively stable condition under the Tokugawa shoguns. Hence admiration for Japanese stability and social achievements was often expressed in British articles and reviews. A typical exponent of such views was the *Times* journalist Alexander Knox who contributed a major review article 'Japan' to the *Edinburgh Review* in October 1852.[1] In the survey Knox wrote 'Everything is so immutable in this empire that things remain at the present in Japan pretty much as they were in Kaempfer's time' (circa 1690).[2] Knox did criticize Japanese 'licentiousness' and 'cruelty', and resorted to biblical and medieval European metaphors to explain Japanese institutions, but overall his views were strongly positive. He saw Japan as distinct from other Asian societies and concluded 'amidst Asiatics the Japanese stand supreme. Can the tribes of India, or the teeming swarms of China for a moment contest the palm with the chivalrous Japanese . . . We can find no nation or tribe in history with whom we might compare the Japanese, but by an effort of misplaced ingenuity'.[3]

By 1859 America's treaty with the Shogun's government had been signed, and Admiral Stirling's first Anglo-Japanese agreement had been followed by the Earl of Elgin's more significant treaty.[4] These Anglo-Japanese diplomatic contacts soon stimulated the writing of popular and serious accounts of contemporary Japan, all of which were based on direct experience. Within a year of Elgin's mission to the Shogun's capital *Blackwoods Edinburgh Magazine* had published a series of articles by Captain Sherard Osborn who had accompanied Elgin on his flagship HMS *Furious*. Despite Osborn's direct experience of Japan, his descriptions echoed Knox's romantic and idyllic tone. A typical passage proclaimed 'Japan shows signs of a high order of civilisation, energy and wealth, which modern Greece decidedly does not exhibit, whatever it did in olden days'.[5] Of particular significance was Osborn's tribute to the intelligence of Japanese officials and their adaptability:

> When one saw how full of intelligence all the higher classes in Japan were – how capable of appreciating the skill and mechanism employed in any of the marvels of scientific labour Great Britain contains. . . . it was a subject of regret that a screw schooner. . . . should have been the only specimen sent of our mechanical or manufacturing skill.[6]

Osborn's experience of Japan may have been the main inspiration for his series of articles but Toshio Yokoyama has suggested that Osborn's cousin did much to edit the manuscripts to satisfy the publisher's desire for a pleasant travelogue which would attract non-specialist readers.[7]

In 1859 Osborn's work was followed by Laurence Oliphant's *Narrative of the Earl of Elgin's Mission to China and Japan in the years 1857, 1858 and 1859*. Oliphant had served as Elgin's secretary and experienced Japan before the onset of anti-foreign violence and arson. Even more significant was his ignorance of the special prior preparation of cities and citizens for the visit of British envoys.[8] Equally influential in the shaping of Oliphant's work was his own awareness of the likely success of a rose-tinted travelogue in attracting readers. The attractions of the book were further enriched by the inclusion of many coloured illustrations. Like Osborn, Oliphant concentrated on many positive aspects of Japanese life and administration. He wrote 'the whole system of municipal government in the cities of Japan, seems very perfect', while he praised the Japanese education system with particular enthusiasm, claiming 'in that respect at all events . . . they are decidedly in advance of us'.[9] Oliphant was often critical of British society and this observation may have reflected his awareness of British educational inadequacies, a decade before the 1870 Education Act.

With the opening of British diplomatic and commercial relations with Japan in 1859 anti-foreign violence became a serious threat to British diplomats and merchants. As a result the next major work on Japan provided a darker and more complex analysis. Rutherford Alcock's *The Capital of the Tycoon*, published in 1862, was an account of the author's three-year term as Britain's first diplomatic representative in Edo. Alcock had travelled more widely in the Japanese interior than previous Englishmen and he admired the cleanliness of country villages. However, his experience of political killings and samurai attacks on foreigners (including the wounding of Laurence Oliphant) led him to view Japan as a feudal society. He wrote 'with the Japanese we take a step backward some ten centuries to live over again the feudal days'.[10] More specifically he likened Japanese political murders to 'scenes of daily bloodshed and murder when Guelphs and Ghibellines fought and slew each other'.[11] Alcock's depiction of Japan as a country of primitive violence and natural disasters was one which would recur in later British accounts of modern Japan.

Despite Alcock's direct experience of Japan, his knowledge of the Japanese language was flawed and limited. In contrast the refined linguistic skills of the ex-diplomat Algernon Mitford led him to a profound empathy with Japan, and a sophisticated understanding which marked a new stage in British perceptiveness. In articles which he contributed to the *Cornhill Magazine* in 1869 Mitford wrote of samurai not as the threatening swordsmen who appeared in Alcock's work but as 'gentlemen' who appeared analogous to British aristocrats. What is more Mitford's eyewitness account of a death by ritual suicide placed emphasis on the 'extreme dignity and punctiliousness' of the occasion rather than its violence and inhumanity.[12] Perhaps such attitudes reflected the increasing emphasis on stoicism and self-control in British public schools and the armed services.

The overthrow of the Shogun's administration in 1868 and the establishment of the Meiji state soon stimulated new appraisals of Japanese politics and society. Indeed, the new government's dramatic series of social, economic and political reforms impressed both experts and globe-trotting visitors. In 1872 Mitford, who had celebrated traditional Japan, now wrote 'Four years ago we were still in the middle ages – we have leapt at a bound into the nineteenth century – out of poetry into plain useful prose.'[13] In the same year the scholar-diplomat W. G. Aston adopted a similar tone in *Macmillans Magazine* and commented 'one edict followed another, many privileges of the upper-class were abolished. . . . and the lower class were raised in position . . . it seems as if a sudden passion had seized up the people to pull down and abolish everything that was old'.[14] Similarly after a short visit, the radical MP Sir Charles Dilke, who had no linguistic expertise, also sensed the melodrama of Japanese change, stating 'What can be, or ever has been, in the history of the world, more singular than the combination of the extreme democracy of spirit of its government with the blind tradition that is personified in the Mikado?'[15]

Rapid architectural and social change was manifestly evident in the townscapes of Tokyo and major ports, but British evaluations of Japanese modernization were also shaped by actions of the Meiji government designed to influence western minds and media.

In 1879 the Liberal MP Sir E. J. Reed, who had designed warships for Japan's new navy, was invited to Japan by the Meiji government as part of a deliberate programme to gain overseas support for treaty revision. Having received generous official hospitality it is hardly surprising that Reed's two-volume work *Japan*, which he wrote on his return, was fulsome in its praise of the current regime.[16] Reed celebrated Japan's supposedly careful pace of change, claiming that its government had resolved 'to make forward neither too swiftly for the peace and security of the nation, nor too slowly for the rapid development of those representative institutions, which, as they know, form the surest basis for internal tranquillity and external respect'.[17]

In contrast, Isabella Bird, the first British women writer to visit Japan, produced a remarkably frank travelogue, *Unbeaten Tracks in Japan*. In 1878 she travelled long distances in Northern Honshu and Hokkaido, areas which were distant from the prosperous towns and villages of the Kanto and Kansai. These northern regions were economically backward, and may have suffered governmental neglect following their support for the Shogun in the civil war of 1868–69. No one could deny Miss Bird's courage or the kindness of her Japanese guide, but her travels would have been impossible without the support of British diplomats in securing a passport for her journeys. These officials may also have seen her as a informal gatherer of useful intelligence. Miss Bird claimed to present a 'faithful picture of peasant life' and dwelt much upon poverty and sickness.[18] In a typical passage she wrote: 'It is painful to see the prevalence of such repulsive maladies as scabies, scald head, ringworm, sore eye and unwholesome looking eruptions, and fully thirty per cent of the village people are badly seamed with small pox.'[19] At a place recorded as 'Kuruma toge' she commented: 'The crowd was filthy and squalid beyond description. Why should the "quiver" of poverty be so very full? One asks as one looks at the swarm of gentle naked . . . children, born to . . . hard toil, to be like their parents, devoured by vermin and pressed hard for tax.'[20] Despite her chronicle of poverty and suffering Miss Bird recognized the good intentions of the Meiji government. Much of what she saw clearly illustrated 'the difficulties which the government has to encounter in its endeavour to raise masses of people as deficient as these are in some of the first requirements of civilization'.[21]

By 1889 Japan was not only served by numerous steamship lines but the fans, prints and lacquerware which she exported had contributed to a widespread view in Britain of Japan as a land of delicate exotic beauty, a view which was expressed to some extant in the Gilbert and Sullivan operetta *The*

Mikado.[22] This view was also conveyed in part, by Rudyard Kipling in his published 'letters' from Japan which he wrote in 1889.

Kipling's family links with the artist Burne-Jones and the Arts and Crafts socialist William Morris probably contributed to his sympathetic view of traditional Japanese dress, pottery and design. However, his long residence in British-ruled India made his evaluation of an *independent* Asian country particularly complex. Kipling's positive responses to Japan's daily life and scenery were also helped by the existence of comfortable western-style hotels, English-language guidebooks and his reading of E. J. Reed's pro-Japanese work; but his lack of linguistic knowledge contributed to very questionable judgements.[23] At his most complimentary he wrote: 'Japan is a great people. Her masons play with stone, her carpenters with wood, her smiths with iron, and her artists with life, death and all the eye can take in.'[24]

However, Kipling was deeply averse to Japan's headlong westernization and as a stern conservative deplored any moves in a liberal political direction. Such views were probably strengthened by his observation of Japan's current political instability. He commented:

> A constitution is the worst thing in the world for a people who are blessed with souls above the average. It makes them vote; it makes them talk about politics, it makes them edit newspapers and start factories . . . the first demand of the artistic temperament is mundane uncertainty.[25]

The 1880s saw further visits to Japan by British admirers of Japanese landscape, craft and design; but by 1894 Japan's successful economic and military development had stimulated a major innovation in British interpretations of Japan.[26] In 1887 and 1892 Lord Curzon visited Tokyo, and in 1894 he published a major political and diplomatic analysis *Problems of the Far East*. Curzon had already established himself as a published authority on *Russia in Central Asia* and *Persia and the Persian Question* and had served in the India Office. Furthermore his status secured him the help of British diplomats during his visit. The Japanese government's ambitious programme of publishing reports and statistics in English were further aids to his purposeful inquiries. The seriousness of this author's intent was clear from his opening statement 'There will be nothing in these pages of the Japan of temples, tea-houses and bric-a-brac, that infinitesimal segment of the national existence which the traveller is so prone to mistake for the whole'.[27] Rather Curzon sought to explore 'the effects of a nation still in pupilage to assume the manners of a full grown man'. This author was not uncritical of many features of Japanese politics, but he was surprisingly willing to acknowledge Japanese virtues and see similarities between problems in London and Tokyo. During Curzon's stay conflicts between the government and the newly formed Diet were often close to deadlock but he interpreted these difficulties as somewhat akin to the conflict between the Lords and the Commons in Britain.[28] More specifically he likened Ito Hirobumi's government to 'a Whig cabinet, composed of the great Whig families, the Cavendishes and the Russells of modern Japan'.[29] Following Japan's victory over China in 1895, Curzon made some amendments to his first edition, but his comments remained sympathetic and restrained. Of Japan's future he wrote 'Endowed not merely with an intelligent and enterprising people but with ample riches – there is scarcely any limit that need be set within a given area, to the commercial expansion of Japan.'[30] Perhaps conscious of the shared interests of an Imperial Britain and a rising Japan in resisting Russian expansion, Curzon was careful to compliment Japan's current rulers on their 'temperate self-restraint' and 'liberal sentiments' before urging upon them 'a friendly understanding with China, interested like herself in keeping at a distance . . . the Muscovite from the north'.[31]

In the first years of the twentieth century Britain's overseas policies and domestic institutions were objects of widespread criticism and reappraisal. Such controversies were given additional intensity by the growth of popular newspapers and the electorate's increased interest in political rivalries and international conflict. The belief that German and Russian expansion threatened Britain's imperial position contributed to the signing of the Anglo-Japanese Alliance in 1902. Fear of German, French and American commercial competition generated a major debate on educational reform and national efficiency. Within this Henry Dyer played a vocal and energetic role. As a young man Dyer had served as the first principal of the Imperial College of Engineering in Tokyo, an institution which pioneered many aspects of engineering education. Enthused by memories of this experience, Dyer published *Dai Nippon, the Britain of the East. A Study in National Evolution* in 1904. This work clearly stated that 'Britain should not be above learning a few lessons from Japan'.[32] More specifically (unconsciously echoing Oliphant's opinions in the 1850s) he noted 'the educational arrangements of Japan are very complete'.[33] Dyer continued 'Those who have had the advantage of them have been fitted to take an active and intelligent part in the great developments which have taken place'.[34] This writer was impressed by Japanese forms of practical education but he was also inspired by what he saw as its psychological or spiritual basis. He concluded

> The chief lesson to be learnt from Japan is the need for a truly national spirit for the accomplishment of great ends . . . Our greatest need is a conscious national aim to which all our efforts would be constantly directed, and to which the latest developments of science would be efficiently applied.[35]

In sections of his work Dyer exaggerated the self-sacrifice, self-control and idealism of the Japanese people, but this is hardly surprising. He retained friendly links with many of his ex-students in Japan and Japan's growing strength was a material reality. Furthermore the creation of the Anglo-Japanese alliance had endorsed Japan's claim to be regarded as a disciplined and successful modern state. Even more significant was Dyer's reliance on English-language materials, many of which were provided by Japanese government officials on Japanophile westerners. Among his most helpful informants Dyer singled out Dr Sakatomi, the Vice-Minister of Finance, who supplied 'all the most important Government publications', and 'my old colleague Captain Brinkley editor of "The Japan Daily Mail".'[36]

From the signing of the Anglo-Japanese Alliance the output of English-language sources from Japanese official agencies increased. Furthermore Japanese writers such as Nitobe Inazo produced works on Japan which sought to evoke favourable responses amongst British readers.[37] Ayako Hotta-Lister has also suggested that the Japanese Foreign Ministry may have given financial support to books which were, ostensibly, commercial publications.[38] Some of these volumes could also serve a second purpose, for they fitted well with the current enthusiasm for the reform of British institutions. The notion of Japan as a possible template for reform received yet further justification from Japan's victory over Tsarist Russia in 1905. A typical contribution to this flow of publications was Alfred Stead's *Great Japan: a Study of National Efficiency*. Stead had travelled widely and was a warm enthusiast for the Anglo-Japanese Alliance.[39] Like other books of this genre Stead's work drew heavily upon books and articles by Japanese authors which had been published in English. Many of these writers, such as Ito Hirobumi and Okuma Shigenobu, were members of the newly created Meiji aristocracy, and their titles 'Marquis' and 'Count' probably gave their words particular resonance in Edwardian society.[40] Stead interwove lengthy quotations from such sources with his own uncritical assessments of Japan's history and recent progress.

He paralleled other Japanophile writers in seeing 'Bushido' and the comprehensive and overwhelming patriotism of the Japanese as the stimuli which had enabled them to achieve a moral modernity. He wrote:

There exists no distinction between the welfare of the individual and the welfare of the State – whoever attacks the state attacks each and every Japanese subject. The Japanese recognise to the full the duties of patriotism as well as the rights and advantages of citizenship. The individual interest always gives way to the national . . . If common thought and anonymous self-sacrifice produce power, the secret of Japanese success in the world is not far to seek.[41]

Of particular power – in view of their topicality – were Stead's references to Japan's moral conduct in her war with Tsarist Russia. Indeed he devoted whole chapters to Japan's 'Humane War', her 'Red Cross Society' and her broad spirit of internationalism. In fact Stead saw Japan as 'The pioneer of

Internationalism', rather than the leader of a pan-Asian movement against the West.[42] According to this view, Japan was not only successful in refined war and open trading but her 'International morals' were 'much higher than those of Europe'.[43] Stead's ideal was 'a new triple alliance . . . when the United States, Japan and Great Britain shall stand together as the guardians of international justice and morality.'[44]

In the years following the Treaty of Portsmouth British opinions of her East Asian ally became more divided and complex. Japan's desire to erect higher tariffs troubled some British journalists, while signs that Japan sought a privileged commercial position in Manchuria and Korea created further anxieties.[45] It was to counter these strands of journalistic and popular criticism, and to promote Japan's exports that the Japanese government gave elaborate and expensive support to the organization of the Japan–British Exhibition at the White City in London in 1910.[46] The exhibition was intended to demonstrate Japan's successful modernization and to transform the Anglo-Japanese Alliance from an alliance of governments into a broad alliance of peoples. However, like many Edwardian exhibitions the White City event also aimed to attract and entertain the public by presenting exotic 'villages'. At the White City there were Ainu, Taiwanese and Japanese 'villages', as well as demonstrations of Sumo and Japanese musicianship. These unusual attractions probably did most to draw eight million visitors, though informed observers paid most attention to the outstanding displays of Japanese fine arts and design. Particularly remarkable was the attempt which the exhibition's organizers made to suggest close parallels between the peoples of the two 'Island Empires'. The *Official Guide* referred to 'the striking similitude between the Japs [sic] and our own people' and confirmed . . . 'the resemblance manifests itself in manner, physical stamp and shape of the head. To anyone acquainted with the principles of phrenology the resemblance is very marked . . . a good augury for the growth of sympathy between the East and the West.'[47]

How successful the Japan–British Exhibition was in reshaping the perceptions of millions of visitors is difficult to determine. But the British press responded favourably and even newspapers in such small provincial towns as Scarborough now accepted that Japan was an advancing and progressive state.[48] Irrespective of its uncertain outcome the Exhibition constituted the first mass encounter of Britons with Japanese history and culture, and the first large-scale attempt by the Japanese government to shape British attitudes towards 'the Island Empire of the East'.

The events of the First World War concentrated the attention of the British press and public on conflict in Europe and the Middle East. However, conceptions of post-war reconstruction produced a pioneering British analysis of Japanese rural society. Believing that Japan's small-scale agriculture might provide lessons for the development of smallholdings in post-war Britain,

W. Robertson Scott left for Japan in 1915. This scholar of agricultural communities had already carried out research in Denmark and the Netherlands and spent more than three years travelling even more widely in provincial Japan than had Isabella Bird in the early Meiji years.[49] The diversity of this researcher's experiences is apparent from his Introduction to *The Foundations of Japan* which he completed in 1922:

> I was present at agricultural shows, at fairs, wrestling matches, Bon dances, village and county councils and the strangest of public meetings. I talked not only with farmers and their families but with all kinds of landlords, with schoolmasters and schoolmistresses, policemen, shopkeepers, priests, cooperative society enthusiasts, village officials, county officials, prefectural officials, a score of Governors and an Ainu chief.[50]

Like other distinguished British visitors Robertson Scott met members of the Japanese academic and administrative elites, but his contacts also included such nonconformist figures as the 'no-church' Christian Uchimura Kanzo. In his lengthy stay this writer appears to have developed some knowledge of colloquial Japanese and enjoyed the assistance of sympathetic interpreters. His web of diverse informants and experiences produced a work which was rich in information, empathy and analysis. *The Foundations of Japan* expressed admiration for progressive aspects of Japanese agriculture and recognized the individuality and variety which was present in rural life. For its author 'Japanese aestheticism, the victorious Japanese army and navy, the smoking chimneys of Osaka, the pushing mercantile marine, the Parliamentary and administrative developments of Tokyo and a costly worldwide diplomacy are borne on the backs of – the Japanese peasant and his wife'.[51] Robertson Scott clearly favoured rural improvement over 'erroneous conceptions of national progress' and, unconsciously, anticipated some of the major economic and political problems of the 1930s. More significantly his advocacy of 'more cooperation', 'improved implements' and 'paddy adjustment' was to be echoed by American occupiers following the Pacific War.[52]

Although the Anglo-Japanese Alliance was ended by 1923, British officials who had worked in Japan in the alliance's heyday retained their pro-Japanese warmth. In 1930 Captain Malcom Kennedy, who had been posted to the Tokyo Embassy during the alliance, published *The Changing Fabric of Japan*. In this work Kennedy employed both Japanese and English sources to present a conservative, yet sympathetic assessment of the social changes which Japan had confronted since the First World War. Despite the rise of labour, the women's movement and the growing power of the press Kennedy believed that social cohesion could be preserved by the pursuit of moderate and balanced policies. Despite his military background and values Kennedy claimed that economic considerations dominated Japanese policy making in 1930. He concluded 'when it comes to the question of a slight naval sacrifice being necessary as the price of a real economic gain, that sacrifice will be made, provided that the requirements of national defence are not made to suffer unduly.'[53]

During the 1930s new domestic and international factors increasingly transformed Japan and British perceptions of her. Japan's military expansion in Manchuria in 1931, and her creation of the satellite state of Manchukuo in 1932, significantly undermined Japan's earlier reputation in Britain as a supporter of international cooperation. Her departure from the League of Nations further deepened popular mistrust at a time when support for 'peace' and 'collective security' was particularly widespread in Britain. Developments in Japanese domestic policies created yet further disenchantment with the Japanese state and its culture. The replacement of civilian leaders by ministers with a military background suggested the general militarization of Japanese society, while the violent activities of exotically named patriotic societies further reinforced this trend. Assassinations of civilian, business and political leaders and the failed military coup of 26 February 1936 all revived notions of Japan as an inherently violent, exotic and unstable society. If anything the events of the early and mid-1930s suggested a return to the samurai violence of the 1860s and 1870s which had preceded and followed the Meiji Restoration.

The significance of such events for British public opinion was deepened by changes in Britain which had followed the First World War. Popular awareness of international affairs had grown and active popular concern at Japanese expansion was more widespread that at any previous time. These attitudes were given even greater intensity by the activities of such organizations as the League of Nations Union; and the rise of new media of mass communication. The development of photojournalism in the popular press, the spread of cinema newsreels and growing radio coverage of foreign affairs coincided with events in East Asia in which Japan appeared to threaten peace, and Britain's political and economic interests; this, at a time when Japanese textiles were increasingly entering British home and colonial markets. The outbreak of the second Sino-Japanese War in July 1937 reinforced popular British antipathy to Japan, and created a perception that China was a victim state in international society.[54] Amid these events not only were the mass media more powerful influences than books written for an elite or general readership but writers who were inherently sympathetic to Japanese life and society found it increasingly difficult to withhold disapproval and disillusion from their work. The Japanophile economist G. C. Allen, who had lectured 'for three years in a Government College at Nagoya' in the 1920s, was but one example.[55] In 1936 he paid a research visit to Japan and held consultations with close and long standing Japanese friends. On his return he wrote *Japan: The Hungry Guest*, a work which was completed after the outbreak of the war in China. Writing of this conflict he sadly observed

> Territorial expansion and the development of a flourishing export trade are to some extent, alternative policies for Japan . . . It is difficult to believe that Japan is strong enough to pursue both of these policies successfully, and she now seems to have trusted her fate to the former.[56]

Clearly the events of the Pacific War produced anti-Japanese propaganda in Britain, but it was the war's realities rather than works of propaganda that had the biggest impact on British perceptions. In 1910 the Japanese government had created the Japan–British Exhibition to engineer the first mass encounter of British citizens with Japan's culture and people. During the Pacific War the victories of the Imperial Japanese Army and Navy resulted in a second large-scale British experience of Japanese culture and conduct. The imprisonment and ill-treatment of tens of thousands of British prisoners of war constituted this experience; and generated widespread hostility to Japan. This hostility reflected both the severity of the prisoners' suffering and the numerical scale of this harsh meeting between British and Japanese servicemen.[57]

In the post-war world British books which describe or analyse Japan have been less significant than the mass media and direct experience in shaping popular perceptions. For more than a decade after 1945 films such as *A Town Like Alice* and *Bridge on the River Kwai* revived and prolonged popular awareness of the suffering of British prisoners of war.[58] In contrast, Japanese films helped to initiate a new enthusiasm for Japanese artistry and aesthetics. By the mid-1950s British critics were hailing Kurosawa's *Seven Samurai* as a modern masterpiece and in the 1960s the works of Ozu, Mizoguchi and Oshima entered the repertoire of the National Film Theatre and cinemas specializing in foreign films.[59] The organization of major Japanese film seasons was often encouraged by such cultural impresarios as Kawakita Kashiko. From 1973 the government-supported Japan Foundation has organized successful film festivals, exhibitions and educational projects, while Japanese corporations donated generously to major British museums.

In the late 1970s, 1980s and 1990s a new amalgam of economic and cultural trends refined and diversified British perceptions of Japan. Rising imports of high-quality Japanese electronic goods impressed millions of consumers, while visits by large numbers of polite and freespending Japanese tourists helped to dissolve notions of Japanese as spartan and inscrutable. Potentially of greater importance was the organization of a new form of mass Anglo-Japanese contact. In the late 1970s, the British and Japanese governments cooperated to establish the JET programme to ensure a continuing and growing flow of British graduates to teach English in Japanese schools.

This ensured the transmission of direct experience of Japanese daily life to many thousands of British citizens.[60] Early Victorian perceptions of Japan were often quasi-fantasies created by a narrow elite for a middle-class readership. In fact elements of exotic fantasy were seen as aids to a publication's commercial success. In the late Meiji period published descriptions were more diverse and approving, and were increasingly influenced by the availability of Japanese government materials in English. This tendency reached its apogee in the years of the Anglo-Japanese Alliance, an alliance which also inspired the holding of the Japan–British exhibition – a pioneering attempt to introduce a broader British public to a three-dimensional representation of Japanese history and culture.

In the interwar and wartime years new mass media and hostile direct experiences created largely critical and bitter perceptions of Japan. However, since the San Francisco Treaty cultural, economic and citizen level contacts have gradually produced more diverse yet sympathetic attitudes. In more recent years information technology, satellite television, jet transport and enlightened cultural agencies have brought variety, complexity and increasing reality to British interpretations of contemporary Japan.

Notes

1. 'Japan', *Edinburgh Review*, vol. 96 (1852), pp. 348–83.
2. Ibid., p. 359.
3. Ibid., p. 351.
4. For an introduction to early Victorian Anglo-Japanese relations see W. G. Beasley, *Great Britain and the Opening of Japan, 1834–1858* (London: Luzac, 1951).
5. S. Osborn, 'A Cruise in Japanese Waters', *Blackwoods Edinburgh Magazine*, vol. 85 (1860), p. 60.
6. Ibid., p. 57.
7. Toshio Yokoyama, *Japan in the Victorian Mind: Study of Stereotyped Images of a Nation, 1850–80* (London: Macmillan, 1987), p. 28.
8. Ibid., p. 54.
9. Laurence Oliphant, *Narrative of the Earl of Elgin's Mission to China and Japan in the years 1857, 1858 and 1859* (Edinburgh and London: William Blackwood and Son, 1859), vol. 2, pp. 139 and 179.
10. Sir Rutherford Alcock, *The Capital of the Tycoon, A Narrative of Three Years' Residence in Japan* (London: Longman Green, 1863), vol. 1, p. xix.
11. Ibid., vol. 1, p. 353.
12. A. B. Mitford, 'A Japanese Sermon', *The Cornhill Magazine*, vol. 20 (1869), pp. 196–204; 'Another Japanese Sermon', Ibid., pp. 356–62; 'The Execution by Hara Kiri', Ibid., pp. 549–54; Ibid., p. 551.
13. A. B. Mitford, 'Wanderings in Japan – II', *The Cornhill Magazine*, vol. 25 (1872), p. 319.

14. 'Japan', *Macmillans Magazine*, vol. 26 (1872), p. 496.
15. C. W. Dilke, 'English Influence in Japan', *Fortnightly Review*, vol. 20 (1876) New Series, p. 433.
16. E. J. Reed, *Japan, Its History, Tradition and Religions, With a Narrative of a Visit*, 2 vols (London: John Murray, 1880). The author's indebtedness to Japanese hospitality and sources of information is outlined in a lengthy Preface.
17. Ibid., vol. 1, p. 354.
18. Isabella Bird, *Unbeaten Tracks in Japan*, Virago Travellers edition (London: Virago, 1984, first published 1880), note 1, p. 100.
19. Ibid., p. 81.
20. Ibid., p. 97.
21. Ibid., note 1, p. 100.
22. First performed at the Savoy Theatre, London, 14 March 1885. It ran for 672 performances.
23. Hugh Cortazzi and George Webb (eds), *Kipling's Japan: Collected Writings* (London: The Athlone Press, 1988), p. 8.
24. Ibid., p. 92.
25. Ibid., p. 106.
26. For example, in 1876–77. The designer Christopher Dresser (1834–1904) visited Japan.
27. George Nathaniel Curzon, *Problems of the Far East* (revised edition) (London: Constable, 1896), pp. xii–xiii.
28. Ibid., pp. 19–20.
29. Ibid., p. 32.
30. Ibid., p. 387.
31. Ibid., pp. 386, 392, 394.
32. Henry Dyer, *Dai Nippon, the Britain of the East. A Study in National Evolution* (London: Blackie and Son, 1904), p. 425.
33. Ibid., p. 426.
34. Ibid., p. 426.
35. Ibid., p. 428.
36. Ibid., pp. ix–x.
37. For example, Inazo Nitobe, *Bushido, the Soul of Japan*, first published in 1905.
38. Ayako Hotta-Lister, *The Japan–British Exhibition of 1910: Gateway to the Island Empire of the East* (Richmond: Japan Library, Curzon Press, 1999), p. 94.
39. For Alfred Stead's life (1877–1933) see *Who Was Who, 1929–1940*, vol. 3 (London: Adam and Charles Black, 1941), p. 1283.
40. These titles were the outcome of the Peerage Act of July 1884.
41. Alfred Stead, *Great Japan. A Study of National Efficiency* (London: John Lane, The Bodley Head, 1906), p. 1.
42. Stead devoted Chapter 14 to 'Humane War', p. 286 ff., Chapter 15 to 'Red Cross Society', pp. 323 ff., and Chapter 19 to 'The Pioneer of Internationalism', pp. 427 ff.
43. Ibid., p. 444.
44. Ibid., p. 475.
45. Ayako Hotta-Lister, *The Japan–British Exhibition of 1910: Gateway to the Island Empire of the East* (Richmond: Japan Library, Curzon Press, 1999), pp. 9–37.
46. Ibid., pp. 74–99.
47. Ibid., p. 178.
48. Ibid., p. 113.

49. For J. W. Robertson Scott's life see E. T. Williams and C. S. Nicholls (eds), *The Dictionary of National Biography, 1961–1970* (Oxford: Oxford University Press, 1981), pp. 889–90.
50. J. W. Robertson Scott, *The Foundations of Japan. Notes Made During Journeys of 6,000 miles in the Rural Districts as a Basis for a Sounder Knowledge of the Japanese People* (London: John Murray, 1922), p. x.
51. Ibid., p. ix.
52. Ibid., p. 370.
53. M. D. Kennedy, *The Changing Fabric of Japan* (London: Constable, 1930), p. 270.
54. The destructive nature of Japanese military action in China was often shown in *British Movietone News* cinema newsreels.
55. G. C. Allen, *Japan: the Hungry Guest* (London: George Allen and Unwin, 1938), p. 9.
56. Ibid., p. 253.
57. A typical work describing Japanese ill-treatment of prisoners of war was Edward Frederick Langley Russell (Lord Russell of Liverpool), *The Knights of Bushido – A Short History of Japanese War Crimes* (London: Cassell, 1958).
58. *A Town Like Alice*, directed by Joseph Janni (1956), *The Bridge on the River Kwai*, directed by David Lean (1957).
59. A major Ozu and Mizoguchi season was held at the National Film Theatre, London in 1963. An Oshima season was held at the National Film Theatre in 1969.
60. See David Chandler and David Kootnikoff (eds), *The JET Programme: Getting Both Feet Wet* (Sheffield: David Chandler, 1999).

2

The Changing Image of Britain among Japanese Intellectuals

Chushichi Tsuzuki

This essay is an attempt, by way of introduction, to present an overview of some salient features of the changing image of Britain in Japanese minds – especially among intellectuals – during the last two centuries. Such images, though sometimes (and particularly in the early period of study) the product of imagination and fantasy, became increasingly linked with actual needs and aspirations in politics and economics. The growth of social and cultural contacts also contributed to emulation, understanding and cooperation between the two countries.

Early images of Britain as a mighty colonial power

In the early years of the nineteenth century it was Britain which emerged as the major threat to Japan from the south. The Napoleonic Wars had repercussions far beyond Europe, and Britain, aspiring to replace the Netherlands in her colonial expansion in South-East and East Asia, sought to obtain a foothold in Japan. However, it was not until the aftermath of the Opium War of 1840–42 that Britain appeared at the centre of the drama of the opening of Japan.[1]

In Japan, Dutch Studies or Western Studies had begun to spread with the lifting in 1720 of the ban on the import of western books (except those dealing with Christianity). Honda Toshiaki (1743–1820), one of the pioneer scholars of this new learning, was perhaps the first to form a view of Britain as the country to be emulated by Japan, though his arguments were based on geographical misconceptions. Honda, of mixed samurai-farmer origin, opened a private school in Edo and his studies and observations resulted in several works, including 'Tales of the West' (*Seiiki Monogatari*) (1798). In this he praised European powers for their wealth and influence, illustrated by the number of overseas dependencies which they had acquired. It is high time to 'retrieve' Ezo, he declared. With the Ezo islands restored, Japan would become one of two wealthy, powerful countries in the world, along with Britain, which, though a small country, had many dependencies.

Honda also developed a theory of population, starting with its natural tendency to multiply, comparable to that of Robert Malthus. Honda's own remedy for an increase in population in excess of the production of food was overseas expansion. From this came his dream of a greater Japan: Japan should move to Kamchatka, located at 51° N, as far north as London, *hence climatically similar to London*, to be named Old Japan, and Japan transplanted to the north, should become increasingly prosperous and surpass Holland which faces north, while Kamchatka faces south. Japan would extend to America to the east, to Manchuria to the west, to the 22 Ezo islands, the island of Matsumae (Hokkaido), Japan itself and the Ryukus to the south. Moreover, the expansion of Japan should take place not through military conquests but by foreign trade and colonization. Obviously his model for Japan's expansion was Britain. He took for granted the need to open Japan, cherished political democracy, of a sort, and even went as far as to criticize the unproductive classes, though he refused to meddle with bakufu rule.

By the time Sato Shin-en or Nobuhiro (1769–1850) lectured to daimyo and wrote for them and for his fellow intellectuals, the seas around Japan were increasingly crossed by foreign vessels. In one of his lectures dealing with 'Sea Defence' Sato, the son of a country doctor in Dewa Province, stated that Japan was very conveniently situated for sea voyages and foreign trade, and would surpass Britain in climate and products; therefore, she should prepare herself with sailing skills and armed ships for overseas expeditions. Japan should conclude treaties for peace and trade with China, Annam and Siam, and further develop Ezo, occupy Russian ports in Kamchatka and trade with America through these north-eastern strongholds. In the South, Japan should develop uninhabited islands in the South Seas, occupy Luzon, and govern Java and Borneo from there. He believed these measures would prevent Britain from plundering the Far East.[2]

His idea of Japan conquering a large part of the world was further elaborated in his work, *Kondo Hisaku* (Secret policy of Intermixing) (1823). However, it is difficult to evaluate just how influential Sato's writings were and what impact they exerted on the generations which were deeply involved in the turmoil of the opening and modernization of Japan. Nevertheless, he represented and even typified this process of turmoil in a most striking form, which some called state socialism and others referred to as a 'totalitarian' structure.

In the second month of 1825 the Shogun's government issued an edict urging the daimyo to expel foreign ships without a second thought. Until this edict was revoked in the wake of the Opuim War, Japan was to go through an extremely xenophobic period, which was to have marked repercussions in the decades that followed. It was to vindicate this edict and to declare a Japan-centred view of a world order that Aizawa Seishisai (1781–1863), the nationalist writer of the Mito school, wrote *Shinron* (A New Thesis) (1825).[3] Part of the inspiration for this book was provided by his experience as an interpreter in dealing with 12 British seamen who 'landed [at Mito beach] and begged for goods [*sic*]', an act which would suggest that 'their contempt for our divine country has gone too far'.

The arrival in 1837 of the American ship *Morrison* with several Japanese castaways on board coincided with the exploration of the Bonin Islands by the British warship *Raleigh*. As soon as the *Morrison* approached, shore batteries at Uraga opened fire in accordance with the decree of 1825. The ship was obliged to leave Edo Bay and returned to Macau. The *Morrison* was misrepresented by a Dutch captain as a British ship, and the British were perhaps more dreaded than the Americans for their expanding empire. Watanabe Kazan, chief samurai officer at Tahara *han* which had a long Pacific coastline, had been warned by a Dutchman to prepare defences against Britain which would seize Japanese islands.[4]

The high-handed manner in which the *Morrison* was expelled alarmed the scholars of the western school. Takano Choei, once a student of von Siebold at Nagasaki, wrote *Yume Monogatari* (A Dream Tale) (1838) and Watanabe Kazan *Shinkiron* (A Cautious Argument) (1838) to express their apprehensions. In his work Choei defended Britain against Dutch allegations that she was the country of pirates: Britain is no enemy of Japan, and to bombard her ships without reason will make Japan an unreasonable and unjust country. He described the British as 'alert and quick-witted, industrious and enduring, steeped in literature, pursuing art and craft, skilled in military arts, giving the first priority to enriching the people and strengthening the nation'. The British had undertaken the colonization of barren lands and carried out the guidance and subjugation of indigenous peoples, who were now four times as numerous as the population of the mother country. As British trade with China began to prosper, the Portuguese and Dutch who had traded there before the British, vilified them from envy.[5] In his book Kazan obliquely condemned the bakufu's seclusion policy. 'In Asia only Japan, China and Persia are independent, and of these three only Japan refuses to communicate with the Europeans. This is a matter of great concern.'[6]

Kazan was made to appear an eager participant in an imaginary colonization plot – fabricated by an Edo constable. Kazan, Choei and several others were arrested in 1839. This resulted in a temporary suppression of Dutch learning, and both Kazan and Choei met a martyr's death.

In 1854, one year after Commodore Perry's arrival, a peace and friendship treaty was concluded with the United States (and also with Britain and Russia in 1854). Hotta Masayoshi, the bakufu's senior councillor, prepared a memorandum for the benefit of other officials, stressing the need for 'friendly alliances', sending ships to foreign countries to 'copy the foreigners where they are at their best' and to strengthen our armaments and 'gradually to subject the foreigners to our influence until in the end . . . our hegemony is acknowledged throughout the globe'.[7] With the opening of

Japan emulation rather than outright hostility became an attitude which was widely adopted by enlightened opinion in the bakufu, and among its enemies in their relations with the western powers, Britain above all.

The Anglo-Satsuma War: from a Britain to be defied to Britain as an ally

As a result of serious damage to property and persons inflicted by *joi* (anti-foreign) terrorists after foreign trade officially began, Britain, one of the main victims, demanded apologies and indemnities (especially for the slaying of the British merchant Richardson at Namamugi near Yokohama) from Satsuma, responsible for such acts of terrorism. Satsuma's prevarications led the British to send a fleet of seven warships to Kagoshima. Large parts of the city of Kagoshima were destroyed but the British fleet also suffered damage and had to withdraw for repairs. Eventually Satsuma paid an indemnity and settled her dispute with Britain.

The Kagoshima War, or Satsuma–British War of 1863,[8] was reported to the still xenophobic imperial court as a victory and was 'generally regarded as a British rout and an act of expelling the barbarians by Satsuma'.[9] But Satsuma's encounter with the British transformed han policies, intimacy replacing defiance in its relations with the British. Satsuma trod the perilous path of opening the country more rapidly than did the rest of Japan. With great secrecy 17 Satsuma students, including Mori Arinori (1847–89), were sent to London in 1865, assisted by Thomas Glover, a British merchant at Nagasaki. Mori, who became the minister of education in the 1880s, was deeply impressed by the spirit of the dignity of man which he found in the casual remarks of his landlady, and also in the institutions for handicapped people which he visited. In a letter addressed to his brother in 1866 he wrote that Japan's traditional laws were in many cases 'cruel and remote from human sentiments' while British laws did not conflict with reason, and it would be difficult to achieve national improvement on the basis of the laws currently enforced in Japan.[10]

Choshu, the only han firmly committed to *joi* action, also sent several young samurai, including Ito Hirobumi (1841–1909) and Inoue Kaoru (1836–1915), to London in connection with the purchase of a British ship. Arriving in the British capital 'the scales were lifted from Ito's eyes' – the magnificent scenes the Choshu samurai saw represented science, progress, and above all power.[11] Choshu's hasty action against foreign ships resulted in a combined force of British, American, Dutch and French ships destroying its forts around Shimonoseki and defeating the Choshu troops which guarded them. It was no accident that Satsuma and Choshu, the two great han which had suffered a defeat by the West, and had learned lessons from it, soon allied themselves together in a civil war against the bakufu.[12]

Liberal Britain and Meiji intellectuals

Fukuzawa Yukichi, perhaps the most prominent representative of Meiji enlightenment, visited Europe in 1862 as a 'translator' for the bakufu delegation. At Hong Kong, where the delegation stopped on its way to the West, he felt that British tyranny surpassed that of the Shogunate. In London he observed banking and postal services with great interest, but Parliament was 'a perplexing institution', for the debates between government and opposition were something beyond his comprehension.[13] Yet, in his book on 'Conditions in the West' (1866), he showed himself greatly attracted to Britain whose 'voluntarism' he admired, while 'freedom or liberty' ('not a Japanese term for it yet') became a focal point of all his new ideas.[14] He praised Britain for her 'generous laws' which 'do not bind people but develop their natural abilities'. Although Britain's army was the least strong among those of European countries, her navy was kept sufficiently powerful to promote and protect her foreign trade, while her taxes were less burdensome to her people than those in other countries. British wealth and power did not depend on her overseas possessions which would be better given their independence (even for the benefit of the mother country); but on trade with foreign countries, including her former colonies. Britain was 'richer, stronger and more civilized than . . . other countries because she was conveniently located. Furthermore, her products were abundant, outstanding individuals were numerous and her politics was fair and just'.[15] After the Meiji Restoration of 1868 Fukuzawa came to see Britain in more relative terms. Now he saw Japan, though lagging behind Britain, as doing her best to advance her civilization to such an extent that he claimed that his own country was already based on the principle that all men are socially equal: only talent and achievement would sustain ranks and distinctions. Japan's advance, however, was slower than he had expected owing largely to 'the ignorance and illiteracy of the people'. Hence he put great emphasis on learning, practical learning which would assure freedom and independence to individuals and also to the nation.[16] These arguments were set forth in his second major publication *Gakumon no Susume* (An Encouragement of Learning) (1872–6) which became 'the text-book of the nation'. His third major book, *An Outline of a Theory of Civilization*, owes much to Francois Guizot and Henry Thomas Buckle, the two historians from whose arguments he developed a theory of his own, retaining a relativist view of civilization, but stressing national independence as the most important factor. His image of Britain had also shifted its emphasis and he termed the British in India, possibly in other colonial territories, 'heartless and cruel . . . in their administration'.[17] When his hopes for Korean independence were disappointed in the 1880s, he began to show a new development in his view of civilization by advocating Japan's 'Exit from Asia, Entry to Europe'.

These were years when some major British works on social and political thought were translated. Nakamura Masanao (1832–91), formerly a bakufu professor of the prestigious Shoheiko school, translated *Self-Help* by Samuel Smiles (1871), and *On Liberty* by John Stuart Mill (1872). Nakamura had accompanied 12 bakufu students sent to London for study in 1866 and returned in the first year of Meiji (1868). He admired Britain and the British:

> everybody there worships a real god, has firm control of himself . . . [and] is engaged in his work as a calling for the benefit of humanity (this is the reason why one's trade and occupation are not despised as vulgar). Everybody is patient and respects independence; people of different ranks and classes work for certain aims, as though parts of a spinning machine all move and turn without causing any obstruction in the process of production.[18]

Baba Tatsui (1850–88), of Tosa samurai origins, and a product of Fukuzawa's school, spent several years in England in the 1870s during which time he was attracted to Disraeli's eloquence and deeply moved by 'the relentless attack made by John Stuart Mill on the prejudices of society'. However, he did not conceal his disappointment with British residents in Japan, who in his view slighted Japanese politics and religion, whereas he, like Fukuzawa, had greatly admired Britain for her practice of equality before the law and justice – unencumbered by class distinctions. He served as editor of the organ of the *Jiyuto* (Liberal Party) and wrote on liberty and people's rights but government persecution of active democrats forced him to choose a life of political exile in America.[19]

Tokutomi Soho (1863–1957), the son of a wealthy farmer in Higo province who was educated at Kumamoto Yogakko (Western School), won sudden fame when, under the influence of Herbert Spencer, he published *Shorai no Nihon* (The Future Japan) (1886). In this book he described the Meiji Restoration as a great turning point from feudal aristocratic militarism to popular productionism in the process of social evolution. Soho concluded that 'in the future Japan should be an industrial country . . . also a democratic country'.[20] Soho's liberal sentiments, however, were soon to be submerged under a new drive to create a greater Japan at the time of the Sino-Japanese War.

Britain and social democracy: Katayama Sen

Meiji social democracy owed a great deal to the United States for its Christian socialist origins as well as for its trade union organizations. It also derived inspiration from European socialism, embodied in the Second International, the British contingents of which exerted an influence far greater than their actual strength, by virtue of the books and newspapers written in English, a language that was familiar to Meiji socialists.

Katayama Sen (1859–1933), of Okayama peasant origins and a Christian socialist, studied at Andover Theological Seminary, Massachusetts. With his fellow students he visited England where he carefully observed the social programmes of Toynbee Hall and Oxford House and also met Tom Mann, who was then associated with the Labour Church movement. In 1896 he returned to Japan after 11 years' study in America and in the following year became director of Kingsley Hall, the first 'settlement' in Japan, which opened in Kanda, Tokyo. Katayama's observations on British society were published in a book entitled *Eikoku Konnichi-no Shakai* (British Society Today) (1897), a record of his visit to Britain from 19 June to 24 August 1894. From Liverpool where he had landed, he proceeded to Birmingham which impressed him with its city council (municipal socialism), the legacy of Joseph Chamberlain. In London he stayed mostly at Balliol House, an institution attached to Toynbee Hall in Whitechapel, among dens of villains and scoundrels and 'famous for Jack the Ripper'. 'Every day I went out to see London, its social conditions, charity institutions, prisons, orphanages, reformatories, in short everything related to social problems.' He emphasized the work of the Salvation Army, its match factory, 'social elevator facilities for ex-prisoners, and lodging houses'. He described prisons, reformatories and industrial schools in great detail. He gave a lively picture of the conditions of the workers living in tenement-houses including the Peabody Buildings. He paid special attention to Canning Town and its shipyard where 'warships of our Japanese Empire' were built. He also gave an account of the dock labourers in this area and the Dockers' Strike of 1889. From London he proceeded to Hull by boat, then to York, and to Edinburgh where he was impressed by the extent of both its slums and its charitable organizations. If Edinburgh was Kyoto, Glasgow must be Osaka, said Katayama. With its municipal trams, electric and gas light, and an advanced sewage system Glasgow was a highlight of his British tour. Manchester was another with its Free Trade Hall, Mechanics' School, and YMCA which promoted immigration, a subject Katayama himself cherished and later put into practice in Texas.

Shortly after his return from America Katayama took his full share in launching the trade union movement in Japan, starting with the Iron Workers' Union whose inaugural meeting was held in the YMCA building in Kanda. While the British Labour Party in the form of the Labour Representation Committee was founded in 1900, the first socialist party in Japan, the Social Democratic Party, was formed in 1901 and was suppressed as soon as it declared its aims. These included universal suffrage and a legal status for trade unions (the latter aim was only attained after Japan's defeat in the Pacific War in 1945). Katayama, who had been disappointed by the deadlock reached so soon by a movement for parliamentary socialism in Japan, welcomed the news that John Burns, an engineer, a member of the London County Council and an MP, had joined Campbell-Bannerman's Liberal government in 1905.

> The status of British members of parliament is honorary and they do not obtain a stipend, not a penny, to say nothing of the 2000 yen received by a Japanese member of the Diet; this is also the case with the members of a city council. John Burns, being a member elected by the working-class constituency called Battersea and having no property of his own, the constituency workers collected the amount of money which he had been receiving as an engineer twenty years before and paid him . . . He mostly walks to Parliament.[21]

'Britain is the world leader', he also wrote:

> Britain has controlled the general trend of the world as its leader because it had many able personalities. British politicians are quick to perceive world trends as well as the conditions of each country. [Here he refers to the 1894 treaty abolishing extraterritorial rights in Japan on the eve of the Sino-Japanese war.] In this way Britain is ever practical, sticks to the positive aspects of the world, carries out innovations in diplomacy, and advances towards new objectives to such an extent that British politicians are always powerful and successful in diplomacy.[22]

Again as for the entry of Burns into the government, he added, 'this is not a case of the cabinet patronizing and pleasing the workers but a product of the time and a definite sign of Britain recognizing the power of the workers'.[23]

Katayama's view of a 'social Britain' was surprisingly similar to Fukuzawa's image of a 'liberal Britain', both practical and rich in outstanding personalities, concerned with the issues of civilization and progress; Britain, however, after decades of industrialization fully recognised the power of the workers whom Fukuzawa had relegated to the limbo of the ignorant, at least in Meiji Japan.

Keir Hardie in Japan

Keir Hardie had emerged as a major figure in the Second International mostly as a result of his strong pacifist convictions. His world tour, partly financed by the Salvation Army, began with a visit to Canada in July 1907. He crossed the Pacific in August. The *Shakai Shinbun*, Katayama's socialist paper, reported Hardie's short stay in Tokyo which was a major event for a handful of Japanese socialists at the time. Katayama met Hardie on his arrival at Shinbashi Station on 21 August. He accompanied his guest in a rickshaw to the British Embassy, and to several government offices. Hardie spent the whole afternoon at Kingsley Hall and answered questions from many visitors regarding his own experiences and the British labour movement.

Hardie spent that night at a Japanese house near Shinjuku that belonged to Sakai Toshihiko, formerly a teacher of English, now a socialist leader who mistrusted Hardie's advocacy of parliamentary socialism. Yet Hardie was cheerful enough to sing *La Marseillaise* for his host and his friends, and slept on a futon under a mosquito net. Early next morning, Kotoku Shusui, the leader of the anarchist section of the movement, came to greet Hardie.[24] In fact, in spite of his 'parliamentarism' Hardie, for the sake of fairness, had defended the right of anarchists to attend the London congress of the International some ten years before. On that morning Hardie, accompanied by Katayama, went to see Count Okuma with whom he had a long interview. 'To the question why the Japanese government persecutes socialists so severely', wrote Katayama:

> the Count answered that the fault is on both sides, some socialists are hot-headed and attempt to carry out at once in Japan those measures about which they read in western books . . . The Count said among other things that the ideals of our sovereign in the past have been socialistic . . . Hardie explained and corrected some mistaken notions on socialism and expounded its aims and principles.[25]

On the afternoon of 22 August there was a reception for Hardie at the Kinkikan Hall, at which the leader of the Labour Party gave a speech for 90 minutes with Katayama as his interpreter. He stated that he was against all wars, the Boer War above all, and emphasized that the number of socialist MPs had increased to 32 at the last election. 'Let the workers dominate the parliament. This is our aim, which is not for our personal fame, but in order to eliminate poverty and suffering in our society today.' He also stressed the need for female suffrage and racial equality. After his departure the split between the direct actionists and the parliamentarians among Japanese socialists became further exacerbated.

The Webbs and Japan

Sidney and Beatrice Webb visited Japan a few months after the Treason Incident, the execution in January 1911 of Kotoku Shusui and his associates for their alleged involvement in a plot against the Meiji emperor. The Webbs' visit naturally caused some unease among Japanese socialists who held their breath for fear of possible consequences. There were protest movements against the executions in major capital cities in America and Europe, including one by local Fabians in London, but obviously the Webbs were in no mood to raise the issue in Japan. In Japan they shunned labour politics altogether but personally enjoyed their stay, 'almost entirely spending our time with Japanese statesmen, officials, philanthropists, bankers, landlords and peasants', as Sidney wrote in a letter to Bernard Shaw.[26] In Tokyo he gave 'a first-rate lecture on "How the administrative experience of the British Empire might be made useful to Japan", which seems to have been much appreciated by an audience of Ministers, officials and professors'.[27] In Kyoto Beatrice observed that the professors of the Kyoto Imperial University

> are all civil servants and have to be careful not to incur the reproach of 'dangerous thoughts' – but certainly in their talks with us they were quite free and easy in their criticisms of the Government and the status quo. Nearly all the professors of Political Economy in Japan are 'Socialists of the Chair'; we were pleased to find that they had all our books, even those on English Local Government![28]

Korea had been annexed to Japan in the previous year and local uprisings against the annexation had been ruthlessly suppressed. The Webbs revealed themselves as social imperialists: 'The Koreans are 12 million dirty, degraded, sullen, lazy, and religionless savages, who slouch about in dirty *white* garments of the most inept kind, and who live in filthy mudhuts', wrote Sidney: 'this race the Japanese have at last annexed . . . to the world's advantage, as there is at any rate law and order now.'[29]

Though Japanese socialists did not make much of the Webbs at the time of their visit, Fabianism remained with them as a convenient term of reference when they felt it necessary to proceed slowly under difficult circumstances, or to be practical by avoiding ideological disputes (though British Fabians were not altogether free from internal discord).

Taisho democracy and Britain

Taisho democracy is the term given to the ideas and movements which were born from the 'defence of the constitution' agitations of 1912–13 against the reassertion of the power of the *Hanbatsu* (the Satsuma-Choshu clique) and the continuation of *Genro* ('elders') politics. As such it was largely a domestic issue of political reform, for which the term 'democracy' was perhaps too advanced, and had to be replaced by a newly coined word *minponshugi* ('people-ism') which seemed compatible with the monarchical Meiji constitution. Kayahara Kazan (1870–1952), a journalist, who stayed in Europe for some five years after the Russo-Japanese War as a newspaper correspondent, was one of the first to use this new term as the concept opposed to militarism. He founded a journal of his own in October 1913 which he named *Daisan Teikoku* (The Third Empire), an empire which would stand for individualism, 'little-Japanism', and joint rule by the emperor and the people, a successor presumably to the first empire of the 'hegemonic' bakufu and the second empire of the Meiji *hanbatsu* oligarchy. The journal was read by students of private universities rather than those of imperial universities, and more by provincial intellectuals than by the metropolitan elite. In fact it was a popular version of the *Toyo Keizai Shinpo* (Oriental Economist) founded in 1895 as a journal specializing in economics and politics like the London *Economist*, and edited then by Miura Tetsutaro (1874–1972) and later by Ishibashi Tanzan (1884–1973) (the future prime minister), both graduates of Waseda University. The *Toyo Keizai Shinpo* took the lead in opposing military expansion and advocating 'little-Japanism', Miura arguing that in Britain advocates of small Britain and those of 'greater Britain' complemented each other, whereas in Japan expansionists alone held sway.[30] Uehara Etsujiro (1877–1962), one of the regular contributors to *Daisan Teikoku*, had studied at the London School of Economics and Political Science. He had become an admirer of representative government in Britain (and later, incidentally, became a minister of state under Yoshida Shigeru in 1946). Uehara Etsujiro developed a constitutional theory far more radical than Minobe Tatsukichi's organ theory of the emperor, for he included the emperor among the people and pleaded strongly for universal suffrage (in the November 1913 issue of *Daisan Teikoku*). An article by Elizabeth Robinson, a suffragette leader, defending women's resistance to oppression in England was translated in one of the earlier issues of the same journal. In another contribution Tagawa Daikichiro compared the manner of Lloyd George replacing Asquith as the head of Britain's Liberal government during the war with that of Marshal Terauchi replacing Count Okuma as prime minister. He commented that (in spite of the author's personal liking for Asquith) British constitutional politics showed its excellence before the whole world, while in Japan the intervention by *Genro* caused unnecessary confusion. This, he continued, 'showed the dignity of the British throne to be superior to that of the Japanese Imperial house' and he added that foreigners (mostly like the British) in Yokohama bet on a new Japanese prime minister, knowing that the emperor would decide as he was told by *Genro*.[31] This issue of the journal was suppressed and its editor, Ishida Tomoji, was found guilty of *lèse-majesté*. In the same issue, Fukuda Tokuzo, an eminent economist, wrote on 'Lloyd Georgeism' as 'pointing to the dawn of a new civilization' in which he maintained that British liberals had to recognize man's right to live, itself a 'protectionism' for the weak guaranteed by a national insurance system. 'Lloyd George, most advanced in this protectionism, deserves his new post as prime minister, and it is natural that this happened in Britain which stands at the apex of civilization.'

Minponshugi was given an authoritative definition by Yoshino Sakuzo (1878–1933), a professor at the Imperial University. In his article 'The Fundamental Principles of Constitutional Politics', in *Chuo Koron* (January 1916), he described it as politics 'for the people' as well as politics that 'takes into serious and final account the will of the people'.[32] His arguments were based largely on British parliamentary practices but his favourable view of Britain did not extend to liberalism.

Yoshino had been in Germany and Austria for more than two years as a government scholar before staying in England for two months on his way home. Being steeped in the German academic tradition of statecraft he regarded the British aversion to compulsion as 'sentimental superstition'. When conscription was introduced in Britain in early 1916, he felt it would never be thorough and would be replaced again by a voluntary system as soon as the war was over. 'In some sense this [liberalism] is a defect of British national character', he remarked, 'yet it is probably because of this that Britain could still maintain the stance of a great nation while losing a war.'[33] It should be noted that at the time this was written Verdun and the Somme were still to come. This is a far cry from Fukuzawa's admiration of a liberal Britain, though Yoshino as well as Kawakami (who will be discussed below) was attracted to a social Britain that had inspired the socialist Katayama at the turn of the century. The fresh discovery of a 'social Britain' by Japanese scholars was due largely to the fact that Great Britain was engaged in a war in which all social classes were to be mobilized.

One day in April 1913 Yoshino visited Toynbee Hall. 'I sincerely hope', he wrote, 'that facilities like the one here should be set up in Japan.'[34] Back in Tokyo he founded a University Extension Society. 'Settlements', and a system of university extension based on a British model, were widely discussed at a time when the Japanese government sought to reorganize and expand higher education.[35]

Kawakami Hajime (1879–1946), a professor at Kyoto Imperial University, had come under the influence of Arnold Toynbee, the economic historian and founder of the university settlement movement in Britain. He duly directed his attention to social policy to remedy the wide gaps between rich and poor, between economics and ethics and ultimately between the West and Japan.[36] Like Yoshino, he spent two years, 1913–14, in Europe as a government scholar, studying German idealist philosophy. When war broke out he moved to London but he found England generally disappointing. Even Bernard Shaw, whom he had admired, turned out to be a bore. Yet the two-and-a-half months he spent in England were crucial in his development as a Marxist economist. Poverty in the midst of the world's greatest wealth became an overriding issue for him. His 'Tales of Poverty', which was serialized in the *Asahi Shinbun* in 1916, was a great success. Wealth was defined as 'the means for a man to become truly a man – the aim of human life. The amount deemed necessary to achieve such a goal is not unlimited.' This was truly a Ruskinian idea. He retained these ethical overtones when he turned to a Marxist analysis of capitalism. His 'moral' Marxism and his martyrdom were inevitable outcomes of his brief encounter with a social Britain during the First World War.

Japanese Fabians

The lively organizational efforts and sharp ideological differences which characterized Japanese labour in the post-First World War years were suddenly brought to an end in 1923. In June the members of the clandestine Communist party were arrested. The Kanto Earthquake in September was accompanied by white terror. Meanwhile, universal suffrage had been on the Diet's agenda for some time, though it was voted down in March 1923 (but passed in 1925). It was under these circumstances that, in January 1924, Abe Isoo (1865–1949), the veteran socialist pioneer, Yamazaki Kesaya (1877–1954), the socialist lawyer trained in America, and Ishikawa Sanshiro (1876–1956), the disciple of Edward Carpenter the libertarian socialist, met and decided to call on all the tendencies, schools and advocates in the social movement to form a study group – possibly to inspire the founding of a social democratic party to deal with new situations. Abe Isoo, a Christian socialist educated at the Hartford Theological Seminary in Connecticut, had participated in the first socialist party, the SDP of 1901, he was also known as the founder of the baseball team of Waseda University where he taught.[37] In his 'Autobiography' Ishikawa referred to the new group as 'an extraordinary collection of people full of verve'.[38] A regular meeting was held at Abe's house, and members included Inomata Tsunao, the Rono-ha Marxist and a member of the first communist party, Iwasa Sakutaro, the anarchist activist (who failed to shoot General Fukuda, the commander of the forces implementing martial law at the time of the Kanto Earthquake), Kikuchi Kan, the popular novelist and dramatist and the founder of the *Bungeishunju* magazine (in January 1923), and Katayama Tetsu (1887–1978), later to be a socialist prime minister under the American occupation.

In its first issue (May 1924), the new group's organ *Shakaishugi Kenkyu* (Studies of Socialism) clarified the position of the society:

> The day for socialism to be treated as a utopia has gone . . . Our attitude . . . is realistic and law-abiding, gradualist but positive. We would like to add that we are tolerant to all socialist thought. We have decided to call our society Fabian. But we have nothing to do with the Fabian Society in Britain. We should not be judged as an imitation of the British model, [though], there is some resemblance in our stance to theirs.

Abe provided figures to show how powerful socialists had become in Europe. 'The precious weapon with which to fight capitalism in the world of capitalism is money', wrote Kikuchi Kan: 'if one is really determined to fight with capitalism, one should go into capitalist society and make money.' This is what Kikuchi did for himself, but whether the cause of socialism advanced with his accumulation of money is another matter.[39] Meanwhile, Japan's relations with Chinese warlords in Manchuria deteriorated. In the Fabian journal Abe declared that Japan should set a good example by stopping the exploitation of China, by selling the South Manchurian Railway back to the Chinese government, and giving up all Japanese interests in Manchuria. If this would save China, the return of our interests to China would not be a loss to us.[40] Abe's arguments were in line with the 'Little Japanism' propagated in *Daisan Teikoku* and the *Toyo Keizai Shinpo*. (They were also in line with the views of Katayama Sen.)

Meanwhile, the Guild Socialism advocated by G. D. H. Cole of the Fabian Research Bureau was taken up by advocates of the cooperative movement like Kagawa Toyohiko (1888–1960) who was attracted to the new British doctrine of industrial democracy. Kagawa, a Christian evangelist known for his work among the poor in a Kobe slum and as the founder of the Kobe consumers' cooperative union, was involved in the trade union movement in the Kansai area and began to advocate 'a new industrial system . . . based on labour'.[41] He pleaded for 'democratic factories' and 'a producers' assembly'[42] and played an active role in the social movements of the day.

By the end of 1925, however, the Japan Fabian Society had been wound up. The grand coalition which its members sought to achieve turned out to be an illusion. Divisions among socialists were deepened rather than eased under the increasingly oppressive conditions created by the growth of militarism and extreme nationalism. For his part Abe became the leader of the Social Popular Party (*Shakai Minshu-to*) when it was formed in 1926, and the first chairman of this party in 1932. He withdrew from it when it joined with other parties to force the resignation of a Diet member Saito Takao who criticized the government's forceful policy towards China in 1940.

Nationalists and Britain: Kuga Katsunan and Kita Ikki

Kuga Katsunan (1857–1907) is remembered in post-Second World War Japan as a pioneer protagonist of a more moderate form of nationalism. At the time of the Sino-Japanese War he advocated a foreign policy of *hokushu nanshin* (defence in the north and advance in the south). He thought that the Trans-Siberian Railway, when completed, could be a spur to Asian development, while in the south Japan should obtain Taiwan as her base and advance into the rest of the world through foreign trade, navigation, emigration and business activity. Furthermore, Japan should take advantage of this opportunity to adjust her relations with Britain, believing that commercial rivalries were pacific in nature and that the interests of Japan and Britain would lead to harmony, not friction.[43] The three-power intervention in 1895, and especially greater Russian involvement in Korean politics, led Kuga Katsunan to invert his political creed and begin to advocate *nanshu hokushin* (defence in the south and advance in the north). Japan, he now felt, should ally herself with Britain and secure her supremacy in the seas around the Korean peninsula.[44]

In the following two decades Japan emerged as a Great Power (although still a probationary one) in East Asia. 'The cause of the preservation of the whole of China and the Anglo-Japanese Alliance are not compatible', declared Kita Ikki (1883–1937), perhaps the most prominent nationalist writer, in his 'Unauthorized History of the Chinese Revolution' (1920). The Alliance lost its *'raison d'être'* continued Kita, 'with the end of the Russo-Japanese war' and after the war

> Japan had been played upon and slighted in the palm of the British hand. Japan made use of Britain in the war with Russia so as to preserve North China. The same cause would compel Japan to fight against Britain for the sake of South China.' Kita, the champion of 'Asian Monroeism', criticized Japan's foreign policy which was geared to British interests (*eikoku hon-gaiko*).[45]

The arguments presented by Kuga and Kita respectively were ahead of their time in the sense that they foreshadowed the foreign policies pursued a generation or two later by Shidehara Kijuro on the one hand and by Takana Giichi on the other. Britain was regarded either as a partner in the economic exploitation of China, or as a rival to be eliminated.

Kawai Eijiro and T. H. Green

Kawai Eijiro (1891–1944), a factory inspector who disagreed with the government on the issue of labour policy at the time of the Paris Peace Conference, resigned his position and joined the newly created Faculty of Economics at Tokyo Imperial University in 1920 to teach western political and social thought. Two years later he was sent to Europe and stayed in Britain until 1925. In spite of the 'great unpopularity in which Britain has been held in Japan', he wrote 'I like this country [which] stands and strides in the forefront of social progress in the world, always devising new institutions', and he regarded 'the remarkable transformation of the Labour party from opposition to government' as 'the greatest event during my study abroad'. The British labour movement, he said, was 'a logical culmination of liberalism', while German socialism 'developed against liberalism'. He noticed that the latest trend of philosophy in Britain was 'the decline of idealism'. He became interested in the idea of collective personality and received invitations more than once from one of its advocates, the young Harold Laski, whom he found to be 'brilliant, erudite and lively'. He visited the Woodbrooke settlement near Birmingham founded by Cadbury and Rowntree (where his Quaker wife stayed), which he called 'the [New] Lanark of the twentieth century'. He attended Fabian summer schools at which he heard E. D. Morel criticizing the Anglo-Japanese Alliance in particular and secret diplomacy in general. At Oxford and Cambridge he was much impressed by the tutorial system which he compared to the private schools which had mushroomed in Japan prior to the Meiji Restoration to train students by a distinguished teacher, for he was concerned about the spread of the 'bureaucratic', 'mass-production system' of education of his own day.[46]

He became a member of the Fabian Society in Britain,[47] and was engaged in the study of Thomas Hill Green and his idealism which he believed would harmonize with the passion for social reform.[48] He is said to have often quoted Green's aphorism: 'Let the flag of England be dragged through the mud rather than the six pence be added to the taxes which weigh on the poor.'[49] Kawai, one of those few courageous professors who upheld liberalism in the difficult days of the late 1930s, was driven from his university position in 1939. Later, he was indicted and tried. He was found guilty and fined in 1943.

The Pacific War and the post-war era

When the Pacific War broke out in 1941, it was a mild surprise for many Japanese to read the term 'USA and Britain' (*beiei*) in that order, in the imperial rescript declaring war. Previously they had been accustomed to the expression *eibei* ('Britain and USA'), although in reality this transposition had been taking place on the world scene since the First World War. In the war years Britain was usually paired with the USA as a junior partner, even in such bellicose slogans as '*Dato Kichiku Beiei*' (Down with the Fiendish America and Britain).

Throughout the decades of the Cold War the image of Britain was apt to be overshadowed by the dominant influence of the two superpowers – the United States and the Soviet Union. There were, however, two cases where Japanese intellectuals sought a British model for their actions: the British Labour Party in power in the period of post-war reconstruction; and the anti-nuclear movement when the Cold War threatened to develop into a nuclear holocaust.

The Britain of the Labour Party

In the early summer of 1947, when the first government led by a socialist (Katayama Tetsu) was formed in Japan, an article appeared in *Chuo Koron* giving a fair account of the history of the British Labour Party. The author of the article (Urabe Toshio) pointed out that Labour's policy of social welfare had been insufficiently appreciated in Japan, though the British electorate now living in austerity gave their support to Labour mainly because of its measures for social welfare: the National Insurance System based on the Beveridge Plan, the National Health Service, town planning, a national land plan, educational reform and new housing.[50]

Japanese assessments of Attlee's Labour government were varied. Earlier in the same year Wakimura Yoshitaro, professor of Economics at Tokyo University, had stressed the fact that the Labour Party had won political power 'peacefully' [through the general election] and had embarked on the nationalization of industries. After a detailed analysis of these measures, Professor Wakimura summarized 'the first period of social planning' by saying that 'the nationalization list of the Labour Party was not based on the selection of those industries that were easy to nationalize, or those that had fallen into difficulties, but aimed at making the national economy socialist by systematically capturing economically strategic heights'. 'When planning for the first period will have been completed,' he added, 'Britain will be more than half way on the road to Socialism even if eighty percent of all her industries remain in the hands of private management.'[51] 'British socialism' now emerged as 'the third way' or 'the middle system between the American system and the Soviet one', wrote Sumiya Mikio, another professor of economics at Tokyo University.[52]

Towards the end of Attlee's government Aneurin Bevan, the leader of the left wing of the British Labour Party, resigned from his post as minister of Labour, protesting against the new charges to be introduced in the National Health Service to meet increased expenditure for rearmament. Five years later, he was designated shadow foreign secretary by the party leader Hugh Gaitskell. At the 1957 Party Conference Bevan came to oppose the left's policy of British unilateral nuclear disarmament. It was some time before this dramatic change in the Labour Party, that Bevan visited Japan to talk with leaders of the socialist (then left-wing socialist) party and *Sohyo* (the General Council of Trade Unions).

The first topic which Bevan dealt with, in an interview arranged with Wada Hiro, secretary of the left-wing socialist party, and Takano Minoru of *Sohyo*, was Japan's rearmament. Bevan argued that under the existing circumstances with American forces stationed in Japan, no matter whether she was armed or not, Japan would be aligned with the policies of the western camp. The vital issue, he said, was for Japan to become truly independent. Then rearmament would be regarded simply as a domestic issue, not one sufficiently important to divide the two socialist parties, left and right.

Wada asked whether nationalized industries would remain sufficiently efficient to keep Britain competitive in foreign trade, a question to which Bevan gave short shrift by alluding to the achievements of the British steel industry.[53] Bevan does not seem to have inspired the Japanese left with his own visions of socialism, but his arguments for Japan's political autonomy or independence had some impact on later events, as will be shown below.

Although it was pointed out by a veteran journalist that Britain was 'seeking to re-establish her leadership in world diplomacy',[54] Japanese interest in the Labour Party waned until Harold Wilson, the new party leader, presented a new rallying point, science and automation allied with socialism – the so-called 'White Heat of Technology', and won the general election in October 1964.[55] Eda Saburo, then the organizing secretary of the Japan Socialist Party, visited Britain and observed the election campaign at first hand. He attended constituency meetings in London, at which he noted that candidates were doing their best to answer all of the questions put to them, and the collection of campaign funds was being made in a modest form ('almost everybody threw money in the tin box, mostly coppers and very few notes'). Some outdoor speeches were made, but not many and not too loud in volume. Door-to-door canvassing was the main form of electoral campaign of individual candidates, while the party headquarters were concerned with the mass media. The amount of campaign funds for each candidate was about 900 000 yen at most, and the figures were inspected by public accountants and published in newspapers. Candidates were not the representatives of local interests, but of the political party, and the electorates would vote for the party and its policies. These details, Eda must have felt, showed a striking contrast to electoral practices in Japan. For 13 years under the Conservative government Britain's international standing had continued to decline. While the Conservatives had sought to maintain Britain's position as a Great Power by means of an independent nuclear capability, Labour, as Denis Healey, the new defence minister, stated in a Fabian speech, believed that Britain was no longer in a position to impose her own will by force, and that her greatness should be derived from her capacity to cooperate with other countries, and to obtain their assent through persuasion and appropriate economic and military aid. Eda felt that the nationalism upheld by Labour was not one of self-assertion against others, but rather 'a national awakening to the need to refashion their own life and country in such a way as be fitted the new development of world history'. Hence Labour's special emphasis on science, technology and educational reform. Eda pointed out that, nationalism apart, the great task for Labour to restore British fortunes was to achieve 'economic growth' which in its turn largely depended on the attitude of the trade unions.[56] Eda's observations were in some way prophetic.

Japanese Fabians for Japan's economic autonomy

Fabianism in Japan had come to mean a gradual and peaceful approach to socialism, similar to that of its British prototype. However, unlike the latter it lacked organizational links with a national labour movement. More than anything else Japanese Fabians aimed to apply the Fabian spirit.[57] The Fabian Research Institute (Kenkyusho), which was formed in May 1950, had no link with the Japan Fabian Society of the 1920s. It was founded under the initiative of Ohara Soichiro (1909–68), the son of Ohara Magosaburo (1880–1943), founder of the Kurashiki Cotton Spinning Company and the

Ohara Institute for the Study of Social Problems (and also of the Ohara Museum of Fine Arts), at a time when deflationary measures for post-war economic recovery led to the dismissal of many workers and to muffled social unrest. This was on the eve of the Korean War, when a peace treaty and an end to the Allied occupation were on the political agenda. The inaugural meeting of the institute was held at the office of Kurashiki Rayon, Tokyo; Arisawa Hiromi, known for the policy of 'priority production' in steel and coal, was chosen as the institute's representative.[58] 'The basic attitude of the institute', read its prospectus, prepared by Tsuru Shigeto, another notable economist, 'is to develop the human capabilities of each individual to the full on the basis of a system no longer encumbered by the private ownership of the means of production . . . and to establish freedom on the foundation of equality.' It emphasized 'a dramatic method' that would preserve 'values worth preservation'.[59]

Japanese rearmament had begun in 1950 and the National Police Reserve (later the security force) developed into the Self-Defence Force in July 1954. Takano Minoru advocated a programme to construct a peaceful national economy.[60] In October 1954, the Fabian Research Institute published a report on Japan's economic autonomy in which it stated that the absence of autonomy was the result of the Japanese economy having been propelled into the US world strategy of an anti-communist military alliances. Arisawa defined the aim of economic autonomy as a higher standard of living that was to be achieved by a positive balance of payments in non-military trade, and stressed the importance of low-cost or cost-competitive plants being established in heavy, chemical industries, because the textile industry alone was insufficient to provide the scale of exports required for economic autonomy. 'New Industries', especially the petrochemical industry, and industrial *combinato* (concentrated zones) were to be established and placed in the framework of the national economy. The problems of economic autonomy, he added, would transcend the existing system of capitalism.[61] Fabianism in post-war Japan served its purpose by providing the frame of reference for a peaceful, gradual transition to a more independent and affluent country, if not to a socialist economy or a neutral Japan. It is of some interest that the last issue of *Fabian Kenkyu* in 1969 was devoted to an analysis of the causes of British economic stagnation in comparison with Japanese economic growth.[62]

The movement for nuclear disarmament

Positive features of the image of Britain in post-war Japan were reinforced by the movement for nuclear disarmament embodied in the CND (Campaign for Nuclear Disarmament) and especially by Bertrand Russell and his Direct Action Committee. In Japan, the only country which had experienced nuclear bombing, it was the American nuclear test at Bikini Atoll in 1954, fatally affecting the crew of a Japanese fishing boat, that helped launch a national movement against nuclear weapons, with a world conference held at Hiroshima in 1955. The Japanese movement, however, suffered from ideological divisions and split, and it took 14 years before a united conference was held again. The British movement was launched in the wake of the first British test of a hydrogen bomb at Christmas Island in 1957. CND was formed in the following year and the annual Aldermaston march became an important event in the history of the movement for nuclear disarmament. Although Japanese interest and participation was slow and restrained, in 1959 one Japanese visitor marched part of the way for the first time.[63] Bertrand Russell and his policy of direct action, rather than CND and its mass movement, attracted the attention of Japanese campaigners against nuclear weapons. Russell kept up his protest campaign by sending an open letter to American and Soviet leaders and by the direct action of his 'Committee of 100' against a US nuclear submarine base in Britain. These were fully reported in Japanese radical magazines such as *Shiso no Kagaku*, *Chuo Koron* and *Sekai*.

The 'London Renaissance'

'For the last twelve years', wrote Ishiguro Hideko in *Chuo Koron* in 1968, 'new songs and new souls sprang up from among the British working classes'. This author referred to the play *Look Back with Anger* (1956) by John Osborne as the beginning of a new British culture, and pointed to the Beatles, the Rolling Stones, Mary Quant, Vidal Sassoon and Twiggy as embodiments of this new mood. Carnaby Street became known in Japan as a symbol of such a 'London Renaissance'. This new culture was termed an 'anti-Victorian spirit' which rejected middle-class hypocrisy and respectability. It was also pointed out that British student protests in 1968, such as that witnessed at the LSE, were less heroic and more restrained than the hysterical scenes witnessed at similar protests in Japan.[64] Maruya Saiichi asked how effective the destructive power of this revolution in fashion and taste would be.[65]

The New Left in Britain, represented by E. P. Thompson in historical studies, has not been sufficiently appreciated in Japan (none of Thompson's major works have been translated). The New Left, by the very nature of its origins, set out to destroy the Old Left, itself a Victorian legacy, and to a great extent it succeeded in doing so. Classless pop culture, itself an offspring of the New Left in some senses, thrived even after the New Left ceased to be an effective force in attempting to overturn old dogmas and respectability. Japanese youth, perhaps more than intellectuals, took pop culture seriously. A classless society in terms of fashion and taste, however, concealed the advance of the middle class or the embourgeoisement of a large section of the working classes. Similar developments were taking place in Japan and the image of Britain as the country of pop culture took root among the younger generation.

Britain in the 1980s and the 1990s

When 'everybody speaks of "the fall of Britain"', wrote *Chuo Koron* in 1968, it means 'the fall of the British empire'. Soon 'everybody' began to talk about a 'sick Britain' which meant, in many cases (especially on the management side), 'sick' industrial relations that culminated in 'the winter of discontent' in 1978–79, and led to the advent of Thatcherism.

Mrs Thatcher's Britain, with its series of privatizations of nationalized industries and public utilities, and its restrictive legislation against trade unions (though perhaps not her poll tax), was favourably received by Japanese business leaders. However, she did attract adverse comment from intellectuals who generally criticized her 'dogma' of the free market. A devastating review of Mrs Thatcher's 'achievements' came from Morishima Michio: 'The reverse turn' attempted by Mrs Thatcher was 'a wild operation worthy of the term "a counter revolution"', wrote Morishima.[66] She sought to introduce the market principle to white-collar workers and saturate education, especially higher education, with the idea of profit-making. Courses which were supposed to serve this principle, such as computer science, accounting and Japanese Studies (at a time when Japan's economic growth seemed miraculous), were encouraged, while more traditional courses were curtailed. Morishima saw the Miners' Strike of 1984–85 as allied to academics' opposition to the introduction of the market principle in universities:

> Mrs Thatcher cannot understand the miners' spirit that would inspire them to go on digging if there remained a shovelful of coal, in the same way that university teachers would not stop lecturing as long as a single student was in the class. They may seem ignorant and heedless of efficiency but they are listening to God, and their calling is their life itself. To make them obey the whim of profit is to turn them into the servants of capitalists.[67]

Morishima, however, has remained an isolated voice in Japan.

The image of Britain among Japanese intellectuals underwent many vicissitudes over the course of the modern era. Fear of Britain was common in the period before and immediately after the Opium War. At the same time the expanding power of Britain was admired, and it encouraged many Japanese to emulate the British for their civilization and industrialization. British parliamentary democracy continued to inspire both politicians and academics, but a Prussian model appeared more attractive to the founding fathers of modern Japan and also to their successors. The image of a liberal Britain, though short-lived before the war, remained a valuable asset. The image of a social Britain, which encouraged Katayama Sen in his support for workers and also gave rise to Japanese Fabianism, remains viable even today. In the post-war era hopes and efforts to grope for a 'third way' in the Cold War drove Japanese intellectuals closer to Britain, especially to the Labour Party, which seemed to embody the ethos of a social Britain. Both nostalgia for and the revolt against Victorian values were readily appreciated by the Japanese. Today, at the start of the twenty-first century, Tony Blair's New Labour, while harking back to the call of Gladstone and his liberalism, looks ahead to a new role in a united Europe. It seems likely that Britain will not cease to be an object of emulation for Japanese intellectuals.

Notes

1. See W. G. Beasley, 'The Foreign Threat and the Opening of the Ports', in M. B. Jansen (ed.), *The Cambridge History of Japan, Volume 5, The Nineteenth Century* (Cambridge: Cambridge University Press, 1989), pp. 259–307.
2. Numata Jiro, Matsumura Akira, Sato Shosuke (eds), *Yogaku, Volume 1, Nihon Shiso Taikei, Volume 64* (Tokyo: Iwanami Shoten, 1972), p. 501; Takimoto Seiji (ed.), *Sato Nobuhiro (Shin-en) Kagaku Zenshu* (Works of Family Learning) (Tokyo: Iwanami Shoten, 1926), vol. II, passim; Koshi Taro, *Sato Nobuhiro* (Tokyo: Shinchosha, 1941), p. 54 f.
3. Imai Usaburu, Seya Yoshihiko and Bito Masahide (eds), Aizawa Seishisai, 'Shinron', *Mitogaku, Nihon Shiso Taikei, Volume 53* (Tokyo: Iwanami Shoten, 1973), p. 78; Bob Tadashi Wakabayashi, *Anti-Foreignism and Western Learning in Early Modern Japan: the New Theses of 1825* (Cambridge, MA: Council on East Asian Studies, Harvard University, 1986; 1991 edition).
4. Sato Shosuke, Uete Michiari and Yamaguchi Muneyuki (eds), *Watanabe Kazan, Takano Choei, Sakuma Shozan, Yokoi Shonan, Hashimoto Sanai, Nihon Shisho Taikei, vol. 55* (Tokyo: Iwanami Shoten, 1975), p. 63.
5. Takano Choei, in *Nihon Shiso Taikei, Volume 55*, pp. 162–4.
6. *Nihon Shiso Taikei, Volume 55*, p. 69.
7. W. G. Beasley, *The Meiji Restoration*, Stanford, Calif., Stanford University Press, 1972, p. 107.
8. Hagihara Nobutoshi, *Satsuei Senso, Toi Kage (Volume 2)* (Tokyo: Asahi Shinbunsha, 1998), p. 46.
9. Ibid., p. 49.
10. Ivan Parker Hall, *Mori Arinori* (Cambridge MA: Harvard University Press, 1973), pp. 88–90.
11. Hamada Kenji, *Prince Ito* (first edition, London: George Allen & Unwin, 1936; reprinted Bethesda, MD: University Publications of America, 1979), pp. 35–6.
12. Albert M. Craig, *Choshu in the Meiji Restoration* (Cambridge, MA: Harvard University Press, 1961, repr. 1978), p. 235.
13. Fukuzawa Yukichi, *The Autobiography of Fukuzawa Yukichi with Preface to the Collected Works of Fukuzawa*, translated by Eiichi Kiyooka (Tokyo: Hokuseido Press, 1981), passim.

14. Fukuzawa Yukichi, *Zenshu* (Works), vol. 1 (Tokyo: Iwanami Shoten, 1958), pp. 289–90.
15. Ibid., pp. 373–4, 376, 378, 380.
16. Fukuzawa Yukichi, *An Encouragement of Learning*, English translation by David Dilworth and U. Hirano (Tokyo: Monumenta Nipponica Monographs, Sophia University, 1969), passim.
17. Fukuzawa Yukichi, *An Outline of a Theory of Civilization*, English translation by David A. Dilworth and G. C. Hurst (Tokyo: Monumenta Nipponica Monographs, Sophia University, 1973), passim.
18. Ishi Tamiji, *Nakamura Masanao Den* (Tokyo: Seiko Zasshisha, 1907), ch. 6.
19. *Baba Tatsui Zenshu* (Tokyo: Iwanami Shoten, 1987–8), vol. 1, 215 ff.; vol. III, p. 75.
20. Tokutomi Soho, *The Future Japan*, trans. by Vinh Sinh (Edmonton, Alberta: University of Alberta Press, 1989), p. 182; John D. Pierson, *Tokutomi Soho, A Journalist for Modern Japan* (Princeton: Princeton University Press, 1980), p. 134.
21. *Katayama Sen Chosakushu*, vol. 1 (Tokyo: Kawade Shobo Shinsha, 1959), p. 150; Katayama, *Bankoku Shakaito* (International Socialist Party), (Tokyo, 1907); *Katayama Sen Chosakushu*, vol. 1, 284 f.
22. Ibid., p. 284.
23. Ibid., p. 286.
24. *Osaka Heimin Shinbun*, 5 September 1907.
25. *Shakai Shinbun*, 1 September 1907.
26. Dated 29 October 1911, Norman Mackenzie (ed.), *The Letters of Sidney and Beatrice Webb, Volume 2, Partnership 1892–1912* (Cambridge: Cambridge University Press for LSE, 1978), p. 336.
27. Beatrice Webb to Lady Courtney, 18 October 1911, ibid., p. 374.
28. Beatrice Webb to Lady Courtney, 19 September 1911, ibid., p. 373.
29. Sidney Webb to George Bernard Shaw, 19 October 1911, ibid., p. 377.
30. *Toyo Keizai Shinpo*, 15 April 1913, quoted in Tanaka Akira, *Shokokushugi, Nihon no Kindai o yominaosu* (Tokyo: Iwanami Shoten, 1999), p. 117.
31. *Daisan Teikoku*, 1 January 1915.
32. *Yoshino Sakuzo, Senshu (Selected Works)*, vol. 2 (Tokyo: Iwanami Shoten, 1996), pp. 35, 43.
33. Ibid., vol. 5, pp. 150, 152.
34. Ibid., vol. 23, p. 338.
35. Henry Dewitt Smith II, *Japan's First Student Radicals* (Cambridge, MA: Harvard University Press, 1972), pp. 35–52; *Daisan Teikoku*, January 1918.
36. Gail Lee Bernstein, *A Portrait of Kawakami Hajime, 1879–1941* (Cambridge, MA: Harvard University Press, 1966), p. 116 f.
37. George Oakley Totten, *The Social Democratic Movement in Prewar Japan* (New Haven: Yale University Press, 1976), p. 46.
38. *Ishikawa Sanshiro Chosakushu*, vol. 8 (Tokyo: Seidosha, 1977), p. 418.
39. *Shakaishugi Kenkyu*, June 1923, pp. 29–35.
40. Ibid., February 1925, pp. 33–5.
41. Robert Schilderon, *Toyohiko Kagawa: Apostle of Love and Social Justice* (Berkeley: University of California Press, 1988), p. 13.
42. George B. Bikle Jr., *The New Jerusalem: Aspects of Utopianism in the Thought of Kagawa Toyohiko* (Tuscon, Arizona: University of Arizona for the Association for Asian Studies, 1976), p. 123 f.
43. *Nippon*, October 1894.

44. Koyama Fumio, *Kuga Katsunan* (Tokyo: Misuzushobo, 1990), p. 189.
45. *Kita Ikki Chosakushu*, vol. 2 (Tokyo: Misuzushobo, 1959), pp. 90–4.
46. Kawai Eijiro, *Zaio Tsushin* (Letters from Europe) (Tokyo: Kaizosha, 1925), pp. 1, 2, 6, 14, 51, 88, 155–7, 166 ff.
47. Hirai Atsuko, *Individualism and Socialism: the Life and Thought of Kawai Eijiro* (Cambridge, MA: Council on East Asian Studies, Harvard University Press, 1986), p. 60.
48. Kawai Eijiro, *Thomas Hill Green no Shiso Taikei* (The System of Thought of T. H. Green), 2 vols (Tokyo: Nihon Hyoronsha, 1930).
49. Hirai Atsuko, *Individualism and Socialism*, p. 92.
50. Urabe Toshio, 'Igirisu Rodoto', *Chuo Koron*, June 1947.
51. *Sekai*, January 1948.
52. Ibid., September 1948.
53. *Chuo Koron*, October 1954, pp. 90–5.
54. Matsumoto Shigeharu, in *Chuo Koron*, April 1958.
55. Harold Wilson, 'The British Labour Party and Scientific Revolution', trans. Amanao Ryoichi, *Chuo Koron*, December 1963.
56. *Sekai*, December 1964.
57. *Fabian Kenkyu*, 15 December 1953.
58. *Fabian Kenkyu*, March 1969.
59. *Fabian Kenkyusho News*, 15 August 1953.
60. *Fabian Kenkyu*, 15 August 1950.
61. *Sekai*, October 1954.
62. *Fabian Kenkyu*, March 1969.
63. *Sekai*, June 1959.
64. Ishiguro Hideko, in *Chuo Koron*, September 1968.
65. Ibid., for Maruya.
66. Morishima Michio, *Sacha Jidai no Igirisu* (Tokyo: Iwanami Shoten, 1989), p. 67.
67. Ibid., p. 122.

Part II
The Nineteenth Century and After

3
Early Japanese Visitors to Victorian Britain

Andrew Cobbing

In the 1860s, after more than two hundred years of cultural isolation, the first wave of Japanese travellers ventured overseas to observe life in the little-known lands of Europe and America. Many of them were samurai, sent abroad on specific missions to investigate western conditions. Fascinated by the extent of British political and commercial influence which they found, they paid particularly close attention to the Victorian world and recorded everything they saw in minute detail. Their diaries and letters chronicle an intriguing cultural encounter with a society far removed from their own experience. Their impressions of an empire at the height of its power also reveal some of the underlying forces at work in shaping images of the West as a whole during this most formative stage in the history of modern Japan.

This essay traces the background to the Japanese discovery of Britain, from perceptions of the outside world in the Edo period to the forces that culminated in the first wave of overseas travellers to the West. Surviving records from these pioneering journeys capture the ordeals of samurai on their travels, from long ocean voyages to the trials of cultural adaptation, and throw light on their own outlook as they searched for solutions to the political and economic crises of the last years of Bakufu rule. As a result of the intensive efforts of some travellers to record what they found in these unexplored lands, within the space of just a few years, a surprisingly in-depth awareness of the Victorian world rapidly emerged in Meiji Japan.[1]

Early travels in the Edo period

Japan's first encounter with Britain is often traced to 1600, when William Adams was summoned to Osaka Castle after being shipwrecked off the Bungo coast. It was there that he spread out a map in front of Tokugawa Ieyasu, and pointed out his native land far to the west. In the last years of the sixteenth century, however, Japanese youths had already been taken to England on at least two occasions when they were captured by Thomas Cavendish on board Spanish galleons in the Southern Seas. These were among the first Japanese travellers to reach Europe; others came in Spanish and Portuguese vessels, invariably motivated by their new-found Christian faith. One convert from Satsuma called Bernardo reached Lisbon as early as 1551. Before the Tokugawa Bakufu imposed its ban on Christianity, two Japanese missions even travelled to Rome and back.

The next Japanese arrivals in England were 11 local sailors from the island of Hirado. After the East India Company set up a factory there in 1613, they were engaged to man the *Clove* on her return voyage to England, and then spent the winter of 1614 in Plymouth before making their way back to Japan. The factory closed down in 1623, however, and shortly afterwards the Bakufu restricted its contact with Europe to Dutch merchants on the man-made island of Dejima in Nagasaki. As a result the Japanese discovery of Britain was to be delayed until the Victorian era, more than two hundred years later. British attempts to reopen trade were all thwarted, notably in 1673 when the *Return* expedition came to nothing, and later during the Napoleonic Wars when Stamford Raffles sent ships to Nagasaki disguised in Dutch colours.

The *sakoku* edicts of the 1630s limited contact with the outside world but did not isolate Japan entirely. In addition to the merchants from China, Indochina and Holland who continued to ply their trade through Nagasaki, large quantities of goods from China and Korea arrived through the Ryukyu and Tsushima islands off the Kyushu coast. Overseas travel was banned, however, and it became a capital offence to leave Japan. Some Ryukyu and Tsushima merchants were permitted to visit China and Korea, but the only Japanese people to reach western shores thereafter were either castaways or the occasional illegal traveller.

Under Tokugawa rule, Japanese attitudes to Britain veered dramatically between extremes of indifference and intense concern. For much of the Edo period, references in geographical works to this former trading partner all but disappeared, in spite of Britain's growing interests in Asia. After interviewing Giovanni Sidotti, an Italian priest captured on the island of Tanegashima in 1708, the influential scholar Arai Hakuseki even claimed that British influence was on the decline because the British monarch had banned traffic with the outside world.[2] When the first warning signs of advancing European colonialism appeared, it was the encroachment of other powers that caught the attention of Japanese scholars. In 1784, Miura Baien wrote of how the Spanish, Dutch and Portuguese had seized lands in Asia. Of Britain, later to be regarded as the archetypal colonial power, there was no mention at all.[3]

In the final years of the eighteenth century, however, the increasing volume of available information brought news of Britain's emerging wealth as a trading power. Some theses argued that commerce along European lines might provide a useful model to enable Japan to overcome its economic problems. Honda Toshiaki, for example, even suggested that the capital of a restructured Japanese empire should be located in Kamchatka as this was on a similar latitude to London in the West.[4] Prompted by their discovery of the commercial wealth of Europe, Honda and other scholars in the early years of the nineteenth century such as Sato Nobuhiro, Takano Choei and Watanabe Kazan were already articulating the framework of strength and prosperity that was later to form the foundations of economic policy in Meiji Japan.

This, however, was not the image of Britain adhered to by the Bakufu authorities. Fear of Russian incursions from the north in the last years of the eighteenth century was followed, with the onset of the Napoleonic Wars, by a growing fear of British advance from the south. This foreign pressure (*gaiatsu*) created a siege mentality in the Tokugawa regime, exacerbated by the growing numbers of foreign ships sighted in the seas around Japan. To Bakufu officials, the British were simply pirates, a notion reinforced by the counsel of the eminent scholar Otsuki Gentaku.

Otsuki thought that he had powerful evidence to confirm his suspicions. Based in Nagasaki during the Napoleonic Wars, he saw several unusual ships arriving in port. These were actually American vessels hired by the Dutch in Batavia. Now that the French had overrun their homeland in Europe, the Dutch had no other ships to sustain their Dejima trade. News of American independence did not reach Japan until 1809, however, and Otsuki was convinced that these ships were British. In 1808, there was the incident involving HMS *Phaeton* when a British man o'war sailed into Nagasaki Harbour in search of Dutch vessels to capture.

Not surprisingly, Otsuki received a negative impression of the British from interviews with the Dutch on Dejima, and subsequent events appeared to justify his belief that they had predatory designs on Japan. When shipwrecked English whaling crews ran amock along the Hitachi coastline in 1824, Takahashi Kageyasu, the official sent to investigate, concluded that 'all their manners are rough, devious and deathly'.[5] The Opium War in particular led to a heightened sense of alarm. Not only had mighty China been defeated, but the subsequent opening of the port of Shanghai brought British merchants, ships and guns uncomfortably close, just a week's voyage away from Nagasaki. By the 1850s, scholars like Yoshida Shoin were increasingly frustrated by the inadequacy of information reaching Nagasaki in Chinese and Dutch. Only through overseas travel, they argued, could they gauge the strengths and capabilities of the Western Powers that were then seeking to open trade relations with Japan.

With the opening of the treaty ports in 1859, the stage was set for the first overseas missions, and the Japanese discovery of the Victorian world. The catalyst was diplomatic: two resident ministers, Townsend Harris and Rutherford Alcock, encouraged the Bakufu to send missions to America in 1860 and Europe in 1862. Ostensibly this was to complete the formalities of the commercial treaties, but it was also an opportunity to impress upon

Japanese officials the benefits of open trade through a series of showcase visits to factories, military installations, hospitals and other wonders of the industrial age.

The Bakufu duly complied, although a wave of terrorist attacks on foreigners in and around the new treaty ports forced somewhat different issues to the fore of Japanese diplomats' minds. The Takenouchi mission in 1862 managed to obtain European consent to postpone the opening of further treaty ports. But the Ikeda mission's visit to France in 1864 failed in its prime objective of securing support for the closure of Yokohama. It did, however, lead to closer ties with France, and in 1865, a smaller delegation under Shibata Takenaka arrived in Paris to negotiate terms for French industrial and military aid. At the same time the Bakufu organized parties of students to study overseas. Initial plans to send a group to America were frustrated by the outbreak of civil war there, and in 1863 they arrived in Holland instead. Other parties left for Russia in 1865, Britain in 1866 and France in 1867, and many of these students were left stranded in Europe when they heard of the overthrow of the Tokugawa regime.

While the Bakufu reserved the right to send its own delegations abroad, the ban on overseas travel remained in place. With the influx of foreign merchants in the treaty ports, however, opportunities arose for illegal travellers (*mikkosha*) to make their escape. There had been isolated attempts even before the opening of these ports, such as when Yoshida Shoin was put ashore on Commodore Perry's orders after stealing aboard one of his ships. Then in the 1860s, as they became increasingly restive over the Bakufu monopoly on foreign trade and overseas contacts, some southwestern domains defied Tokugawa law to send whole parties of samurai to the West.

In 1863, a young Ito Hirobumi, Inoue Kaoru and three other Choshu officers reached London after sailing from Yokohama with the help of S. J. Gower, the local Jardine Matheson & Co. representative. Contrary to popular belief, Thomas Blake Glover, the Scottish merchant in Nagasaki, did not engineer their escape, but he was responsible for the flight of 25 Japanese officers to Britain in 1865. One group was a major expedition of 19 men from Satsuma. He also helped three Choshu officers leave from Shimonoseki, and then three more, two from Hizen (Saga) and one from Aki (Hiroshima), who slipped out of Nagasaki beneath the gaze of Bakufu officials later that year.[6] In 1866, under growing pressure from the treaty powers, the Bakufu finally removed the ban on overseas travel. Anyone could now apply for a passport, as long as they were going abroad for study or trade. This presaged the first real boom in Japanese travel abroad in modern times, as students and troupes of performing artists made their way to cities in the West. In the first year, by far the single most popular destination was Paris, because of the international exhibition held there in 1867. In addition to a Bakufu party, separate delegations from Satsuma and Hizen took part, and attracted considerable interest in France as they vied to sell their wares. Then, after the short civil war (1868–69) that finally destroyed Tokugawa power, there followed an unparalleled rush of Japanese travellers. In the early 1870s, this culminated in the Iwakura Embassy, a small army of more than one hundred officials and students, including several prominent Meiji leaders, which spent nearly two years abroad touring America and Europe.

The voyage to Europe

For early Japanese travellers, the most striking and lasting impressions of Victorian life were often received not in Britain at all, but from their experiences on the long voyage to Europe. From the moment they stepped on board European ships in Yokohama or Nagasaki, they were immersed in an alien world. It was during the two or three months they spent at sea and at ports of call on the way that they were first exposed to Victorian culture, from their diet, fashions and social customs to their steam engines and hotels.

There were two direct routes to Europe. A few travellers had little choice but to endure a long uninterrupted voyage on merchant ships around the Cape of Good Hope, but most booked their passage via Suez and stopped at several ports on the way. These would often include brief stays in Shanghai, Hong Kong, Singapore, Galle and Aden. Until the opening of the Suez Canal in 1869, the next stretch across the desert to Alexandria was a journey by rail.

The last leg of the voyage, through the Mediterranean Sea, sometimes featured stops at Malta and Gibraltar, so the voyage could amount to nothing less than a guided tour of the jewels of the British Empire. This point was not lost on British diplomats when making travel arrangements for delegations from China and Japan. In 1876, for example, Dr Halliday Macartney expressly changed a Chinese mission's booking from a French vessel to a P&O passenger ship. This, he reasoned, would have 'a profound effect upon the members of the Embassy who could not but be impressed at seeing the British flag flying in every port of call they came to see and thus girdling half the globe'.[7]

Early travellers' impressions of life outside Japan can be gleaned from their diaries. They were often written in a somewhat hybrid form, combining the traditional poetic features considered essential to the travel records of educated men in Tokugawa Japan with a growing concern for scientific observation. This new trait was inherited from the increasingly sophisticated geographical works available in Japan towards the end of the *sakoku* period. Manifest in the liberal use of statistics, it reflected the perceived need for an in-depth investigation into conditions in the West.

Diaries written in the 1860s convey the pioneering spirit of men keenly aware of the unprecedented opportunity they had to explore far-off lands for themselves. They also reveal their intense interest as they encountered what to them were novel facets of the outside world. By the 1870s, such travel journals were already becoming more sophisticated, and, as cultural familiarity set in, they conveyed less of a sense of naïve wonder at the curiosities of Victorian life. No longer was amazement recorded, for example, at the thundering steam engines they saw en route, because, in treaty ports at least, these were also rapidly becoming part of everyday life in early Meiji Japan.

The first port of call on the voyage to Europe was often Shanghai or Hong Kong. Almost with one voice, early Japanese travellers were appalled at the servility they witnessed among the native Chinese populations there. In 1862, for instance, Takasugi Shinsaku noted with disgust how people in the streets of Shanghai made way to let the Europeans past. Moreover, the city gate was manned by British and French soldiers, not Chinese, and one samurai traveller was even refused passage when he was mistaken for a native of Shanghai.[8]

Such attacks could be quite venomous. To varying degrees, Japanese visitors were already making a conscious effort to culturally dissociate themselves from China, reflecting a growing anxiety for the future of their own homeland, lest the fate that had befallen Shanghai and Hong Kong be visited on Japan. Others bound for the United States expressed similar views in Hawaii and San Francisco, where they recorded with surprise how Chinese merchants were treated like slaves by the American population.

By the end of the voyage, most Japanese travellers were suitably impressed by the extent of British power in Asia. On the one hand, they resented this foreign dominion over 'civilized' cultural neighbours like China and India. At the same time, they could not conceal a certain admiration for British authority in the colonies. As samurai warriors, they respected the exercise of power and reserved their fiercest criticism for the servility of the ruled masses. The result was frequently a potent blend of jealousy and esteem. By the late 1860s, many were freely using terms such as 'the height of progress' or 'strength and prosperity' in their diaries to describe the distinguishing features of the Victorian world.

Such observations were invariably prompted during the voyage by the first experiences of western technology at work. Travellers came across gas lights in Hong Kong, steam trains in Suez, and telegraph lines along the railway track on the way to Alexandria. Nothing stretched Japanese diarists' powers of description as much as these encounters with the age of steam. The speed of the machines they saw was a revelation, because the fastest mode of transport in the Tokugawa world was still the horse. The first full-size steam train to arrive in Japan was the *Iron Duke* in Nagasaki in 1865, and the first passenger service between Shinbashi and Yokohama did not open until 1872. Between 1871 and 1874, a national telegraph network was built, linking Tokyo to Nagasaki in the south, and Tokyo to Aomori in the north. But in the 1860s, the Japanese abroad were incredulous at the speed of telegraph communications, and dismayed by the sense of haste and impatience this induced in fellow European travellers.

The voyage was also memorable for the encounter with Victorian customs and social manners. Samurai travellers were bemused by the outwards signs of chivalry, and some pointed out what they considered to be the inordinate respect shown to women. This was often most apparent at the dinner table, where men were not even allowed to sit down and eat until their lady companions were ready. Through a combination of trial and error, they gradually discovered the small details of etiquette that had to be observed in Victorian society. As Nakai Hiroshi noted during his voyage across the Indian Ocean in 1866, 'It is best to steer clear of the ladies on deck. They care not for light chatter, and you cannot even smoke in their presence.'[9]

Encounters with European food frequently posed problems, a challenge intensified by the constraints of sea travel. Some Japanese travellers were impressed by the fare served on P&O ships, and novelties like ice cream and pineapples were among the most pleasant discoveries of the entire voyage. Scholars of Western Studies in particular made great efforts to like the food, as if to justify their training through a European diet. Nevertheless, three oily helpings of meat every day soon proved too much for most, and before long they often admitted to cravings for *sashimi* and other native dishes.[10]

During these voyages in fact, travellers were put under considerable pressure to adapt in a number of ways, particularly if they were planning on staying in Europe for any length of time. The trials of an unfamiliar diet would soon be followed by the inevitable question of clothes and hairstyle. The attention that their samurai attire inspired in foreign observers ranged from benign curiosity to ridicule. While their traditional swords were usually admired with evident respect, their *chonmage* topknots were more often the objects of undisguised mirth, and many increasingly felt obliged to exchange their native dress for the mode of a Victorian gentleman.

As official representatives of Japan, travellers on early Bakufu missions were under strict orders to wear samurai clothes, and they often attracted large crowds in Europe and America curious to catch glimpses of their exotic attire. Those who were abroad to study, however, were soon persuaded to cultivate a less conspicuous style of dress. On their arrival in Hong Kong in 1865, the Satsuma students even stayed on board ship for three days waiting for their newly ordered clothes to arrive before they summoned the courage to step ashore and explore.[11]

The Japanese in Britain

Whether arriving by train from Southampton, Dover or Liverpool, the principal destination and terminus of the long journey from Japan was London. As the largest city in the world and the nerve centre of a far-flung empire, the Victorian capital was a natural focus of interest. Travellers would usually spend their first nights there in hotels; students often stayed in modest lodgings such as the Kensington Hotel, while diplomatic officials might be able to afford the luxury of the Langham Hotel at six times the price.[12]

Now that they had finally arrived, the first chinks would begin to appear in the façade of Victorian prosperity that the passage to Europe had invariably reinforced in their minds. In spite of all the miraculous steam machinery and evidence of British colonial power which they had found in ports of call, some were surprised to discover that, in the streets of London, there were visible signs of social deprivation. In 1867, Nakai Hiroshi caught a glimpse of Victorian charity when he was taken along one morning to watch soup being served to the poor. 'These extremes of poverty are an unchanging norm all over the world,' he concluded bleakly, 'and even in such a developed and prosperous nation as this.' Similarly, in 1872, Kido Takayoshi was moved by a visit to the docks in the East End to declare: 'The poor people here are even more destitute than ours.'[13]

Japanese visitors were certainly impressed, however, by the scale and prodigious energy of London. Not so grand in layout as Paris but more imposing than New York, the Victorian capital was a hive of activity with its bustling thoroughfares and rapidly growing transport networks. Trains ran high overhead along viaducts and bridges, and the world's first underground railway had opened in 1863. It was the sheer volume of traffic in particular that caught their imagination. In 1868, Sano Tsunetami recorded in his diary: 'I saw steam trains crossing a bridge, and there were no gaps at all between one train and the next.'[14] They were amazed by the hectic scenes at stations like Charing Cross. As Kume Kunitake, the official chronicler of the Iwakura embassy, observed: 'Passengers boarding cluster together like bees, while those getting out scatter in all directions like ants.'[15]

For diplomatic delegations, these glimpses of city life were caught in passing during the course of their often exhaustive tours of observation in and around the capital. Few failed to visit the showcase splendours of the day, from older historical sites like St Paul's Cathedral and the Tower of London to modern wonders of the Victorian age such as the Crystal Palace, the Thames Tunnel and Madame Tussauds. The Foreign Office and the War Office often arranged further visits to Parliament and Woolwich Arsenal and day trips to see military manouevres or inspect naval installations in ports on the south coast. In their quest to fathom the secrets of Britain's prosperity, and encouraged by their Victorian hosts' enthusiasm to display their achievements, a number of parties also ventured to the industrial north to see ironworks and mines, the cotton mills of Lancashire and the shipyards of Tyneside and Glasgow.

In the course of these tours, official Japanese delegations would move daily from one hotel to another, before leaving London for Dover and the next stop on their European itinerary. For students intent on a longer stay in

Britain, however, the time had come to make arrangements for a course of study, and to move out of their hotels into cheaper accommodation elsewhere. They might stay for a while with some generous host family or perhaps rent their own lodgings, possibly in Bayswater, Notting Hill or Camden, where distinct Japanese student communities were to emerge in the early Meiji years.

At this stage of their travels, Japanese students were heavily dependent on the arrangements made by their Victorian mentors. The merchants who engineered the illegal escapes of the first Choshu and Satsuma students in 1863 and 1865, for example, put them in touch with Professor Alexander Williamson of University College London, and he then allowed them to attend his Analytical Chemistry classes. Some of them stayed at his house in Belsize Park, or in the homes of other members of college staff.

University College went on to enrol more Japanese students than any other college in the West.[16] In fact, there were more Japanese students in London than any other city outside Japan. They also settled elsewhere in the British Isles; in the 1860s, for example, at least 12 Japanese visitors stayed in Aberdeen, the hometown of Thomas Glover. In the 1870s, they could be found studying at universities in Glasgow, Edinburgh, Oxford and Cambridge, training at various shipyards around the coast, and attending local schools in towns and villages in Wiltshire and County Armagh. The Japanese now comprised the largest Asian student population in Britain, even outnumbering students from India.[17]

Most students spent at least a year abroad, and some stayed for the better part of a decade. The majority were able to make plans for the voyage back to Japan, but an unfortunate few never saw their native land again. In polluted European cities, consumption was a common complaint, while cholera was a frequent visitor at ports of call on the voyage there and back. The first such casualty in Britain was Yamazaki Kosaburo from Choshu who died in London in March 1866. He and three other Japanese students were buried in Brookwood Cemetery near Woking in Surrey. In the 1870s, several other Japanese travellers also died in and around the shipyards in the northeast of England.[18]

Return to Japan

The boom in overseas travel following the opening up of Japan really took off when the Bakufu removed its long-standing restrictions in 1866. This did not necessarily mean, however, that there was a progressive increase in the numbers of travellers to the West in the second half of the nineteenth century. On two occasions in these early years, their numbers were in fact decimated as students cut short their research to return to their homeland. These were mostly samurai who had been sent abroad by the central government or their respective domains. No matter how far away they were themselves, their paymasters were in Japan, and they were always susceptible to the effects of political instability at home.

Firstly, when news of the overthrow of the Tokugawa regime reached Europe early in 1868, Bakufu diplomats and students alike were forced to hurry back. Many travellers who had been sent abroad by their domains also felt duty-bound to return and play their part in the civil war that followed. Secondly, and on a somewhat grander scale, there was an exodus of Japanese students from the West in the mid-1870s that effectively curtailed the headlong rush for overseas knowledge of the early Meiji years. Encouraged by senior government officials such as Okubo Toshimichi, many of them had been sent abroad by individual domains (*han*), but when these feudal realms of the old Tokugawa world were dismantled by the *haihan chiken* act of 14 July 1871, responsibility for their studies fell on the new Ministry of Education (Monbusho) in Tokyo instead. At one stage, the cost of supporting all these overseas students accounted for 21 per cent of the entire Monbusho budget.

Unable to sustain this burden, the Meiji government launched investigations into the state of Japanese students abroad. These were largely carried out by officials attached to the Iwakura embassy. At the time, this embassy seemed to be the latest development in a continually expanding search for ideas from Europe and America, but it actually presaged an end to this first era of Japanese studies in the West. Starting in 1873, regulations were put in place for the systematic recall of all but a handful of overseas students. Much was made in the Meiji press of their academic failings, as many of them had been sent abroad by their domains with little thought given to their aptitude for research. In spite of some resistance, most were forced to return over the next few years, although examinations initially devised for them upon their arrival back in Japan met with such fierce opposition that they soon had to be abandoned.

By 1876, the new order was in place. Now there was a closely monitored turnover of restricted numbers of students drawn from the elite at the Kaisei Gakko College and the Imperial College of Engineering in Tokyo. They were already specialists in their own right, so much so that Sugiura Jugo, a student who arrived in Britain in 1876, had already identified the only experts in his chosen field that he felt were capable of furthering his education.[19] Thus the rich variety of political backgrounds that had characterized early Japanese travels in Britain were already a fading memory. As such, the large numbers of Japanese students there in the early 1870s were not so much a phenomenon of the new political order, but more representative of the volatile conditions in the last years of Bakufu rule, as individual domains struggled to reinvent themselves before they were swept away altogether by the centralized Meiji state.

Returning travellers made their mark in various fields, but most prominently in government posts, journalism, published works and education. Such was the plurality of the age that some dexterous Meiji statesmen were involved in some or all of these fields at any one time. Travellers' career prospects depended to a great extent on their political loyalties and the timing of their reappearance in Japan. Factional interests ensured that some from domains like Satsuma, Choshu, Tosa and Hizen had easier access to senior posts in the Meiji administration. This was particularly the case immediately after the fall of the Bakufu when a number of illegal travellers from southwestern domains found that, in spite of their youth, their rare experience of the outside world made them indispensable to the new government.

It was these circumstances that enabled men like Ito Hirobumi, just 28 years old in 1868, to rise so quickly to prominence in Meiji Japan. The first diplomats to represent Japan in western capitals, for example, were veterans of the Satsuma expedition to Britain in 1865, and still in their early twenties. Key posts in the ministries of Public Works and Financial Affairs often fell to men from Choshu and Hizen who had been students in Britain during the 1860s. Similarly, factional interests were apparent in the Imperial Army and Navy, with senior posts often held by men from Choshu and Satsuma respectively.

In contrast, while some former Bakufu diplomats and students possessed valuable overseas experience which soon led to government appointments, few were readily admitted to positions of authority. Moreover, by the mid-1870s, returning travellers were no longer such a rarity in Meiji Japan, and even if they had impeccable connections, they faced such a high level of competition in an already established administrative system that many were obliged to work their way up through lower government ranks.

Many returning travellers conveyed their ideas in the Meiji press, either by founding newspapers or by contributing articles to the numerous journals that appeared in the early years of the new regime. In particular, the access that they had to liberal thought in Victorian Britain led some to play prominent roles in the campaign for liberal rights in Japan. Notable examples were students from Tosa such as Baba Tatsui and Ono Azusa who transplanted the debating societies they had seen and organized in London directly to Tokyo. Others wrote books, such as Nakamura Masanao, one of the Bakufu students in London, who assuaged the disillusionment of many former servants of the Tokugawa regime like himself with his published translation of Samuel Smiles' *Self-Help*. This was so successful that he went on to translate other works, including John Stuart Mill's *On Liberty*. The fact that such ideas could be diffused at all bears testimony to the revolution in Japanese awareness of the outside world that had accompanied the first years of overseas travel.

Japanese images of Victorian Britain

In the 1850s, scholars such as Yoshida Shoin still felt frustrated by the inadequacy of information to hand on Britain. Yet by the end of the 1870s, many Japanese readers had become increasingly familiar with western ideas and quite accustomed to finding detailed reports on Victorian life in books and journals. This quantum leap in cultural awareness was made possible by a series of ambitious research projects during the early years of overseas travel. These were *tansaku* works, studies that drew upon the existing tradition of geographical research on the outside world from the *sakoku* period, and added the experience of first-hand observations to present all-encompassing surveys introducing the West as a whole to readers in Japan. Close attention was paid to conditions in France and the United States, but they consistently focused in the greatest depth on life in Victorian Britain.

The first such study was compiled during the Takenouchi mission's travels in 1862, when five experts in Western Studies, including a young Fukuzawa Yukichi, were ordered to prepare reports on conditions in Europe. These were then edited after their return to Japan under the supervision of a Bakufu official called Fukuda Sakutaro. The result was a series of reports on six European countries, the most detailed of which was *Eikoku Tansaku*, an 'Investigation of Britain'.

Eikoku Tansaku represented a significant advance in Japanese understanding of life in the Victorian world. In place of the often-dated scraps of information handed down in Dutch to generations of scholars who had never left Japan, here for the first time was a systematic analysis of conditions in Europe based on the first-hand observations of overseas travellers. At the same time, these appointed experts were limited by the parameters of their training, for they were still dependent on Dutch for much of their information, and also by the constraints of life on a Bakufu mission. They spent just six weeks in England, and they were never allowed out of their hotel without a Bakufu official to monitor their activities. Moreover, their investigations were confined by the *tansaku* order, the research brief which they had received just before they left Japan. This showed little interest in British culture as such, but concentrated largely on matters of defence and the management of Japan's newly opened treaty ports.

This agenda gave rise to some singular observations in *Eikoku Tansaku*. Only the refusal of the volunteer militia to cooperate, it claimed, had prevented a full-scale invasion of Japan in 1861 after a terrorist attack on the British legation building at Tozenji in Edo. There was nothing equivalent to Japan's treaty ports in Britain, it concluded, because foreigners were not confined to specially prescribed settlements, although they were allowed to mingle freely with the native population.[20]

There were also some important discoveries. It was during their visits to factories, hospitals, schools and coal mines, as they looked for the secrets of

Victorian prosperity, that these Japanese experts stumbled across the notion of a commercial stock company. Unlike Japan, where the samurai marshalled the activities of peasants and merchants on behalf of their daimyo lords, in Britain large-scale projects – from the construction of railways and telegraph lines to the management of hospitals and schools – were organized by private companies, operating to varying degrees outside government control. The absence of any apparent class restrictions also fed the imagination of these young scholars whose own career prospects in Japan were limited by the rigid hierarchy of the Bakufu administration. Government officials in Britain, they declared with enthusiasm, were chosen according to their merits, and not because of their rank.[21]

Temporarily at least, such revolutionary ideas were destined to remain concealed following the Takenouchi mission's return to Japan early in 1863. During their absence, the political climate had changed dramatically as the *joi* campaign to expel foreigners gained momentum, so that *Eikoku Tansaku* and the other volumes on Europe were kept hidden away in Nijo Castle. For the time being, the young scholars who had compiled these reports kept their own counsel, aware that *joi* activists could turn their wrath on anyone with conspicuous sympathies for the foreign invaders.[22]

It was not until Fukuzawa Yukichi compiled his best-selling *Seiyo Jijo* (Conditions in the West) that some of these ideas saw the light of day. Published early in 1867, much of the first volume was based on his observations in Europe four years before. He later attributed the success of this work to its timing, likening the minds of samurai readers at the time to blank sheets of paper as they groped for ideas to help them shape the future of Japan. The clarity of his writing enabled them to form a clear image of political and social organization in the West.[23]

Fukuzawa wished to portray the diversity of life in Europe and America, and to dispel the popular image of the West as a monolith solely bent on the exploitation of Japan. He was an avid admirer of Victorian progress in particular, and argued that the reason for British successes in devising such ingenious new machinery lay in the social freedom they enjoyed to develop their natural talents. Anxious to convey the benefits of Victorian technology, he gave glowing descriptions of the trains, telegraph lines and gas lights of the industrial age, so much so that he fought shy of mentioning any of their disadvantages.

Like other scholars of his generation, Fukuzawa relied primarily on information in Dutch, and the notes he wrote in Europe reveal no interviews in English. In later volumes of *Seiyo Jijo*, however, he took to translating English books that he had obtained during his travels. This enabled him to transcend the Dutch perspective of Britain still apparent in many Japanese impressions of the Victorian world, only to replace it with British views of the world at large. In one section, for example, he related how people in India preferred the stability and trading benefits they enjoyed under British rule to the chaos they would have to endure if they achieved independence. Of the Indian Mutiny, there was no mention.[24] Moreover, although Fukuzawa certainly introduced a broader agenda than *Eikoku Tansaku*, it was hardly comprehensive. As far as possible, he omitted facets of society that might complicate his presentation of political and financial structures in the West. He assiduously avoided the subject of religion, for example, perhaps because he did not wish to confuse his readers, or perhaps because his own travels had never really exposed him to daily life in Europe. Students returning from abroad in the late 1860s would arrive to find *Seiyo Jijo* attracting considerable interest in Japan, but they might have been disappointed to see how little it conveyed any sense of everyday life in Britain or anywhere else in the West.

This was partly why one returning student called Nomura Fumio felt moved to write his own account, *Seiyo Bunken Roku* (Record of Observations in the West), the first volume of which appeared in 1869. The fact that he felt able to write such a work at all based almost exclusively on a two-year sojourn in Aberdeen is indicative itself of the importance attached to Victorian Britain in the early Meiji years. Even so, whereas Fukuzawa's work still reflected the constraints of short-term diplomatic visits spent largely confined to hotel lobbies and group excursions, *Seiyo Bunken Roku* did convey the increasingly sophisticated awareness of Japanese students who had some experience of living in Britain.

Nomura's prime concern was the field of human relations, grounded in his belief in the homogeneity of mankind. People in the West, he argued, were essentially the same as the Japanese, notwithstanding the effect of anomalies in climate, geography and culture. Although not as fluent a writer as Fukuzawa, the strength of his work lay in the copious statistics he presented to support his arguments, and in his numerous examples of contradictions and peculiarities he had found in Victorian society. He portrayed the benefits of western machinery, but also gave figures indicating the high number of casualties in railway accidents. Not only did he describe the Victorians' rules of etiquette and their bewildering notion of chivalry, but he also touched upon their religious sensibilities, explaining the horror they showed, for example, when they read newspaper reports on ritual suicide in Japan. There was a multitude of voices in his writing, recollections of interviews and conversations from his student days abroad. The result was a richly textured portrait of Victorian customs and attitudes, enabling Japanese readers to conjure up vivid images of daily life in Britain.[25]

A much grander and more polished work was the exhaustive analysis of Victorian Britain in *Tokumei Zenken Taishi Beio Kairan Jikki* (A True Record of the Special Ambassador's Travels in America and Europe). This was the official chronicle of the Iwakura Embassy's epic adventures, compiled by Kume Kunitake and published in five volumes in 1878.

Originally a Confucian scholar, Kume became a student of western affairs by appointment rather than design. Unlike many specialists, however, his background gave him a long-term perspective which he used to particularly good effect in portraying the historical impact of the industrial revolution. After all, many of the factories that the Iwakura Embassy visited had only been founded a matter of decades before. This discovery greatly impressed Okubo Toshimichi, one of the vice-ambassadors, allowing him to envisage rapid industrial growth in Japan.[26] Kume's elegant style and impressive command of classical Chinese also appealed to more traditional readers. He even contrived to describe modern industrial processes in classical terms which, however impenetrable they may look today, struck a chord in early Meiji Japan, where many people were struggling to reconcile their own cultural background with the suddenly fashionable ideas from the West.

Inevitably, Kume's text reflected the official concerns of the Meiji state. Although the ambassadors had seen numerous factories during their visit to Britain in 1872, for example, they were most concerned with questions of operation and management, and showed no real interest in labour relations. In contrast, there is an interesting case of a student in Cambridge at the time called Baba Takeyoshi, who visited Rochdale to investigate the cooperative movement, and later campaigned to set up such an organization in Japan.[27]

Nevertheless, Kume succeeded in creating a multilayered portrait of life in Britain. Although no expert in Western Studies himself, he was able to draw on works already in print, and had opportunities to consult not only other members of the embassy, but also various Japanese students he met in western capitals. The assistance of his travelling companion Hatakeyama Yoshinari (then known as Sugiura Kozo) was particularly invaluable, as Hatakeyama was a veteran of the first Satsuma expedition to Britain in 1865, and already had several years' experience of living both in London and America.

In Kume's work, there finally emerged a rationale of political dynamics in Victorian life. While readers of Fukuzawa's *Seiyo Jijo* may have inferred that Parliament was governed by some pattern of consensus, Nomura described the individual parties in his *Seiyo Bunken Roku* and explained how they settled debates through majority votes. Partly due to his official position, Kume presented a more conservative portrait than either Fukuzawa or Nomura, but he also gave due emphasis to a symbiotic balance in the two-party system between tradition and innovation, with alternating regimes complementing each other over time to regulate political development.[28]

Kume was not a pioneer of Japanese research on the West, but *Beio Kairan Jikki* was nevertheless a milestone in the progress of Japanese thought on the outside world. In range and depth, it can be seen as the culmination of the first wave of overseas research following the opening of Japan. It was also a formidable achievement, and one that did not invite imitation, so that subsequent studies tended to fragment into separate disciplines, particularly as students were increasingly trained to a high standard in their respective fields before they left Japan.

During the early years of overseas travel in the 1860s and 1870s, research carried out in Britain was a central component in the Japanese discovery of the West. Victorian political and commercial power held a pre-eminent place in the world that returning travellers, from Fukuzawa to Kume, presented to their readers in Japan, and London became a natural focus of interest for Japanese students abroad. The growth of British influence in Asia had been viewed in Japan as a threat to national security, and the research of early overseas travellers was initially developed as a response, resulting in images of Victorian power and prosperity as potential models for imitation. Experience of life in Britain increasingly modified this agenda, prompting the discovery of a deep-seated political heritage, a powerful Christian tradition and some of the social problems as well as the achievements of the industrial age. In the early Meiji years, this tempered earlier images of civilization in the West with a growing awareness of Victorian society and political culture that has underpinned Japanese perceptions of Britain ever since.

Notes

1. This essay is based on A. Cobbing, *The Japanese Discovery of Victorian Britain* (Richmond: Japan Library, Curzon Press, 1998).
2. Matsumura Akira, Bito Masahide and Kato Shuichi (eds), *Arai Hakuseki – Nihon Shiso Taikei*, vol. 35 (Tokyo: Iwanami Shoten, 1975), p. 36.
3. Ayusawa Shintaro, *Sakoku Jidai no Sekai Chirigaku* (Tokyo: Hara Shobo reprint, 1980), p. 78.
4. Tsukatani Akihiro and Kuranami Seiji (eds), *Honda Toshiaki, Kaibose Iryo – Nihon Shiso Taikei*, vol. 44 (Tokyo: Iwanami Shoten, 1970), p. 141.
5. Inuzuka Takaaki, *Meiji Ishin Taigai Kankeishi Kenkyu* (Tokyo: Yoshikawa Kobunkan, 1987), p. 43.
6. Cobbing, *The Japanese Discovery of Victorian Britain*, pp. 28–9, 31–2.
7. J. Frodsham, *The First Chinese Embassy to the West* (Oxford: Clarendon Press, 1974), p. xxxix.
8. Cobbing, *The Japanese Discovery of Victorian Britain*, p. 54.
9. Nakai Hiroshi, 'Kokai Shinsetsu', in Meiji Bunka Kenkyu Kai (ed.), *Meiji Bunka Zenshu*, vol. 7 (Tokyo: Nihon Hyoron Shinsha, 1928), p. 286.
10. Ibid., p. 283. Kawaji Ryoko, *Kurofuneki* (Tokyo: Hosei Daigaku Shuppankyoku, 1953), p. 163. Nomura Fumio, 'Josa Nichiroku', in Tokyo Daigaku Meiji Shinbun Zasshi Bunko (ed.), *Maru-maru Shimbun* (Tokyo: 1982), pp. 19, 30.
11. Matsumura Junzo, 'Yoko Nikki', in Koshaku Shimazuke Henshusho (ed.), *Sappan Kaigunshi*, vol. 2 (Tokyo: Sappan Kaigunshi Kankokai, 1928), p. 921; Hatakeyama Yoshinari, 'Yoko Nikki', *Kagoshima Kenritsu Tanki Daigaku Chiiki Kenkyusho Kenkyu Nenpo*, no. 6, 1978, pp. 63–4.

12. Shibata Takenaka, 'Futsuei Ko', in Numata Jiro and Matsuzawa Hiroaki (eds), *Seiyo Kenbunshu, Nihon Shiso Taikei*, vol. 66 (Tokyo: Iwanami Shoten, 1974), p. 409. Matsumura Junzo, 'Yoko Nikki', p. 932.
13. Nakai Hiroshi, 'Kokai Shinsetsu', p. 295. S. Devere Brown and A. Hirota (trans.), *The Diary of Kido Takayoshi*, vol. 2 (Tokyo: University of Tokyo Press, 1985), p. 261.
14. Sano Tsunetami, 'Meiji Gannen Zai – O Nikki' reproduced in A. Cobbing, *Bakumatsu Saga Han no Taigai Kankei no Kenkyu* (Saga: Nabeshima Hokokai, 1994), p. 169.
15. Kume Kunitake, *Tokumei Zenken Taishi Bei – O Kairan Jikki*, vol. 2 (Tokyo: Hakubunsha, 1878), p. 40.
16. 'Faculty of Arts Register, Faculty of Medicine Register', University College London. Between 1864 and 1876, at least 65 Japanese students were registered there. A monument now stands in the central quad in memory of the first arrivals from Choshu and Satsuma.
17. Cobbing, *The Japanese Discovery of Victorian Britain*, pp. 37, 116–24. S. Lahiri, 'Metropolitan Encounters: a Study of Indian Students in Britain' (PhD dissertation, SOAS, London, 1995), pp. 12, 15. Higashi Fumi no Miya, the first member of the Japanese Imperial family to study abroad, spent several months in Warminster in 1871. His stay included perhaps the first recorded Japanese visit to Stonehenge. Rev J. J. Daniell, *The History of Warminster* (London: Simpkin Marshall & Co., 1879), pp. 83, 148.
18. Cobbing, *The Japanese Discovery of Victorian Britain*, pp. 141–2. There is now a monument in Brookwood Cemetery commemorating the four Japanese students buried there.
19. Meiji Kyoikushi Kenkyukai (eds), *Sugiura (Shigetake) Jugo Zenshu* (Otsu: Sugiura Jugo Zenshu Kenkyukai, 1983), p. 674.
20. Fukuda Sakutaro, 'Eikoku Tansaku', reproduced in Numata Jiro and Matsuzawa Hiroaki (eds), *Seiyo Kenbunshu Nihon Shiso Taikei*, vol. 66 (Tokyo: Iwanami Shoten, 1974), pp. 497, 544.
21. Matsuzawa Hiroaki, 'Samazama na Seiyo Kenbun', ibid., p. 650.
22. Jijishinposha (eds), *Fukuzawa Zenshu* (Tokyo: Kokumin Tosho, 1926), vol. 14, pp. 29–30.
23. Ibid., p. 407.
24. Ibid., pp. 410–11, 429.
25. Murata (Nomura) Fumio, *Seiyo Kenbun Roku*, reproduced in *Meiji Bunka Zenshu – Gaikoku Bunka Hen*, vol. 7, pp. 202–7, 260.
26. Nihon Shiseki Kyokai (ed.), *Okubo Toshimichi Monjo*, vol. 4 (Tokyo: Nihon Shiseki Kyokai, 1928), pp. 448–9, 468.
27. Nohara Kazuyoshi, 'Kyoryoku Shoten Soritsu no Gi – Baba Takeyoshi Kenkyu Noto', *Kyoryoku Shoten Kumiai Tosho Shiryo Senta Shiryo Shu*, no. 9 (Tokyo: 1995), p. 62.
28. *Fukuzawa Zenshu*, vol. 1, pp. 370–1; *Meiji Bunka Zenshu*, vol. 7, pp. 220–2; Kume Kunitake, *Kairan Jikki*, vol. 2, p. 79.

4

The Rituals of Anglo-Japanese Diplomacy: Imperial Audiences in Early Meiji Japan

John Breen

A historic audience

The date is Friday 26 March 1868. The place is the Shishinden chamber of the Kyoto palace. The emperor reclines south-facing against a chair placed on the *michodai*. He is clad in Heian court garb, his eyebrows shaved, his cheeks rouged and his lips painted red and gold. To the emperor's left sits Sanjo Sanetomi; Iwakura Tomomi is outside the canopy to the emperor's left. Both men are first ministers in the new government. Yamashina no miya, head of the Foreign Bureau, stands to the emperor's right. The daimyo and nobles of *gijo* rank sit in relative proximity to the emperor, according to court rank (Plate 1).

Shortly after noon, Sir Harry Parkes, the British minister, enters the chamber to the strains of *gagaku* music. Clad in gold embroidered coat, with plumed hat in hand, and boots on his feet, Parkes approaches the emperor, bowing twice. He steps up on to the specially constructed dais and bows a third time. The emperor stands and whispers a greeting. Yamashina repeats the greeting at greater volume, which Ito Hirobumi translates:

> I hope your sovereign enjoys good health. I trust that the intercourse between our respective countries will become more and more friendly, and be permanently established. I regret deeply that an unfortunate affair, which took place as you were proceeding to the palace on the 23rd, has delayed this ceremony. It gives me great pleasure, therefore, to see you here today.

Parkes replies:

> Sire, Her Majesty the Queen is in the enjoyment of good health. I shall have great pleasure in reporting to my government Your Majesty's inquiries and assurances of friendship.

Parkes congratulates the emperor on adopting 'the system of international law' and, with regard to the unfortunate affair of the previous week, he insists the memory of it will be 'effaced by the gracious reception which Your Majesty has given me this day'.[1] Parkes departs the imperial presence, leaving the Shishinden via the western staircase.

The problem

Parkes later reported to London that 'the etiquette observed on the occasion conformed, as closely as circumstances would permit, to that obtaining at European courts'.[2] But this is too brief and too matter-of-fact a reference to what was, in reality, a momentous event. For this was the first audience ever granted by a Japanese emperor to western diplomats. To this extent its historical import might bear comparison with the much better-known audience granted by the Qing emperor to Lord Macartney in the 1790s. But this was also the first state ritual of any sort in modern Japan. Catherine Bell has articulated the vital role of ritual action not only in the projection but the construction of power relations, and in the consequent defining of identity and status.[3] Since power relations – internal and external – and issues of identity and status were of fundamental concern to the leaders of Restoration Japan, early Meiji imperial audiences deserve to be better known and understood.

My proposal is that a careful study of these audiences in the first decade of Meiji will shed light on three issues in particular: Firstly, such a study promises to bring into relief the dynamic reorganization of internal power relations, between three key groups in the Restoration period: the imperial institution; the power axis of Iwakura Tomomi, Kido Takayoshi and Okubo Toshimichi; and conservatives within and beyond the court. Secondly, we might expect imperial audiences of different sorts to shed new light on the construction of power relations not only between Restoration Japan and the West but also between Japan and its Asian neighbours. Finally, a study of imperial audiences promises to disclose the complex and contested process whereby the image of the Meiji monarch was defined and projected for public consumption. My analysis begins with the third of these.

The emperor

Kyoto

The emperor's clothes were anything but new; they were of Heian heritage, as was his make-up. The Shishinden, the *michodai* and a range of other symbols all recalled the rituals of ancient Japan. However, the actions of emperor and Parkes, and their words, too, disclosed the onset of a dramatic transformation in the Japanese imperial institution.

Before 26 March, the young emperor had granted numerous audiences to senior bureaucrats. They would take place in the Kogosho chamber of the palace. The emperor would occupy the upper level of the multi-levelled Kogosho, seated upon a raised mat; he would be concealed kami-like behind a screen and so beyond the gaze of his subjects. They would kneel on entering his presence, proceed on their knees in his direction – always at an angle to avoid 'confrontation' – and stop twice to prostrate themselves fully, before withdrawing.[4] The stillness of the emperor, his silence and aloofness, his withdrawal behind a screen, were perhaps fitting for the sort of emperor idealized by late Edo theorists like Okuni Takamasa. For Okuni Takamasa, the emperor was sacred and unique by virtue of his descent from the Sun Goddess; he was thus incomparably superior to the sovereigns of all other nations, too. He should never engage in politics and, that he should ever encounter a foreign diplomat face to face, let alone speak to one, was unimaginable.[5]

Ritual space on 26 March was structured differently of course. Unlike the multi-levelled, matted Kogosho, the cypress-floored Shishinden was an open, undifferentiated space. No doubt this was why it was selected as the site for the audience. True, the emperor occupies the elevated space of the *michodai*, but Parkes also occupies elevated space in the form of the specially constructed dais. The emperor, no longer a merely passive presence, stands to greet Parkes; both men are of roughly similar height. Most importantly, the emperor is now fully exposed to Parkes' gaze. Note, finally, that the emperor's rising to his feet as Parkes bows for a third time conforms precisely to diplomatic protocol as established by the Congress of Vienna. In short, by his ritual actions, the emperor is being drawn into a community of western sovereigns.

His ritual words underscore the same point. Takagi Shozo has stressed the silence of the emperor in early Meiji audiences.[6] But the emperor here was not silent; he spoke. His whispered tones were entirely on account of nerves. The language employed by both emperor and Parkes is highly revealing. The emperor asks after Queen Victoria's health and hopes for the deepening of friendly relations. Parkes, for his part, refers to queen and emperor as 'Her Majesty' and 'Your Majesty' respectively. There is a parity between sovereigns and their states implicit in the exchange, and it was later restated in the *Dajokan Nisshi* report of this event, where Japanese emperor and British queen are both styled *kotei*.

Just how decisive a step this ten-minute audience constituted in the western progress of the Japanese emperor was underscored by Algernon Mitford, who accompanied Parkes into the Shishinden as interpreter:

> We were standing in the presence of a sovereign whose ancestors for centuries had been to their people demi-gods. Now suddenly the veil of the temple had been rent and the Boy-God, in defence of whose divinity

myriads of his subjects were ready gladly to lay down their lives, had descended from the clouds to take his place among the children of men. Not only that, he had allowed his sacred face to be seen . . . by 'The Beasts from Without'.[7]

The further progress of Japan's new, western-style sovereign can be tracked with considerable precision over the next few weeks, months and years.

Osaka

In May 1868 the emperor was in Osaka on an 'imperial expedition'. The leadership had been anxious to cut him loose from the stifling influence of conservatives in the Kyoto court, especially that of his mother, Nakayama Yoshiko.[8] The expedition was to play a vital role in relocating the emperor at the political centre. Parkes demanded an audience with the emperor in Osaka and, on 22 May, he was received in the Kakarisho chamber of the Higashi Honganji. For Parkes, this was still more significant an event than the earlier Kyoto audience since, as he put it, 'it brought the young Mikado for the first time into direct relations with Foreign Sovereigns'. He referred here to the purpose of the audience: his presentation of credentials to the emperor.[9]

Parkes, who had Admiral Keppel bring several gunboats up to Osaka to 'give eclat' to the occasion, proceeded to the Honganji accompanied by two hundred marines from HMS *Rodney* and HMS *Ocean*.[10] As he and his entourage entered the Kakarisho, he bowed once, and the emperor rose to his feet. He bowed once more at the foot of the dais on which the emperor stood, and a third time on ascending the dais. As they stood face to face, Parkes placed the letter from Queen Victoria directly into his hands. For such was stipulated under Congress of Vienna provisions for diplomatic audiences. Parkes offered a greeting; the emperor once again tried but failed to articulate a response and Yamashina no miya interceded.[11]

The credentials themselves are of great symbolic import since they articulate the nature of the drama that was unfolding. Queen Victoria's letter began: 'To the Most High, Mighty and Glorious Prince, His Imperial and Royal Majesty, the Mikado of Japan, Our Good Brother and Cousin, Greeting!' It went on to advocate 'the improvement of relations of Friendship and Good Understanding which happily subsist between our respective Empires'. Having requested the Emperor give credence to all Parkes might represent to him, the Queen signed it: 'Your Imperial and Royal Majesty's Affectionate Sister and Cousin, Victoria R.'[12]

Note how, in accepting the queen's letter the emperor, born of the Sun Goddess, divine and so incomparably superior to foreign sovereigns, is adjusting himself into an international family where sovereigns are all human: they are 'brothers', 'sisters' and 'cousins'. Note, also, how with this new familiarity comes the promise, the symbolic confirmation, perhaps, of yearned-for status parity. Victoria and Meiji are both sovereigns; both rule over empires; both are engaged in a shared endeavour to promote friendship and commercial activity for mutual benefit.

Tokyo

In early summer the following year, Parkes reported to Iwakura that Queen Victoria's son, the Duke of Edinburgh, wished to visit Japan on his tour of Asia.[13] The duke's request for an audience with the Qing emperor had been rejected, and Japanese leaders saw here an opportunity, as Date Munenari put it, to 'enhance Japan's reputation [overseas]'.[14] The duke's audience, as it turned out, was constructed from start to finish very much as a meeting between two distant cousins, between men of equal standing. This was what Iwakura had meant when he told Parkes that a new type of ceremonial would be observed for the occasion, one that would reflect the emperor's personal view that all sovereigns of the world were equal.[15] This was first evident on the duke's journey from Yokohama to Tokyo. Algernon Mitford, who accompanied the duke, was particularly struck by his reception en route. 'The shutters of upstairs rooms were sealed so that no Peeping Tom should look down on the [duke's] August Person . . . The people who thronged the roads fell prostrate [as the duke passed], touching the earth with their foreheads.'[16]

The encounter proper – in official documentation it was styled not *ekken* or audience, but *settai* or reception – took place on 4 September in the Tokyo palace's Ohiroma chamber. In the first of two ritual sequences, the 17-year-old emperor stood to receive the boot-clad duke, eight years his senior, on the upper level of the Ohiroma, where formal greetings were exchanged. An informal sequence followed as the duke left the imperial presence to stroll through the palace gardens. He took tea in the Momiji teahouse, and proceeded to the Takimi pavilion where the emperor awaited him. Sanjo Sanetomi greeted him on the verandah and, as they entered, the emperor rose to his feet, bowed and begged his Royal Highness to be seated.[17] Tea and cakes were served and the two men, with Mitford as interpreter, conversed on world affairs as equals and intimates.

Finally, here, brief mention needs to be made of two audiences with foreign dignitaries – the Russian Prince Alexis and Parkes once more – that took place after the abolition of the domains in 1871, and while the Iwakura embassy was still touring Europe. Each marks further developments in the construction of the informal, personal dimension to the Meiji imperial image.

In 1872, the playboy prince, Alexis, visited Japan and sought an audience with the emperor. On this occasion, the increasingly dynamic emperor – he had just returned from a tour of the central provinces of Japan – went by carriage to greet Alexis at his Hamagoten residence, and they drank wine and smoked tobacco in the Nakajima pavilion. The next day they rode together by carriage to Hibiya to observe a military parade there. Never before had the Meiji emperor been seen in public with a foreign dignitary. Three days later, emperor and Russian prince went by carriage to Yokohama to observe a naval display.[18] Finally, what was notable about the audience offered Parkes in 1873, on his return to Japan after a three-year sojourn in Britain, was that the emperor received him with the empress at his side. Hereafter this became the norm.[19]

It goes without saying that the construction of the modern monarch was a highly complex and contested process. It is certainly not one that can be grasped by studying the rituals of diplomacy alone. Indeed, another, more discrete process closely paralleled the one we have been observing. It was one that sought to authorize the particularistic, nativistic dimension of the imperial institution. The imperial oath of April 1868 was a key moment here since it cast the emperor in the manner of Jinmu, the mythical first emperor who celebrated state rites before the Sun Goddess even as he oversaw the political realm. This oath took place just ten days after Parkes' audience in the same Shishinden chamber. Parkes and other diplomats were excluded from it and remained quite ignorant of it.[20] The emperor's historic pilgrimage to Ise in 1869 was a second key moment. The Meiji Daijosai of December 1871 was a third. The dramatic tensions between these two imperial constructs demand our close attention, of course. It seems clear, however, that early Meiji imperial audiences played a vital role in reconstructing and projecting the Meiji emperor in the image of western sovereigns.

The ritual structuring of international relations

One of the most pressing problems confronting the Restoration leadership was the redefinition of power relations of two types: with foreign powers – the western Powers as a first priority – and within government. The definition and projection of the imperial image discussed above needs to be understood within the contest of these primary concerns. As Bell has argued, ritual situations are vitally linked to power concerns, and play a vital role in the construction of power relations. It was precisely in order to give form to relations between the new Japan and the foreign powers that, in January 1868, Ernest Satow pressed upon the new leadership the need for diplomatic audiences; it was for the same reason that Iwakura applied himself so vigorously to their realization.

The reality of Japan's relations with Britain and the other powers was one of blatant inequality. The 1858 treaties' provisions for extraterritoriality, low import duties and 'most favoured nation' status contrived to fix Japan in what was tantamount to a semi-colonial rut. More symbolic still were the gunboats anchored in Japanese ports, the foreign troops stationed on Japanese soil, the armed escorts that accompanied Parkes to his several audiences with the emperor. The power differential was huge and vividly so. There was the day-to-day bullying and interference of diplomats like Parkes;

the wearing of boots in the Shishinden, the Osaka kakarisho and the Tokyo Ohiroma – which Parkes knew breached Japanese norms of etiquette – was also symbolic of the essential inequality. Yet, if one looks again at, say, the first audience in Kyoto back in March 1868, it is striking for the equality of status that its symbols appear to project. To be sure, it was an equality on uniquely western terms – as the boots suggest – but an equality between nations and their sovereigns nonetheless. Parkes' actions – in bowing three times on his approach to the emperor – accorded the emperor respect equal to any European head of state in the nineteenth century. His words – in addressing the emperor as 'Your Majesty', and referring to Queen Victoria as 'Her Majesty' – denied all status distinctions between sovereigns.

This relationship of promised parity was none other than that proclaimed by international law. Indeed, when Parkes concluded his address to the emperor in March by congratulating him on 'adopting the system of international law universally recognised by other states', he was effectively casting the audience as Japan's *rite de passage* into the new order. Parkes was not the only one who so interpreted the audience. International law and its promise of equality and empowerment animated government discussions throughout February and March. When Higashikuse Michitomi wrote to Sanjo about 'the great fortune that would accrue to our imperial nation' from the audiences, and when Date Munenari wrote of the audience's unsurpassed benefits to Japan, it was to the promise of international law they referred. In the famous petition of 1 March penned by Matsudaira Shungaku, Yamanouchi Yodo and Date Munenari, specifically to prompt debate about the whole audience question, the authors insisted it was required by international law.[21] The petition demanded the abandonment of the 'stupid practice' of referring to westerners as 'dogs, sheep and barbarians', the establishment of 'rites that would confer on Westerners status equivalent to that which Japan once granted to China', and the reception in audience of foreign representatives 'according to the principles of international law'.

When the emperor granted the audiences to Parkes and to other foreign diplomats it signified, of course, not only Japan's accommodation within a new international order, but also Japan's departure from the world order of early modern Asia. This was a complex, hierarchically structured order in which the Chinese occupied the centre and other states, Japan, Korea and the Ryukyus amongst them, occupied the subordinate periphery. There was no sense of sovereign independence, rather each state was tributary to China. As Ronald Toby and others have shown, the Tokugawa Japanese reimagined this order, locating themselves at the centre with Korea, the Ryukyus and Holland at its periphery. In either case, power relations in Asia were conceived hierarchically, in terms of centre/periphery. The concept of sovereignty and independence did not exist. International law, however, conceived of power relations as horizontal, and it was here in this horizontality that Japanese leaders imagined new possibilities of equality with the Western Powers.

There was a striking symbol in the Shishinden audience on 26 March of the beginnings of Japan's reorientation to a new order. The Shishinden was renowned for the *kenjo no shoji*, the sliding panels depicting the 32 sages of Han-period China that line the inner-facing northern wall. The panels are strangely absent from the illustration by Hiroshima Koho; in their place are other panels with a nondescript colour wash. This proves not to have been error of the painter's, but the outcome of a 'curious episode' recalled by Matsudaira Yoshinaga, one of those responsible for ritual arrangements:

> Someone or other . . . expressed the opinion that it would be altogether unfortunate to expose these Chinese paintings to the Western gaze. As a result, we had the front part of the sliding panels depicting the Han [sages] turned around so that they became the rear; the [plain] rear side was made to face inwards.[22]

In the context of early 1868, we might suggest 'curious' hardly does justice to the episode. This was a symbolic denial, rather, of Japan's Asiatic past, a turning away from China. It marks a hesitant step into a new international order, with new rules of diplomacy. It is an early manifestation of the phenomenon that came to be known in mid-Meiji as *datsua nyuo*.

The differences in the possibilities offered Japan by the new and old orders were symbolized by an incident that erupted the following year. I refer to Japan's diplomatic approaches to Korea in New Year 1869. These were met with a Korean rebuttal on account of Japan's use in diplomatic correspondence of the characters *ko* and *choku* for the emperor. *Ko* and *choku* were for the exclusive use by the emperor of China, the central kingdom.[23] The attitude towards the new imperial Japan by Britain and Korea was thus strikingly different. While for Britain, the Japanese sovereign was emperor and, indeed, cousin to the Queen, and Japan was an empire; for Korea, by contrast, Japan's assumption of imperial airs was both insult and threat.

Japanese diplomacy in Asia

Japan quickly mastered the ritual techniques of international diplomacy, and began to deploy them as a means to structuring its own power relations with Korea and with China in the 1870s. In the remainder of this section, I examine two historic audiences: that granted to Soejima Taneomi by the Qing emperor in June 1873, and that granted by the Japanese emperor to the Korean emissary Kim Ki Su in 1876. Their implications for Japan's power relations in Asia are my concern.

Japan and China, 1873

In the spring of 1873 Soejima left Japan for China as Ambassador Extraordinary and Minister Plenipotentiary. The ostensible purpose of his mission was to exchange ratifications of the Sino-Japanese Treaty of 1871, and present a personal message from the Japanese emperor to the young Chinese monarch. In summer 1873, 29 June to be precise, Soejima achieved something remarkable: he became the first foreign diplomat to be received in audience by a Qing emperor since Lord Macartney in 1793. Moreover, he was the first ever to be received according to what Soejima referred to as the 'principles of international law'.[24] His mission broke through decades of Chinese diplomatic intransigence, but in reality what he achieved was more momentous still: the structuring and projection, through his ritual words and actions, of a new power relationship with China. The event was as historic for East Asia as the Meiji emperor's first audience with Parkes in March some five years before.

Soejima's rank as Ambassador Extraordinary and Minister Plenipotentiary made him the highest-ranking diplomatic agent in China. One can imagine his satisfaction when, in accord with international protocol, he received official calls from lower-ranked diplomats from Britain and other western nations while in Peking and when, for the same reasons, he was the first among them to be received in audience. There was clearly some substance to the principle of parity under international law; it promised a measure at least of empowerment to those who conformed to its practices.[25] More momentous, of course, were the audience's implications for Japan's power relations with China. Soejima swept aside impassioned Chinese pleas that he perform the three bows and nine prostrations of the kowtow, that symbol of traditional power relations in Asia. He rejected too the foreign compromise of five bows, apparently acceptable to the Chinese. Three bows was the norm under international law, insisted Soejima. And Soejima had his way.[26]

Early in the morning of 29 June 1873, Soejima entered the imperial presence in full western diplomatic attire, complete with gold embroidered jacket, feathered hat in hand, boots on his feet and sword by his side. He bowed three times on the approach and handed over the message from the Japanese emperor. It began 'The Great emperor of Great Japan (*Dainihon daikotei*) addresses the Great emperor of Great China (*Dai shinkoku daikotei*) . . .'.[27] The Qing emperor stood and offered a short reply. Soejima must have been keenly aware he was making history. China was no more the centre of Asia, its emperor no more the supreme heavenly ruler to whom tribute was due; China, Japan and their sovereigns were now equals in international law. Japan was proclaiming its departure from Asia; the old Asian order was over.[28]

Japan and Korea, 1876

Soejima's role in levelling the relationship between Japan and China had – and was meant to have – profound implications for Meiji Japan's already tense relationship with Korea. If China and Japan now had parity of status in East Asia, how could China insist that its rights over Korea were greater than Japan's? Japan's overtures had been rejected, as we saw, in 1869, and

Korea remained a problem for Japan. In 1873, the Meiji government was in crisis over Korea; at issue was the timing rather than the fact of a Japanese naval attack. In 1875, the Meiji government dispatched a warship, the *Unyo*, to the island of Kokado on the West coast of Korea to provoke retaliation. They succeeded, and an armed flotilla left Japan under Kuroda Kiyotaka in February 1876 to settle the incident in the manner of international gunboat diplomacy. Kuroda's mission resulted in Japan imposing on Korea what is known as the Koka treaty. The first article declares Korea to be 'an independent state, with rights equal to Japan' and as a sign of amity between the nations each would deal with the other deploying 'rites and ceremonies that speak of fundamental equality'. Yet Article 2 on the opening of Korean ports and Article 3 on extraterritoriality disclose the Koka treaty to be every bit as unequal as those the US, Britain and other powers forced on Japan some 20 years before.[29] What merits consideration here is the audience granted by the Meiji emperor to the Korean emissary Kim Ki Su following treaty ratification later in the year.

There is some lack of clarity about *precisely* what happened at this historic audience, but conflating different sources, it is possible to hazard a reasonable guess. The audience took place in the emperor's Akasaka retreat, following the fire in the Tokyo palace in 1873. It was replete with innovations, symbols and symbolic moments that served to underscore the vanity of Korean aspirations for relations of parity with Japan. Kim was first led into a temporary waiting room, the *kazoku shikoma*, where he was required to 'adjust his formal attire'. He then moved into the Kogosho chamber and 'bowed solemnly' before being requested to 'adjust his hat'. At the threshold to the Akasaka Ohiroma, Kim prostrated himself fully, his forehead touching the ground; he got up, advanced and the emperor stood to greet him. Kim bowed, and offered a greeting. As the official record of the encounter notes, 'The emperor replied [to the greeting] in silence.' Kim then left the emperor's presence and prostrated himself once more before departing the Ohiroma.[30]

In his introduction to modern Japanese diplomacy, Iguchi Kazuki writes that Japan's first concern was to transform its relations with Korea so that they conformed to the western model.[31] But the ritual dimension to Japan's diplomacy with Korea suggests some qualification is required if only because there is no equality idealized here and no parity promised. Ten days after the audience, Moriyama Shigeru of the Foreign Ministry, who had been involved in the negotiations for the Koka treaty, wrote to the Korean government, possibly in response to a complaint. He offered his thanks for Kim's visit, the first from a Korean emissary in some 60 years and, before concluding with wishes for long years of intimate relations, commented: 'I cannot set out in any detail here the programme for the audiences [the emperor offers] to foreign dignitaries, but I hope you will appreciate that [Kim's audience] was an expression of our profoundest feelings of friendship.'[32]

Imperial audiences and internal relations of power

It goes without saying that the construction of a new imperial identity for Japan and the establishment of a new set of international relations exerted a profound influence on internal power relations in early Meiji Japan. The intimate linkage between ritual and identity and ritual and power relations guarantees that opposition is generated. Those who oppose are aware of rituals' transforming effect. But in the case of early Meiji Japan, the relative lack of resistance is striking; such resistance as there was came less from the leadership – for they came to understand quickly enough the empowering possibilities of imperial audiences. It came rather from conservatives within the court and radicals on the streets. This resistance bears examination; Japan's standing in the international community – its very independence – depended on the ability of its leaders to overcome it.

On 23 March 1868 Sir Harry Parkes, Ernest Satow and Algernon Mitford set off from the Chion'in temple in Higashiyama shortly after noon. Their party was headed by 300 samurai from Higo. There was a mounted escort of the Metropolitan Police, a guard of the 9th Regiment and some 2000 samurai taking up the rear. Passing through throngs of spectators lining both sides of Shijonawate, they turned right, and as they did so two masterless swordsmen appeared 'as if from nowhere, charging down the cavalcade hacking with their swords'. In the melee, one assailant was killed, another arrested and much blood was spilt. Parkes' audience with the emperor was abandoned. This was, of course, the 'unfortunate incident' to which the emperor referred in his speech to Parkes, when the audience finally took place on 26 March.[33]

The attack was a salutary reminder of the deep, widespread and enduring anti-foreign sentiment at large in the aftermath of the Restoration. Saegusa Shigeru, the assailant arrested, typified the prevailing sentiment when he wrote in his confession of his fury at the foreign powers for their continuous slighting of the imperial dignity. Even today, he lamented, with the emperor and his court restored to power, their arrogance remains unchanged.[34] Men like Saegusa had welcomed the Restoration as the opportunity for realizing the emperor's wishes to expel the foreigners. There was nothing in the court's 3 January declaration (*Osei fukko fukoku*) to dampen their expectations. This historic document mentioned the emperor's wish to return to the age of Jinmu and restore national dignity, but foreign affairs did not feature in it. Men like Saegusa were bewildered by the new government's declaration of 8 February that the emperor intended fully to adhere to the treaties. Things got progressively worse when, in mid-March, the government announced that the emperor would indeed receive foreign representatives in audience in the palace. The perpetrators of the Kobe and Sakai incidents – both involving attacks in foreign residents – were then executed as common criminals. All of this engendered an anti-foreign atmosphere in and around Kyoto in late March, at the time of Parkes' audience, that was said by a contemporary to be 'close to boiling point'.[35]

What is important to understand is that the performance of the first imperial audience was not for the sole benefit of the foreign powers alone; it was targeted also at men like Saegusa and their sympathizers in the imperial court. They were designed to underscore several points to these conservatives: that a unified government now existed; that it was an imperial government, not one dictated to by the men of Satsuma and Choshu and, finally, that the emperor personally desired not the expulsion of foreigners (*joi*) but a new era of friendly relations (*washin*). No one who witnessed the audience or read about it in the *Dajokan Nisshi* could deny friendship was the emperor's sincere wish; nor could they deny the government was a truly imperial government. The anti-foreign radicals within the court and beyond it were not yet silenced, but this audience made it clear at a single stroke that their aspirations did not fit with the new Japan and its monarch.

Hiroshima Koho's painting of the Shishinden audience depicts a government, an imperial government, comprising daimyo and nobles, celebrating the onset of a new international era. The most drastic reordering of government and court had been necessary, however, to bring this event to fruition. Matters came to a head on 8 March when a series of court councils was convened to debate the aforementioned Matsudaira petition. The challenge for Iwakura was to win over the court, but especially the emperor's maternal grandfather, Nakayama Tadayasu and his daughter, the redoubtable 33-year-old Nakayama Yoshiko, who was the emperor's mother. Other resistance was offered by Ogimachi Sanjo, Nakamikado Tsuneyuki and Ohara Shigetomi, men who had been close to Iwakura before the Restoration but whom he had progressively isolated on account of their intractable anti-foreignism.

Iwakura chaired the first and critical court council on 8 March. Present were the three most senior ranks in government, the *sosai*, *gijo* and *sanyo*, and at least some of their number were persuaded by Iwakura's arguments. Matsudaira Shungaku later recalled that the daimyo of *gijo* and *sanyo* rank were 'not that dismayed' at the prospect of foreign audiences, but that Nakayama Tadayasu and other courtiers of *gijo* rank appeared to 'plummet to the depths of despair'.[36] Angry exchanges took place now about whether the emperor, descended from the Sun Goddess, would be required to shake diplomats' hands and what dress he should wear. The meeting dispersed, with much reassuring left to do.

A commotion erupted later in the day as word reached Nakayama Yoshiko that the audiences were to go ahead within days. Iwakura asked Higashikuse Michitomi to calm her down; her hysteria might disturb the emperor, and without his cooperation national shame might result. Higashikuse found Yoshiko in a state of hysteria. To have foreigners come to Kyoto, to the imperial palace, and be received in audience by Emperor Komei's son, would be to have the son commit an unpardonable act of unfiliality, she wailed. Higashikuse soothed her by saying that to him, too, the very thought of audiences was defiling. To refuse, however, would be to insult foreign sovereigns; and this would lead to 'armies of the six nations' overrunning Kyoto. Foreign troops would seize all Japanese women, he added pointedly, and take them off to foreign lands. Kyoto and the imperial palace would be razed to the ground. 'How can we not allow foreigners into the imperial presence?' Gently Higashikuse suggested that for the emperor to refuse would be an even greater act of unfiliality. Unable to counter Higashikuse's arguments, Nakayama Yoshiko cried herself to sleep that night.[37] Later it was reported that several courtiers took their lives.[38]

How the emperor himself was finally persuaded is unclear. The *Iwakurako jikki* records that at some time on the 8th Iwakura and Matsudaira both explained to him it was 'international practice' for sovereigns to receive foreign representatives. They had him summon Nakayama Tadayasu and, in Iwakura's presence, order him to assume charge of the arrangements for the audiences.[39] Of the emperor himself we hear little more. Presumably he was kept well away from his mother because she remained inconsolable. She anyway soon became involved in a plot with the court doctor, Fujiki Seikan, to have the emperor declared unfit for duty. The emperor was suffering from a fever, and was out of sorts, Fujiki reported to Nakayama Tadayasu; he would be unavailable for state duty on the required date. Tadayasu conveyed the information to Iwakura who was 'greatly surprised', and had the emperor checked by another doctor who declared him to be 'in perfectly good health'. Yoshiko grew steadily less stable as the historic day approached. She stopped eating about a week beforehand and, on the eve of the audiences, submitted her final lament: 'What can I possibly, possibly say about the barbarians being received in audience tomorrow? It is the end of the world. I can do nothing but weep and wail.'[40] However, the Restoration leadership was not diverted from its course. With the performance of the first historic audience in the Shishinden later in March, Nakayama Tadayasu, and others like Ogimachi, Nakamikado and Ohara, lost all influence over the construction of the imperial image and the redefining of Japan's relations with the foreign powers. Resistance continued to smoulder, of course. Sasaki Takayuki wrote in his diary of widespread outrage in summer 1869 that the Duke of Edinburgh was to be allowed access into the Tokyo palace's inner garden.[41] But these were the laments of men who had already lost all influence.

Unlike the conservatives in court and their radical activist allies in the streets, there is little evidence of concerted resistance by the leadership to the idea of the emperor granting audiences to foreign diplomats. Saigo Takamori suggested it might be advantageous to wait until the emperor had matured; he was concerned lest the young emperor bring embarrassment upon Japan. For the rest, however, the leadership was keenly aware that imperial audiences were Japan's passage to the new order in which international law prevailed; here alone lay the promise of parity and equality of status; here alone lay the hope of a swift revision to the unequal treaties. It is not the case, however, that imperial audiences prompted no resistance at all. Indeed, in spring of 1870 a potentially damaging dispute erupted precisely over ritual practice. It was prompted by Sir Harry Parkes.

On the morning of 15 April 1869, Admiral Hornby was ushered into the imperial presence in the Tokyo palace for his first and only audience with the Meiji emperor. Parkes accompanied him. Hornby paid his respects to the seated emperor, who responded in kind and, as was custom, issued a short message (*chokugo*) expressing his hopes for the excellent health of Hornby's sovereign. The message was read out by Iwakura Tomomi and translated into English by Alexander Siebold. No sooner had Siebold finished, however, than Parkes stepped forward insisting Siebold translate his every word. To the amazement of all present, he addressed himself directly to the emperor: 'Until you cease to refer to Queen Victoria as *teio*, as you have just done in your message, and until you substitute the title *kotei* for *teio*, you will be guilty of disrespect towards my sovereign.'[42] Parkes, accompanying Admiral Hornby, walked out.

This was the prompt not only for the resignation of Sawa Senka, the Foreign Minister, but for intense debate about titles for Japanese and western sovereigns and a range of other symbolic issues relating to imperial audiences: foreign dignitaries' use of armed escorts on the way to audiences, their wearing of shoes in the imperial palace, and the question of whether the emperor should stand to receive all or only some foreign dignitaries. As a result of a succession of heated debates, *kotei* was agreed upon as the Japanese term for foreign sovereigns. An attempt by Terajima Munenari to have foreigners refer to the Japanese emperor as *tenno* floundered when the German minister insisted that, if the emperor merited that distinctive title, then so should his sovereign. Hereafter the Japanese dropped the use of *tenno* in diplomatic correspondence but prefaced *kotei* with a set of particularistic adjectives: 'The Great Japanese emperor who has succeeded to the everlasting throne and who reigns with divine assistance' (*tenyu o hoyu shi, bansei ikkei no teiso o fumitaru Nihonkoku Dai Kotei*). For Terajima, the armed escorts accompanying diplomats rendered Japan 'tantamount to a subject state and were responsible, more than anything, for destroying Japan's national dignity'. A conclusion of sorts was agreed in 1872 with agreement on an escort of ten men, armed for ceremonial purposes only. The question of shoes was only resolved after much debate with the Foreign Ministry, which insisted it was the height of insult. The ministry granted, however, that to enforce the removal of shoes would be rather like 'us [being made to] forego a cap when we don full court dress'. The Foreign Minister proposed, by way of compromise, that the *tatami* be removed from the Ohiroma audience chamber of the palace, and replaced with more durable wood-panel flooring. Finally, agreement was reached that, unless the emperor were granting audience to a minister or a member of a foreign royal family, he might indeed remain seated.[43] What is clear is that all of these disagreements, with the exception of the last – which had anyway been earlier agreed by Parkes – were resolved in favour of the foreign powers; in line, that is, with the principles of international law.

Conclusion

Scholars of ritual have curiously overlooked ritual's diplomatic dimension. This is curious since diplomacy is about nothing so much as power, status and identity, the very concerns of the field of ritual studies. Students of diplomacy, with the exception of Hevia's ground-breaking work on the Britain–China encounter in the late eighteenth century, have similarly over-looked the ritual dimension to international relations.[44] Here I have sought to suggest that, especially, perhaps, in the critical early phases of interna-tional relations, the ritual dimension is critical to a rounded understanding of diplomacy's dynamic. In his book on modern Japanese diplomacy, *Japan and the Wider World*, Akira Iriye writes that the study of international relations begins with certain key considerations: 'How a country defines itself . . . ; how national leaders view regional and global realities; and what meanings they . . . give to their country's place in the history and geo-graphy of the world.'[45] An exploration of the ritual dimension to diplomacy promises a fuller answer to Iriye's fundamental questions than would otherwise be possible.

Any discussion of Japan in its relations to Britain and other nations, both western and Asian, in the nineteenth century cannot overlook the imperial institution in which the meanings of the new state were invested. In recent years, there have been several book-length studies in Japanese of the progress of the Meiji emperor: Asukai Masamichi's *Meiji taitei*, Yasumaru Yoshio's bril-liant *Kindai tennozo no keisei*, Toyama Shigeki's *Tenno to Meiji ishin* and Iwai Tadakuma's *Meiji tenno*. In English there is T. Fujitani's *Splendid Monarchy*. None, however, locates the development of the imperial construct in the context of early Meiji diplomacy. My preliminary exploration of the realm of ritual diplomacy suggests that this is an oversight and that imperial audi-ences granted to British and other diplomats in the 1860s and 1870s were of definitive importance in the creation of the Meiji monarch in all his complexity.

Notes

1. The audience is fully described in Naikaku Kiroku Kyoku (ed.), *Hoki bunrui taizen, Gaikomon, Gaihin seppan* (hereafter *Gaihin seppan*), p. 101. See also Ernest Satow, *A Diplomat in Japan* (London: Seeley, Service and Co., 1921), pp. 359–62.

The reader is referred to the 1931 painting by Hiroshima Koho which is on permanent display in the Seitoku Kinen Kaigakan, Tokyo. The painting in fact shows not Parkes' audience but that of the Dutch minister. As will be seen, Parkes' audience had to be postponed.

2. Parkes was referring to the etiquette normalized after the Congress of Vienna in 1815, and disseminated in such handbooks as Baron Carl von Martens' *Guide Diplomatique* (Leipzig, 1832) and J. C. Bluntschli's *Le Droit International Codifié* (Paris, 1886).

3. Catherine Bell, *Ritual Theory, Ritual Practice* (Oxford: Oxford University Press, 1992), pp. 197–223.

4. Such was the experience of Date Munenari just a few days earlier. He describes his experience in Nihon Shiseki Kyokai (ed.), *Date Munenari zaikyo nikki* (reissue: Tokyo: Tokyo Daigaku Shuppankai, 1972). See also Satow, *A Diplomat in Japan*, p. 358.

5. On Okuni Takamasa, see in English John Breen, 'Shintoists in Restoration Japan', *Modern Asian Studies*, vol. 24, no. 3 (1990) pp. 579–602. Okuni Takamasa was, it should be noted, a keen advocate of open-country politics. See, for example, his treatise on international law ('Okuni Takamasa's Shinshin kohoron', translated and annotated in Tetsuo Najita (ed.), *Readings in Tokugawa Thought, Select Papers*, vol. 9, translated and annotated by John Breen (Chicago: University of Chicago Press, 1995).

6. Takagi Shozo, *Tenno no shozo* (Tokyo: Iwanami Shoten, 1998), p. 9.

7. Lord Redesdale, *Memories*, vol. 2 (London: Hutchinson and Co., 1915), p. 460.

8. As detailed later in this chapter.

9. FO 46 series Parkes to Keppel, 29 April 1869. None of Parkes' diplomatic rivals had had the foresight to send for their credentials back in 1867.

10. Satow, *A Diplomat in Japan*, pp. 370–1.

11. Satow, *A Diplomat in Japan*, p. 371. See also Parkes' account of the audience in FO 46 series Parkes to Stanley, 30 May 1869.

12. Gaimusho chosabu (ed.), *Dai Nihon gaiko monjo* (hereafter *DNGM*) (Tokyo: Nihon Kokusai Kyokai, 1939), pp. 632–3.

13. On the duke's visit see, in English, Hugh Cortazzi, 'Royal visits to Japan in the Meiji period, 1868–1912', in Ian Nish (ed.), *Britain and Japan: Biographical Portraits*, vol. 2 (Folkestone: Japan Library, 1997).

14. Cited in *Gaihin seppan*, p. 230.

15. FO 46 series Parkes to Stanley, 23 August 1869.

16. Lord Redesdale, *Memories*, vol. 2, p. 495.

17. Lord Redesdale, *Memories*, vol. 2, pp. 495–501. See also 'Memorandum by Mr. Mitford', *DNGM*, p. 404. The Foreign Ministry had hoped the emperor might be persuaded to come to the veranda himself to greet the duke.

18. Details of the reception for the Russian prince are to be found in *Gaihin seppan*, pp. 249–50.

19. *Hoki bunrui taizen, Gaikomon, Zoto*, pp. 83–4.

20. On the Oath, see John Breen, 'The Imperial Oath of April 1868: ritual, power and politics in Restoration Japan', *Monumenta Nipponica*, vol. 51, no. 4 (1996), pp. 407–29.

21. Kunaicho (ed.), *Meiji Tennoki*, vol. 1 (Tokyo: Yoshikawa Kobunkan, 1970), p. 626.

22. Matsudaira Yoshinaga, *Itsujishi ho*, p. 374.

23. Iguchi Kazuki, *Nihon kindai shi 4: Chosen, Chugoku to teikoku Nihon* (Tokyo: Iwanami Shoten), 1995, pp. 8–9.

24. For a full discussion of Soejima's strategy, the reader is referred to McWilliams' excellent study: Wayne C. McWilliams, 'East meets East: the Soejima Mission to China, 1873', *Monumenta Nipponica*, vol. 30, no. 3 (1975), pp. 243, 257, 259.
25. McWilliams, 'East meets East', pp. 259–60. For fulsome estimations of Soejima's performance in Peking, see pp. 260 and 270–1.
26. McWilliams, 'East meets East', p. 260.
27. *NGKM*, vol. 5, pp. 30–1.
28. McWilliams observes 'Soejima was in effect declaring Japan's new identity; no longer was Japan to be identified together with China as a tradition-bound, exclusive and isolationist Asian country beyond the pale of modern international intercourse' (p. 275).
29. Rekishigaku kenkyukai (ed.), *Nihon shi shiryo 4: kindai* (Tokyo: Iwanami Shoten, 1997), p. 115.
30. See *Gaihin seppan*, pp. 199 and 206–7. The information about the emissary prostrating himself is contained in the Imperial household ministry's much more detailed programme for the audience of Kim Honjip in 1880. It is reasonable to assume that the procedures were also followed for Kim's 1876 audience.
31. Iguchi, *Nihon kindai shi*, p. 12.
32. *Gaihin Seppan*, pp. 199–200.
33. On this incident see especially see Oka Yoshitake, *Reimeiki no Meiji Nihon* (Tokyo: Miraisha, 1964), chapter 1.
34. Ibid., p. 35.
35. Ibid.
36. Matsudaira, *Itsujishi ho*, p. 360.
37. Ibid., p. 257.
38. Soejima Taneomi, 'Shishin nikki', *Nihon gaiko monjo*, vol. 6, p. 149.
39. Iwakurako Kyuseki Hozonkai (ed.), *Iwakura ko jikki*, vol. 2 (Tokyo, 1906) p. 320.
40. 'Nakayama Yoshiko kengon', 1 February 1869 (*Ishin shiryo kohon*).
41. Tokyo daigaku shiryo hensanjo (ed.), *Hogohiroi: Sasaki Takayuki nikki* (Tokyo: Tokyo daigaku shuppankai, 1973), p. 140.
42. On this incident see Sawa Nobukazu, 'Eikoku genshu keisho mondai no tenmatsu', in Shidankai (ed.), *Shidankai sokkiroku*, vol. 30 (Tokyo: Hara Shobo, 1975), pp. 133–42; see also 'Igirisu koshi ekken no sai no futsugo no shidai ni kansuru ken' in *DNGM*, vol. 3.
43. On these various issues, see *Gaihin seppan*, p. 101; Sawa, 'Eikoku genshu keisho mondai', p. 140; *DNGM*, vol. 3, p. 520 see also *DNGM*, vol. 3, pp. 637–8.
44. James Hevia, *Cherishing Men from Afar: Qing Guest Ritual and the Macartney Embassy of 1793* (Durham, NC and London: Duke University Press, 1995).
45. Akira Iriye, *Japan and the Wider World* (London: Longman, 1997), p. vii.

5

For the Triumph of the Cross: A Survey of the British Missionary Movement in Japan, 1869–1945

Hamish Ion

> I have a considerable distrust of Japanese Christianity. I believe the day may come, and before long when they will be tired of Europeanism and will throw us over and our Christianity at the same time.
>
> (Archbishop of York to Archbishop of Canterbury, 4 January 1896)[1]

This survey concerns the many hundreds of British men and women missionaries of different denominations who were a continuous presence in Japan from 1869 until the end of the Second World War and beyond.[2] It assesses the contribution of a voluntary movement of Britons abroad supported by contributions of hundreds of thousands of British people from every walk and station of life. The activities of the missionary movement expanded as the onward march of British power generated the spread of British civilization. Its decline as the twentieth century progressed can be taken as an early harbinger of the declining national resources and flagging energy underpinning Britain's overseas endeavours in East Asia. In a limited space, however, it is difficult to do full justice to a complex phenomenon which touched upon an impressively broad range of different aspects of Japanese culture and society. Indeed, the importance of the British missionary movement to Japan as a subject of academic study lies precisely in the breadth of its contact with Japan. For those interested in Anglo-Japanese cultural relations, the history of British missionary relations with the Japanese is a particularly rich and fascinating field of study because it is not only marked by reciprocal misinterpretations and misunderstandings across cultural boundaries, but also by genuine efforts to bridge cultural differences.

The realm of ideas, especially religious ones, is not as easily transmitted across the cultural divide as other aspects of a culture, such as sports, fashion, food and drink, which are less culturally challenging. While British missionaries converted relatively few Japanese (the apostates were more numerous and perhaps more influential in Japanese society than Christians), the negative cultural implications of Christianity for Japan have had an immense impact on political, social, and religious development of that country. The response of Japan to Christianity (or its perceived threat to Japanese culture) led to a profound Japanese effort to restore, rejuvenate or re-invent political, social and religious forms from the mid-nineteenth century onwards.

There is a natural tendency to give too much credit to missionaries for bringing about changes or moulding opinions in Japan. It is probable, for instance, that pre-1941 Hollywood feature films had a much greater influence in shaping the Japanese image of Britain and British people than the presence of hundreds of British missionaries in the towns and countryside of Japan. In terms of Britain, however, the enormous canon of literature and reports published in church magazines and journals did constitute a major source of information about Japan. Indeed, it could well be that the British missionary movement was more important for its impact upon British thinking and knowledge about Japan, than its achievements in Japan itself. It might also be suggested that British knowledge about Japan, especially rural Japan, was deeper prior to 1941 as result of many years of missionary reports than it was until the return of large numbers of Britons to rural Japan with the Japan Exchange and Teaching (JET) Programme. If there was a major failure on the part of British missionaries, it was their inability before 1941 to remove at the highest level of their own church in Britain that 'considerable distrust of Japanese Christianity' which the archbishop of York admitted to in 1896.

This survey concentrates on the work of missionaries who belonged to the two major Church of England missionary societies, the Church Missionary Society (CMS, low church Anglican) and the Society for the Propagation of the Gospel in Foreign Parts (SPG, high church Anglican). These missions began work in Japan in 1869 and 1873 respectively. Together with the American Church Mission (Protestant Episcopalian), these two British missions established the Nippon Seikokai (NSKK, the Anglican Church of Japan) in 1887. As well as records of the various missionary societies, the survey makes use of the papers of successive archbishops of Canterbury to help assess opinion about Japan at the highest level of the Church of England. The prime focus of this study is the relationship between British missionaries and the Japanese Anglican Church – a relationship which illuminates the changing tide of Anglo-Japanese relations. Before examining the three different phases of the British missionary endeavour in Japan, it is appropriate to make some general comments about the achievements of this movement which will indicate the vast scope of activity that missionary work encompassed.

The achievements of the voluntary British missionary movement in Japan were considerable. British missionaries founded churches, schools and hospitals, and other specialized institutions. The British and Foreign Bible Society helped to make Christian literature available in Japan. The social work of the Salvation Army among the poor and deprived in the slums of

Tokyo and other Japanese cities and their campaigns for temperance and against prostitution drew the attention of the Japanese authorities to these hitherto neglected areas. This was also true of the leper work of Anglicans such as Hannah Riddell and Nellie Cornwall-Legh,[3] or that of Anna Maria Tapson, who founded a garden home for tuberculosis sufferers. Even in their recreational activities, British missionaries had a significant impact on Japanese society; they helped to popularize Karuizawa as a summer resort, introduced hiking and mountaineering as a leisure sport into Japan and focused interest in youth activities such as the Girl Guides.[4] Missionaries were also among the pioneers in Japanese studies, and active in supporting the Asiatic Society of Japan.[5] Missionaries themselves wrote books, many of lasting interest, about Japanese Buddhism,[6] Ainu customs and language,[7] tales of the Japan of yore,[8] the early English settlement of the Bonin Islands,[9] and everyday life in Japan.[10] Amidst all this literary activity, some missionaries also found time to play a part in the translation of the Bible into Japanese.[11]

British missionaries were also involved in education. They founded the Koran Jo Gakko in Tokyo, the Shoin School in Kobe and the Poole Jo Gakko (Bishop Poole Girls' School) in Osaka in order to provide Christian education for girls. The often long-serving English gentlewomen who taught at these institutions, such as Kathleen Woolley (sister of the famous archaeologist Sir Leonard Wooley) and Mary Hailstone at the Koran Jo Gakko, Ethel Hughes and Leonora Lea at the Shoin School, Katherine Tristam and Loretta Shaw at the Poole School, had an abiding influence on succeeding generations of students at these schools.[12] It was not simply English, mathematics and good manners which were taught – physical fitness and sports was also stressed. Koran Jo Gakko, for instance, was the first school in Tokyo to play hockey, a sport which remains popular among young women at university in Japan.[13] CMS missionaries in Osaka established the Momoyama School for boys.[14] While the mission schools were a visible reminder of British missionary work in Japan's major cities, much missionary work and effort was also invested in kindergartens and Sunday schools in smaller cities and towns like Odawara and Otaru where British missionaries also lived. A stream of British women missionaries worked for many years with very little recognition in these schools or as evangelists attached to parishes: Susan Ballard (the sister of the famous literary vice-admiral), the Bosanquets Amy and Nora, Jane Staveley and Jessie Voules, to name a few of hundreds who served in Japan, provided the backbone and missionary presence at the local level.[15]

Even though many missionaries spent their whole working lives in the Japanese empire, they remained British in their lifestyle, habits and outlook and they propagated a Christianity with a British flavour. The NSKK was a church for Anglophiles. It was the church of those, like Theodora Ozaki, the wife of the politician Ozaki Yukio, who were attracted to British culture and supported strong ties between Japan and Britain. But the NSKK also had a place for the villagers of Shimosa Fukuda, in rural Chiba prefecture.[16] The NSKK was a church that conducted work among the Ainu in Hokkaido, Chinese students in Tokyo, and the English-speaking settlers of the Bonin Islands. In its overseas missionary work, the NSKK sought to serve the spiritual needs of the Japanese community in Manchuria and to participate in the evangelization of Taiwan in the wake of Japan's annexation of that island.

While their primary task was the evangelization of the Japanese, SPG and CMS missionaries also served the British community by providing priests for the British congregations in Tokyo, Yokohama and Kobe as well as manning the Seamen's Missions in the latter two ports. They also catered for visiting Japanese seamen to the port of London. Albeit small, there was also an English Mission School in Kobe diocese for western children. St Andrew's, Shiba was the church of the British Embassy, and three missionaries Alexander Croft Shaw,[17] Lionel Cholmondeley and Kenneth Sansbury[18] served as chaplains to the Embassy. The British congregations in Japan gave generously to the Japan side of the work, both financially and in the donation of their professional services. The latter was the case with Sir Josiah Conder,[19] the architect, who designed St Barnabas, Ushigome and St George's, Bonin Islands. Old Japan hands, such as Sir Ernest Satow, who retired to England, continued, through organizations like the Guild of St Paul, to support British missionary work in Japan. Bishop Montgomery, the long-time secretary of the SPG, clearly recognized that it was also important for British prestige that the Church of England was seen to be sending and maintaining missionaries in Japan and Korea.[20] During the late nineteenth century, British Anglicans definitely benefited from the fact that they were from the Church of England, which was identified with the most powerful western nation in East Asia. Indeed, as Cyril Powles has pointed out, the so-called Shiba Sect of SPG missionaries in Tokyo 'preferred to serve Japan as the Established Church of England served its own society, by engaging in a wide variety of social and cultural pursuits'.[21] Indeed, a major attraction of the Shiba Sect to young Japanese was that they were *gakusha* (scholars), as the literary work of the Oxford-educated Arthur Lloyd and other members attests.

It was in the late 1930s that the British connection came to threaten rather than help both the Salvation Army and the NSKK, for they became particular targets of the Japanese authorities because of the Japanese perception that Britain was 'finished' as a great power. As one of his gaolers told Samuel Heaslett during his imprisonment following the outbreak of war in December 1941, his case was 'not a question of right or wrong, but a question of patriotism. "Patriotism," the gaoler said, "is above questions of right or wrong."'[22] Certainly, missionaries and missions of other nationalities were also harassed by the Japanese authorities. Likewise, especially during the 1930s, other religious groups, most notably Hitonomichi Kyodan, Tenrikyo and Omotokyo, suffered even greater persecution than Christians because of their supposed heterodox beliefs.[23] Yet, even though Canon Archibald C. Hutchinson of Fukuoka[24] goes to some length to deny any real hostility among ordinary Japanese towards British people, and argues that missionaries voluntarily withdrew in order to save Japanese Christians from police harassment,[25] there is no denying that Anglophobia, as distinct from general xenophobia, was a potent force behind the victimization of British missionaries, the Salvation Army and the NSKK by the Japanese authorities.

British missionaries in Meiji Japan

The CMS began its missionary work in 1869 at a time when Christian work and faith among the Japanese was still prohibited. Indeed, as George Ensor discovered after baptizing Futagawa Ito (Kojima Ito), Japanese who defied the prohibition faced imprisonment or worse.[26] The persecution of the Urakami crypto-Christians beginning in the spring of 1868 (to which the punishment of Futagawa was related) led to sharp diplomatic protests. This was, John Breen has suggested, 'the single greatest diplomatic problem faced by the Meiji government after the Restoration'.[27] When Shaw and William Wright[28] arrived in Yokohama to begin SPG work in Japan in 1873, the Japanese authorities had already responded to western pressure on the Iwakura embassy by relaxing the enforcement of the proscription against proselytizing among the Japanese. However, the reassessment of the impact of the Iwakura embassy on the religious policy of the Meiji government, which John Breen has undertaken, points not to a new openness toward Christianity (the standard interpretation of Japanese Christian history since Guido Verbeck)[29] but rather to a confirmation of the Meiji leadership's anti-Christian stance, and also to the rise in the fortunes of Buddhism.[30] Given the emphasis that Meiji leaders placed on the importance of religion to the modern state and the necessity of countering Christian activity,[31] it is plain from 1873 that Christianity had no great chance of success in Japan.

However, the Meiji oligarchy was unable to control the flood of new ideas that entered Japan after 1873 through the medium of the English language. These were then synthesized and adapted to the Japanese intellectual milieu by Japanese opinion makers and specialists in Western Studies. The English language was the major medium through which Protestant Christianity was first introduced to the Japanese.[32] Christianity was viewed as *yosai* (western learning of a technical type).[33] The subsequent history of the expansion of Christianity during the late nineteenth century closely parallels the vicissitudes of changing Japanese attitudes to the English language.[34] Given this fact, the pool of potential converts, that is those who understood English, was very small. This was so, in part, because the window of opportunity for Japanese to learn English sufficiently well in order to qualify as members of the initial generation of the English language elite proved to be very narrow, largely limited to those of samurai background who were born five years on either side of 1861.[35] Furthermore, for those sufficiently linguistically and intellectually gifted to become members of the English language elite, conversion to Christianity jeopardized future prospects, at least, in the secular world. Thus, what is surprising is not how few Japanese became Christians during the 1870s, but rather how many of the English language elite were attracted to Christianity.

This was, of course, not apparent to Shaw or Wright when they seized the opportunity to begin SPG work in Tokyo. Happily for them, during the early 1870s, when the vogue for English-based western learning was at its height there was considerable interest in Christianity. This conveniently coincided with the influx of missionary reinforcements and the removal of the proscription edicts. Shaw was invited by Fukuzawa Yukichi to live in his home in order to teach his children English.[36] Fukuzawa also allowed Shaw to teach ethics and Christianity at his private school, Keio Gijuku in Mita, Tokyo. Keio students were also drawn into the Sunday school classes that Shaw and Wright held in the Daishoji temple including Ozaki Yukio (Gakudo) (later one of Japan's most famous parliamentarians) and Tajima Jutaro (later elected to the first Diet) both of whom Shaw baptized at Christmas 1875.[37] Shaw stayed with Fukuzawa and his family for two years. The link to Keio did not end, however, when Shaw moved into a home of his own. In 1876 Fukuzawa gave Alice Hoar, the first female SPG missionary in Japan, 'the use of the upper part of his house, where he opened a small school for her to use in teaching Christianity'.[38] Despite the fact that Fukuzawa was publicly, at times, virulently anti-Christian, the personal friendship between Shaw and Fukuzawa remained intact and led to a succession of SPG missionaries teaching English at Keio through to the 1920s. Indeed, the connection with the students at Keio was a major reason why the SPG did not attempt to establish their own boys' school in Tokyo.

Yet, if Shaw was able to capitalize on his opportunity to reach the students at Keio, CMS missionaries at either end of Japan came tantalizingly close, but ultimately failed to be the missionaries who converted the members of what were to become two of the most famous Christian bands in Japanese Christian history. Japanese Christians working with Herbert Maundrell[39] in Nagasaki had close ties with the young students at the Kumamoto Yogakko who would later form the Kumamoto Christian band, and indeed Maundrell had visited the school in the vain hope of convincing them to be baptized in the Anglican communion.[40] Likewise, Walter Dening in Hakodate had contact with the students at the Agricultural College in Sapporo who would later form the Sapporo Christian band.[41] Theobald Palm, the medical doctor belonging to the Edinburgh Medical Mission, met with considerable success in Niigata and its environs but later withdrew from Japan having decided that there was little need for medical missions there.[42] If missionaries tried to make the most of the spread of English to the peripheries of Japan by emphasizing the connection between

Christianity and western civilization or medical science, those at the centre found themselves doing battle with foreigners and Japanese who preached their belief in evolutionary thought with almost missionary fervour. In combating this, Henry Faulds, the Scottish Presbyterian missionary doctor associated with the Tsukiji hospital, locked horns with E. S. Morse, the American proponent of evolutionary ideas in Japan, and attempted to counter his arguments.[43]

The same group of Japanese intellectuals led by Kato Hiroyuki[44] at Tokyo Imperial University after 1878, who supported Morse and championed Darwinian ideas, were also in the vanguard of those determined to reduce the influence of the English language elite at the university, as well as to rid it of English-speaking foreign teachers with Christian leanings. Kato himself would appear to have had an obsessive hostility toward Christianity and continued to publish anti-Christian tracts almost to the end of his life.

Other than theological and religious arguments against the acceptance of Christianity, the Achilles' heel of Japanese Christians was the doubt that was cast into the minds of non-Christian Japanese about their loyalty to Japan, and even their 'Japaneseness' when they became Christians. The difficulty of being both Japanese and Christian proved to be extremely taxing for many Japanese converts. This stands in contrast to Japanese Buddhists who did not suffer from a similar conflict between their religion and their Japanese identity. Already, by the end of the Meiji era, the desire for an independent Christianity in Japan had begun to suggest the creation of a Japanese Christianity (*Nipponteki Kirisutokyo*) distinct from the Christianity propagated by British or other western missionaries. Further, nationalism coupled with the demands of patriotism led the Japanese Christian movement to be identified as supporting Japan's expansionism overseas especially after the Russo-Japanese War. It was by their support of Japanese imperial and military ambitions in continental East Asia that Japanese Christians could demonstrate their loyalty to Japan to counter the doubts about their Japaneseness raised by their adherence to a foreign religion identified with the West.

The importance of countering the criticism of Christianity coming from the Imperial University was one reason for the establishment in 1887 by the SPG in Tokyo of the Missions of St Andrew and St Hilda, with the Guild of St Paul in England to help support them. The intention of these two missions, the former designed for university graduates and the latter for 'ladies of culture as well as of devotional life and zeal', was to reach out to the educated classes in the capital and to serve as centres for general evangelistic work.[45] St Andrew's Mission Brotherhood served to train deacons and priests. It also sought to reach students and office workers through English-language classes and lectures held in its night school. Further, the Mission tried to strengthen the Japanese Anglican congregations in Tokyo through pastoral work.

The person responsible for the creation of St Andrew's and St Hilda's was Edward Bickersteth, who took up office as the second British bishop of Japan in 1886.[46] The appointment of Bickersteth was welcomed by both the SPG and CMS. He saw his task in Japan as the creation of a strong and independent Anglican church. In this, Bickersteth received the necessary and enthusiastic support of Bishop Channing Moore Williams of the American Church mission and together they paved the way for the formation of the NSKK in 1888 by the union of two British Anglican missions and one American Church mission. One reason for the creation of the NSKK was Bickersteth's impression that the Protestant denominations in Japan would soon unite into a single Japanese Protestant Church. He felt that if Anglicans were to influence the nature of this union church, it was necessary for them to have already established their own independent Japanese church.[47] When, at his instigation, the 1888 Osaka Anglican Conference placed on record 'the desire for the establishment in Japan of a Christian Church which by imposing no non-essential conditions of communion, shall include as many as possible of the Christians in this country', it met with little support from other missions in Japan.[48]

Bickersteth would modestly take little credit for the creation of the new Church.[49] Yet it would seem highly unlikely that the NSKK would have been created at that time and in the form it was without his determination and energy. Bickersteth had realized from the start

> the impossibility of acting in an independent country like Japan, which has never known a Master and all whose people are zealous asserters of independence, exactly as would be suitable in India, where there is British rule and an Establishment, and whose people have not for nearly a thousand years been without an 'overlord.'[50]

Bickersteth was impressed by Japanese Christians. Writing to the archbishop of Canterbury, he noted rather patronizingly that they

> are as a rule independent of foreign help in getting a livelihood, educated, and many of them, as our Conference proved, thoroughly able to debate a question, with a keen appreciation of the points at issue. On the other hand they are ready to accept sympathetic guidance and teaching.[51]

To Bickersteth perhaps the last point was the really important one. Nevertheless, he made it clear that the different circumstances in Japan required a response from missionaries different from that suitable in India or elsewhere under British colonial rule. His aim, however, was to entrench British Anglican values into the new Japanese church.

In 1887 Bickersteth had suggested the formation of an ecclesiastical Province of China and Japan by joining the dioceses of Victoria, Mid China,

North China and Japan together. The aim of this was that when Japanese bishops were consecrated (and Bickersteth thought that they soon would be) they would not be wholly independent of an Anglican espicopate.[52] While Archbishop Benson of Canterbury reluctantly agreed to the formation of the NSKK (he did not see the need for it to be created so speedily), he refused to countenance the creation of an ecclesiastical Province of China and Japan. This was ironical, for one who was so intent on the establishment of an independent Japanese Church. During the 1890s, Bickersteth oversaw the creation of a church structure that led to the consecration of many foreign bishops representing the interests of the SPG, CMS and American Church mission but with no Japanese bishops. Indeed, by 1896 there were four British and two American bishops associated with the NSKK and the number of bishops continued to grow in the future.

There was also a deeper concern than simply consecrating too many bishops. The archbishop of York damningly wrote of his considerable distrust of Japanese Christianity.[53] After ten years as bishop and as the major missionary force for change in the Japanese Anglican Church, Bickersteth (who now held the title of bishop of South Tokyo as a result of the creation of the new bishops) must bear some responsibility in failing to remove that 'considerable distrust of Japanese Christianity' among the highest church authorities at home. There was an unease about Japan which would not disappear until 1945.

Bickersteth's desire to see the rapid creation of an independent Japanese Church was predicated on a very positive attitude toward the transformation of Japan into a modern state. The open gratitude of Fukuzawa Yukichi and other prominent Japanese to Shaw for his early advocacy of Anglo-Japanese treaty revision, as well as an overall improvement of Anglo-Japanese relations after 1894 reinforced his optimism about Japan. British missionary attitudes to Japan often followed the changing nature of Anglo-Japanese relations. During the late nineteenth century, missionaries supported the rapid changes that were taking place in Japan insofar as those changes were seen to be helping the cause of Christianity. Sometimes this meant going against official British policy, as was the case with Shaw's advocacy of treaty revision. But, in general, missionaries in Japan stood aloof from political debate. Powles has suggested that Shiba Sect missionaries were so fascinated with Japan's modernization, which to them was indistinguishable from westernization, that their attention was diverted from the nature of the people who were bringing about this change.[54] Bickersteth was, at times, unable to see that cultural differences between Japanese and British might lead to difficulties. An obvious case was the prayers to the emperor in the NSKK Prayer Book which bore a great similarity to those offered to the British Royal Family, and failed to take into account different shades of meaning across cultural bounds.[55] This failure, it has been suggested, made Japanese Anglicans much more susceptible to bend to the pressures of the

Emperor system.[56] Bickersteth and other Anglican missionaries approved of the Meiji state, and tolerated its imperialist expansion into Taiwan (indeed, the NSKK followed in the wake of Japanese colonialism and established its own mission in Taiwan in 1895). They optimistically affirmed what they found in Japanese culture, pointing out, as Imai Judo did after the Russo-Japanese War, that Japan needed Christianity in order to make Japanese traditional values perfect.[57] Instead of threatening to destroy Japanese values, the grafting of Christianity to the root of Japanese culture would serve to allow that culture to flourish. Christianity could act to purify *kokutai* (the national polity).[58] Indeed, Japanese Anglican leaders 'considered it the function of the Church to identify itself with society in order to purify it'.[59] Once the Anglo-Japanese Alliance had been signed, British missionaries became much less sanguine in their attitudes toward Japan.

One reason for this was that after 1902 Japan's behaviour, both international and domestic, was perceived to reflect directly upon Britain's reputation as Japan's ally. Another reason was the religious policies of the Japanese government, particularly the 'fabrication of a new religion' in the promotion of State Shinto after the Russo-Japanese War, which was viewed as a direct challenge to Christian work. Yet the death of Bishop Bickersteth in 1897 and that of Archdeacon Shaw in 1901 proved to mark the end of an era of expansive growth which had seen the NSKK steadily expand through the 1890s when virtually all other churches had suffered a period of retarded growth.[60]

Growing unease

In 1904 Herbert Moore, who had served as an SPG missionary during the 1890s, noted in his popular account, *The Christian Faith in Japan*, that 'it is good to be zealous in a good cause, but zeal must be according to knowledge; and a careful observer would be hardly likely to anticipate the speedy triumph of the Cross'.[61] The evangelistic work of British missionaries revealed that they anticipated no such rapid triumph. Indeed, the first three decades of the twentieth century saw a steady decline in British missionary work, which was only partially attributable to the financial and personnel difficulties stemming from the First World War. Other causes were ones which the missionaries brought upon themselves.

These latter difficulties stemmed in part from the absence of missionary bishops who had the dynamism and authority of Edward Bickersteth. There was also an evident lack of zeal for evangelization among the Anglican clerical missionaries, and especially among SPG missionaries. The hesitation and indecision detected among SPG missionaries in Japan suggests a deep malaise and a loss of will. This was a harbinger of the greater loss of self-confidence which was symptomatic of the decline and growing weakness of Britain overseas. The paradigm of missionary decline as an early manifestation of British imperial decline can also be extended to the lessening of British missionary influence within the NSKK. However, the British decline at this time was partially masked by the addition of the Canadian Anglicans who began work in 1889 at the instigation of Bishop Bickersteth. In contrast the American Church mission grew steadily in importance and influence. This was dramatically illustrated in 1923 when two converts of the American wing of the NSKK became the first Japanese Anglican bishops.[62]

Following the First World War, innovations in evangelism were introduced, but the adoption of new methods and techniques such as newspaper evangelism was slow and hesitant because of the conservatism of the missionary societies.[63] Although individual missionaries in Japan speculated on the methods and philosophy of missionary work, there was little sympathetic discussion of these topics in the British missionary community, partly because of the prevailing attitude that converts were made as a result of hard work and there were no short cuts. Nevertheless, British missionary work in the new century was characterized by more than mere inertia. The Pan Anglican Conference held at Lambeth in 1907 was regarded as important by the missionaries in Japan, and led to the creation of a Central Theological School for the NSKK (prior to this, the three Anglican missions had operated their own theological training centres). Furthermore, following the Edinburgh Conference of 1910, the worldwide missionary movement exuded a buoyant confidence.

However, the atmosphere in Japan was becoming increasingly difficult for Christianity. In 1910 Bishop Cecil Boutflower of South Tokyo told the archbishop of Canterbury that 'The present influence of what at home we should call "The Crown" is quickly but decidedly antagonistic.'[64] Boutflower felt that the Imperial Household Department, the Education Department and the Army Department were the three major centres of this anti-Christian hostility which was based on:

> a feeling that Xty endangers the central fiction on which their constitution rests, and at which the most educated Japanese (e.g. Baron Kikuchi in his European Lectures on Education) in this 20th century seem willing to play – that the Emperor is of 'divine' descent, and for Japanese the highest conceivable Being! This too is why the 'state-religion' maintained is Shinto, which is essentially a very rudimentary nature worship, but as it provides the Emperor with a Sun-Goddess as ancestress and has taken on ancestor-worship, it is eminently useful for patriotism; while in the same breath Government has sought to make it easy for all by declaring (with same breath that it is not 'a Religion' at all – or be registered as such like Buddhism or Xty)![65]

Missionaries were acutely conscious of official policies to encourage the emperor cult, which they correctly saw as hindering the progress of

Christianity. Yet it was extremely difficult for them to respond to this challenge except to recognize it as an attempt 'to identify religion and patriotism and to make the person of the Emperor, rather than the Imperial ancestors, the focus of devotion and sacrifice'.[66] As late as the summer of 1937, it was pointed out that

> Japan may be the deciding factor between peace or war in the world. Can Christianity show this great nation the way of peace through Christ? Japan hungers for something which cannot be met by Shinto worship, Buddhism, or materialism. Japan needs Christ, the Prince of Peace.[67]

The position of British Anglicans had not changed from Bishop Boutflower's day – that the divinity of the emperor was a simple fabrication, and what Japan really needed was Christianity. Yet British Anglicans did not consider it their role to be critical of government policies, even though they might defy common sense, as the emperor cult did (in their opinion). They were prepared to accept government reassurances to Christians and Buddhists that visiting State Shinto shrines was not a religious act but merely a patriotic gesture.

The First World War was a turning point in missionary attitudes towards Japan. There was a belief that Japan had not supported Britain strongly enough during the war. In 1917 Bishop Boutflower complained of 'the varnished admiration of German powers which goes on openly behind the secure screen of a language whose press none of the other civilised countries can read'.[68] In 1915, in explaining the war to an audience of Japanese Anglicans, Harold Steele, an SPG missionary in Okayama, said it was a 'Holy War for England' and that Germany, who had engineered the war, had repudiated 'Christianity and all that Christ stood for'.[69] In seeing the Great War in those terms, it is difficult to see how British missionaries could not but have been disappointed by Japan's support of Britain.

Further, it was becoming increasingly clear as Japan industrialized during the First World War that the modernization of Japan was not creating a society that was any more open to the Christian message than that of the 1870s. Indeed, even before the end of the war, it was becoming evident that British missionaries did not find modern Japan or the modern Japanese attractive – it was the Japan of the countryside where traditional values remained pure – that appealed to missionaries. This can be seen in the literary work which has already been alluded to: that of John Batchelor on the culture and language of the Ainu, the concern of Lionel Cholmondeley with the Bonin Islands, the love of the Japan Alps and its mountain folk manifested by Walter Weston and later Murray Walton, and even the earlier study of Buddhism and Confucianism by Arthur Lloyd. All of these can be seen as a search for purity in dying societies or in the historical past away from the reality of modern Japan as it emerged out of the Meiji period. Herbert

Kelly, the Anglo-Catholic monk who taught at the Central Theological College during the First World War, noted in the early 1920s that 'few missionaries really sympathise with the Japanese. Some – for example France – are very anti. – J. Shortt was the only really pro – J. I knew I thought him silly (Lafcadio Hearn is the type).'[70] In June 1921 Walter France, an SPG missionary in Tokyo, did condemn the changes taking place in Japan and compared them unfavourably with the stable world of the closing years of the Meiji period. He believed that the disintegration of past standards and ideals could be summed up in the word 'democracy'.[71] Yet those British missionaries who had served in Japan for any length of time tended to view the country with deep affection. This feeling of great attachment to Japan was evident when France wrote after leaving Japan about Mount Fuji. In 1929 France wrote to a young SPG missionary that

> Mt. Fuji was my most important parishioner for some seven years. I lived alone in Numadzu and almost worshipped the marvellous beauty and mystery of it. I would give anything to have a sack on my back, tabi and Waraji on my feet and be off showing you Fuji and most particularly the Izu and Hakone country. It's my very own. I know its ills and hills and nillywaws and typhoons and moods and tenses.[72]

This does underline, however, the close affinity that British missionaries felt with rural Japan. Further, their attachment to the Japan of the countryside made it difficult for missionaries to understand the changing moods of industrialized and urbanized Japan.

After the Great War, British Anglican missionaries were increasingly uncertain of their aims and role in the evangelization of Japan. Indeed, in 1924 the situation was perceived to be so grave that Archbishop Randall Davidson of Canterbury was obliged to appoint Bishop Arthur Knight of London to travel to Japan in order to survey Anglican Missionary activity. Before Knight's report (which called for a renewal of the British commitment to Japan). there was even some doubt as to the advisability of continuing work in Japan. One of the distressing facts at this time was the weakness of the SPG which had not been able to appoint a clerical missionary from England to Japan for some 15 years.[73] One of the casualties of the SPG's failure to reinforce Japan was the closure of St Andrew's Missionary Brotherhood in 1921. Bishop Knight's recommendations, however, resulted in new missionaries and new bishops being appointed to Japan including Basil Simpson, an SPG missionary, as bishop of Kobe, and Gordon John Walsh, a CMS missionary, as bishop of Hokkaido.[74] For the time being the missionary crisis was resolved.

During the early 1930s, the British missionary movement in Japan was faced with unprecedented challenges owing to the extraordinary nature of the social, political, economic and military problems which confronted

Japan at home and abroad. Missionaries called for patience. In 1934, in the aftermath of the crisis over Manchuria, but also at a time when the idea of a new Anglo-Japanese alliance was being mooted, Bishop Arthur Lea of Kyushu stressed that

> as Britishers we have a great responsibility toward Japan, because of this friendship which, on both sides, stood the test of war: on Britain's side during the Russo-Japanese war, and on Japan's side during the great World War . . . She still believes that in ideals she has many points in common with Great Britain; and herein lie our responsibility and opportunity.[75]

At the same time, Lea recognized that 'there is about the Japanese people a reticence, suggestive of mystery, if not secretiveness, which militates against complete understanding'.[76] Yet the positive and pro-Japanese stance of British missionaries in Japan was difficult to sustain in the face of reports by missionaries in north China and Manchuria concerning Japanese actions. However, missionaries were much hampered in their efforts to explain the Japanese point of view regarding the East Asian crisis by the attitude of the Japanese government toward them.

In August 1936 in a letter to the British ambassador, Sir Robert Clive, Samuel Heaslett, the presiding bishop of the NSKK, complained that 'there is a tendency all around to curtail privileges and rights granted by treaty, and to confine us to the beaten tracks, This is a reversal of the conditions under which we were encouraged to found and expand our work in this Empire', and it was making mission work impossible and missionary withdrawal inevitable.[77] Clive's view was that 'the long and short of it is that the Japanese would like to see the last of the foreign missionaries. They won't kick them out but they may, by making life intolerable for them,' cause the missionaries to leave.[78] It was the Foreign Office view that missionaries could only hang on and hope that the Japanese government's attitude towards them might change. On the surface, the departure of missionaries from Japan would not seem to be important except to demonstrate that the Japanese authorities could rid Japan of a foreign presence without suffering any obvious consequences. However, what the Japanese government failed to realize (which the Chinese government under Chiang Kai-shek fully understood) was the important influence of missionary opinion on western Christian opinion about Japan and the East Asian crisis. In alienating western missionaries in Japan, the Japanese government was ensuring that Japan would lose the support of the international Christian community as far as its position in the East Asian crisis was concerned.

Yet, despite everything, during the early 1930s, the NSKK still continued to grow, reaching a peak of 43 000 in the jubilee year of 1937.

War and reconciliation

One of the keys to the difficulties that confronted British missionaries in the years immediately before Hong Kong and Khota Bharu was the Japanese response to the role of Cosmo Lang, the archbishop of Canterbury, as the chairman of the famous Albert Hall meeting of October 1937 protesting against Japanese actions in north China. Understandably, in light of their own government's consistent attempts to control religion and to utilize it in support of state policies, the Japanese chose to misinterpret the archbishop's actions (after all, he was the spiritual head of the established Church of England) as revealing British government attitudes toward the war in China. Early in March 1937, Lang had spoken out in the House of Lords against the massacres in Ethiopia and had urged the government to protest against the use of poison gas by the Italians. At the end of September 1937 he was asked by Gerald Barry, the editor of the *News Chronicle*, to chair a meeting at the Royal Albert Hall in early October in order to protest against the indiscriminate bombing of civilians in China. Barry believed that if Lang took part in this meeting it would set the seal on British national protest as nothing else could.[79] Prior to the Albert Hall meeting, Prime Minister Neville Chamberlain had asked to see Lang in Downing Street and had warned him about the possible adverse impact that Lang's chairing the meeting might have. However, Chamberlain did not expressly forbid the archbishop from taking part in the protest.[80] Lang could use this to justify his actions.

In explaining his decision to chair the meeting to the Japanese ambassador, Yoshida Shigeru, Lang noted that 'it was scarcely possible for me holding my position as a representative of moral and especially Christian opinion in this country to refuse to give some expression to those feelings though I hope I shall do so with fitting moderation'.[81] A similar sentiment was expressed by A. C. Don, the archbishop's chaplain, in a letter to Viscount Kano.[82] Yet, it goes without saying that the impact of the archbishop's action in participating in the Albert Hall meeting was to raise Japanese suspicions of British missionaries dramatically. Kenneth Sansbury later reported that Bishop Matsui Yonetaro of Tokyo went so far as to say that the archbishop's actions meant 'the end of our connection with the English Church'.[83] Tsukada Osamu has pointed out that the Albert Hall incident not only intensified the desire of some Japanese Anglicans for complete independence for the NSKK, but also brought the church to the attention of the military police and the Tokko Keisatsu which ultimately led to the arrest of Bishop Heaslett and others on spy charges.[84] It could be argued that British missionaries brought these difficulties upon themselves because they had failed to transfer power in the NSKK from western bishops to Japanese bishops during the 1920s and early 1930s. However, nothing could have prepared the British missionaries for the crisis which followed the Albert Hall incident.

One immediate result for the NSKK, and the Japanese Christian movement as a whole, at the opening of the 1937 Sino-Japanese War was the government's call for the spiritual mobilization of all religious bodies behind the war effort. Japanese Anglicans quickly expressed their support of Japanese government actions in China and this support would remain constant. In 1939 it was noted of the view of the Japanese Anglican delegation to the Madras Anglican Conference that

> it is true that the Christian conscience is grieved over much that happens, and that the Christian heart is stirred with a real desire to help China in many ways and, especially, when peace shall have been restored. Ardent patriotism, war time enthusiasm, and intensive propaganda, however, have combined to unite the people in support of the Government.[85]

The efforts of the government turned from the voluntary spiritual mobilization of religions to legislation in the form of a Religious Bodies Act which was seen to threaten the episcopalian system of church organization on which the NSKK was founded. In early 1940 Bishop Basil Simpson of Kobe was scathing in his reaction to the lack of Japanese Anglican protest to this Religious Bodies Act, stating that 'like all Japanese, they find opposition to officials almost impossibly difficult'.[86] Such an opinion was certainly not welcomed by the Japanese. The end for the British element in the NSKK was close at hand. It was precipitated by the arrest of British and Japanese Salvationists in August 1940 on charges of spying. Worried that the NSKK would be compromised if British missionaries were allowed to continue to hold positions of authority, Bishops Naide and Matsui demanded the resignation of all English and American bishops from the House of Bishops at the end of August 1940. Heaslett, who saw no alternative but to acquiesce to Japanese demands (there was a complete lack of courtesy about the way in which Naide and Matsui went about forcing Heaslett and the western bishops out), thought this action marked the end of missionary activity in Japan.[87] While Heaslett would continue to remain in Japan in order to look after the English congregations in Yokohama, after October 1940 neither he nor any of the other western bishops had any official connection with the NSKK. Indeed, the withdrawal of British missionaries from Japan was beginning to take place in earnest.

British missionaries were not involved in the negotiations between the various Protestant organizations which led to the formation of the Nippon Kirisutokyodan, the government-sponsored union Protestant church, in 1941. Heaslett was strongly opposed to the scheme. In September 1941 he wrote:

I have met with nothing but scepticism about the future of this Union. It has no spiritual basis, and is *really* an attempt to satisfy the Government's modern craze for getting all parties engaged in the same kind of work under one umbrella. As far as I can gather each Church is carrying on its work as before and paying no attention to the new Church order. But *outwardly* there are now four Christian groups – RC: Greek Orthodox,: [N]SKK: Union Church.[88]

A schism took place in the NSKK regarding whether or not to join the Nippon Kirisutokyodan with Bishops Naide and Matsui, together with newly consecrated Japanese bishops, leading the pro-union group. A rump of the NSKK, led by Bishop Sasaki Shinji and Bishop Yashiro Hinsuke, remained outside the union Church even though this meant a loss of government recognition of the NSKK as a religious body and led to very considerable hardship during the war. Those Japanese who remained Anglicans in defiance of the wishes of the Japanese government did so out of patriotism for Japan. They dared to oppose officials because they felt that the episcopal system which the NSKK represented was a better form of religious organization than the one which the Nippon Kirisutokyodan offered Japanese Christians. Even though they were prepared to suffer imprisonment for their religious beliefs, it was not a question of a lack of nationalism or patriotism but rather the reverse that led them to keep the NSKK in existence during the traumatic years of war.

The majority of British missionaries withdrew from Japan before the commencement of hostilities in December 1941. Those who remained in Japan were interned, or imprisoned like Heaslett, and later exchanged. A few remained in Japan for the duration of the war among whom was Leonora Lea who lived quietly in Kobe with the help of Japanese friends, including Bishop Yashiro.[89] Indeed, Lea's adulation of Yashiro and his indomitable struggle to maintain the NSKK in the face of difficulties was one reason why Bishop Yashiro has such an impeccably high reputation in British and Japanese Anglican circles. The need to discover what had happened in Japan during the war led Archbishop Fisher to send out Bishops Heaslett and J. C. Mann as special emissaries in early 1946.[90] What is surprising, given the unpleasant atmosphere that existed for British missionaries in Japan in the period from 1937, was the spirit of forgiveness and reconciliation which marked the dealings of the Church of England with the NSKK and Japanese Anglicans when the war was over. There was no feeling that there was a need for retribution concerning anyone's conduct before or during the war. Indeed, those who had caused the schism in the NSKK by joining the Nihon Kirisutokyodan were welcomed back into the NSKK if they wished to rejoin, as many did. In October 1947, it was agreed that one of the conditions of the independence of the NSKK which had been proclaimed in 1940 was that all diocesan bishops had to be Japanese.[91] While western bishops would be elected in the future, they would always serve as assistant bishops to Japanese ones. Even though the independence of the NSKK from western control had been wrested in 1940 during a time of great turmoil, British and American missionaries were prepared to allow this to stand. If nothing else, the period from 1937 had seen the NSKK achieve full independence, and after 1945 the Church of England was not about to attempt to take it away.

Conclusion

The war had clearly shown that Bishop Bickersteth and the many other British Anglicans who had served long years in Japan had been successful in building a strong church both in its Christian beliefs and its organizational structure – a church which proved capable of withstanding the most intense pressure to cease to exist. The missionary movement symbolized the desire of British Christians to share with Japanese their religious ideas and in doing so to improve the well-being, both physical and spiritual, of Japanese people. In wanting to do so, British missionaries and their constituents at home also learnt a good deal about Japan and the Japanese. More than other connections between Britons and Japanese, the missionary movement did lead to a foundation of goodwill between the two countries at the person-to-person level. What the missionary movement could not do was prevent the breakdown of relations between the two countries in the 1930s. Yet, it could, and did, take a lead in bringing about reconciliation between Christians in Britain and in Japan after the war had ended. Even though Japanese Anglicans still wait for 'the triumph of the Cross', the NSKK still continues to give spiritual comfort to those Japanese who choose to be members of it and is a living reminder of the patient work of many Britons in the past who wanted to help to construct a better Japan.

Notes

1. Lambeth Palace Library (hereafter cited as LPL). Archbishop Edward White Benson Papers (hereafter cited as Benson Papers), volume 141, Archbishop of York to Benson, 4 January 1896.
2. For a recent general survey of British missionary work in Japan, Korea and Taiwan, see A. Hamish Ion, *The Cross and the Rising Sun, Volume 2: The British Protestant Missionary Movement in Japan, Korea and Taiwan, 1865–1945* (Waterloo: Wilfrid Laurier University Press, 1993). Of very considerable value in terms of British Anglican missionary activity in Tokyo during the Meiji period is Cyril Hamilton Powles, *Victorian Missionaries in Meiji Japan: The Shiba Sect 1873–1900* (Toronto: University of Toronto–York University Joint Centre on Modern East Asia, 1987). Helpful in revealing the differences between British Anglicans and other Christian missionary groups in Japan is Cyril Hamilton Powles, 'Foreign

Missionaries and Japanese Culture in the Late Nineteenth Century: Four Patterns of Approach', in *Northeast Asia Journal of Theology* (1969), pp. 14–28. A short but useful overview is Helen Ballhatchet, 'British Missionaries in Meiji Japan', in Ian Nish (ed.), *Britain & Japan: Biographical Portraits* (Folkestone: Japan Library, 1994), pp. 33–44. A brief account of British missionaries in Japan up to 1883 can be found in Grace Fox, *Britain and Japan 1858–1883* (Oxford: Clarendon Press, 1969), pp. 502–31. There are many Japanese-language general histories of Christianity in Japan, among them, although dated but still valuable, is Ebisawa Arimichi and Ouchi Saburo, *Nihon Kirisutokyo shi* (Tokyo: Nihon Kirisutokyodan Shuppankyoku, 1971). A more recent study dealing with the problems of Christianity in the early Showa era is Kaneta Kyuichi, *Showa Nihon Kirisutokyokai shi: Tennosei to jugo nen senso no moto de* (Tokyo: Shinkyo Shuppansha, 1996). The standard history of the Anglican Church in Japan remains Nippon Seikokai rekishi hensan iinkai, *Nippon Seikokai hyakunen shi* (Tokyo: Nippon Seikokai Kyomuin Bunsho Kyoku, 1959) (hereafter cited as *Nippon Seikokai hyakunen shi*). A useful recent survey is the chapter by Oe Mitsuro, 'Nippon Seikokai shi', in Doshisha Daigaku Jinbun Kagaku Kenkyujo hen, *Nihon Purotesutanto sho kyokai no kenkyu* (Tokyo: Kyobunkan, 1997), pp. 17–73. Also highly useful are Tsukada Osamu, *Nippon Seikokai no keisei to kadai* (Tokyo: Seikokai Shuppan, 1979), and also by the same author are *Tennoseika no Kirisutokyo: Nippon Seikokai no Tatakai to Kunan* (Tokyo: Shinkyo Shuppansha, 1981) and *Shoki Nippon Seikokai no keisei to Imai Judo* (Tokyo: Seikokai Shuppan, 1992). Among histories of the CMS, Eugene Stock, *The History of the Church Missionary Society. Its Environment. Its Men and Its Work* (London: Church Missionary Society, 1899), 3 vols, and Gordon Hewitt, *The Problems of Success: a History of the Church Missionary Society 1910–1942: Volume Two Asia: Overseas Partners* (London: SCM Press, 1977) are particularly useful. For the SPG, see H. P. Thompson, *Into All Lands: the History of the Society for the Propagation of the Gospel in Foreign Parts, 1701–1950* (London: SCM, 1950). As well as British Anglicans, other missionary societies from England and Scotland were involved in work in Japan. The English Baptists began a short-lived Japan Mission in 1879, see A. S. Clement, 'The Baptist Missionary Society in Japan', *Baptist Quarterly*, vol. 26, no. 2 (April 1975), pp. 68–73. The United Presbyterian Church of Scotland began their Japan Mission in 1874 among whose members was the missionary doctor, Henry Faulds (1843–1930, in Japan, 1874–83), and the clergymen, Robert Davidson (1846–1909, in Japan 1874–1901) and Hugh Waddell (1840–1901, in Japan 1874–1900). For Faulds, see Nihon Kirisutokyo Rekishi Dai Jiten Henshu Iinkai, *Nihon Kirisutokyo Rekishi Dai Jiten* (Tokyo: Kyobunkan, 1988) (hereafter cited *NKRDJ*), pp. 1195–6; for Davidson, see *NKRDJ*, p. 896, and for Waddell, see *NKRDJ*, p. 1547. The Scottish Presbyterians supported missionaries in Japan from 1873 until 1901 but their work lost its distinct identification through its amalgamation with American and other Presbyterian missions beginning in 1877 to form a union Presbyterian Church in Japan (Nihon Kirisuto Ichi Kyokai). For the United Presbyterian Church Mission see Elizabeth G. K. Hewat, *Vision and Achievement, 1796–1956: a History of the Foreign Missions of the Churches United in the Church of Scotland* (Edinburgh: Thomas Nelson, 1960). The Edinburgh Medical Missionary Society supported Dr Theobald Palm (1848–1928) in Niigata between 1875 and 1883. For Palm, see *NKRDJ*, p. 1131. The Royal Navy supported the Loochoo Naval Mission which supported Bernard Jean Bettelheim (1811–70) as a missionary at Naha in the Ryukyu Islands between 1846–54. C. H. Moreton, a missionary affiliated with the

London Missionary Society, was in the islands between 1854 and 1855. For a brief biographical note on Bettelheim, see *NKRDJ*, p. 1262. See also *NKRDJ*, p. 93 for a summary of the Loochoo Naval Mission.

3. For Hannah Riddell (1855–1932, honorary CMS in Japan 1889–1932) see *NKRDJ*, p. 1500. For Nellie (Mary) Cornwell Legh (1857–1941, honorary SPG in Japan 1908–41) see *NKRDJ*, p. 546. See also Nuki Taminosuke, *Kornworu Ri Joshi no Shogai to Igyo* (Tokyo: Konworu Ri Denki Kanko Kai, 1954).

4. Archdeacon Alexander Croft Shaw (1846–1902, SPG in Japan 1873–1902) is generally considered to be the first westerner to popularize Karuizawa as a summer resort. See Cargill G. Knott, 'Notes on the Summer Climate of Karuizawa', *Transactions of the Asiatic Society of Japan*, Series I, XIX (1891), pp. 565–77 (p. 565). See Cyril Hamilton Powles, 'Trinity's First Man to Japan', *Trinity*, vol. 9, no. 2 (1971), pp. 6–7. See also *NKRDJ*, p. 669. Walter Weston (1861–1940, honorary CMS in Japan 1887–95, 1902–05, 1911–15) was instrumental in popularizing mountaineering as a recreational pastime in Japan, see A. H. Ion, 'Mountain High and Valley Low: Walter Weston (1861–1940) and Japan', in Sir Hugh Cortazzi and Gordon Daniels (eds), *Britain and Japan 1859–1991* (London and New York: Routledge, 1991). See also Walter Weston, *Collected Works*, 4 vols (Bristol: Ganesha Press, 1999). See also *NKRDJ*, pp. 161–2. Mariel Greenstreet established the first Girl Guide pack in Japan at the Koran Jo Gakko in Tokyo in 1920. Koran Jo Gakko hyakunenshi no ayumi hensan iinkai, *Koran Jo Gakko hyakunen no ayumi* (Tokyo: Koran Jo Gakko, 1988), p. 51.

5. Among the many British missionaries who were members of the Asiatic Society of Japan during this period, Arthur Lloyd (1852–1911, SPG in Japan 1884–92, 1895–1911) stands out as one who frequently published articles in the *Transactions of the Asiatic Society of Japan* and served for a number of years as one of its officers. For Lloyd see *NKRDJ*, p. 1521.

6. Of particular interest because of their pioneer nature (although they can be disparaged because of their basic western outlook) are the works of Arthur Lloyd. Among Lloyd's studies are *The Creed of Half Japan: Historical Sketches of Japanese Buddhism* (London: Smith Elder, 1911) and *The Wheat among the Tares: Studies of Buddhism in Japan* (London: Macmillan, 1908). Even though Lloyd's views of Buddhism must now be considered flawed, his books and also his many articles must be regarded as a significant pioneering effort However, Lloyd's most satisfactory book was his observations on Japanese society, chiefly that of Tokyo, entitled *Every-day Japan. Written after Twenty-five Years' Residence and Work in the Country* (London: Cassell, 1909). Increased knowledge about the nature of Japanese Buddhism can be seen in the later work of Ronald D. M. Shaw, the missionary son of Archdeacon Shaw as illustrated in his *The Gospel and Japanese Buddhism* (London: SPG, 1931).

7. Archdeacon John Batchelor (1854–1944, CMS in Japan 1877–1941) was considered a pioneer scholar of Ainu customs and language (although his works might now be discounted as primitive and lacking scientific rigour). Among Batchelor's works are *An Ainu–English–Japanese Dictionary (Including a Grammar of the Ainu Language)* (Tokyo: Methodist Publishing House, 1905) and *Ainu Life and Lore: Echoes of a Departing Race* (New York: Johnson Reprint Corporation, 1971). For Batchelor, see *NKRDJ*, pp. 1117–18. For a brief overview of evangelistic work among the Ainu and also research into the Ainu, see *NKRDJ*, pp. 13–14.

8. See Walter Dening, *Japan in Days of Yore: Human Nature in a Variety of Aspects* (London and Sydney NSW: Griffith Farran, 1887). Walter Dening (1843–1913,

CMS missionary in Japan 1874–83) was a missionary in Mozambique and then in Japan before resigning to become a teacher and journalist in Japan. For Dening, see *NKRDJ*, p. 900. See also Helen Ballhatchet, 'Woruta Deningu: Meiji Shoki Ni Okeru Senkyoshi no Katsudo', *Azia Bunka Kenkyu*, 16 (November 1987), pp. 21–55; Helen Ballhatchet, 'The Missionary Approach to Japan: Walter Dening, A Case Study', in Peter Lowe (ed.), *Proceedings of the British Association for Japanese Studies. Volume 1: History and International Relations* (Sheffield: Centre of Japanese Studies, Sheffield University, 1976), pp. 38–59.

9. See Lionel Berners Cholmondeley, *The History of the Bonin Islands from the Year 1827 to the Year 1876, and of Nathaniel Savory, One of the Original Settlers; To which is Added a Short Supplement Dealing with the Islands after their Occupation by the Japanese* (London: Constable, 1915). For Cholmondeley (1858–1945, honorary SPG in Japan 1888–1921), see *NKRDJ*, p. 868. See also A. Hamish Ion, 'Lionel Berners Cholmondeley: a Chaplain in Japan 1888–1921,' in Ian H. Nish (ed.), *Britain and Japan: Biographical Portraits Volume II* (Folkestone: Japan Library, 1997).

10. See Henry Faulds, *Nine Years in Nipon: Sketches of Japanese Life and Manners* (Wilmington, DE: Scholarly Resources Inc. Reprint, 1973).

11. In 1878 A. C. Shaw for the SPG, Charles Warren (1841–99, CMS in Japan 1873–99) and John Piper (1840–1932, CMS in Japan 1874–80) for the CMS had participated in the Prayerbook Committee for the Anglican Church. Because of their late arrival in Japan, British missionaries did not play a large part in the translation of the New Testament into Japanese, a task which was completed by 1880. However, John Piper until 1880, and, most especially, Philip Fyson (1846–1928, CMS in Japan 1874–1908) after 1882 played a key role in translating the Old Testament in Japanese which was virtually completed by 1887. See Ebisawa Arimichi, *Nihon no Seisho: Seisho honyaku no rekishi* (Tokyo: Nihon Kirisutokyodan, 1981), pp. 273–6. For Warren see *NKRDJ*, pp. 1548–9. For Piper see *NKRDJ*, p. 1098. For Philip Fyson see *NKRDJ*, p. 1185.

12. Amy Kathleen Woolley (1887–1976, SPG in Japan 1915–1942, 1948–64), Mary Elenor Hailstone (1889–1970, SPG in Japan 1920–42, 1947–65), Ethel Mary Hughes (1875–1968, SPG in Japan 1906–21), Katherine Alice Tristam (1858–1948, CMS in Japan 1888–1939), Loretta Shaw (?–1940, CMS in Japan 1904–24), Leonora Edith Lea (1896–1971, SPG in Japan 1927–?).

13. Alfreda Arnold, *Church Work in Japan* (Westminster: Society for the Propagation of the Gospel in Foreign Parts, 1905), p. 78.

14. For a history of Momoyama Gakuin, see Momoyama Gakuin hyaku nen shi hensan iinkai, *Momoyama Gakuin hyaku nen shi* (Osaka: Momoyama Gakuin, 1987).

15. Susan Ballard (1863–1945, SPG in Japan 1892–retired 1935), Amy Caroline Bosanquet (?–1950, CMS in Japan 1892–1932), Nora M. Bosanquet (1871–?, SPG in Japan 1908–17), Jane Anne Staveley (1898–1963, CMS in Japan 1928–61), Jessie Elizabeth Voules (1869–1952, SPG in Japan 1913–41).

16. The evangelization of this village, beginning in the late 1870s, is an example of conversion along extended family lines and also the role of economic dependency as a factor in the decision to convert within a close-knit rural society. See Nishiyama Shigeru, 'Shimosa Fukuda Seikokai no keisei to tenka', *Shingaku no koe*, vol. 19, no. 2 (June 1972), pp. 10–27.

17. Of interest because of Shaw's key role in the establishment of St Andrew' s Church is C. Kenneth Sansbury, *A History of St Andrew's Church, Tokyo (English Congregation) 1879–1939* (Tokyo: Sei Andoru Kyokai, 1940). See also Shirai Takako, *Fukuzawa Yukichi to Senkyoshitachi: Shirarezaru Meiji no Nichi-Ei Kankei* (Tokyo:

Miraisha, 1999); A. Hamish Ion, 'The Archdeacon and the Bishop: Alexander Croft Shaw and Edward Bickersteth and Meiji Japan', in J. E. Hoare (ed.), *Britain and Japan: Biographical Portraits, Volume III* (Folkestone: Japan Library, forthcoming).

18. Kenneth Sansbury (1905–93, SPG in Japan 1932–8).

19. Josiah Conder (1852–1920, in Japan 1877–1920) designed many church buildings, the most famous being the Russian Orthodox Nicolai Cathedral in Kanda, Tokyo. For Conder, see *NKRDJ*, p. 549.

20. United Society for the Propagation of the Gospel in Foreign Parts Archives (hereafter cited as USPGA), Bishop H. H. Montgomery Papers (MP) H9 'Journal of Tour of the Far East 1911', typescript, p. 120. When the USPG Archives were consulted they were located in Tufton Street, Westminster, subsequently they have been moved to the Rhodes Library, Oxford.

21. Powles, *Victorian Missionaries*, p. 9.

22. Samuel Heaslett, *From a Japanese Prison* (London: Student Christian Movement Press, 1942), p. 45. Samuel Heaslett (1875–1947, CMS in Japan 1900–42, 1946) was long-time bishop of South Tokyo and then presiding bishop of the NSKK during the late 1930s. In December 1941 he was imprisoned by the Japanese authorities on the outbreak of war, and held for four months before being released into house arrest and eventually repatriated on an exchange ship.

23. The persecution of so-called new religions by the authorities is vividly described in Sharon Garon, *Molding Japanese Minds: The State in Everyday Life* (Princeton: Princeton University Press, 1997), pp. 70–87.

24. Archibald C. Hutchinson (1884–1981, CMS missionary in Japan, 1911–41) was born in Nagasaki and, together with his younger brother Ernest G. Hutchinson (1889–1973, CMS in Japan 1916–1939), likewise born in Japan, continued the evangelical work of their father, Archdeacon Arthur Blockey Hutchinson (1841–1918, CMS in Japan 1882–1918) in Kyushu. See A. B. Hutchinson, *NKRDJ*, pp. 1120–1. Other examples of families being involved in missionary work can be seen in A. C. Shaw and his son R. D. M. Shaw (1883–1972, SPG in Japan 1907–42), Bishop Arthur Lea (1868–1958, CMS in Japan 1897–1935) and his daughter Leonora Lea, and the three members of the Warren family, Archdeacon Charles Frederick (1841–99, CMS in Japan, 1873–99), Charles Theodore Warren (1865–1949, CMS in Japan 1890–1910), and Horace George Warren (1869–1950, CMS in Japan 1893–99).

25. A. C. Hutchinson quoted in Gordon Hewitt, *The Problems of Success*, p. 328.

26. For George Ensor (1842–1910, CMS in Japan 1869–72), see *NKRDJ*, p. 201. For Futagawa Ito (1845/48–1930/4), see *NKRDJ*, pp. 1222–3. Details concerning Futagawa's baptism and subsequent imprisonment can be found in Ozawa Saburo, *Nihon Purotesutanto shi kenkyu* (Tokyo: Tokai Daigaku Shuppansha, 1964), pp. 284–6. Futagawa would later help Walter Dening, the CMS missionary, when he first began missionary work in Hakodate. In terms of the persecution of Japanese Christians, Professor T. Fujitani notes, in his study of the Japanese monarchy, that in 1869 a plan had been suggested in order to deal with the threat of Christianity 'to tattoo, brand, and condemn all Christians to hard labor'. T. Fujitani, *Splendid Monarchy: Power and Pageantry in Modern Japan* (Berkeley: University of California Press Paperback, 1998), p. 259n.

27. John Breen, '"Earnest Desires": the Iwakura Embassy and Meiji Religious Policy', *Japan Forum*, 10 (2) 1998, pp. 151–65, p. 152. See also John Breen, 'Beyond the Prohibition: Christianity in Restoration Japan', in John Breen and Mark Williams (eds), *Japan and Christianity: Impacts and Responses* (Basingstoke: St Martin's Press, 1996), pp. 75–93, 89–90.

28. For William Ball Wright (1843–1912, SPG in Japan 1873–82), see *NKRDJ*, pp. 1482–3.
29. G. F. Verbeck, 'History of Protestant Missions in Japan', *Proceedings of the General Conference of Protestant Missionaries of Japan held at Osaka, Japan, April, 1883* (Yokohama: R. Meiklejohn, 1883), pp. 23–186, pp. 53–4. Verbeck noted about the removal of the edicts against Christianity from public view that

> although the Government by no means intended publicly to declare by its actions that the prohibition of Christianity had now been abrogated and religious toleration granted, yet the event itself conveyed, in the general estimation of the people, the idea that liberty of conscience was henceforth to be allowed, and it virtually amounted to as much.
>
> (Verbeck, 'History', p. 55)

30. Breen, 'Earnest Desires', p. 152.
31. Ibid., p. 162. A more moderate position is taken by Cyril Powles who suggested that

> it seems fairly clear that the Meiji leaders did not quite know what to make of the religion from the West. They were resolved not to allow it to become a divisive factor in public affairs. As a 'private religious opinion' they had no strong feelings against it. In line with the ancient principle of *saisei itchi* (unity of government and cult), they would even be willing to give it limited recognition if it appeared that it would support social order and personal morality. But the new religion refused to fit into any of their categories.
>
> (Powles, *Victorian Missionaries*, p. 24)

32. It should also be remembered that Chinese language was second only to English in terms of its importance of introducing Christianity and its ideas to educated Japanese in the late 1860s and early 1870s. Dohi Akio has stressed the importance of Chinese-language Christian books in helping to convey Christian ideas to the Japanese as well as the concepts of heaven and of a Supreme Being that intellectuals of samurai background, particularly those with a grounding in revivalist forms of Neo-Confucianism or Oyomei, could garner from Confucianism. See Dohi Akio, *Purotesutanto Kirisutkyo shi* (Tokyo: Shinkyo Shuppansha, 1982), p. 48.
33. Tsukada, *Tennoseika no Kirisutokyo*, p. 230. See also Alan Suggate, *Japanese Christians and Society* (Bern: Peter Lang, 1996), p. 73.
34. For a useful study of Japanese attitudes toward English language, see Ota Yuzo, *Eigo to Nihonjin* (Tokyo: Kodansha, 1995 edition).
35. Ibid., p. 74.
36. USPGA. Letters and Papers Bombay, Colombo, Labuan, North China, Victoria 1868–1874. Shaw to Bullock, 14 May 1874.
37. *Nippon Seikokai hyakunen shi*, p. 60. It was more good manners in not wanting to disappoint Shaw, rather than actual lasting Christian conviction which was the reason why Ozaki allowed himself to be baptized.
38. Takako Shirai, 'Yukichi Fukuzawa and Early Missionaries in Japan', *Japanese Friends of the Bodleian Newsletter*, 7 Winter 1993/94, p. 4. Alice Eleanor Hoar (?–1922, SPG in Japan 1875–retired 1897).
39. For Archdeacon Herbert Maundrell (1840–96, CMS in Japan 1875–93), see *NKRDJ*, p. 1415.

40. See F. G. Notehelfer, *American Samurai: Captain L. L. Janes and Japan* (Princeton: Princeton University Press, 1985), p. 207.

41. Dening baptized Ito Kazutaka (1859–1929) in 1876 in Sapporo. Ito, a student at the Sapporo Nogakko, would play an influential part in the development of Christian fervour at the College which would lead to the formation of the Sapporo Christian Band. For Ito Kazutaka, see *NKRDJ*, p. 119. For a brief overview of Dening's work in Hokkaido and his contact with the Christians in Sapporo, see Nippon Seikokai Hokkaido Kyoku rekishi hensan iinkai, *Nippon Seikokai Hokkaido Kyoku kyu ju nen shi* (Sapporo: Nippon Seikokai Hokkaido Kyoku, 1966), pp. 8–23, especially pp. 17–21.

42. An enthusiastic description of Palm's work in Niigata in 1878 can be found in Isabella L. Bird, *Unbeaten Tracks in Japan: an Account of Travels in the Interior, Including Visits to the Aborigines of Yezo and the Shrine of Nikko* (London: John Murray, 1893), p. 121. For Palm's views on medical work in Japan, see Theobald Palm, 'The Position of Medical Missions', *Proceedings of the Osaka Conference, 1883*, pp. 310–21 (p. 321).

43. Kozaki Hiromichi, the famous Congregationalist pastor, expressed his indebtedness to Faulds for making 'many helpful suggestions in the realm of philosophy and science. He was a Hegelian; and he expounded the philosophy of Comte, Kant and Hegel, as well as Darwin's theory of evolution' to Uemura Masahisa, Motora Yujiro and Kozaki. See Kozaki Hiromichi, *Reminiscences of Seventy Years: the Autobiography of a Japanese Pastor*, Kozaki Nariaki, translator (Tokyo: Kyo Bun Kwan, 1935), p. 373.

44. For Kato Hiroyuki (1836–1916), see *NKRDJ*, pp. 305–6.

45. Alfreda Arnold, compiler, *Church Work in Japan* (London: Society for the Propagation of the Gospel in Foreign Parts, 1905), p. 62.

46. The first British bishop of Japan was Arthur William Poole (1852–85, CMS in Japan 1883–84). Seriously ill when he was consecrated bishop, Poole was not bishop long enough to leave a lasting mark on the work in Japan. See *NKRDJ*, p. 1243. Edward Bickersteth (1850–97, SPG in Japan 1886–96) was the son of the bishop of Exeter and the grandson of an influential secretary of the CMS. Prior to coming to Japan, he had been invalided from missionary work in India, where he had been instrumental in establishing the Cambridge Mission to Delhi. See *NKRDJ*, pp. 1154–5.

47. LPL Benson Papers, volume 41. Bickersteth to Benson, 21 September 1886.

48. Henry St George Tucker, *The History of the Episcopal Church in Japan* (New York: Charles Scribner's Sons, 1938), p. 139.

49. LPL. Benson Papers, volume 52. Bickersteth to Fenn, 11 March 1887.

50. Ibid.

51. LPL. Benson Papers, volume 52. Bickersteth to Benson, 10 March 1887.

52. LPL. Benson Papers, volume 65. Bickersteth to Benson, 26 August 1887. Memorandum on the formation of an Ecclesiastical Province in China and Japan.

53. Ibid.

54. Ibid., p. 115.

55. For a discussion of this issue and its implications in regards to Japanese Anglican views of *tennosei*, see Tsukada Osamu, 'Nippon Seikokai kitosho ni "Tenno no tame" no sho kito no keifu', *Kirisutokyo*, 25 (December 1983), pp. 69–92.

56. See Tsukada, *Shocho Tennosei to Kirisutokyo*, especially pp. 121–6.

57. Tsukada, *Shoki Nippon Seikokai no keisei to Imai Judo*, p. 84.

58. Powles, *Victorian Missionaries*, p. 124.

59. Ibid., p. 125.
60. Powles notes that the NSKK had 8753 members in 1900 with 45 Japanese clergy, 222 Japanese lay workers, 219 churches or preaching stations and 148 missionaries (including Canadian Anglicans and American Church missionaries as well as the British Anglicans). See Powles, *Victorian Missionaries*, p. 162.
61. *The Christian Faith in Japan* (Westminster: Society for the Propagation of the Gospel in Foreign Parts, 2nd edition, 1904), p. 123. Herbert Moore was acknowledged as the author of this book.
62. These were Motoda Sakunohin (1862–1928) who became bishop of Tokyo and Naide Yasutaro (1866–1945) who became bishop of Osaka. For Motoda see *NKRDJ*, p. 1403, and for Naide see *NKRDJ*, pp. 970–1.
63. Canon W. H. Murray Walton (1890–1980, CMS in Japan 1916–33) was an early advocate of newspaper evangelism and achieved considerable success with it during the 1920s.
64. LPL. Archbishop Randall Thomas Davidson Papers (hereafter cited as Davidson Papers), volume 393 Japan 1910–24. Cecil Boutflower to Davidson, 15 August 1910. For Cecil Henry Boutflower (1863–1942, SPG in Japan 1909–21) see *NKRDJ*, p. 1291.
65. Ibid. Baron Kikuchi Dairoku, the Cambridge graduate, who had lectured recently in Britain on Japanese education, was a particular bête noire of Boutflower.
66. Arthur Lea, 'Understanding Japan', *Journal of the Royal Central Asian Society*, vol. XXI (October 1934), Part IV, pp. 561–77 (p. 575).
67. *CMS Missionary Outlook*, June 1937, pp. 138–9.
68. USPGA. Bishop Boutflower Papers. Cycle-letter no. 36, 15 November 1917.
69. USPGA. SPG Series E 1915, H. T. Steele, June 1915. Harold Thomas Steele (SPG in Japan 1901–21).
70. LPL. Davidson Papers, volume 393, Herbert Kelly to Davidson, 24 August 1923. Herbert H. Kelly (1860–1950, SPG in Japan 1913–19) played an important role in introducing Anglo-Catholic theological ideas into the NSKK. Among Japanese Anglicans influenced by Kelly were Sasaki Shinji (1885–1946), Nose Hidetoshi (1892–1974) and Yashiro Hinsuke (1900–70), who became leading figures in the NSKK during and after the Second World War. The two missionaries to whom Kelly referred were Walter F. France (1887–1963, SPG in Japan 1910–23) who became a secretary of the SPG after his departure from Japan, and Charles H. Shortt (1858–1948, Canadian Anglican in Japan 1900–18). When Kelly called France anti-Japanese, it can be assumed that it was his lack of sympathy with modern Japan that he was referring to. According to Kelly, missionaries were not alone in being anti-Japanese, he also felt that the British community in Kobe was very anti-Japanese.
71. UPGA. SPG Series E 1921, W. F. France, June 1921.
72. UPGA. Far East Letters Sent 1928–1931. W. F. France to J. H. Dickinson, 22 October 1929.
73. LPL. Davidson Papers, volume 394. Memorandum from S. P. G. [Bishop H. H. Montgomery] after a long talk with Mr. J. H. Oldham, 12 June 1924.
74. John Basil Simpson (1880–1942, SPG in Japan 1910–41) and Gordon John Walsh (1880–1972, CMS in Japan 1923–40).
75. Arthur Lea, 'Understanding Japan', pp. 561–2.
76. Ibid., p. 562.
77. PRO. FO 371/20291 S. Heaslett to R. Clive, 1 August 1936. Enclosed in Clive to Orde, 7 August 1936.

78. Ibid.
79. Among the speakers at this meeting were Lord Lytton, Herbert Morrison, Lady Violet Bonham-Carter, Rev. Sidney Berry, and Professor Chang Peng-Chun.
80. LPL. Archbishop Cosmo Lang Papers (hereafter cited Lang Papers). Volume 6: China. Memorandum of Meeting with the Prime Minister, October 1937.
81. LPL. Lang Papers. Volume 6: China. Lang to Yoshida Shigeru, 4 October 1937.
82. LPL. Lang Papers. Volume 6: China. A. C. Don to Viscount H. Kano, 5 October 1937.
83. USPGA. South Tokyo Letters Received 1938. Kenneth Sansbury, circular letter no. 1, 7 October 1938.
84. Tsukada, *Nippon Seikokai*, p. 185.
85. *The C. M. S. Outlook*, vol. 66, no. 781, April 1939, p. 73.
86. USPG Archives. Kobe Letters Received 1940. Simpson to Bishop Hudson, 23 March 1940.
87. Heaslett's opinion is contained in a telegram sent by the American Ambassador to his superior in Washington. See National Archives, Washington, DC, USA, US State Department, 394.0063/1 J. Grew to Secretary of State, telegram, 24 August 1940.
88. LPL. Lang Papers. Volume 185: 1942. Letter from Bishop Samuel Heaslett, 16 September 1941.
89. See, for instance, LPL. Archbishop Geoffrey Francis Fisher Papers [hereafter cited as Fisher Papers]. Volume 8. Lea to Fisher, 18 September 1945.
90. L. P. L. Fisher Papers. Volume 16. Fisher to Heaslett and Mann, 29 January 1946.
91. Church Missionary Society Archive Microfilm. File 52: Japan Mission, 1935–49. G1J3 Nippon Sei Ko Kai: general correspondence and future policy 1935–49. CMS Secretary to Heaslett, 11 October 1947.

6
Theatre Cultures in Contact: Britain and Japan in the Meiji Period

Brian Powell

The development of Japan's dramatic literature owed much to the works of William Shakespeare during the Meiji period, principally through the mediation of Japan's first Shakespeare translator, Tsubouchi Shoyo. In this way Britain has contributed greatly to modern Japanese theatre and this contribution is often discussed in writing on drama in Japan. This present volume includes a study, by Mark Williams and David Rycroft, of the problems of conveying essential Shakespeare to an audience conditioned to accept kabuki as the norm. Much less attention has so far been paid to the question of whether the way in which plays were presented in Japan in the late nineteenth century owed anything to contact with western, here specifically British, theatre cultures. Seen from today's perspective, when Japanese theatre companies are often to be seen in British theatres and Japanese acting methods are widely discussed, one might assume also that some mutual influence might have taken place. The method adopted here in trying to assess how much each theatrical culture contributed to the other will be to consider the recorded impressions of those who visited the other country; and to look for hints in their subsequent theatre work that the impression had been internalized and made part of their view of practical theatre. 'Contact' is therefore the key word in this approach.

British visitors to or residents in Japan around the beginning of the Meiji period and visitors from Japan to Britain at about the same time occasionally recorded their impressions of the local theatre that they saw. The earliest account of a British visitor is that of Sir Rutherford Alcock, who was not able to watch theatre in Edo 'because no person of rank can be seen in such places, and it would have been a breach of all rules of society for a Minister to visit a theatre'. However, Alcock did manage to watch some kabuki-like popular theatre in Osaka thanks to the Dutch commissioner having insisted on seeing theatre each year on his way to and from Edo.[1] It was 'kabuki-like' in my phrase because reference to a drop curtain meant that the scale was smaller than in the big, more institutionalized kabuki theatres of the time, which used draw curtains, but even so Alcock was

103

surprised that 'the *mise-en scène* was very much less crude' than he had expected and impressed by the revolving stage and frequent changes of scene.[2] He was, however, not impressed at all at the action on the stage and expressed some wonder at the attitude of the audience.

> We arrived between ten and eleven, and stayed about an hour and a half, during which time a piece something like the 'Miller and his Men' or the 'Forty thieves,' with a little coarse love-making and a great deal of murder and fighting were got through, apparently to the entire satisfaction of a numerous, if not a very nicely discriminating audience.[3] [And] . . . when the piece proceeded, and a scene of indescribable grossness was going on, it was marvellous to see with what entire unconcern man and woman, young and old, looked on, either with amusement or indifference, but perfectly unembarrassed, with no sense of indecency or indecorum.[4]

In general the theatre that Britons saw in Japan in the first two decades of the Meiji period struck them as being very different in form from what they were used to in the West. The theatres are open all day and a 'regular Japanese play-goer will sit it out the whole time, having his meals brought to him'.[5] One does not know what type of theatres such visitors would have frequented in England, but the generally boisterous atmosphere of the early Meiji theatres is often commented on. Some of these comments, rather unflattering at times, indicate that the image of theatre that such visitors had brought with them was a somewhat sedate one. There was no doubt, however, that theatre was a favourite pastime in Edo and Osaka and one only had to watch the faces of the spectators to observe how enthusiastic they were about their theatre.[6] Writing about Yokohama theatre in the 1880s, Sir Ernest Satow has the impression that in Japan theatre has always been

> a place of amusement and distraction, where people of all ages and sizes go to enjoy themselves without caring one atom whether the incidents are probable or proper, so long as there is enough of the tragic to call forth the tears which every natural man sheds with satisfaction on proper occasions, and of the comic by-turns to give the facial muscles a stretch in the other direction.[7]

There is an air of wonderment about these early accounts of theatre actually seen in Japan. Taking one's shoes off at the entrance, allowing children to gambol about the stage during intervals, expressing one's appreciation by calling out the actor's name rather than by applauding, unconcernedly sleeping through whole scenes – all these aspects of Meiji theatre are observed with slightly amused detachment and with no hint that what these

Englishmen were watching might be part of a theatrical heritage that was of relevance to the theatre of Britain.

The situation of early Japanese visitors to Britain was quite different. They were visiting the most powerful country in the world at the time and representing a country which was well aware of its own military weakness compared to Britain and the other Western Powers. One should not be surprised that, however sure some of them were of their own values, they observed all aspects of the countries in the West which they visited as potentially contributing to the success of those countries, at least as defined by the standards of the day. Although Alcock rightly described the theatre as a place where no one of any social status would go, and although it is probable that none of the early Meiji visitors to Britain had ever seen theatre in Japan, they were receptive to the idea that theatre might be one link in the chain that had resulted in the West making such progress.

Several missions were sent to the West by the bakufu in the last years before the Meiji Restoration and as early as 1862 a book was published by an official bakufu interpreter on theatregoing in Paris.[8] Members of these missions often found themselves being taken to the theatre as part of the official programmes for their visits. Language was a serious barrier to their full enjoyment of the experience, not that many of the English plays of the period would have merited close attention anyway, and they sometimes slept through performances. They did, however, notice the theatre buildings, their interior decoration, the scenery and the manners of the audiences and these made a deep impression on them.[9] One such visitor's description of a London theatre was reported in the *Kyoto Shinbun* in March 1872. This was an 'extremely imposing and beautiful' structure 'facing the Houses of Parliament'.[10]

This seemingly innocuous comment may be significant in that this was probably the Lyceum Theatre, which had just begun nearly three decades of glittering success through the actor and later actor-manager Henry Irving (1838–1905).[11] If so, Wellington Street off the Strand, which was where the Lyceum was situated, could hardly be described as being near the Houses of Parliament. But whether this visitor knew the geography of London or not, there were no London theatres very near the Houses of Parliament and the very fact of mentioning government and theatre in the same sentence provides a stark contrast to Japan at the time. From 1841 until 1868 only three theatres had been allowed in the Edo area and these were confined to a marshy area well to the north of the city centre and next to the Yoshiwara pleasure quarter. In 1868 the government had ordered these three theatres to move into central Tokyo, but none had done so. In 1872 an enterprising manager, Morita Kan'ya XII (1846–1897), had taken the lead in moving his theatre, and the Morita-za, now renamed the Shintomi-za, operated henceforth from Shintomi-cho in Kyobashi, probably as close to the seat of government as the Lyceum was in London. In addition, in response to official encouragement to foster a more elevated social role for theatre, Morita Kan'ya installed ten seats specially for the use of foreigners (Japanese theatregoers still sat on *tatami* mats).[12] From now on in Tokyo government and theatre were to be geographically close and contact between these two institutions, so inimical to each other throughout the Tokugawa period, was to become frequent. In the 1879s Morita Kan'ya played an important part in this, encouraged and supported by a few influential figures in government and journalism who had seen theatre in the West.

The most active of these was Fukuchi Ochi (real name Gen'ichiro, 1841–1906), who visited Britain four times between 1862 and 1873. His first visit to Europe awakened an interest in journalism and in 1868 he was the joint founder of one of Japan's first newspapers. Fukuchi is best known for having been president of the company that founded *Tokyo Nichinichi Shinbun* in 1874. He is credited with having set the pace for the development of newspaper journalism in Japan and the leading articles of *Tokyo Nichinichi Shinbun* encouraged public debate of a kind unknown before. Of particular relevance to this essay is the campaigning for a reform of Japanese theatre that Fukuchi conducted in the columns, especially the editorial columns, of his newspaper.

In December 1871 Fukuchi left Yokohama as a member of the Iwakura Embassy. At the port he was introduced by Okubo Toshimichi to Morita Kan'ya, who had assiduously developed contacts among the official elite and had made sure he would be noticed in the send-off party at Yokohoma. The Iwakura Mission lasted 21 months, spending just over eight in the United States, five in Britain, two in France, with various short trips to other European countries.[13] During their stay in Britain they went to the theatre in London and the provinces at least six times. The mayors of Liverpool and Manchester both entertained their Japanese guests at theatres in their cities, the former also seeing fit to take them to the circus.[14] If nothing else, this must have impressed on the Embassy that theatregoing as relaxation was not confined to metropolitan high society. Even in northern cities, which the mission primarily knew and visited as centres of industry, official receptions were complemented by invitations to the theatre. One may speculate that the mayors' wives were also present, and there would otherwise have certainly been ladies present in the theatre. In fact visits to the theatre by married couples was something that Fukuchi was later to espouse in *Tokyo Nichinichi Shinbun*.[15]

Fukuchi covered a whole range of aspects of theatre reform through his journalism from pleading for theatre to be allowed to continue to exist through to quite detailed proposals for the development of a new type of history play, which would replace the flamboyant and unconcernedly anachronistic kabuki *jidai-mono* with something that would dramatize historical events with more accuracy and authenticity. How much the ideas developed here were due to his theatregoing experiences in Britain is not known, as the Embassy visited the theatre in other countries and he himself had an interest in Schiller as a playwright.

He was, however, instrumental in providing a first for Britain in 1879 when an adaptation of Bulwer Lytton's play *Money* was performed by kabuki actors. The playwright was Kawatake Mokuami (1816–93), the leading playwright of the era. With the encouragement of Fukuchi and government officials such as Ito Hirobumi, who had seen theatre in Britain, Mokuami was attempting to bring a modicum of realism to kabuki. Fukuchi Ochi had explained the plot of *Money* to Mokuami, who found the sentiments of the play so congenial that he was able to set it in Meiji Japan. The shining honesty of the main character was familiar to Japanese audiences from previous Mokuami plays, and his final magnanimity after demonstrating to his venal friends and relatives the wickedness of their ways satisfied the authorities' wish to see the theatre depict virtue being rewarded and vice punished.

Ningen Banji Kane no Yononaka (In All Human Affairs it is a World where Money only Counts), as *Money* was translated, was also one of the first plays in Japan to be played under gas lights. This was in the Shintomi-za, which Morita Kan'ya had extensively refurbished in 1878. There had been frequent contacts between Fukuchi Ochi and Kan'ya and Fukuchi was able to explain how theatres were organized as places of entertainment in Europe. In April 1878 Matsuda Michiyuki, then Governor of Tokyo, invited a number of people connected either with the kabuki theatre or with government to his residence. Ito Hirobumi was present, as was Kan'ya and the leading actors of the day, Ichikawa Danjuro IX and Onoe Kikugoro V. Ito explained to this group that in the West theatre audiences were respectable, the actors occupied a high social position and were persons of considerable culture and that their plays were noble and refined (it must be said that his examples were drawn mainly from France). Fired with enthusiasm by this, Kan'ya set about refurbishing his theatre and in June the same year the reformed Shintomi-za was given a glittering opening ceremony. The gas lights were part of this rapid modernization, and changes such as a more rational system of payment for tickets, entrance only through the front of the theatre, and the provision of services such as toilets and restaurants inside the theatre began a gradual tendency towards making the act of going to the theatre more like that experienced in the West. At the opening ceremony Kan'ya and all his staff, actors and playwrights included, wore frock coats.

One person who missed this significant theatrical event was Suematsu Kencho (1855–1920), a journalist on Fukuchi Ochi's newspaper who had been introduced to Ito Hirobumi by his employer.[16] Suematsu was attached to the Japanese legation in London and, although ostensibly sent to Britain to study, acted as an informant on world affairs for Ito by writing him frequent letters. From 1881 until the end of his stay in 1886 he spent most of his time studying law at Cambridge. While he was living in London,

Suematsu often went to the theatre and in letters to Ito and to his family he describes what he saw:

> The construction of the stage and the selection of the scenery do not come up to the standard of Japanese theatre. Since the period is very short, usually from eight to twelve in the evening, there are seldom any plays on a grand scale. Therefore where the plays are concerned, Japanese dramas are far superior, and the actors' skills are not necessarily much inferior. However Japanese plays are not as good as European ones in that the dialogue on stage lacks the kind of style and emotion that touches people's hearts, and the movements of the actors are too artificial, so that on the contrary they often inhibit true sentiment.[17]

Although Suematsu travelled to continental Europe during his stay, his ideas on theatre were mainly shaped by his experiences in London. On his return to Japan in 1886 he quickly became the leader of what was known as the Drama Reform Movement (*engeki kairyo undo*). He and a few supporters formed the Drama Reform Society (Engeki Kairyo-kai) in August and issued a manifesto for the society in the pages of a kabuki magazine. While few would have seen it there, Fukuchi Ochi also had it published in the *Tokyo Nichinichi Shinbun* and gave public support to its aims in an editorial. The list of signatories to the manifesto included Inoue Kaoru, the foreign minister, Mori Arinori, the minister of education, and Fukuchi himself, and the list of 47 (perhaps calculated to recall the Chushingura *ronin* with their great courage and unerring emotional integrity) supporters included Ito Hirobumi, Iwakura Tomomi and Okuma Shigenobu.

The manifesto included three main aims:

1. To reform the evil conventions of hitherto existing theatre and cause the realization of good theatre.
2. To cause the writing of plays for the theatre to be an honourable profession.
3. To build a properly constructed auditorium which will be used for theatre performances, music concerts, song recitals, etc.

Suematsu subsequently developed his views on drama reform in a public lecture that he gave in Tokyo in October of the same year (1886).[18] This too was given full coverage in the press. He clearly regarded kabuki as unsuited to the modern age, in spite of the rather moderate views he had expressed from England. He seems to have blamed this on the way in which the kabuki theatre had always been dominated artistically by the actors and he hoped that by encouraging a perception of the playwright as a man of literature, as in the West, a closer identification of theatre and high culture would result. He thought that the institution of the *onnagata* should be abolished and female parts be played by actresses. He wanted plays to be more realistic and to reject the conventional didacticism. All the crudity of kabuki should be stripped away, so that no one would be shocked by what they saw. Perhaps he did not know that twenty years earlier Alcock had observed Japanese spectators being very far from shocked, but Suematsu was thinking of audiences from a different social class, who remembered the strict rules on public deportment that operated for the samurai during the Tokugawa period.

Most of what Suematsu was advocating had to do with the externals of theatrical performance. The Society did encourage the writing of so-called 'plays of living history' (*katsurekigeki*), which Fukuchi had been calling for, but they were not popular among kabuki audiences and it needed the development taking place in literature at the same time, led by Tsubouchi Shoyo, to establish the basis for a new historical drama. As many of Suematsu's critics, among them Tsubouchi, pointed out, his was a superficial attempt to change theatre, and it seems likely that the support of so many public figures was due to reasons unconnected with the theatre. 1886 saw a intensification of political activity over treaty revision and the theatre was destined in the eyes of government to be a part of the now flourishing Rokumeikan culture.[19]

Much of Suematsu's missionary energy was devoted to advocating the building of a new theatre. He was quite specific about the features that he wanted this building to have and, if it had materialized, it would have been very similar to theatres he had seen in London, particularly as a suitable British architect was also identified. Suematsu did not suggest that this theatre could be the theatrical equivalent of the Rokumeikan, but it would have had all the necessary facilities for preparing to watch and actually watching theatre that would be conducive to a quiet, politely sociable outing. Suematsu's theatre was never realized as he intended. Financial backers could not be found for a thoroughly western-style theatre and Suematsu had to be content with the Kabuki-za, Japan's largest theatre to date, which was opened in 1889. This had what is referred to as a western exterior, although westerners see much that is oriental in it, but inside it was a pure kabuki theatre. The reforms that Kan'ya had introduced in theatre management at the Shintomi-za were taken further in the new theatre, but the performance and auditorium space left audiences in no doubt that the theatre was intended for traditional Japanese theatre.

The Drama Reform Society withered away at the end of 1887, but not before Suematsu had marked up the singular achievement of arranging for the Meiji emperor to watch kabuki for the first time. It is hardly necessary to comment on what an extraordinary change in official perception of kabuki must have occurred for this to have been allowed to take place. Not twenty years earlier kabuki actors had been classed as outcasts, and the kabuki theatre had attracted much condemnation during the early years of

Meiji for the salaciousness of its performances. The emperor and empress did not stoop to attending a theatre; instead the leading actors of the time were summoned to the residence of Inoue Kaoru where they performed on a specially constructed stage in the garden. The plays performed were, with one exception, from the classical repertory.

A theatre building answering to Suematsu's requirements was not finally built until 1911, when the Imperial Theatre (Teikoku Gekijo) was constructed in Marunouchi. Much of the impetus for this large project was occasioned by the visit of Prince Arthur of Connaught to Japan in February 1906 to present the Order of the Garter to the emperor, the so-called Garter Mission. There was some consternation when it was realized that a projected visit to the theatre would mean using the Kabuki-za. The occasion was sponsored by the Tokyo financial world and they spent some 10000 yen making the Kabuki-za more like a western theatre by such devices as building pillars and arches at the entrance.[20] A number of mishaps occurred during Prince Arthur's time in the theatre – there was a power cut, the Kabuki-za had not been able to provide an interpreter to translate the Japanese speeches of welcome – and there were suggestions on the Japanese side that the royal guest from the 'Alliance Country' was not entirely happy, although he managed a few affable comments for the press.[21] Mitford, by contrast, seemed to think that he enjoyed himself greatly.[22] Newspaper reports stressed the importance for Japanese theatre of the attendance of a visitor of Prince Arthur's status and expressed the hope that the dismal shortcomings revealed by it would be speedily rectified. Japanese audiences were especially criticized for behaving badly in the theatre and having no standards of dress or politeness.

The plans for the Imperial Theatre were announced in August the same year and they incorporated a number of innovations that were designed to ensure that Japanese audiences learned to deport themselves as their counterparts in the West. For example, it was to be an all-seat theatre (thus doing away with the traditional four-to-six-person stalls boxes (*masu*) where much loud socializing regularly took place); each seat would be numbered and each ticket would bear a seat number (thus minimizing confusion and preventing competition for the best positions); cutting the length of performances to about four hours was also stated as an intention and this too would have inhibited the perception of the theatre as a place to spend a sociable day out.[23]

In this way Britain had a part, quite an important, part in the transformation of kabuki theatregoing from the lively, participatory existence it had at the beginning of the Meiji period (whose passing, it must be said, is regretted intensely by some theatre historians) to the rather sedate form that it takes now. Kabuki is, however, only one of several theatre genres that developed in the first half century after the Meiji Restoration and we may ask whether Britain aided in the development of these in any way.

During the Meiji period the main alternative to kabuki was a type of theatre referred to as *shimpa*. The name is significant as literally translated it means 'new school' and it was applied to indicate a contrast with the 'old school' (*kyuha*) which was kabuki. The fact that both genres were regarded as part of one whole may explain both why its practitioners thought of themselves as pioneers of modern theatre and why, when some of them performed in the West, their art was referred to as kabuki. Kabuki was the only referent for aspiring pioneers in the 1890s, when *shimpa* developed, and it was natural that it was looked to as a model.[24] *Shimpa* acting was close to kabuki acting; not nearly as polished because it was mainly performed by actors who had not received rigorous training from their kabuki actor fathers since childhood, but with many of the mannerisms and movement patterns. Both women and men played female roles.

Shimpa was theatre performed by outsiders – that is, people outside the acting and other theatrical families that had controlled kabuki for two hundred years. It had been the involvement of 'outsiders' such as Fukuchi Ochi and Suematsu Kencho and the various politicians interested in the Drama Reform Society who had established the principle that the theatre world need not be a closed one.

One part of the *shimpa* movement in the 1890s became set in a fixed mode of production which has tended to define *shimpa* ever since. Performing adaptations of popular novels serialized in newspapers, this type of *shimpa* provided its audiences with tales of Meiji figures, mainly pairs of lovers, who were subject to the same tension between *giri* (social obligation) and *ninjo* (human emotions) that had been gripping kabuki audiences of the *sewa-mono* domestic tragedies for many decades. As repetition has never been a problem in Japanese theatre, the constant repetition of this type of play gave the actors and actresses a kind of professionalism that began to gain them critical acceptance.

Kawakami Otojiro (1864–1911), on the other hand, did not think this was the way the new drama should be developing. Uniquely among theatre people active in the 1890s he had seen theatre in the West, having been sponsored by Ito Hirobumi to go to France in 1893. He took a company of 19 actors and actresses, including his ex-geisha wife Sadayakko, on a long tour to the United States, Britain and France between 1899 and 1901. In Boston he met Henry Irving, and the great English actor gave him a letter of introduction which enabled him, in spite of exiguous financial resources, to take out a contract with the Coronet Theatre in Notting Hill. Kawakami's performance there in the spring of 1900 was greeted coolly by those critics who made their way to Notting Hill. For a week the theatre was empty, but then 'the fashionable and artistic public, which has a habit of ignoring the professional critic, became aware of the fact that a miniature comedy and tragedy of rare delicacy and charm, as naif as they were beautiful, could be seen'.[25]

These words were written by Osman Edwards, author of the first book on Japanese entertainments, which he wrote after a trip to Japan in 1899. He met Fukuchi Ochi several times and inclined to his views on the necessity to reform kabuki. He was full of praise for Kawakami and Sadayakko. Of the former he wrote: 'As an actor he is certainly free from the painful mannerisms of the older generation: his elocution is more even, his action more quiet and sudden, his facial expression less exaggerated.' Sadayakko, he wrote, 'combines with much physical attraction of voice and face the secret of supremely graceful movement. Her dances were revelations of the witching of Salome's art. Her histrionic powers are not less remarkable.'[26]

News of this unusual theatrical event reached Buckingham Palace and the prince of Wales sent a messenger to the Coronet to invite Kawakami and his company to give a private performance for him and his friends. Kawakami was consulted in detail about the type of stage on which he wanted to perform and no expense was spared by the Palace to provide a suitable performance space, including a *hanamichi*. The occasion was a great success and the company were granted an audience with the prince of Wales after the performance.

From today's perspective it appears unfortunate that London (and Paris) audiences were introduced to kabuki through Kawakami and Sadayakko. Osman Edwards thought that Kawakami deserved praise for 'lopping away several excrescences which disfigure the drama of his native land'.[27] Now that kabuki is appreciated in the West for the highly accomplished theatrical art that it is, we might be inclined to blame Kawakami (and Edwards to some extent) for inhibiting the development of a sensitivity to the integrating role that the 'excrescences' played in the totality of kabuki theatre. In mitigation, however, one can agree with Edwards' relief that British theatregoers had seen something at least close to the theatre that was most popular in Japan. He had written in a tone close to despair: 'one shudders to reflect on the unfortunate fact that English playgoers, until quite lately, derived most of their ideas about Japan from The Mikado of Mr W S Gilbert and The Geisha of Mr Owen Hall'.[28]

Kawakami's trips abroad strengthened him in his conviction that the hallmarks of kabuki – especially the continuous background music and the use of onnagata – had no place in *shimpa*, and on his return he initiated what he called a movement to establish 'correct drama' (*seigeki*). There was no background music; coloured gels were used in the lights; the *hanamichi* was ignored. In this he is seen by one Japanese theatre historian as having helped to lay the foundation of *shingeki* (new drama), the genre usually regarded as the modern drama of Japan.[29]

Japanese theatre people were now beginning to travel abroad and over the next twenty years most, but not all, of them spent time in London. Disentangling the contribution that London theatre made to their thinking on their art is difficult, as they usually made short stays in the theatrical capitals of continental Europe, where much that was pioneering in western theatre was taking place. They therefore returned to Japan with multiple impressions and only rarely can one discern an especially British influence.

For instance, the kabuki actor Ichikawa Sadanji II (1880–1940) made a grand tour between December 1906 and August 1907. The son of the great Sadanji I, who had died in 1904 after a career as one of the three most famous kabuki actors of the Meiji period, Sadanji II was judged to be a poor actor and his performances with his father's company were derided by the critics in Japan. He knew Kawakami and heard from him about theatre in the West, and this had whetted his appetite to see this for himself, perhaps thus finding the inspiration that would set his career on an upward path. In August 1906 he took the name Sadanji II, much to the disgust of purists, and made so much money out of the performances to celebrate this (again criticized in the reviews) that he was able to afford an extensive trip abroad.

He reached London in April 1907 during a Shakespeare festival. He was impressed by a performance of Hamlet by the actor-manager Beerbohm Tree, noting that when Tree added his own bits of business (such as kneeling by Ophelia's grave and throwing flowers into it) he did not add to Shakespeare's text some suitable lines to accompany the actions. Sadanji much admired this act of restraint in not tampering with the text.[30] Kabuki actors were still accustomed to having the right to require changes in plays that did not suit them, although changing a classic play would have been unusual. Sadanji's comment may indicate how little effect the Engeki Kairyo-kai had had in its insistence that the playwright's work should be regarded highly. Sadanji was also full of praise for the discipline of the actors playing the crowd in *Julius Caesar*, something with which the later *shingeki* movement had some difficulty when, unlike in kabuki, all actors hoped to be able to play lead parts one day.

Sadanji met Johnstone Forbes Robertson, Squire Bancroft and Ellen Terry, the last of whom invited him to observe tuition at her acting school. Sadanji went to the school almost every day for three weeks and was very interested in what he saw. He comments on how each part of the body was trained separately before the teacher allowed full body movement. He also describes singing exercises, which he thought very logical and observed to be con-centrated on producing the voice from the throat. In the end, however, he concludes that, although he of course learnt a lot, training such as he saw there was simply not suited to 'theatre in our country'.[31] Here was an example of a British model being specifically rejected. Sadanji was confident that the acting techniques of kabuki that were still the norm in Japan were adequate to meet the challenge of new plays reflecting the changing times. On his return he set about testing this confidence by having them perform a new historical play by Matsui Shoyo (1870–1933), his mentor and com-panion on his travels (during which it appears they quarrelled several times). At the same time he initiated at his own theatre, the Meiji-za, the reforms in theatre management and organization that were planned for the Imperial Theatre, thus anticipating the latter by three years and in the process antagonizing many of his own fans. Matsui was deeply worried by all this and took the extraordinary step of addressing the actors at a rehearsal of his new play and warning them that a brief trip to the West by their leader was not going to change Japanese theatre at a stroke. To some extent Matsui was vindicated, as some of Sadanji's reforms were unsuccessful and traditional practices were reintroduced early in the month's run. For example, the new prohibition on eating and drinking in the theatre could not be sustained because the much publicized theatre restaurants could not cope with the numbers involved.[32] On the other hand, Sadanji had the gratification of being invited to host a 'welcome home' performance the next month (February 1908) for the outgoing Japanese Ambassador to Germany. Six hundred of the metropolitan business, political and academic elite gathered at the Meiji-za for the occasion.[33]

Sadanji later joined a young theatre enthusiast, Osanai Kaoru (1881–1928), in forming one of the two companies usually credited with establishing the *shingeki* movement in Japan. Perhaps significantly in view of Sadanji's experiences in London, this company used kabuki actors and expected them to adapt their acting technique to perform translated western plays and new plays by Japanese playwrights. This was the Jiyu Gekijo (Free Theatre) and it mounted its first production, of Ibsen's *John Gabriel Borkmann*, in 1909, performed entirely by male kabuki actors. Jiyu Gekijo is said to have been modelled on the Incorporated Stage Society, which was a theatre club formed in 1899 expressly to produce in club conditions modern plays that had been refused a licence for public performance.[34] The Stage Society was certainly active while Sadanji was in London, but he does not mention it in his account of his London stay. Osanai, however, probably knew about it from his extensive reading in western theatre. Like the Stage Society Jiyu Gekijo mounted a number of private productions of new plays and it attempted, unsuccessfully in the end, to sustain its finances through a similar membership system. Jiyu Gekijo aroused much interest, not to say excitement, among intellectuals over the succeeding few years, and encouraged several young Japanese playwrights, but the enthusiasm of its kabuki actors waned quickly and it stopped regular activity in 1915.

Jiyu Gekijo's rival as a pioneer *shingeki* group was Bungei Kyokai (the Literary Arts Association). Originally a literary society attached to Waseda University, Bungei Kyokai was later to be reorganized into virtually a theatre company under the leadership of Tsubouchi Shoyo and a pupil of his, Shimamura Hogetsu (1871–1918). Bungei Kyokai also combined private with public productions. Its first public production, in 1911, was of *Hamlet*, directed by Tsubouchi. During Bungei Kyokai's short life in this form productions of Shakespeare alternated with those of the most modern playwrights in the West: Ibsen, Sudermann and Shaw. Tsubouchi directs

Shakespeare; Shimamura assists Tsubouchi in his Shakespeare productions, but is clearly more interested in modern European drama, as he directs Ibsen and Sudermann (but not Shaw). His case again illustrates the problems of assigning specific influence from abroad. Shimamura spent from May 1902 to July 1904 in Oxford studying philosophy and aesthetics and going frequently to the theatre in London (over one hundred times).[35] He subsequently stayed in Berlin for ten months where he went to the theatre more than fifty times. But apart from his known impatience with the kabuki-like acting style that Tsubouchi imposed on the amateur actors and actresses of Bungei Kyokai, there was nothing specifically English or German in his directing style either during his time in Bungei Kyokai or in his own company later.

The story of the Japanese discovery of British theatre continues in this vein. *Shingeki* theatre people go to the West, make a grand tour of Europe that includes London and return to Japan to direct plays that draw widely from the European tradition. Apart from Shaw, who is performed occasionally, British playwrights were not in the forefront of development in European theatre and it may not be surprising that Britain is mainly looked to, if at all, as the country that produced Shakespeare. Osanai Kaoru, Sadanji's partner in Jiyu Gekijo, makes such a tour in 1912 and 1913. This includes a short stay in London, but his subsequent activity shows that seeing the new year in at Stanislavski's home in Moscow and the Russian director's productions that he watched made the strongest impression on him.[36]

There is little to indicate that British theatre found anything to adopt from Japan during the Meiji period. Japanese theatre throughout this time was dominated by kabuki and the British theatre had only the haziest notion of what that was. Although Henry Irving had met Kawakami and Ellen Terry had met Sadanji, neither thought the encounter of sufficient interest to include it in their autobiography. It seems that British theatre during the last few decades of the nineteenth century was so confident of its own standards – and with some justification given the array of superlative actors that it had at its disposal – that it had no need to consider whether those standards would benefit from closer contact with Japan. In Japan in the 1870s some in the kabuki theatre had that confidence, but others were convinced that there had to be wide-ranging reform. The latter probably had an influence out of proportion to their ability to carry their audiences with them because they enjoyed the backing of powerful figures in the worlds of politics and finance.

Answering to the requirements of the latter that theatregoing become more respectable, the social organization of the audience areas of theatres changed considerably, but at least in the case of kabuki the actor's art remained much the same. Someone like Kawakami Otojiro, who had broken away from kabuki, returned from the West convinced that he was right, and others later travelled abroad to seek to reaffirm their convictions that the

West had something to offer Japanese theatre. All began to perform in theatres whose atmosphere was changing rapidly and it may not be fanciful to suggest that Britain gave decisive encouragement in that direction through having a monarchy that enjoyed the theatre.

Notes

1. Rutherford Alcock, *The Capital of the Tycoon*, vol. 2 (London: Longman, Green, 1863), p. 113.
2. Ibid., p. 114.
3. Ibid., pp. 112–13.
4. Ibid., p. 114.
5. R. M. Jephson and E. P. Almhirst, *Our Life in Japan* (London: Chapman and Hall, 1869), p. 187.
6. Ibid., p. 187.
7. Ernest Satow, *A Diplomat in Japan* (Oxford: Oxford University Press, 1968), p. 51.
8. Matsumoto, Shinko, *Meiji Zenki Engekiron-shi* (Tokyo: Engeki Shuppan-sha, 1974), p. 25.
9. Ibid., p. 30.
10. Ibid., p. 29.
11. Ibid., p. 29.
12. Akiba, Taro *Nihon Shingeki-shi*, vol. 1 (Tokyo: Riso-sha, 1971), pp. 7, 71–7.
13. D. W. Anthony and G. H. Healey, *The Itinerary of the Iwakura Embassy in Britain*, Research Papers in Japanese Studies (Cardiff: Cardiff Centre for Japanese Studies, 1996), pp. 9–13.
14. Ibid., pp. 21–8.
15. Quoted in Matsumoto, *Meiji Engekiron-shi* (Tokyo: Engeki Shuppan-sha, 1980), p. 35.
16. Margaret Mehl, 'Suematsu Kencho in Britain, 1878–1886', *Japan Forum*, vol. 2 (October 1993), p. 174.
17. Ibid., p. 181.
18. Matsumoto, *Meiji Zenki Engekiron-shi*, pp. 287–307; R. P. H. Mason, 'Suematsu Kencho and Patterns of Cultural and Political Change in the 1880s', *Papers on Far Eastern History*, vol. 20, September 1979, pp. 20–40.
19. Mason, Suematsu Kencho', pp. 33–5.
20. Matsumoto, *Meiji Engekiron-shi*, p. 794.
21. Ibid., p. 746.
22. A. B. Mitford, *The Garter Mission to Japan* (London: Macmillan, 1906), p. 87.
23. Ibid., pp. 751–2.
24. Ozasa, Yoshio, *Nihon Gendai Engeki-shi, Meiji Taisho-hen* (Tokyo: Hakusui-sha, 1985), p. 51.
25. Osman Edwards, *Japanese Plays and Playfellows* (London: Heinemann, 1901), p. 65.
26. Ibid., pp. 66–7.
27. Ibid., pp. 66–7.
28. Ibid., p. 61.
29. Ozasa, *Nihon Gendai*, p. 58.

30. Ichikawa, Sadanji, 'Sadanji Jiden,' in Saeki Shoichi et al. (eds), *Nihonjin no Jiden*, vol. 20 (Tokyo: Heibon-sha, 1981), p. 350.
31. Ibid., p. 351.
32. Matsumoto, *Meiji Engekiron-shi*, p. 757.
33. Ibid., p. 760.
34. Toita, Koji, *Engeki Gojunen* (Tokyo: Jiji Tsushin-sha, 1956), p. 57.
35. See Iwasa, Soshiro. 'West End no Hogetsu', *Hikaku Bungaku Nenshi* XXVII, Waseda Daigaku Hikaku Kenkyushitsu, March 1991.
36. Kubo, Sakae. *Osanai Kaoru* (Tokyo: Kadokawa Shoten, 1955), p. 75.

7
'To Adapt, or Not to Adapt?' *Hamlet* in Meiji Japan

Mark Williams and David Rycroft

> Translation is, of course, a rewriting of an original text. All rewritings, whatever their intention, reflect a certain ideology and a poetics and as such manipulate literature to function in a given society in a given way.[1]

Susan Bassnett and André Lefevere open their general editors' preface to the Routledge Translation Studies series with this explicit challenge to all those who have tended to judge works of literature in translation on the basis of their 'accuracy' and of their 'fidelity' to the original text. The challenge has not gone unheeded and the past decade has witnessed a series of critical studies of various texts premised on the notion that all such 'rewritings' result in a new original, whether this assumes the form of a translation, an adaptation, a literary history or whatever. These new texts, whilst certainly open to comparisons with the original, have rightly been subjected to critical evaluation as pieces of discrete, internally consistent literature, and questions concerning the new insights offered and the extent to which these new interpretations relate to and illuminate the concerns of the audience, have inevitably been at the forefront of critical discussion.

Implicit within such discussions, however, is an acknowledgement, not only of the responsibility, but also of the power that is invested in the individual responsible for this rewriting. For, as Bassnett and Lefevere continue, 'Rewriting is manipulation, undertaken in the service of power' (ibid.). The liberties taken with this power and the extent to which the rewriter chooses to adapt the form of the original: these will be integral in shaping the reception of a work or an author in a receiving culture different from the culture of origin of the text. For whereas, on the one hand, such rewritings can be used to introduce new concepts, new genres and new literary devices, equally they can be used to subvert – to 'repress innovation, distort and contain' (ibid.). Furthermore, the more the expectations of the receiving culture differ from those of the source, the greater the scope afforded to the rewriter to manipulate this reception.

It follows from the above that, confronted by a translation and charged with the task of critical evaluation, we do our industry a great disservice if we limit ourselves to discussions of *how* a text has been translated. There are other, equally salient considerations – questions relating to why a particular text or author has been selected, the identity of the translator and his/her success in meeting a series of translational aims. For, as Lefevere argues, 'Contrary to traditional opinion, translation is not primarily "about" language. Rather, language as the expression (and repository) of a culture is one element in the cultural transfer known as translation' (ibid., p. 57). There is, in short, a process of negotiation at work here – a dialogue between two (or occasionally more) cultural codes and systems – and translation, as the product of transcoding different cultures, comes to represent much more than merely the consequences of crossing linguistic barriers.

The role of the receiving, or target, culture in all this is clearly integral as, to a large extent, it is the dominant poetics of the day in this receiving culture that will determine the strategy of translation to be adopted. To be sure, the status of the original in the source culture will be in part responsible for determining which texts will be translated. Equally significant as an influence on the entire process of translation, however, will be issues relating to the target culture – its self-image at the time of translation, the types of texts it deems acceptable, the levels of 'acceptable' diction, the configuration of the prospective audience and the cultural scripts to which that audience is accustomed and which it is willing to accept. Such considerations are difficult to overemphasize, a point made forcibly by Lawrence Venuti in his study of the history of translation,

> The viability of a translation is established by its relationship to the cultural and social conditions under which it is produced and read.
>
> This relationship points to the violence that resides in the very purpose and activity of translation: the reconstitution of the foreign text in accordance with values, beliefs and representations that pre-exist it in the target language . . . Translation is the forcible replacement of the linguistic and cultural difference of the foreign text with a text that will be intelligible to the target-language reader.[2]

To Venuti, 'a foreign text is the site of many semantic possibilities that are fixed only provisionally in any one translation, on the basis of varying cultural assumptions and interpretative choices, in specific social situations, in different historical periods'.[3] Seen thus, translation represents a process of cultural negotiation – with the choices confronting the potential translator indeed bewildering. In broad terms, however, as Romy Heylen has noted in his study of six French versions of *Hamlet*, these options can be delineated as approximating to one of the following three text types. Firstly, the rewriter may take the text and, by adapting it to a certain dominant poetics or ideology in the target culture, may seek to integrate the resulting text as part of the receiving tradition. Alternatively, a cultural compromise may be sought, a balance between various characteristics from both sets of poetics and ideologies. Finally, however, out of dissatisfaction with the dominant poetics of the receiving literature, the rewriter may import the foreign text with little or no attempt at acculturation. In so doing, in retaining the text as an exotic 'other', he or she may use the foreign text as a means to attack canonical forms within the receiving culture.[4]

The three categories are clearly not designed to be mutually exclusive and, as Lefevere also insists, any approach to rewriting 'which rests content with decreeing which translations ought to exist and which ought not is very limited indeed. Rather, it should analyze texts which refer to themselves as translations and other rewritings and try to ascertain the part they play in a [given] culture'.[5]

At this point, we should turn to a specific source text and a specific receiving culture. But, as we consider the reception of Shakespeare, and of *Hamlet* in particular, in Japan during the Meiji era (1868–1912), let us bear in mind the issues relating to strategic decision-making and manipulation of an original as outlined above. Much has been written on the subject of *Hamlet* in Japan, the majority of it in Japanese, and much of it subsumed into the seminal study of the topic, Kawatake Toshio's *Nihon no Hamuretto* (*Hamlet in Japan*). All the factual detail relating to the attempts of the Meiji literati to produce a Japanese *Hamlet* is incorporated into this monograph and we acknowledge our indebtedness to the scrupulous attention to detail exercised by Kawatake. However, this essay intends to achieve a more specific focus, one that acknowledges more fully the element of manipulation – the exercise of power – involved in the process of introduction of Shakespeare's drama to a Japanese readership. More specifically, we shall be shining the spotlight on two particular rewritings of the play: *Hamuretto: Yamato Nishiki-e* (A Japanese Print of *Hamlet*), which represents the first completed adaptation published by Kanagaki Robun (1829–94) in 1886, and the version, produced and staged by Tsubouchi Shoyo (1859–1935) in 1911, which represents the first complete translation of the entire text to appear on stage (see Figures 7.1 and 7.2).

As will be evident from our introductory comments, the distinction between the adaptations (that characterized the vast majority of the early Meiji attempts to produce a Japanese version of *Hamlet*) and the more literal translations (spawned by the pioneering work of Shoyo in particular during the latter part of the era) is perhaps not as significant as many traditional commentators would have us believe. We are talking here, less of two discrete genres, but of two variants of the art of 'rewriting', variants which, in both cases, will respond to the same critical evaluation as regards 'fidelity' to Shakespeare's original, internal consistency, and so forth. For, as Adrian

Figure 7.1 Shoyo surrounded by students rehearsing a scene from Shakespeare circa 1913

Figure 7.2 Hamlet with his mother in the Bedroom Scene – when the ghost appears (Act III, Scene IV, line 105). *'Save me and hover o'er me with your wings, You heavenly guards'* (trans. Shoyo)

Pinnington has argued convincingly in his discussion of 'two versions of *Hamlet* in Japanese dress' (those by Odashima Yushi and Munakata Kuniyoshi),

> there is no clear set of rules which allows us to array translations tidily along an axis of greater and lesser fidelity to the original. A translation or adaptation may be truer to Shakespeare's original in one sense and by the same token ignore or suppress some other equally vital aspect of the work in question, just as a contemporary production may make visible some quality of a play while obscuring other elements.[6]

Here, we shall be taking this logic one step further – in suggesting that there will be occasions when the literal translation may well be less 'faithful' to the original than the 'spirited' adaptation which, while radically overhauling the form of the original, may occasionally be more effective in capturing its underlying 'spirit'. In both cases, the important point is that we are confronted with a 'new' original – and it is on these terms, as unique texts firmly rooted in the prevailing literary poetics of their respective day, that they will be considered. In so doing, rather than offering a mere comparison of the works of two of the most significant dramatists on the Meiji literary scene, we shall use the differences in approach to rewriting of these two to highlight the dramatic shift in poetic norms that occurred during the quarter century that separated the two experiments.

Commentators of the intervening period – the 1890s and early years of the new century – are quick to identify this as an era of rapid reassessment in Japan. With the rush towards modernization that had characterized the early Meiji era now tempered by an acknowledgement of the need for a more measured approach to all things western, and with the political institutions so ardently advocated by the freedom and people's rights movement now in place, here was a period marked by reflection upon the significance of various native institutions. In the sphere of literature, the result was a burgeoning of literary activity that has been cited by the prominent critic, Karatani Kojin, as representing the 'origins of modern Japanese literature'.[7] In the theatrical world, this was the period in which the efforts of the 'Engeki kairyokai' (Theatre Reform Group), founded in 1886 with the express intent of bringing reform to the Japanese dramatic tradition, began to bear fruit and the efforts of the 'new school' (*shimpa*) to produce a stage language that approximated more closely the contemporary vernacular were much in evidence. In short, between 1886 and 1911, there was a concerted challenge to the prevailing literary climate. Our comparison of these two Japanese versions of *Hamlet* is designed to highlight the extent to which both represent manipulations – rewritings designed to 'make them fit in with the dominant, or one of the dominant ideological and poetological currents of their time'.[8]

As Kawatake is at pains to stress in his study, Robun and Shoyo were by no means alone in their attempts to introduce the drama to a wider Japanese readership. From the outset of the Meiji era, both were embroiled in a much wider, more concerted attempt to create a literature better suited to the tenor of the times. More specifically, both were increasingly caught up in the move to devise a viable successor to the *gesaku* (popular) literature tradition with its unflagging reliance on the formula of *kanzen choaku* (encourage good and chastise evil) that had predominated in the latter part of the preceding Tokugawa era. For all their interest in literary reform in general, however, it was in the sphere of drama in particular that both were to concentrate their efforts and, by the early 1880s, both men were at the vanguard of a movement which sought a radical reappraisal of the dramatic tradition in Japan by means of selective importing of the western 'classics'. For some, the determination to emulate such western forms derived from simple dissatisfaction with the newly perceived limitations of the vernacular tradition. For others, however – and it is to this latter category that both Robun and Shoyo belong – there was a more ambivalent attitude to western knowledge. Initially, at least, theirs was a predominantly utilitarian approach whereby they sought to integrate the best of the western dramatic tradition with their indigenous theatrical institutions – in an attempt thereby to revive the fortunes of the latter. The distinction is significant. What we see here, in effect, is the conflict which Lefevere discerns in

> nearly all non-western [literary] systems in the nineteenth century: the struggle between the traditional poetics intent on keeping the system closed to Western influence and a new poetics trying to strike a balance between the traditional and the imported, which is perceived as either potentially liberating or potentially subversive depending on the ideological position taken.
>
> (pp. 35–6)

For the vociferous minority opposed to all contact with the literary legacy of the West, the struggle entailed, quite literally, the defence of the Japanese nation and culture from colonial subjugation. Such isolationism was, however, anathema to the burgeoning majority, including Robun and Shoyo, who came under the sway of those reformers, such as Fukuzawa Yukichi, who advocated education as the means to improve the native tradition. Theirs was a 'culture with a low self-image' which, in keeping with Lefevere's prediction, 'welcome[d] translation (and other forms of rewriting) from a culture or cultures it consider[ed] superior to itself' (p. 88).

Lefevere's thesis provides a useful pointer in our search for answers to the first of the issues, highlighted in our introduction, as crucial to the process of textual rewriting: why is a particular author – in this case, Shakespeare – selected for adaptation or translation in the first place? With the need to revamp the poetics of Kabuki, the dominant theatrical genre of the day, all too apparent even to those intent on resisting the 'pernicious' flow of western imported literature at all costs, here was a model which had withstood the test of time in its source culture and yet which, particularly with the benefit of a modicum of judicious adaptation during the process of rewriting, could be readily accepted by Kabuki audiences in early Meiji Japan.

Much has already been written about the prominence accorded to the work of Shakespeare in this process of rapid importation – and Kawatake is by no means alone in citing as highly significant in this regard the intrinsic similarities between the world of the Kabuki theatre and the Elizabethan stage.[10] Indeed, as far back as 1911, the critic Robert Porter was suggesting that 'comparison of English and Japanese stage history elicits the curious fact that in both countries the rise of popular drama dates from the same period'.[11] A number of similarities has been suggested, but some of these are, at best, coincidental, at worst rather contrived or superficial. Coincidence or not, however, the fact remains that Kabuki did represent a defining force in the reception of Shakespeare into Japan – the first non-Kabuki complete translation of any Shakespeare play was not until Tozawa Koya and Asano Hyokyo's translation of *Hamlet* in 1905 – and its influence was to remain evident even in many of the later, purportedly more 'literal' translations. The trend is that as described by Lefevere,

> The genre that is dominant in the target culture defines to a great extent the readers' horizon of expectation with regard to the translated work that tries to take its place in that target culture. If it does not conform to the demands of the genre that dominates the target culture its reception is likely to be rendered more difficult.
>
> (p. 92)

Having identified Shakespeare as a logical target of interest for these Meiji rewriters, however, the question still remains, 'Why *Hamlet?*' It is at this point that the similarities in terms of theme and style between the Elizabethan stage and Kabuki appear to offer significant insights. Not only would the themes of civil war, of rivalry and betrayal within families, of deeds of heroism and of revenge, and of the failings of great historical figures whose lives end in tragedy, have found ready parallels in the Kabuki tradition; of equal significance in this regard is the figure of Hamlet himself. For, in dominating every scene in which he appears, revealing different facets of his complex personality depending on the people with whom he is interacting, and consequently causing all other characters to seem to exist, not so much in their own right but as foils to the protagonist – as butts of his wit or targets of his moral outrage, Shakespeare's hero would appear to possess a ready parallel, in terms of dramatic theory, in the *tateyaku*, the leading actor of Kabuki drama.

Let us turn now to consider the rewriter's success in meeting a series of translational aims which need to be explicitly addressed before every new attempt at rewriting, regardless of the relationship between source and target language. By way of example, one could cite one of the key decisions confronting all translators of Shakespeare: whether to historicize or to modernize. The choice in such cases is clear: either the rewriter will attempt to invoke both the historical flavour and language of the original by selecting comparable historical solutions on the linguistic, literary and sociolinguistic levels, or the original will be rendered in a more contemporary setting in an attempt thereby to focus on the universal qualities of the original text. The implications of this decision are considerable. For, it is the decisions made in this regard that will determine to a large extent the strategies adopted with regard to various related problems raised by elements in the universe of discourse of the original. How to deal with dialects? How to deal with allusions to events or persons that would have been familiar to contemporary audiences of the original but which would mean little to a target audience with a very different cultural heritage? How to retain the full range of meaning of the double entendre, or of the expression with a particular connotation to a particular audience? These and other related problems must be addressed by all seeking to rewrite a text for a foreign audience. And it is on the basis of the solutions adopted in response to these issues that assessments as to the 'fidelity' of a given rewriting will be made.

In the case of rewritings of Shakespeare into Japanese, however, such problems are clearly exacerbated by the need to operate in a target culture further removed from the source culture (not merely in terms of linguistic origins but also of literary and cultural heritage) than is traditionally the case. Indeed, as Andrea Nouryeh has argued in her study of 'Shakespeare and the Japanese Stage': 'Unlike European translations which can draw from common Christian symbols, climate, and topography, and have linguistic correlatives, Japanese translations must be adaptations in which much of the verse, imagery, humour and cultural context of the original plays is lost.'[12] Nouryeh is not alone in her assessment of the specific problems confronting the Japanese translator of Shakespeare.[13] Indeed, even by the end of the Meiji period, doubts were being expressed as to the suitability of Japanese for a drama turning on intellectual dilemmas and involving long soliloquies.[14]

For critics of this persuasion, it is the fundamental prosodic differences between English verse, with its stress-timed metrical pattern, and Japanese, with its syllable-timed rhythm, that render all attempts at 'faithful' translation well-nigh impossible. Confronted with the blank verse of Shakespeare's original, argues Niki Hisae in her study of Shakespeare translation in Japan, the Japanese translator is in no position to replicate this, whether mimetically or analogically. Instead, he or she is limited, either to an approach based on the semantic factors of the original, in which the poetry is allowed to 'take on its own unique poetic shape as the translation develops', or to one in which 'the substance of the original is retained but the form is

changed' (pp. 51 ff). For many of the Meiji adapters, the 'changes' introduced into their rewritings may not have been deliberate attempts to create
'Japanese versions of *Hamlet*'. In choosing to render the iambic pentameter
of the original into the traditional 7–5 metre, in determining to reproduce
the 'To be, or not to be' soliloquy in terms designed to recast the psychological uncertainty betrayed by Hamlet as a classic example of the individual torn by the conflicting tensions of *giri* (duty) on the one hand and
ninjo (human feelings) on the other . . . subconsciously or not, these Meiji
adapters were selecting various illocutionary strategies designed to enable
the end product better to conform to the prevailing poetics in their receiving culture at the time of their particular adaptation. The resulting texts
rarely stand close scrutiny as translations, if by that we restrict our assessment to the success or otherwise of the attempt to find precise linguistic
equivalents for Shakespeare's original in the target language. If, however, we
view these as interpretative parallels of the original with the aim of evoking
a similarly imaginative response in the reader to that experienced by a reader
of the original, then several of these 'new' Meiji texts are surely worthy of
more serious critical appraisal than that to which they have been subjected
to date. With this in mind, let us turn then to the two rewritings of *Hamlet*
that did most to capture the poetic spirit of Meiji Japan.

Kanagaki Robun

By the time Robun produced the first complete 'rewriting' of *Hamlet* in
Japanese in 1886, the general synopsis of the play would have been familiar to the Meiji literati as a result of the pioneering efforts of a series of earlier
aficionados.[15] Shakespeare's name became widely known, largely through
references found in Nakamura Keiu's celebration of Samuel Smiles' *Self-Help*.
Three years later, the earliest known translation of Hamlet's speech, 'To be
or not to be', written in romanized Japanese and clearly intended to be
amusing, appeared in *The Japan Punch*. It is generally attributed to the British
artist and journalist Charles Wirgman and Japanese scholars have speculated
at length as to whether it might have been occasioned by an actual performance which Robun, at the time working in Yokohama as Inspector of
Public Sentiment, might have seen. He certainly knew of Wirgman and may
have worked on the script of a production at the new Minato-za theatre in
1874 for which Wirgman painted the scenery. And he later acknowledged
his debt to Wirgman, a keen amateur cartoonist, for his interest in producing *manga* for illustrated newspapers which dates from this time. At any rate,
in 1875, Robun started serializing his first Kabuki adaptation of *Hamlet* in
the *Hiragana e-iri shimbun*.

Serialization of this *Seiyo Kabuki Hamuretto* (A Western Kabuki *Hamlet*)
began on 7 September 1875 with a brief introduction to the plot and a list
of the characters given in *ateji* (phonetically equivalent Chinese characters).

However, after only two further instalments, Robun abandoned this project, a decision he was subsequently to attribute to 'adverse public reaction' and the 'unfavourable tenor of the times'.[16] Clearly, with the new Meiji oligarchy only just beginning to make its mark, plays which flouted the traditional dictates of *kanzen choaku* were liable to attract public disapproval.

By the mid-1880s, however, the times had changed considerably. Some of the more pernicious consequences of the 'Three Principles' that had been issued by the Kyobusho (Ministry of Religion) in 1872 in an attempt to encourage authors to think seriously about 'the uses of literature in an enlightened society'[17] had been ironed out and Shoyo's treatise on the 'Essence of the Novel' (*Shosetsu shinzui*, 1885) had triggered considerable debate on the method of effecting a radical reconsideration of the role of literature in general. In the sphere of drama in particular, the period had seen the founding of the 'Engeki kairyokai' (Theatre Reform Society) in an 'attempt to modernize and sanitize Kabuki in line with theatre practice'.[18] And, by way of initial attempts to implement such reforms, at much the same time, Shoyo had begun his experiments with adapting western plays into a traditional Japanese format as a means of enriching a dramatic tradition to which he remained so attached – starting with *Shizaru kidan* (Julius Caesar, 1884) and an unfinished version of *Hamlet* under the title *Denmaku no oji: Hamuretto monogatari* (1885).

Given the nature of these advances, it is not surprising that Robun felt more confident about his second attempt at a Kabuki version of *Hamlet* produced some 11 years later. Equally, however, there is clear evidence in this *Hamuretto Yamato Nishiki-e*, which was serialized in the autumn of 1886 in *Tokyo e-iri shimbun*, of considerably more attention paid by Robun to the tastes and requirements of a mid-Meiji theatre audience. The changes effected by Robun for this second attempt offer significant clues as to the problems he discerned in the earlier version; at the same time, however, they represent a sustained attempt to conform more closely to 'the demands of the genre that dominate[d] the target culture of the day'.

Robun introduced his new *Hamlet* with an admission that, in the new version, he 'had revised the style of the former and imitated the style of a *joruri imbon* (the text of a piece in *joruri* style) of the Toyotake school'.[19] This is accompanied by the title of his drama printed in a manner clearly reminiscent of a Kabuki signboard:

Above this is included the description: '*Gekijo no kairyoan wa igirisu no jidai-kyogen: shijo no kairyomen wa waga kuni no jidai-kyogen*' (Proposal for improving the theatre by adapting an English historical play: the text takes the form of our country's *jidai kyogen*). Robun's readership would have been well versed in this form of Kabuki with a historical theme as its subject. It would also have empathized with his depiction of this piece as a '*shohontei*', a word used to describe the text used to prepare a Kabuki performance.[20] The intent was clearly to create the illusion for his audience that it was attending a real Kabuki performance[21] – and this illusion would have been enhanced by the decision to provide the drama with a Japanese historical setting.

The decision to remove the setting for the drama from Elsinore to the castle of the house of Shiba and to locate this in the Nambokucho era (when the Imperial Court was divided between the southern and northern courts (1336–92)) would have been one with which Robun's audience could readily identify. Thereafter, as the action begins, a more precise location – near the town of Sakata in modern-day Yamagata Prefecture – is suggested by references to Mogami Castle and to the area surrounded by three famous mountains, Dewasanchi. On the second day of serialization, Robun includes a complete dramatis personae, the names, though still cited in *ateji*, largely corresponding with Shakespeare's originals. On the following day, however, arguing that the list was a vestige from the previous failed attempt, he plunges into the new version in which these phonetic names are largely abandoned, replaced by Japanese names designed to help the audience to understand the family relationships involved. Thus, as the curtain rises, it is the Lord of Mogami, Minamoto Kaneyori, who has suddenly died and his brother, Kanehisa, who has succeeded him.

Another change, readily apparent from the first day of serialization, concerns the transformation of Shakespeare's drama, designed from the outset with actors in mind, into a version that is halfway between a novel and a script for the theatre. Not only did Robun offer a substantial introduction, but the lines to be spoken by actors or by the *gidayu* chorus, though clearly indicated, are embedded in passages of narrative and interspersed with occasional comments, many of a humorous or self-deprecating nature, from Robun himself. Robun's use of the *gidayu* chorus is of particular interest in this regard. For it was by availing himself of this technique, drawn straight from the Kabuki theatre (where it replaced some of the dialogue by recounting what an actor is saying or thinking at a particular juncture), that he sought to offer insights into the inner lives of the characters and to portray their suffering, not as unique, but as a facet of the universal. The resulting characters may appear less complex psychologically. As a result of the commentary offered by the *gidayu*, however, their motivations for actions possess a coherence sometimes lacking in Shakespeare's original: in removing some of the ambiguity surrounding Shakespeare's characters, Robun succeeds in recasting these into figures of considerable internal consistency.

Let us turn then to a consideration of some specifics with regard to Robun's characterization.[22]

Perhaps the key to Robun's interpretation of Shakespeare's drama concerns his treatment of the figure of Polonius, recast in *Nishiki-e* as Muneharu. The traditional interpretation of Polonius on the western stage tends to be that of the loyal, old retainer whose only fault is his overzealousness in his master's affairs.[23] He may be a man addicted to manipulating others and spying on them and there is an unpleasantness in his elaborate instructions to Reynaldo to spy on the former's son in Paris. But there is a certain humanity to Polonius too. He is aware of the power of young love and feels sympathy for the lovers. As a former thespian, he is embarrassed by the emotion of the actor's speech and concerned for the actor. More importantly, he is ignorant of Claudius' fratricide. His own death is accidental, Hamlet's action being portrayed as opportunistic and a mistake ('I took thee for thy better'). And Laertes' passionate filial devotion and energetic pursuit of revenge, while important for the contrast they provide with Hamlet's own inaction, still do not elevate Polonius' death to the status of the tragic.

In contrast, Robun's Muneharu is evil personified. He certainly tries to curry favour with his new lord, Kanehisa (Claudius), and to come across as the ever-faithful retainer. And he seeks to justify his ambition by criticizing the old lord as inadequate to defend the country in difficult times. All along, however, he betrays a willingness to work for the elimination of Hamuramaru (Hamlet) if this were to his advantage, and he struggles to conceal his desire to establish his own son, Reinojo (Laertes), as Kanehisa's successor in the hope thereby of usurping the castle in one fell swoop. Learning of Kanehisa's plot to kill Hamuramaru, therefore, he perceives this as an ideal opportunity to drive them to kill each other. He is, in short, even more treacherous than Kanehisa himself.

Confronted by such treachery, Robun's audience would have recognized this as conforming to the time-honoured tradition of the *o-iemono* (part of the Kabuki repertoire dealing with hereditary rights and obligations). And as a necessary corollary to this came the need to add complexity to the relationship between Muneharu and his children. In Shakespeare's original, the relationship between Polonius and both Ophelia and Laertes remains relatively uncomplicated – with a result that both Laertes' antagonism towards Hamlet and Ophelia's madness are seen as perfectly natural human emotions. In contrast, those between Muneharu and his children, Reinojo and Mikariya-hime (Ophelia) appear less natural; they owe much to the clash between *giri* and *ninjo*, discussed earlier as so characteristic of the Edo drama.

In keeping with this template, both Reinojo and Mikariya-hime seek to remain loyal to Kanehisa, their lord and master. The contrast between Laertes and Reinojo is particularly marked. Sympathy for the former, a man who has suffered keenly from the death of his father, is conspicuous by its absence; Shakespeare does not allow Laertes the status of a tragic hero. Too easily influenced by Claudius, he becomes a willing partner in a murderous conspiracy and it is only in his final lines that we sense the poignancy of the joint deaths of two young men who could have been brothers:

> Exchange forgiveness with me noble Hamlet.
> Mine and my father's death come not upon thee
> Nor thine on me!

> (*Hamlet*, V. ii, 334–6)

Reinojo, for his part, realizes his father's treachery and is deeply troubled. His challenge to Hamuramaru, murderer of his father, to a duel may lack for enthusiasm. But his belief that 'even if a father is not a father, the son must continue down the path of the son' remains unwavering and he feels no choice but to seek revenge (*Hito*, 1936, p. 36). Even if successful in avenging his father, however, he sees no future for himself following such an act of disloyalty and so, when Hamuramaru disembowels himself, Reinojo feels obliged to follow suit. This may appear similar to the fate that befalls Laertes; the fundamental difference, however, lies in the fact that Reinojo was prepared for this all along.

It is out of a similar sense of contradiction that Mikariya too is forced to suffer. Like Ophelia, she too appears harshly treated by Hamlet and is driven mad by a combination of this and the sudden death of her father. In other ways, however, her relationship with Hamuramaru is very different to that between Hamlet and Ophelia: the two may be joined by the same pure love – but, for Mikariya, there is the added awareness that she is engaged to Hamuramaru as a result of the wishes of deceased ancestors. As a consequence, she is torn between, on the one hand, a sense of duty, of *giri*, to her ancestors and to her own father of whose plot to kill Hamuramaru she is all too well aware and, on the other, her natural feelings (*ninjo*) towards Hamuramaru whom she is forbidden even to see. It is therefore little wonder that she is unable to respond with the innocent madness of a naïve young woman as betrayed by Ophelia in her famous song of love (*Hamlet* IV, scene v). Instead, she appears fully aware of the potential consequences of her actions:

> As she sits down, she starts to sing a song in the *imayo* style which sounds like the voice of the nightingale flying out of the valley to announce the arrival of spring.
> Even a departed spirit was an ordinary person before:
> In the end we will all be spirits . . .
> Although spirits have power to meet and combine body and soul,
> There's a gap between these two spirits which is sad . . .

Although I am here in the old capital, even Asajigahara is deserted
And the light of the full moon is shining clearly
As the keen autumn breeze cuts into me.

(ibid.)

The Mikariya who confronts the audience at this point is caught in an impossible impasse from which only death can release her. The audience, recognizing the familiar 7–5 metre of her song, would have responded to this much as they responded to the *michiyuki* scenes in which two lovers walk to their deaths in the traditional *shinjū* (love suicide drama).

A similar element of inevitability is introduced into the characterization of Hamuramaru himself. To be sure, Robun is at pains to retain the tragic sense of waste that a young prince of Hamlet's grace and potential, 'the expectancy and rose of the fair state', has to die. Both protagonists are victims of a fallen world, whose tragic duty is to 'set it right'. In other respects, however, the difference between the two is marked, particularly at the end of the respective dramas. Gone is the serious student from Wittenberg whose philosophizing on the problems with which he finds himself confronted, particularly in the soliloquies (which Robun chose to delete), is so integral to development of the drama. Instead, Robun's pro-tagonist is a more tragi-comic figure – depicted by Kawatake as a '*tsukuri-aho*' (jester) (p. 172) – one far more in keeping with the *o-iemono* tradition with which his audience could more readily identify and one better placed to accept the destiny which he knows will befall him. As the drama nears its conclusion, therefore, Hamuramaru's resignation is of a different order to that of Hamlet; there is no belief in the 'special providence in the fall of a sparrow'. As he enters the final scene of the drama, he knows exactly what is going to happen, whereas Hamlet believes he is simply facing Laertes in a friendly contest. Hamuramaru knows, even as he contemplates the skull at the side of Mikariya's grave, that he has to die. And unlike Hamlet who, by his own admission, so often 'unpacks his heart with words', Hamuramaru's pain is communicated through silence and reserve.

Another character to be revamped by Robun in an attempt to render the play more in keeping with the traditional dramaturgical mould is Gertrude, here recast as Serido no Mae. Lacking any of the maternal affection and com-passion in her dealing with Hamuramaru, here is a lady who, at least until 'the play within the play' scene, appears devoid of remorse for her com-plicity in the death of her former husband. Her conscience is nevertheless pricked by the drama that unfolds before her on this occasion and she takes her leave, before Kanehisa, on account of her 'feeling unwell' (*Hito*, p. 30). It is, however, not until she sees the ghost of her late husband – an appari-tion denied to Gertrude – that the pangs of conscience begin to influence her actions and, even then, her response is by no means immediate: she is still all too aware of her status as lady of the Shiba family and as the wife of a samurai. Instead, her reparation is delayed until the final scene – in which she drinks from the poisoned chalice intended for Hamuramaru, not by mistake as the original suggests, but in a deliberate and premeditated manner, whereupon she confesses her complicity in all that has gone before and seeks atonement. For Robun's audience, echoes of the tradition of the *modori* of classical drama (whereby a character, previously portrayed as villainous, is ultimately revealed as possessed of integrity) would have been readily identified.

The list of concessions made by Robun to his 1880s audience is by no means exhaustive. There remains, however, one further departure from Shakespeare's original in Robun's text which, while designed to reassure his contemporary Kabuki audience, nevertheless represents an interesting challenge to those who sought comfort in the tried and tested. At first glance, the inclusion of a series of villainous characters, absent from Shakespeare's original, who overhear Hamuramaru's plan to have revenge on his uncle and who seek to thwart him appears as yet another concession to the dominant poetics of the day – would have been an ideal opportunity for Robun to conclude his drama with the depiction of Hamuramaru having faithfully fulfilled his filial obligation. And yet here we have no traditional ending in which 'goodness is encouraged and evil chastised'. Hamuramaru and Reinojo may perform their double suicide, but the Fortinbras-type figure who rides in astride a white horse does not accord Hamuramaru a hero's funeral. Instead, we are left with the image of what appears to be a neighbouring lord taking advantage of the confusion at Mogami Castle – and the suggestion that the entire family will be destroyed. Evil may have perished; but so too have those whose motives have been revealed as pure. Instead of the conventional Kabuki-style ending, we are left with a literal tragedy in which everything has been destroyed.

Having considered some of the concessions made by Robun to his contemporary Japanese audience, and some of the ways in which he had built on the traditional model using new material in an attempt to create a new form of drama incorporating elements of both the western and eastern dramaturgical tradition, however, the question of fidelity to Shakespeare's original still remains. On the one hand, Robun's drama betrays an interest in interpreting the changes taking place within society and in elucidating, in easily accessible language, the literary values of the new Meiji oligarchy as enshrined in the abovementioned 'Three Principles'. The result is a drama, embedded very clearly within a Japanese context and in which the balance between the depiction of the characters and theme and basic ideals of the original has been subtly, yet significantly, shifted. On another level, however, Robun's determination to rekindle interest in the essential plot of the original has resulted in a rewriting, still in five acts, with a similar division of scenes in which he retains most of the main events of the original. The appearance of the ghost, the feigned madness of the protagonist, the drama within the drama, the admonition of the protagonist by his mother, the drowning of the object of the protagonist's affections, the earthy humour of the gravediggers ... all are provided with ready parallels in Robun's 'Japanese print of *Hamlet*'. Of much greater significance when considering Robun's approach to Shakespeare's original text, however, is the manner in which both Shakespeare and Robun make masterly use of the resources available to them by their respective languages and cultures. Both use their own poetic traditions to create an inner drama which complements the action on the stage and, where Shakespeare creates a mass of powerful images within the dialogue, Robun combines and re-combines emotive conventional elements in his choric *joruri* commentary. Robun's version may lack the romantic fascination of a Hamlet who talks about life, and talks about it with so much eloquence and insight that we are moved to identify with him, to be excited and amused by him. But if one sees *Hamlet* as a play about a young man of great potential who, through no fault of his own, is placed in an intolerable position, 'in a world where appearances belie reality, where integrity and innocence bring disaster, where evil seems dominant, where order and "degree" are threatened or overthrown' and who, in trying to resolve the impossible demands placed upon him, tries to act honourably and morally even though this will lead to his own death and the death of those he loves, then its kinship with *Nishiki-e* can be clearly seen.

Tsubouchi Shoyo

Robun was by no means alone in working on Shakespeare – and on *Hamlet* in particular – during the 1880s. The ensuing years saw the appearance of various partial translations – most notably those by Yamada Bimyo (1888) and Mori Ogai (1889), two prominent members of the literary establishment – and a couple of new attempts at adaptation, by Kawatake Shinshichi III (1889) and Fukuchi Ochi (1891). As noted above, these were formative years in the emergence of a modern Japanese literature and these reworkings can be seen as ushering in a new phase in the assimilation of *Hamlet* into Japan. Gone was the utilitarian approach to the text that had marked the majority of the early encounters – to be replaced by a new interaction with the original in which the protagonist came increasingly to be perceived as a role model for those engaged in addressing the issue of self-identity in their literature. For Kitamura Tokoku and Shimazaki Toson – indeed for all those who were part of the coterie centred on the journal *Bungakkai* in the 1890s seeking to come to terms with the concept of the *kindai jiga* (modern self) – *Hamlet* became essential reading, its influence readily discernible in such works as Tokoku's *Horaikyoku* (The Song of Paradise, 1891) and Toson's *Hakai* (Broken Commandment, 1906) and *Haru* (Spring, 1908).[24]

By the turn of the century, then, Shakespeare's characters had been introduced into Japan's poetry and fiction – and even into the political debates taking place within Japanese society. As yet, however, none of these attempts to produce a Japanese version of *Hamlet* had resulted in a full staged pro-

duction. This honour was to fall to Kawakami Otojiro who, in 1903, produced and directed the first performance of *Hamlet* – in the *shimpa* style that
his troupe had been so influential in fostering. The performance was an
immediate success – as much, argues Kawatake, a result of its revolutionary
intent as of its intrinsic merit. To Kawatake, this production represents the
'fusion' of the two trends that had been evident in *Hamlet* studies in Japan
to that date – the moment when the preference for adaptations in the old
style on the one hand came together with the move towards drama in translation on the other (pp. 205 ff). The claim is readily supported: in contrast
to the dialogue which is rendered, for the most part, into relatively literal
Japanese, the setting itself represents an adaptation – but an adaptation not
in the style of the *jidaimono* as preferred by Robun and the other early Meiji
adapters, but into a modern-dress Meiji setting in which many aspects of
the traditional staging were removed.

Buoyed by the success of this latest development, in 1905 two more
Shakespeare scholars of the period, Tozawa and Asano succeeded in producing the first complete and literal translation of the entire text of *Hamlet*,
one from which traces of either adaptation or the *marubon* style that had
characterized the earlier attempts had largely been excised. But it was
Tsubouchi Shoyo, who, from his earliest encounters with the problems of
creating a Japanese version of *Hamlet* in the 1880s, remained steadfast in
his determination to produce and direct a complete scholarly version of
the drama. His efforts culminated, on 20 May 1911, with the first staged
performance of a complete translation, the first to seek to replicate an
authentic western dramatic style.[25] Let us turn then to consideration of the
contribution of this man who, more than any other Shakespeare 'rewriter'
in Japan, lived most acutely the contradictions inherent in the process of
the modernization of Meiji Japan.

Born Tsubouchi Yuzo in 1859, Shoyo's career can be seen not simply as a
mirror of developments on the literary scene in Meiji Japan, but as a pre-
cursor and instigator of so many of these changes. Educated at Tokyo Kaisei
gakko (the forerunner of Tokyo University), he quickly found himself iden-
tifying with those 'enlightenment scholars' of the early Meiji era who, while
retaining a fascination with the *gesaku* tradition of popular Tokugawa literature, devoted themselves to the creation of a modern Japanese literature
and drama. For Shoyo, as for so many of his contemporaries on the literary
scene, traditional Japanese drama was in urgent need of reform. His rejection of the efforts of his forebears was perhaps nowhere more in evidence
than in his dismissal of the *jidaimono* of Chikamatsu Monzaemon, traditionally celebrated as the epitome of such art,

> In general, one may say of Chikamatsu's *jidaimono* that they are tales of
> a dream-fantasy (*mugen*) land, which borrow from reality hardly more
> than the names of places and people . . .

In what way do these plays resemble dream-fantasies? In their absurd plots, their incidents which have not the least basis in fact, their unnatural characters, their illogical construction, their diffuse relationships or, again, their plethora of metamorphoses and inconsistencies, their lack of unity of interest, their unexpected complications and their exaggeration of the materials – in every respect they are fantasies within a dream.[26]

As already noted, initial attempts at reform of the Kabuki tradition assumed the form of compromise – in the aborted attempts, in the 1880s, to produce Japanese versions of various Shakespearean classics, most notably *Julius Caesar* and *Hamlet*. Both assumed a distinct *joruri* style and included a series of concessions to the contemporary poetics in Japan; but this should be seen less as a reaction against all things western, than as indicative of a willingness to meet the plays halfway – to render them more accessible to a Meiji audience by reworking the plots in a familiar framework. For Shoyo, primary amongst his artistic concerns was to show that he could understand, not just western texts, but the western approach to literature – but this was always in the hope that he could discern thereby a means to revive his native literary tradition. Compared with Shakespearean drama, therefore, Shoyo saw the Kabuki theatre as lacking psychological interest, unity of action and seriousness of intent – and it was this, rather than any determination to expunge Japan's dramatic tradition, that led to the decision, shortly after these initial unsuccessful attempts to adapt Shakespeare into a Japanese context, to seek to introduce such western drama on its own terms – by working on a translation of the bard's complete works. In Shakespeare, Shoyo discerned a blueprint for reform, one which, given the inherent similarities between the two forms, could serve as an ideal catalyst for advance. As Shoyo himself acknowledged,

Most [plays written abroad] were basically incompatible with Kabuki. Only the plays of Shakespeare bore curious resemblances to Kabuki in their dramatic form, though there was no comparison in literary value. It occurred to me that, if this was indeed the case, much could be fused together. I came to feel that research into Shakespeare might be the most useful means of improving the Japanese drama, not only for me personally, but for the Japanese as a whole.[27]

Although he abandoned his attempts to create a new literary genre which could fuse the two traditions, it is still ultimately enrichment rather than the overthrow of the native tradition which lay at the heart of Shoyo's translation project, a venture which occupied him until shortly before his death in 1935. And, as he argued shortly after commencing the project, he saw this as eminently attainable, on condition that various provisos were met.

In particular, he advocated the need for the retention of the distinction between narrative and dramatic poetry, unity in terms of the action of the play and consistency in ensuring that all actions stem from the character of the persons in the play. Drama, he suggested, should deal seriously with the moral laws governing human life, characterization should be realistic and plots, while retaining a rational structure and development, should serve to reflect accurately natural human emotions.[28]

It is hard to exaggerate the significance of Shoyo's call on a theatrical world which, by the turn of the century, had seen traditional Kabuki largely unable to respond to the new public demands that accompanied the burgeoning national self-confidence that followed victory in the Sino-Japanese War. Its replacement – in the form of *shimpa* productions, many of which incorporated dramatic celebrations of national triumphs – may have been rapturously received. Largely absent from these productions, however, was communication of those qualities on which Shoyo had come to set such store – and it was this, rather than any inherent determination to jettison the pillars of traditional Japanese drama, which led to the decision to rewrite Shakespeare, not in the form of Japanese adaptations, but as more literal, scholarly translations.

The decision to devote the rest of his life to a translation of the complete works of Shakespeare was clearly epochal. Of equal significance at the time, however, was the concomitant realization of the need for translators to be involved in the stage production of the new dramas they produced. The requirements of a translated dramatic text are actability (it has to be spoken by actors and understood aurally by the audience), imaginative impact (the text when spoken must excite an imaginative response in the theatre audience which should be similar to that evoked by the original work), and faithfulness to the original (where literal accuracy is not possible, the version offered should be true in spirit to the perceived intentions of the original). Shoyo would certainly have recognized these requirements and, aware of the number of aborted attempts to stage *Hamlet* in something close to its original form, he determined to oversee all stages of his project. The result was the founding, in 1906, of his own repertory group, the Bungei kyokai (Literary Arts Association), with the express aim of trying his hand at western-style drama – with Shakespeare at the fore of his plans. The group itself was short-lived and disbanded in 1913. However, in this short time, it succeeded in transforming the nature of Shakespeare performance in Japan and 'had the historic effect of carrying reform of the modern Japanese theatre into the technical field'.[29] Within months of its creation, the group was ready to put on a gala performance at the Kabuki-za in Tokyo, which included the trial scene from *The Merchant of Venice*. The following year, between 22 and 26 November, a programme of scenes, including Shoyo's translation of *Hamlet* in a three-act version, was presented under Shoyo's direction. This was followed, on 20 May 1911, by a full five-act performance at the Imperial Theatre, with the celebrated Matsui Sumako as Ophelia and Doi Shunsho as Hamlet.

The performance was new in so many ways. Some differences, such as the use of actresses in place of *onnagata* (although others, including Kawakami, had pioneered this reform), immediately became the focus of critical debate. But, as the first full-length production in Japanese of any Shakespearean play, audiences would have been equally struck by a performance far removed from the traditional Kabuki style to which they were accustomed, one which resembled instead the realistic modulation and tempo of contemporary drama. Here was a performance in which the emphasis was less on form, more on the heart and where the goal was for a natural portrayal of the action – for the creation of a single, unified artistic space rather than, as was increasingly the case with Kabuki, for granting a platform to individual artists on which to perform.

For Shoyo himself, however, the intent was, if anything, even more ambitious and, in an article written to accompany the performance, he argued,

> Our main intent is to effect a fundamental change in artistic technique – that is, in elocution, movement and expression . . . Therefore, in this translation we have tried as far as possible to avoid the conventional 7–5 style and, in recognition of the musical quality of the original, we have sought to introduce a suitable rhythm.[30]

The choice of the tone of the language to be adopted was, in Shoyo's estimation, of crucial significance. Well aware that, to an English-speaking audience, the distinctive quality of Shakespeare's language derives, in part at least, from the fact that it is *not* the language of everyday speech – that much of it assumes the form of dramatic poetry highly charged with imagery and written in verse and that those parts which are colloquial have the charm of also being archaic, Shoyo struggled in particular with the question of how much of his text should be rendered in the modern colloquial language. On the one hand, he was acutely aware of the need to allow his audience, who had no access to Shakespeare's original, to judge the power that could be effected by the theatre. To this end, and particularly if he were to succeed in his aim of revitalizing traditional Japanese theatre by rendering his text more 'relevant' to his early twentieth-century audience, the temptation to capitulate to the calls for a literary language that replicated the spoken (his had, after all, been an integral, if temperate voice in the *ge-bun ichi* ('the unification of spoken and written languages') movement) was ever-present. With a consensus still to be reached as to the exact form this 'unification' should assume, with the considerable acting skills of Doi at his disposal and with Shoyo's previous contributions to the dialogue on both literary and theatrical reform now widely acknowledged, he was ideally situated to develop a new dramatic style. Equally pressing, however, was the desire to determine a style that would adequately reflect the language of the original, one that would effectively convey the richness and variety of Shakespeare's text.

The struggle was a source of genuine concern for Shoyo. A study of the text that appeared as part of his 'Complete Works of Shakespeare' (1928), however, reveals the extent to which Shoyo remained gripped by a deep affinity to the classical tradition. The result is a rhythmic, literary style containing numerous echoes of the language of Kabuki in rendering Shakespeare's blank verse and in which unnecessary colloquialisms have been scrupulously avoided. For all the express determination 'to effect a fundamental dramaturgical change', here was a language that appears to be a mix of the Kabuki and *kyogen* traditions – a compromise involving a variety of elements from the existing classical tradition. As Shoyo himself argued,

> Shakespeare's tone is much more elevated, it has more breadth and depth than Chikamatsu's – and so there are occasions when his works cannot be translated merely with resort to Chikamatsu's language. One sometimes has to go back to the language of the *Taiheiki, Seisuiki* or even the *Heike monogatari* . . . Without approximating either too much, Shakespeare's genius lay in his ability to steer a course between the historical drama (*jidaigeki*) and the personal drama (*sewamono*).[31]

It is hardly surprising that the stage performances derived from the text, while widely acknowledged as ground-breaking, were nevertheless criticized for their use of language which was, according to one critic, *tenga ni sugite, mimi de kiku ni wa endokatta* (over-refined and hard to distill aurally).[32] Shoyo's response to such criticism is highly revealing. On the one hand, in the immediate wake of the performances, Shoyo felt compelled to issue a robust defence of his project,

> There are those who have criticized my use of the *kyogen* style in my recent *Hamlet*. But this was a decision taken following careful deliberation. Those who argue that the language of *kyogen* should be restricted to use by servants are doing a great disservice to Japanese literature . . . And even if the words themselves are taken from *kyogen*, the expressions into which these have been incorporated have been carefully reworked.[33]

For all his defence of his style, however, there is no doubt that Shoyo was stung by such criticism and it was this, plus the rapid increase in the range and quality of the various western Shakespeare editions and commentaries available to Japanese scholars during the last decade of his life that led to the decision, in 1928, to embark on a complete revision of his translations, not just of *Hamlet*, but of his entire Shakespeare corpus. This new edition was published between 1933 and 1935 by Chuokoron-sha and contains some of Shoyo's final thoughts on translation after more than fifty years of experimentation. Most interesting in this regard is the final chapter of this series, entitled *'Jibun no hon'yaku ni tsuite'* (Concerning my own Translations), in which Shoyo divides his approach to the Shakespeare text into five stages. By this stage, he was well into the fifth and final stage, a period in which he claimed to be seeking to remove some of the arch-classical style and archaisms of his earlier translations and to increase the extent to which he employed a colloquial style. The approach he summed up as follows,

> Translated in a literary style, or even in a style free of literary expressions, using words which have special associations, the text tends to be hard to understand, carries an unwelcome Japanese flavour or assumes an archaic quality; but if it is translated using modern expressions, it is not necessarily so. Those famous lines, so complex and sometimes so dreadfully concise, bound up with ancient events and full of metaphor, written in old grammar and which even English people cannot digest without notes, in some strange way seem to me vividly alive and somehow every word touches my heart directly.[34]

The implication here would appear to be that, in moving away from a style which echoed traditional dramatic language to one which reflected contemporary speech one can achieve something closer to the impact and directness of Shakespeare's original. But he still dismissed the colloquial style attempted by some of his contemporaries,

> At least as far as Shakespeare is concerned, attempts at translation into the contemporary vernacular are misguided. We are talking here of Shakespeare who is recognized as possessing a richer range of vocabulary than any other writer in the history of English literature. To try and translate this into contemporary colloquial Japanese, which is recognized as most barren in this respect, is totally impossible.[35]

The challenge confronting Shoyo is clear, the compromises he made to his critics – and those he resisted – perhaps nowhere better illustrated than in his approach to the soliloquies. As already noted, before Shoyo's attempts at a complete translation of the text, these had tended to be dismissed by earlier rewriters as presenting a unique problem and, as such, best either translated and published in isolation or deleted from versions of the whole drama. Confronted with this tradition, Shoyo's initial response, in the draft translation performed by Bungei kyokai in 1907, was to omit many of these, including 'To be, or not to be'. By 1911, however, he appears convinced of the necessity to incorporate these in a 'complete' translation, his response to the 'To be' soliloquy in particular revealing the extent to which, as translator, he was obliged to consider the various nuances of the original before eventually opting for one, less ambiguous alternative. The alternative selected by Shoyo is well documented,

> *Nagarauru? Nagaraenu? Sore ga gimon ja ... Zannin na unmei no yadama o hitasura tae-shinode oru ga daijobu no kokorozashi ka, aruiwa umi nasu kannan o mukae-utte, tatakote ne o tatsu ga daijobu ka?*

The opening character, only readable as *'nagarauru'* as a result of the phonetic gloss inserted over the character normally pronounced *'son'* (existence), represents an interesting example of Shoyo's attempt to capture the richness and subtlety of the original, to allow for two shades of meaning to coexist in the reader's eye. The verb *'nagarauru'* (now *nagareru*) is normally written with different characters suggesting the passage of time and is thus used to connote the sense of 'to continue living' or 'to live out one's life'. By selecting the character *'son'* (with its variant reading of *aru*), however, Shoyo was in a position to superimpose onto this the more abstract idea of 'existing'. Dissatisfied with this compromise, however, he replaced this, in the 1935 version, with the phrase *'yo ni aru'* (rendered with the character more commonly used for *'aru'*), resulting in the more specific implication of 'To exist in the world, or not to exist in the world, that is the problem'.

In the next phrase, Shoyo employs an elegantly elliptical phrase, composed of the characters for 'stone' and 'arrow'– and again the pronunciation of *yadama* is only clear from the phonetic gloss – to convey Shakespeare's 'slings and arrows'. The expression represents an interesting compromise: instantly intelligible to his readers due to the meaning-specific Chinese characters employed, the term would have been equally readily understood by his theatre audience – as a result of the existence of a homophone with the meaning of 'arrows and projectiles'.

The compromises continued, another interesting example coming with the use of the characters glossed, redundantly it would seem, as *daijobu*. The pronunciation may now be fixed; to Shoyo's generation, however, particularly to those familiar with the language of Kabuki, the more common reading of these three characters would have been *'masurao'*, an old word meaning 'manly' and used here, with *'kokorozashi'*, to render Shakespeare's phrase 'nobler in the mind'. The advantage for the younger generation ends, however, with the pronunciation: Shoyo clearly intends to convey the meaning of 'manly, noble' and the combination of these characters with this reading serves as another interesting and, to Shoyo's contemporary audience, startlingly effective compromise that captured, in part at least, the levels of complexity of Shakespeare's original.

Examples of Shoyo's unique blend of classical and contemporary styles clearly proliferate throughout his text. In the final assessment, however, the text that eventually appeared, in the Chukoron-sha 'definitive' version betrays evidence of an author, willing to heed the widespread calls for a version of *Hamlet* that more closely corresponded to the contemporary vernacular, but nevertheless determined not to sacrifice what he saw as the richness of Shakespeare's language. As he argued in the aforementioned consideration of his own style,

> My problems with the contemporary colloquial translations relate to the way that they make unquestioning use of both everyday vernacular slang, popular expressions and even dialect and, on the other hand, various literal translations which can in no way be considered correct Japanese. Translators tend to use these things without thinking and then problems occur. The colloquial translations of *Hamlet* are a case in point. Ophelia's words sometimes take on the tone of a barmaid whereas in fact she is a princess, the equivalent in *joruri* style of someone higher than Yukihime or more like Tokihime or Yaegakihime. In other examples, depending on the translator, the queen's words seem more in keeping with those of a hostess at a cheap hotel. The same holds true for the prince: the sons of the contemporary aristocracy might refer to themselves as *boku*; but a prince from the feudal era? It is all very well to use words in contemporary use. But, at the same time, one must not forget to replicate the times, customs and the rank and personality of the characters in the original text.[36]

It is this ability to replicate the tone of Shakespeare's original that marks Shoyo's version out for particular attention. The result is indeed a 'modern' drama – not in the conventional sense, but in its very ability to strike an effective balance, a synthesis of the various dramaturgical trends to date and a starting point for future work on *Hamlet* in Japan. With this, the *shingeki* (new drama) tradition assumed a new respectability and, as a result of Shoyo's pioneering work, the trend in the ensuing decades would be towards rewritings of other European plays to be staged in Western style.

Conclusion

Reference was made at the outset of this study to the three broad choices available to the prospective translator as identified by Romy Heylen. A cursory analysis of the two Japanese versions of *Hamlet* discussed in this essay would suggest a relatively straightforward categorization. Robun's *Nishiki-e*, it would appear, is a classic example of a rewriting in which the text has been adapted to the dominant poetics or ideology in the target culture, this in an attempt at integration into the receiving tradition. Equally uncontentious, at first glance, is the assignation of Shoyo's 'literal' translation to the category of foreign text imported with little or no attempt at acculturation, this out of a dissatisfaction with the same dominant poetics and in an attempt to preserve an exotic 'other'. As suggested by the closer textual analysis that followed, however, the case is surely not so clear-cut. What of the extent to which Robun has striven to retain the 'spirit' of the original through the introduction of characters immediately identifiable with their Shakespearean parallels and through his retention of many of the issues integral to the original? Conversely, what of the decision by Shoyo to adopt a language which is neither a faithful replica of that of the original nor a contemporary vernacular translation but which draws, instead, on the very Kabuki tradition for which he sought reform? It is in this respect that Heylen's third alternative – a cultural compromise in which various characteristics from both sets of poetics and ideologies are balanced – comes to appear of greater relevance; the claim that we are confronted here by two variants of the art of rewriting now assumes an added significance.

On the one hand, as critics, we cannot but highlight the differences between the two with regard to the nature of their 'fidelity' to the original and the manner in which its main themes are preserved. There is quite clearly a fundamental difference in terms of the respective approaches to the art of rewriting between Robun and Shoyo. Rather than as a natural consequence of a fundamental distinction between the translation and the adaptation, however, these differences can be attributed, in part at least, to the shift in poetic norms that occurred in Japan between 1886 and 1911 and to the natural tendency, identified by Lefevere, that 'if the original enjoys a highly positive reputation in the target culture, the translation is likely to be as literal as possible' (pp. 90–1). Both rewriters contributed considerably to the burgeoning interest in Shakespeare in Meiji Japan and it is as reflections of this – as manipulations designed to concur with the dominant poetics – that they assume their place as two moments, equally significant, in Japanese Shakespeare studies.

Notes

1. André Lefevere, *Translation, Rewriting and the Manipulation of Literary Fame* (London and New York: Routledge, 1992), p. vii.
2. Lawrence Venuti, *The Translator's Invisibility: a History of Translation* (London and New York: Routledge, 1995), p. 18.
3. Ibid.
4. Romy Heylen, *Translation, Poetics, and the Stage* (London and New York: Routledge, 1993), pp. 21 ff.
5. Lefevere, *Translation*, p. 96.
6. Adrian Pinnington, '*Hamlet* in Japanese Dress', in *Shakespeare Worldwide*, vol. 11 (1986), p. 53.
7. This is the title of Karatani's seminal study, *Nihon kindai bungaku no kigen* (Tokyo: Kodansha, 1980).
8. Lefevere, *Translation*, p. 8.

9. For example, Suematsu Kencho and Fukuchi Gen'ichiro, both of whom studied western drama extensively, but concluded that 'in coming home, we find nothing left in our brain which might serve as an incentive or a watchword for our future career' (cited in R. Porter, *The Full Recognition of Japan* (Oxford: Oxford University Press, 1911), p. 527).

10. See also, for example, Andrea Nouryeh, 'Shakespeare and the Japanese Stage', in D. Kennedy (ed.), *Foreign Shakespeare: Contemporary Performance* (Cambridge: Cambridge University Press, 1993), pp. 254–69.

11. Porter, *Full Recognition of Japan*, pp. 527 ff.

12. Nouryeh, 'Shakespeare and the Japanese Stage', p. 254.

13. Cf. also Kawatake Toshio, *Nihon no Hamuretto* (Hamlet in Japan) (Tokyo: Nansosha, 1972) and Niki Hisae, *Shakespeare Translation in Japanese Culture* (Tokyo: Kenseisha, 1984).

14. Cf., for example, Hiraki Teruo, 'Western Drama on the Japanese Stage', in *The Japan Magazine*, vol. 1 (1913).

15. In preparing this essay, we have relied both on the 1936 version of *Yamato Nishiki-e* that appeared in the journal *Hito* in 1936 and on Orita's scenario for the 1991 Japan Festival performance. We were also able to study a video of a TV performance of this and attended a live performance in Kyoto.

16. This assessment was included as a preface to Robun's second, successful attempt to produce a Kabuki version of *Hamlet* in 1886. See Kawatake, *Nihon no Hamuretto*, p. 69. Clearly, one cannot discount the possibility of Robun having bowed to the fear of formal censure, but there is little direct evidence of official intervention.

17. Donald Keene, *Dawn to the West: Japanese Literature in the Modern Era* (New York: Holt, Rinehart and Winston, 1984), p. 21.

18. James Brandon, *The Cambridge Guide to Asian Theatre* (Cambridge: Cambridge University Press, 1993), p. 151.

19. 7 October 1886 edition.

20. Ibid.

21. Despite the fact that the text was not staged until 1991, there is plenty of evidence, as we shall see, that Robun was writing with a theatre audience very firmly in mind.

22. The ensuing discussion of characterization in *Yamato Nishiki-e* is indebted to Kawatake's meticulous study.

23. For some dissenting interpretations, see the chillingly paranoiac Polonius by Ron Moody in a modern-dress 'banana republic' version of the play and Kozintsev's powerful Russian film version which again cut most of the humanity from the character of Polonius.

24. For further discussion of this topic, see Sato Saburo, 'Hamlet, Polonius and Ophelia in Meiji Japan', in *Comparative Literature Studies*, vol. 22 (1985), where he argues that '*The Broken Commandment* shows remarkable similarity with *Hamlet* in theme and motifs, such as the father–son relationship, . . . moral paralysis and the ultimate acceptance of the self' (p. 31). See also Toson's alter ego in *Haru* who feels that, 'thanks to his friends' guidance and inspiration, he had come to understand the tragic spirit of the mad prince more profoundly than he had thought possible' (cited in ibid.). For an interesting discussion of other novels of the time influenced by *Hamlet*, see Kawachi Yoshiko, '*Hamlet* in Japan: From Drama to Novel', in *Hamlet Studies*, vol. 8 (1986), pp. 65 ff.

25. For detailed discussion of this performance, see B. Powell, 'One Man's *Hamlet* in 1911 Japan: The Bungei Kyokai Production in the Imperial Theatre', in Sasayama,

Mulryne and Shewring (eds), *Shakespeare and the Japanese Stage* (Cambridge: Cambridge University Press, 1998), pp. 38–52.
26. Cited in Donald Keene, *Dawn to the West: Poetry, Drama, Criticism* (New York: Holt, Rinehart and Winston, 1984), p. 411.
27. Ibid., p. 413.
28. The above is an encapsulation of Shoyo's ideas contained in *Waga kuni no shingeki* (Japanese *shingeki*, 1893) and *Shingakugekiron* (On the Theory of the New Musical Theatre, 1904).
29. Yanagida Izumi, 'Pioneers of Modern Japan, III: Tsubouchi Shoyo', in *The Japan Quarterly*, vol. 2 (1964), p. 353.
30. Cited in Kawatake, *Nihon no Hamuretto*, p. 282.
31. Ibid., p. 258.
32. This was the opinion of Kawatake Shigetoshi, cited in ibid., p. 292.
33. Cited in ibid., p. 290.
34. 'Jibun no hon'yaku ni tsuite', in *Shekusupiya kenkyu shiori*, vol. 16 (Tokyo: Waseda daigaku shuppambu, 1928), pp. 321–2.
35. Shekusupiya atto randamu' (Shakespeare at Random), in *Shoyo senshu bessatsu*, vol. 5. (Tokyo: Daiichi shobo, 1977), p. 286.
36. Ibid., p. 296.

Bibliography

Brandon, James, *The Cambridge Guide to Asian Theatre* (Cambridge: Cambridge University Press, 1993).

Heylen, Romy, *Translation, Poetics, and the Stage* (London and New York: Routledge, 1993).

Hiraki, Teruo, 'Western Drama on the Japanese Stage', *The Japan Magazine*, vol. 1 (1913).

Kawachi, Yoshiko, '*Hamlet* in Japan: From Drama to Novel', in *Hamlet Studies*, vol. 8 (1986), pp. 65–76.

Kawachi, Yoshiko, 'Shakespeare and the Modern Writers in Japan: Translation and Interpretation by Shoyo, Ogai and Soseki', in *Shakespeare Translation*, vol. 9 (1982), pp. 29–45.

Kawatake, Toshio, *Nihon no Hamuretto* (*Hamlet* in Japan) (Tokyo: Nansosha, 1972).

Keene, Donald, *Dawn to the West: Japanese Literature in the Modern Era* (New York: Holt, Rinehart and Winston, 1984a).

Keene, Donald, *Dawn to the West: Poetry, Drama, Criticism* (New York: Holt, Rinehart and Winston, 1984b).

Kishi, Tetsuo, '"Bless Thee! Thou Art Translated!": Shakespeare in Japan', in Habicht et al. (eds), *Images of Shakespeare: Proceedings of the Third Congress of the International Shakespeare Organisation* (Newark: University of Delaware Press, 1988).

Kodama, James, 'Shakespearian Translation and the Japanese Language: Some Difficulties', in *Shakespeare Translation*, vol. 9 (1982), pp. 19–32.

Lefevere, André, *Translation, Rewriting and the Manipulation of Literary Fame* (London and New York: Routledge, 1992).

Minamitani, Akimasa, '*Hamlet* in Japan', *Japan Quarterly* (April–June 1990), pp. 176–93.

Niki, Hisae, *Shakespeare Translation in Japanese Culture* (Tokyo: Kenseisha, 1984).

Nouryeh, Andrea, 'Shakespeare and the Japanese Stage', in D. Kennedy (ed.), *Foreign Shakespeare: Contemporary Performance* (Cambridge: Cambridge University Press, 1993), pp. 254–69.

Orita, Koji, 'Kabuki Hamuretto joen ni tsuite' (Concerning the Performance of a Kabuki *Hamlet*), programme notes for 1991 Japan Festival performance of 'Hamuretto Yamato Nishiki-e'.

Pinnington, A. J., '*Hamlet* in Japanese Dress', *Shakespeare Worldwide*, vol. 11 (1986), pp. 51–72.

Porter, Robert, *The Full Recognition of Japan* (Oxford: Oxford University Press, 1911).

Powell, Brian, 'One Man's *Hamlet* in 1911 Japan: The *Bungei Kyokai* Production in the Imperial Theatre', in Sasayama, Mulryne and Shewring (eds), *Shakespeare and the Japanese Stage* (Cambridge: Cambridge University Press, 1998), pp. 38–52.

Rycroft, David, 'A Japanese Print of *Hamlet*', in Marta Gibinska and Jerzy Limon (eds), *Hamlet East–West* (Gdansk: Theatrum Gedanense Foundation, 1998), pp. 196–219.

Sato, Saburo, 'Hamlet, Polonius and Ophelia in Meiji Japan', *Comparative Literature Studies*, vol. 22 (1985), pp. 23–33.

Toyoda, Minoru, 'Shakespeare in Japan: an Historical Survey', *Transactions of the Japan Society of London*, vol. 36 (1939).

Tsubouchi, Shoyo, *Shekusupia-geki no hon'yaku* (Shakespeare's Plays in Translation) (Tokyo: Waseda University Press, 1928).

Tsubouchi, Shoyo, 'Jibun no hon'yaku ni tsuite', in *Shekusupiya kenkyu shiori*, vol. 16 (Tokyo: Waseda daigaku shuppanbu, 1928).

Tsubouchi, Shoyo, 'Shekusupiya atto randamu: Shaoyaku zenshu no fukyuban o shinkan suru ni tsuite' (Shakespeare at Random: To Mark the Publication of a Popular Version of the Complete Works of Shakespeare in Translation), in *Shoyo senshu bessatsu*, vol. 5 (Tokyo: Daiichi shobo, 1977), pp. 281–319.

Venuti, Lawrence, *The Translator's Invisibility: a History of Translation* (London and New York: Routledge, 1995).

Yanagida Izumi, 'Pioneers of Modern Japan, III: Tsubouchi Shoyo', *The Japan Quarterly*, vol. 2 (1964).

8

The British Discovery of Japanese Art

Yuko Kikuchi and Toshio Watanabe

Introduction

This chapter examines the British perception of Japanese art after Britain's discovery of it in the mid-nineteenth century. It will focus on the British evaluation of Japanese art rather than on the history of collecting or on how British artists integrated elements of Japanese art into their own. Where possible, it will also try to highlight where the British view differed from other western views of Japanese art. The first four sections, which attempt to provide overviews of various aspects of the subject, are written by Toshio Watanabe. The last section on Bernard Leach is written by Yuko Kikuchi. It tries to give a more detailed account of one of the most celebrated Anglo-Japanese relationships in art and also demonstrates that the simple term 'discovery' cannot adequately cover such mutual cultural interactions.

In the West before the middle of the nineteenth century most Japanese art and artefacts were regarded as ethnographical curiosities, though Japanese lacquer and porcelain were highly prized for their aesthetic qualities. Both were exported from Japan to the West and had a big impact on western culture in the seventeenth and eighteenth centuries. From the arrival of William Adams in Japan in 1600, the British had direct contact with Japan until they voluntarily left the British East India Company station at Hirado in 1623. Even during this short period the lacquerware which was imported from Japan apparently brought about a Jacobean vogue for lacquer objects.[1] This is also the time when lacquerware as a craft began to be called simply 'Japan'. Very soon western imitation lacquer came to be generally known as 'japanning'. The 1688 DIY guide *A Treatise of Japanning and Varnishing* by John Stalker and George Parker is a good example of this identification of Japan with the craft of lacquer. This publication also contains an early and rare laudatory comment on Japan:

> Let not the Europeans any longer flatter themselves with the empty notions of having surpassed all the world beside in stately Palaces, costly

Temples and sumptuous Fabricks; Ancient and modern Rome must now give place: The glory of one Country, Japan alone, has exceeded in beauty and magnificence all the pride of the Vatican at this time, and the Parthenon heretofore . . .[2]

However, this comment seems to rely more on Marco Polo's comments about Japan being a land with abundant gold than on any direct knowledge of the country or its artefacts.

From about the middle of the seventeenth century, porcelain became the dominant Japanese export artefact and large quantities of it was brought to Europe by Dutch traders. Certain styles of Japanese porcelain, such as the so-called *kakeimon* style, appealed strongly to western taste and were widely imitated by English craftsmen; they eventually became incorporated into the repertoire of English bone china. Japanese lacquerware and porcelain became fashionable in aristocratic circles and remained popular throughout the seventeenth and eighteenth centuries, as can be seen in many stately homes today. However, except in a limited way in the case of the lacquerware, these were largely subsumed under the broader phenomenon of Chinoiserie. Japanese art was rarely acknowledged as a separate entity by the British and even as late as 1851 Japanese items were included in the Chinese section in the Great Exhibition held at the Crystal Palace.

From ethnographical specimen to work of art: mid-nineteenth-century recognition of Japanese art

The period of the 1850s and 1860s was a crucial time for the change in western attitudes towards Japanese art, when we see the beginnings of an appreciation of Japanese art as art in spite of the almost total lack of art-historical knowledge of it. Furthermore, it was the British who made the most important contribution to this shift.

Very few items of what the West would regard as fine art were accessible in Europe as a whole. In general at this time the West relied mainly on various western illustrated publications for their very limited view of Japanese fine art.[3] The first half of the nineteenth century was already presenting the West with a much more varied view of Japan and its art than before, though still only sporadically. Quite a number of illustrations published during this period are clearly based on Japanese originals, though often distorted by the western copyists. Compared to the mostly diagrammatic and crude black-and-white line drawings prevalent in the seventeenth and eighteenth centuries, the quality of execution becomes more sophisticated and sometimes even colour illustrations are used. In addition, during this period access to certain types of original Japanese art became easier in the West, especially in Holland. The Dutch had had a trade link with Japan since the early seventeenth century and were the only westerners who the Japanese allowed to continue to trade at Nagasaki.

A Dutch collector, J. F. van Fisscher, states in his book *Bijdrage tot de Kennis van het Japansche Rijk* (A contribution to the Knowledge of the Japanese Empire), published in 1833, that Japan's pictorial arts are of such importance for the foreigner because these products enable him to form a better notion of a country and its people and give the eager researcher the opportunity to satisfy his interest and curiosity, which would otherwise not be possible due to Japan's isolation from the rest of the world. This statement is characteristic of the attitude of western collectors of Japanese art during the first half of the nineteenth century.

The privileged position of the Dutch regarding the collecting of Japanese art was eroded by the opening up of Japan in 1854 negotiated by Commodore M. C. Perry of the United States Navy. An important shift in the western appreciation of Japanese art can already be detected in the official report of the Perry expedition, *Narrative of the Expedition of an American Squadron to the China Seas and Japan* (compiled by Francis L. Hawks and published in 1856). The Reverend Francis Hawks, who had not been to Japan, was asked to make a synthesis of the journals and other material provided by Perry and his officers. In the introduction a summary and rather negative assessment of Japanese art is given, and several points are made which were shared by many other visitors to Japan in the 1850s and 1860s: the lack of sculpture and architecture and the ignorance of perspective and anatomy are highlighted, there is praise for applied art but contempt for Japanese 'high art'.

However, there is an exception to this general tone in the discussion of the illustrated books and prints in chapter XIII of Hawks's report. Here the comments contradict those in the introduction, stressing instead the simplicity, freedom and vigour of Japanese art, and even praising the use of perspective and knowledge of anatomy! At the end of the chapter Hawks acknowledges Professor Duggan of the Free Academy of New York for his remarks on 'the specimens of Japanese art' which 'were submitted to him with a request that he would examine them artistically'. That Hawks should think the 'specimens of Japanese art' merited an artistic examination is in itself notable and is an early sign of the shift in the western appreciation of Japanese art; but the favourable comments mentioned are thus in all probability not by Hawks nor a member of the expedition but by Professor Duggan. Professor Duggan was, in fact, an Irishman, Peter Paul Duggan (1810–61), who was an artist then principally working in crayon drawing mainly in New York. Thus, what is possibly the earliest enthusiastic appreciation of Japanese pictures by a western artist seems to have been contributed by a man from the British Isles.

The Perry expedition report offers another important piece of evidence for the shift in the appreciation of Japanese art, namely, the illustrations. The

Figure 8.1 A reproduction of Hiroshige, *Oigawa kachi watari* (February 1853), *Illustrated London News*, 13 December 1856

two fold-outs are reproductions of Hiroshige prints: *Yodogawa* (The river Yodo) from about 1834 (Plate 2) and *Oigawa kachi watari* (Fording the river Oi on foot) from February 1853 (Figure 8.1). As can be seen in the case of *Yodogawa*, the colours are somewhat brighter and cruder than in the original and some small details are omitted, but the fidelity of the lines is quite remarkable. This is one of Hiroshige's most poetic works and the reproduction does convey at least part of the essence of Hiroshige's art. This reproduction has been criticized in the past by a specialist in Japanese prints, but within the context of western facsimiles of Japanese art up to 1856, the publication date, this is an outstanding achievement.

The important fact in our context is that these fold-out colour reproductions are inserted exactly where the text is discussing Japanese art. They are examples of Japanese art and not used to give ethnographical information. Care has been taken to reproduce them faithfully and T. Sinclair from Philadelphia is credited with the lithography. The third colour reproduction of a Japanese print in this book makes this point even clearer in a negative way. It is taken from Yoshikazu's (or Yoshisada's?) illustrated book *Asakura Togo ichidaiki* (The life story of Asakura Togo), but is neither presented as a fold-out nor used as an example of Japanese art. Rather, it is used to make observations on the crucifixion in the picture. Its execution is much cruder and the lithographer is not credited.

The Perry expedition report was enormously influential and immediately after its publication became the standard work on Japan. In fact, the reproduction of Hiroshige's print *Oigawa kachi watari* was reproduced, this time in black and white only, in the *Illustrated London News* of December 1856, where the Perry expedition report was reviewed. However, it is an almost full-page spread and looks very striking. Furthermore, most of the last third of the review is directly taken from a passage in the book where Japanese art is favourably discussed. Here again the reproduction is meant as an example of Japanese art rather than simply as a depiction of Japanese life.

Similar attitudes can also be observed in the case of Sherard Osborn, who was the captain of the frigate HMS *Furious*, the flagship of Lord Elgin's mission to China and Japan from 1857 to 1859. He collected, among other things, Japanese prints and used these to illustrate his *Japanese Fragments*, which was serialized in the magazine *Once a Week*. When this was published in book form in 1861, he added six new colour facsimiles of Japanese prints. These are all by Hiroshige. Osborn writes in his introduction that,

> For a time, I could not find a publisher who would produce them in a manner likely to do justice without flattery to the skill of the Japanese artists, but at last the good taste of my friend the editor of *Once a Week*, together with the enterprises of Messrs. Bradbury and Evans, enabled me to place before the Public of England a series of perfect facsimiles, which throw my humble letter-press, as I would desire, into entirely a secondary position. (p. xxii)

As he states, Osborn took great care over the faithful reproduction of these prints which indeed are of good quality. Though in the main text Osborn uses Japanese prints to illustrate Japanese customs and traditions, in the case of the colour facsimiles it is important to note that Osborn chose them as examples of Japanese art and discusses them as such in the text. One of them is Hiroshige's *Hoki* from his series *Rokujuyoshu meisho zue* (Famous places from more than 60 provinces) (1853–56) (Plate 3), and is one of the most poetic and evocative in his late period. Here again we can observe the discriminating choice of a print in spite of the complete lack of art historical knowledge.

The British seem to have been particularly strong in their concern for facsimiles of Japanese prints as works of art. The French were more interested in Japanese pictorial motifs and their reproduction, rather than recreating a Japanese print as a work of art. A striking example of British interest and expertise in Japanese art at this time is the book *Recollections of Baron Gros's embassy to China and Japan in 1857–58* by Marquis de Moges, published in London and Glasgow in 1860. The French original, published in the same year, has no illustrations and the English edition acknowledges that 'the last two lithographs are copied from native tinted engravings contained in a series of volumes said to be school books, lent by the Earl of Elgin to the South Kensington Museum'. Many other British publications on Japan which appeared during the 1860s contain numerous black-and-white illustrations, many from Hokusai's illustrated books, which are quite faithful to the original. This abundance contrasts sharply with what was available elsewhere in Europe and America.

Above all, Osborn's illustrations and a number of others where Japanese art is regarded as such and not simply as an ethnographical tool, show an important shift in attitudes, which has implications for the future.

Design theorists at international exhibitions (1860s–1870s)

The single most important event in the British 'discovery' of Japanese art was the Japanese section at the 1862 International Exhibition at London (Figure 8.2). Though there were some contributions from the Japanese government, such as specimens of timber and paper, the then British Minister to Japan, Rutherford Alcock, sent most of the items, which he had systematically collected for this occasion. Thus, it reflected a British view of what Japanese art was, rather than a Japanese view. The items also included tools such as surgical instruments and there is still a strongly ethnographic overtone in some of the exhibits such as a straw raincoat or wooden clogs. Alcock himself was largely ignorant of the history of Japanese art and most of

Figure 8.2 Japan Section, International Exhibition 1862, *Illustrated London News*, 20 December 1862

the items are likely to have been of recent origin. Nevertheless, this section was crucial for the British appreciation of Japanese art in three important respects.

First, it contained a large quantity of artefacts within a clearly identified Japanese section. During the 1850s there were limited opportunities to see Japanese artefacts, for example, at the Great Exhibition of 1851 in London, the Exhibition of Industrial Art in Dublin in 1853, the Pall Mall Exhibition in 1854 or the Art Treasures Exhibition in Manchester in 1857. However, they were either not distinctly presented as a coherent group or were so small-scale that the exhibits lacked the impact of the 1862 section, which contained well over 600 items.

Second, the number of visitors to the 1862 exhibit was probably so large that it exceeded that at any previous display of Japanese art in Britain or anywhere else for that matter. As mentioned above, Japanese lacquerware and ceramics were known and cherished in Britain, but only by a small elite of connoisseurs, aristocrats and collectors. There were also various earlier exhibitions of good quality Japanese art in Holland, but they lacked mass impact. In the 1862 Japanese section a distinctly identified group of Japanese artefacts were presented for the first time to a very large mass audience not restricted to the elite. Though there were no precise figures for visitor numbers to the Japanese section, the International Exhibition itself attracted over six million visitors (Plate 4).

Third, this Japanese section spawned an unprecedented wealth of critical response to Japanese art by art experts. Most previous British comments on Japanese art had been by travellers, diplomats or journalists. However, in 1862 this situation changed and it was the British art profession which now took serious note of Japanese art. Most of the analytical comments came from design critics and theorists and these were overwhelmingly positive. It is striking to note that during the 1860s it is extremely rare to find any negative comments on Japanese art in British publications.

To understand this we need to examine the crisis which British design was experiencing at this particular moment. Since the 1830s design reform had been a major concern of Britain industrially, politically and educationally. Even the Great Exhibition of 1851, seen as the great triumph of the British industrial revolution in general, was regarded by the design experts as a failure of British design. Already during the 1840s and 1850s a number of design reformers saw Oriental design as one of the best sources from which to improve British design. For example, the seminal book by Owen Jones, *The Grammar of Ornament* published in 1856, contains a disproportionately large quantity of Oriental design for students to emulate.[4] As yet this publication did not include any Japanese design, but by the time the design experts encountered Japanese artefacts at the 1862 International Exhibition, the ground had been prepared for a favourable reception of Japanese art.

Even taking this into consideration, the enthusiasm with which Japanese art was greeted in 1862 is rather startling. Another unexpected element of this welcome was that many of the writers were exponents of the Gothic revival. The architect William Burges is a good example. He organized the Medieval Court in the 1862 International Exhibition, but recommended the Japanese section as follows:

> I hope I have said enough to show the student of our reviving arts of the thirteenth century, that an hour, or even a day or two, spent in the Japanese department will by no means be lost time, for these hitherto unknown barbarians appear not only to know all that the Middle Ages knew, but in some respects are beyond them and us as well.[5]

He also wrote that 'truly the Japanese Court is the real medieval court of the Exhibition'[6] thus equating Japanese art with medieval art. This is an extension of the logic propounded by Owen Jones, that is to say, the Orient did not suffer the post-Renaissance degradation in art which the West had suffered, thus retaining the ideal conditions for art which were to be found both in the Orient and the western Middle Ages. At times the debate gives the impression that some critics saw no difference between the Orient and the medieval West. This gives an interesting twist to the theory of Orientalism propounded by Edward Said. Whereas Said sees Orientalism as a form of western domination over the Orient, according to these Gothicists the Orient is superior because it did not suffer from the post-Renaissance decline. Their aim is to rescue the West by aspiring not only to medieval art but also to Oriental art.

The writers on Japanese art during the 1860s had little historical knowledge of Japanese art, but some of their comments are surprisingly perceptive. For example, John Leighton, a design theorist, while discussing the widely acknowledged Japanese preference for asymmetry, comments that the Japanese *do* use symmetry 'to give dignity, a majesty obtainable by no other means' (Figure 8.3).[7] Another anonymous writer comments in *The Builder* that 'the groups of ornamental forms . . . are frequently of a . . . symmetrical character; but these groups are *applied* with great irregularity'.[8] Indeed, this interest in the formal rather than the exotic aspects of Japanese art is strongly reflected in the Japonism of such designers and architects as William Burges, E. W. Godwin, William Eden Nesfield, Thomas Jeckell and Christopher Dresser.

Japanese art and British Aestheticism (1870s–1880s)

Compared to the design experts fine art cognoscenti had a much more ambivalent attitude to Japanese art. For example, the premier art periodical

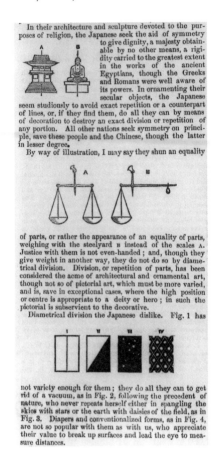

In their architecture and sculpture devoted to the purposes of religion, the Japanese seek the aid of symmetry to give dignity, a majesty obtainable by no other means, a rigidity carried to the greatest extent in the works of the ancient Egyptians, though the Greeks and Romans were well aware of its powers. In ornamenting their secular objects, the Japanese seem studiously to avoid exact repetition or a counterpart of lines, or, if they find them, do all they can by means of decoration to destroy an exact division or repetition of any portion. All other nations seek symmetry on principle, save these people and the Chinese, though the latter in lesser degree.

By way of illustration, I may say they shun an equality of parts, or rather the appearance of an equality of parts, weighing with the steelyard B instead of the scales A. Justice with them is not even-handed ; and, though they give weight in another way, they do not do so by diametrical division. Division, or repetition of parts, has been considered the acme of architectural and ornamental art, though not so of pictorial art, which must be more varied, and is, save in exceptional cases, where the high position or centre is appropriate to a deity or hero ; in such the pictorial is subservient to the decorative.

Diametrical division the Japanese dislike. Fig. 1 has not variety enough for them ; they do all they can to get rid of a vacuum, as in Fig. 2, following the precedent of nature, who never repeats herself either in spangling the skies with stars or the earth with daisies of the field, as in Fig. 3. Diapers and conventionalized forms, as in Fig. 4, are not so popular with them as with us, who appreciate their value to break up surfaces and lead the eye to measure distances.

Figure 8.3   John Leighton, *On Japanese Art, Journal of the Society of Arts*, vol. 11, page 597

of the time, *The Art Journal*, reported little on Japanese art in comparison with more design or architecture-orientated periodicals. The first major article on Japanese art in the *Journal* was written by the American critic James Jackson Jarves and published in the July 1869 issue (pp. 182–3). Though he was generally sympathetic to Japanese art on artistic grounds, he became a fiercer critic when discussing it within the context of culture. Instructive is his comparison of Phidias and Hokusai. He praises both as masters of the human figure, but the Greek is praised for evoking the god-like in man, whereas the Japanese is criticized for indulging 'in the mystical, transcendental, or sentimental, . . . as grotesqueness and diabolism, or to invent supernal ugliness . . . to be admired for its own sake' (p. 182). He further comments that the Japanese artists 'are far from being incompetent or ignorant, but their taste is faulty, owing to wrong culture' and that they have 'no sense of the beautiful' (p. 182). This breathtaking Euro-centrism shows that Jarves has trouble with Japanese art on religious and moral grounds. In fact he has other interesting and original things to say about Japanese art, but this negative verdict on its taste and morals was not unique to him, and was shared by many British intellectuals and fine art commentators. This provides a stark contrast to the design theorists of the 1860s, none of whom seem to have had any such reservations.

An artist and theorist who rattled the moral cosiness in British fine art was the American painter, James McNeill Whistler, who moved in 1859 to London from Paris, where he had belonged to the avant-garde circle of the realists and the artists of nascent impressionism. His Japan-inspired works of the early 1860s broke new ground in challenging the theory of mimesis fundamental to post-Renaissance western art. His compositions introduced subtle inconsistencies or exaggerations for formal effect. He started to manipulate colour away from simply trying to emulate local colour towards a more abstract use to unify the surface of the painting. Though he was deeply affected by the realism of Courbet, he gradually reduced narrative elements in his paintings. Judged with the historical hindsight of the late twentieth century, the actual paintings may look not that different from other contemporary paintings of the time, but during the late 1850s and 1860s these were very radical moves. In our context it is of prime importance to note that for Whistler Japanese art played a catalytic function for the change of his artistic direction. Whistler thus shares with the Gothic Revivalists the moving away from the tenets of post-Renaissance art and the use of Japanese art as a catalyst.

Whistler's enthusiasm for Japanese art predated the 1862 International Exhibition in London and he became the prime advocate of Japanese art among the fine artists active in London. From the early 1860s into the 1870s his way of taking inspiration from Japanese art went through subtle changes. However, it is his theoretical contributions which are crucial to the new direction in the appreciation of Japanese art in Britain.

In order to understand Whistler's attitude to Japanese art, we need to examine his theory of art, which is expressed in a most condensed way in *The Red Rag* published in 1878.

> Art should be independent of all clap-trap – should stand alone, and appeal to the artistic sense of eye or ear, without confounding this with emotions entirely foreign to it, as devotion, pity, love, patriotism, and the like. All these have no kind of concern with it.[9]

This is a manifesto of pure aestheticism. Here he opposes narrative art and argues against such types of paintings as genre painting, historical painting or religious painting. For him the formal and sensory elements have priority over the content of a picture and this opens up possibilities of wider reference points for his art and theory. This is clearly expressed in his famous *10 O'clock Lecture* of 1885, where he ends his talk with the following words: '[T]he story of the beautiful is already complete – hewn in the marbles of the Parthenon – and embroidered, with the birds, upon the fan of Hokusai – at the foot of Fusiyama.'[10] Here he claims that the beautiful transcends history and geography. He does not accept progress in art. Art is not bound either by time or place.

This view is radically different from that of Jarves discussed above. Both Whistler and Jarves use Phidias and Hokusai as examples, but to very different ends. In order to achieve maximum effect from an elite but sympathetic audience, Whistler contrasts the Parthenon sculptures, regarded as one of the noblest examples of western art, with a humble painted fan by Hokusai. As in the case of the design theorists Whistler does not let moral issues enter the discussion of art. This theory has a levelling effect on the choice of the models for art. As long as it is beautiful, it can be from anywhere and any time. The artist can now pick and choose as she or he likes from a wide range of past examples including those from the East, just as in *The Grammar of Ornament* by Owen Jones.

A position somewhat between Whistler and Jarves was taken up by the Pre-Raphaelite critic, William Michael Rossetti. He was a more consistent admirer of Japanese art than his brother Dante Gabriel and wrote a perceptive article on Japanese art in 1863, an early date for such writing by a fine art critic. A revised version of this article was then published in his 1867 book *Fine Art, Chiefly Contemporary*. In this he agrees with Jarves about the lack of moral beauty in Japanese art and states that 'there is nothing throughout the designs in the least suggesting moral beauty' (p. 387). However, then he moves on to say that 'we have no business, nor any disposition, to moralise' (p. 387). Having made light of the moral aspect, he goes on to eulogize Japanese art, saying that it 'assuredly belongs in various respects to the greatest order of art practised in our day in any country of the world' (p. 363).

With the development of the Aesthetic Movement during the 1870s and 1880s, other practitioners of fine arts, including Royal Academicians, also became influenced by Japanese art. Artists such as Albert Moore, Dante Gabriel Rossetti, Simeon Solomon and Frederick Sandys experienced Whistler's Japonisme in close proximity, but others, such as James Tissot, Edward J. Poynter and Lawrence Alma-Tadema, were also participants in the prevailing culture of Japonisme.

The vicissitudes of the British perception of Japanese art (1880s–)

The Aesthetic Movement spread the fashion for things Japanese not only among artists and patrons, but among a considerably wider range of people in Britain. This 'Japanese craze' even permeated popular culture, as can be seen in Gilbert and Sullivan's operetta *The Mikado* (1885). However, this extreme popularity also created a backlash. Now one can hear increasingly strident voices criticizing the prevailing taste for Japan and Japanese art.

For some, Japanese art signalled a threat to western identity and culture. For example, Ruskin, the arch-enemy of Whistler, disliked Japanese art. A letter to the artist and poet Dante Gabriel Rossetti demonstrates that, as early as 1865, Ruskin did not wish even to look at Japanese art.[11] It was also reported that the antiquarian bookseller Quaritch had received a letter from Ruskin 'not to send any more of those Japanese works, as they disturbed him'.[12] Some of Ruskin's followers showed an ambivalent attitude to Japanese art. William Morris, for example, seems to have owned Japanese paintings,[13] but in 1893 he wrote that the 'Japanese have no architectural, and therefore no decorative, instinct'.[14] This is a quite surprising verdict, considering that for most Japanophiles the 'decorative instinct' was a forte of Japanese art.[15] Another artist and writer Walter Crane, a key figure within the Arts and Crafts Movement, was obviously heavily indebted to Japanese prints for the illustrations in his innovative children's books of the late 1860s and 1870s (Plate 5), but seems later to have made negative comments about Japanese art.[16]

By the 1890s the oversupply of cheap Japanese fans, ceramics and lacquerware and the association of Japan with such musical plays as the immensely successful *The Geisha* (1896) with its unprecedented 760 performances at Daly's Theatre in London seems to have created a backlash against Japanese art (Plate 6). The critical comments by Morris and Crane should be seen within this context.

However, on the whole Japanese art was still identified as something of high aesthetic value. This can be seen in many paintings in which Japanese art objects are used as props within the picture to enhance the beauty of the environment, the sitter's own beauty or his or her credentials as an aesthete. Many late Victorian and Edwardian still lives, such as Samuel John Peploe's *Flowers and Fruit (Japanese Background)* (c. 1916, Kirkcaldy District Museum and Art Gallery), portraits, such as *James Strachey* by Duncan Grant (1910, Tate Gallery), or pictures of women, such as *A Girl Reading* by Theodore Roussel (1886–87, Tate Gallery) (Plate 7), include Japanese prints, screens or kimonos. This aspect is poignantly expressed in George Bernard Shaw's *Pygmalion* (1912), when the heroine Eliza appeared in a kimono after being scrubbed and cleaned of Covent Garden grime. There the kimono functions as a metaphor for her transformation and her now revealed beauty.

An important development aiding the appreciation of Japanese art in late Victorian and Edwardian Britain was the increasing knowledge of its history. During the 1860s and 1870s it was Japanese prints and craft objects that dominated the image of Japanese art in Britain. However, from about the 1880s it became clear that these were only a small part of the artistic treasures Japan could offer. Religious art, such as Buddhist sculpture, was already available in small quantities at places such as the British Museum, but the more than one thousand-year tradition of Japanese Buddhist art only became known gradually during this period. For the growth of this knowledge the publication of the English version of the periodical *Kokka* (1905–18) and the series of art books published by Shinbi Shoin either in an English version or with English texts included, played a key role.[17] It is particularly relevant that, according to Murakado Noriko the early Shinbi Shoin books had the aim of propagating Buddhist ideas in the West rather than simply introducing Japanese art to the West.[18]

The deeper knowledge now available in Britain of Japanese Buddhist art, and also of Japanese ink painting, revealed that for these types of art (now regarded by many as superior to prints and craft objects), China was a major source of inspiration. This insight relativized the position of Japanese art within the western estimation of various types of 'Oriental' art, from that of the undisputed pinnacle to just one of the great arts of the Orient side by side with China, and in some cases inferior to its big neighbour.

Most early travellers to China and Japan had praised Japanese art at the expense of that of China. For example, E. B. De Fonblanque, one of the more interesting early observers of the Far East, wrote that '[In] minuteness of detail and patient labour, the Chinese carvers of ivory undoubtedly surpass the Japanese – but the former are simply skilled mechanics, the latter are artists'.[19]

This rather snide comment was fairly typical of the attitudes of British travellers to Japan during the 1860s and 1870s. With the increasing knowledge of the history not only of Japanese but also Chinese art, the early twentieth century saw a shift in the assessment of the relative strengths of the art of these two countries. Finally, in 1935, at the large exhibition of Chinese art at the Royal Academy, British people could see great examples of Chinese art for themselves. During the second half of the nineteenth century the British image of China in general had been very negative, but this changed from about the 1890s[20] and the re-evaluation of its art was part of this process. H. A. Giles, who held the Chair of Chinese at Cambridge University from 1897 until 1932, was seen by one contemporary writer as 'set[ting] out to transform current European ideas about China as a country of mystery and barbarism' to an image of a 'country with an unsurpassed record of civilisation and culture'.[21] Clearly this was a very different attitude from that prevailing during the second half of the nineteenth century.

While this rehabilitation of Chinese culture was taking place in Britain, there was a strong push for a re-evaluation of Rimpa art, both by Japanese and western cognoscenti of Japanese art. Rimpa art was regarded as genuinely Japanese and with little Chinese influence, thus making it an ideal candidate for representing the worth and individuality of Japanese art on the world stage. Tim Clark has pointed out that as early as 1883 Louis Gonse had characterized the artist Korin as 'le plus Japonais des Japonais',[22] whereas

William Anderson, the British surgeon and collector of Japanese art, who worked in Tokyo from 1873 to 1880, had a more negative view of Rimpa artists, criticizing their 'delineation of the human figure and quadrupeds'[23] and saying that '[t]he pictures of Kuwaurin [Korin] and Hauitsu [Hoitsu] have too much mannerism and too little resemblance to nature to please the European eye . . .'.[24] This shows an interesting discrepancy of perception between a cutting-edge art connoisseur in Paris and a non-specialist Briton with a conventional aesthetic viewpoint. Anderson still considered the resemblance to nature in painting an essentials ingredient for the European appreciation of paintings, whereas Gonse was much more aware of the values of nascent modernism. In my view, the increasing appreciation of Rimpa around the turn of the century has two important features. First, it is closely connected with increasingly nationalistic tendencies in Japan. Second, it also connects with the rise of modernism – that is, with a positive evaluation of pictorial decorativeness breaking away from the narrative content-driven paintings of the previous generation.[25]

In 1910, a large-scale Japan–British exhibition was held at Shepherds Bush in London. This contained a representative exhibition of contemporary Japanese art. The quality of exhibits marks a stark contrast to the Japanese section of the 1862 International Exhibition in London. By now scholarship on the history of Japanese art had reached an international standard, and there was a mutual flow of information. This ironically made the impact of the 1910 Japanese art exhibition less strong than that of the 1862 exhibition, in spite of the superior quality of the former. The Japan–British Exhibition was also a forum for the mutual display of the imperial prowess of the two nations, and the annexation of Korea by Japan in the same year darkly foreshadowed the coming years.

At the 1996 Sunningdale workshop of the Anglo-Japanese History Project on Anglo-Japanese relations during the interwar years, discussions focused on negative British views of Japan during this period. Interestingly this was mostly argued by the military and political historians, whereas cultural historians presented contrary evidence.

Laurence Binyon, poet, scholar and curator at the British Museum, was one of those who presented a positive view between the wars. There is almost a sense of innocence or naivety about his genuine admiration of Japanese art. An illuminating episode was his first visit to Japan in 1929 when he was already 60 years old.[26] This was actually financed by a Binyon Reception Committee in Japan. He took with him a selection of English watercolours borrowed from private collectors, and created an exhibition in Tokyo. The Reception Committee even financed a lavish catalogue for this exhibition.[27] It is also remarkable that so many private owners of these watercolours agreed to allow them to be taken to such a distant venue which was not a very politically desirable place. Binyon also gave a series of lectures to packed audiences, which was by all accounts such a great success that it was even reported to the prime minister, Ramsay MacDonald, as a diplomatic triumph. The lecture series was not on Japanese art, but on landscape in English art and poetry and the Japanese audience evidently received it enthusiastically. This episode seems to indicate that at least in 1929 there was still a great deal of good will and mutual admiration between the British and the Japanese.

The post-1945 period saw a gradual recovery from the damage inflicted by war on cultural relationships between the two countries. For example, in 1958 a remarkable exhibition, *Art Treasures from Japan*, was staged at the Victoria and Albert Museum (Plate 8). The 'Foreword' of the catalogue by Philip Jones boasts that it is 'even finer than the famous exhibition of Japanese art held in Berlin in 1939'.[28] It was packed with canonical works of National Treasure status from across a whole span of Japanese art.

However, the real 'discovery' of Japanese art for the post-war generation in Britain was that of contemporary Japanese art and its diversity. The 1964 Tokyo Olympics propagated a new image of Japan as a bearer of modern culture and civilization. It was the image of the bullet train that epitomized this new era. The poster designs for the Olympics by Yusaku Kamekura (Plate 9) reinforced this image of sophisticated Japanese design. The sleek Sony transistor radio and later the ubiquitous Walkman replaced the Fujiyama-Geisha image of the older generation. Japanese electronic goods and motorcycles permeated every corner of the British Isles.

From that time on, Japan has been producing international canonical figures in contemporary art and design, particularly in the fields of fashion and architecture. Londoners now have access to the boutiques of most of the top Japanese fashion designers. The British no longer say that the Japanese have no architecture. On the contrary, architects such as Kurokawa Kisho or Ando Tadao are feted by the Royal Institute of British Architects. Another area of Japanese design which has a rich tradition of British appreciation throughout the twentieth century, is that of garden design. This interest has increased in recent years with the formation of the Japan Garden Society, which consists mainly of British garden designers and enthusiasts. Japanese gardens are now being created in large numbers in Britain, with varying degrees of craftsmanship and associative relationship with Japan.

In the field of popular culture *manga*, Japanese comics, and *anime*, Japanese animation, are having a huge impact across the world and Britain is no exception to this trend. In the field of fine art the situation of the 1990s is considerably more complex. Fine artists with an international reputation, such as Miyajima Tatsuo or Mori Mariko, have received great acclaim for solo shows in London. But does this still come under the heading of a British 'discovery' of Japanese art? Mori Mariko was trained at the Chelsea College of Art and Design in London, joined the Whitney Program in the USA, and then featured in the Norwegian Pavilion at the Venice Biennale. Can she be claimed to form a part of Japanese art? London now boasts an almost constant stream of exhibitions by artists of Japanese origin. However, many of them have been trained in Britain and have never exhibited in Japan. The London Institute, of which Chelsea College of Art and Design is a constituent college, trained more than 600 Japanese art and design students in 1998–99 and many of them will become part of the current British scene. Thus the question of the British 'discovery' of Japanese art is becoming a non-question.

Bernard Leach and the Anglo-Japanese aesthetic relationship

In the twentieth century, one of the most important Anglo-Japanese relationships in modern art and design was that between Bernard Leach and the *Mingei* movement in Japan and the studio pottery movement in Britain. A fruitful cross-fertilization was created through the close friendship and cultural exchange between core members of the *Mingei* movement, including Yanagi Soetsu Muneyoshi (1889–1961), a philosopher and leader of the movement, Bernard Leach (1887–1979), a potter/designer, Tomimoto Kenkichi (1886–1963), the potter Hamada Shoji (1894–1978) and others.

Leach's Orientalism and modernism

Bernard Leach was born in Hong Kong in 1887 and spent his childhood in Japan and Singapore. After training at the Slade School of Art and the London School of Art, his nostalgic memories of the Far East led him back to Japan in 1909 and he lived there until 1920, except for the years 1915–16 when he was in Beijing. Leach arrived there at the crucial moment when modern art was about to come into full bloom. He was involved in the Shirakaba (White Birch) group,[29] through the etching classes he held in Tokyo and then through wider group activities. While in Japan, he learned pottery with Tomimoto Kenkichi under Kenzan VI and they were both given the title of Kenzan VII after only a year's study. This effectively constituted 'Leach's mythic "grounding" in Japanese ceramics'.[30] Leach held several exhibitions in Tokyo during his stay in Japan, contributing to the development of the modern Japanese art movement.[31]

Leach's contribution to the world of Japanese modern art is manifold. One of the most interesting aspects of his cross-cultural fertilization is found in his role as a transmitter of 'modernity' from Britain. It was Leach's Orientalism and primitivism which was transformed and localized in the modern Japanese context. Leach defined the Japanese essence in applied arts as their 'exquisite decorative concept', 'cleanness and sensitivity', 'lightness and characteristic lines'[32] but did not credit them with the 'dynamism', and 'strong beauty' of Chinese art.[33] This made young Japanese intellectuals and artists aware of Euro-American views on Japanese art and helped them to invent their cultural identity with an essential 'Orientalness' and 'Japaneseness' under Euro-American cultural dominance.

Leach came to Japan equipped also with the modern aesthetic notion of the primitive. As Edmund de Waal has pointed out, when Leach went to Japan, he had already mediated images of Japan as 'child-like', 'mystical' and 'spiritual', which were largely constructed from the fantasy world of Lafcadio Hearn.[34] Speaking of Hearn's overwhelming influence on him, Leach said 'I saw everything with Hearn's eyes. Wherever I go, I felt Hearn'.[35] Leach also had a 'dream of Japan' highly charged by James McNeill Whistler's artistic Chelsea, where Leach had also lived. Leach had sketched 'Nocturne' and admired Oriental asymmetrical composition.[36] Tomimoto Kenkichi[37] also wrote an account of Leach's admiration for the primitive beauty of 'savage art' at the Colonial Exhibition held in Japan in 1912, where Leach and Tomimoto shared a fascination for the beauty of the 'primitive savage art' of Korea, Taiwan, Manchuria and that of the Ainu.[38] This reflects the Orientalism and primitivism of European Modernism in early twentieth century expressed in Post-Impressionism and its introduction to Britain in the 1910s[39] by people such as Roger Fry, C. Lewis Hind[40] and Frank Rutter.[41] In the particular British context, it is also often perceived as a continuation of Victorian Japonisme.

Another contribution by Leach was his introduction of Arts and Crafts ideas, in particular his strong inclination toward John Ruskin[42] and William Morris who inspired the first generation of Japanese studio potters such as Tomimoto Kenkichi and Hamada Shoji. Leach wrote in his diary in 1911 of his idea for 'the formation of a group somewhat on William Morris lines by Takamura, Tomi, self and a few others. Painting, sculpture, porcelain, lacquer, etc., to be exhibited in our own gallery'.[43] Leach's Morrisian ambition of creating an 'art of the people' by beautifying daily life by means of a total concept of applied art were successfully presented at the *Bijutsu Shinpo* exhibition of small works by young progressive artists in 1911.

Wallhangings were stencil-designed by Leach and rush chairs were designed by Tomimoto Kenkichi, another Morrisian artist trained in Britain. They also sold their inexpensive early works of *raku* pottery. In 1919 Leach exhibited furniture as well as his pottery at Ruitsuso. His furniture was received by Japanese artists and designers with enthusiasm because of its modernity and 'Japaneseness'. They included his three-legged chairs epitomizing modern Arts and Crafts ideals, but including such Oriental symbols as the form of the shrine gate for the back of his chairs made of Japanese cedar in a peculiar Anglo-Japanese 'hybrid' style.[44] There was also a chair upholstered in material inspired by Japanese firemen's quilted coats. This had a great impact on such artist-craftsmen as Hamada, who described them as 'very close to life, to living, and very exotic and unusual' (Figure 8.4).[45] Chairs were important objects for the modern 'life of culture' (*bunka seikatsu*) at that time, symbolizing the culture of the Occident, modern and 'rational' living and above all an exciting project for new artist-craftsmen as part of a new field called 'interior design'. As part of their artistic expression,

Figure 8.4 Bernard Leach, table and chairs, *c.* 1916–19

many Japanese designers experimented in designing chairs in a peculiar hybrid style and integrated them into modern Japanese living.

Complementary 'hybrid' discourses: Yanagi's *Mingei* theory and Leach's Anglo-Japanese philosophy

Bernard Leach also played an extremely significant role in Yanagi Soetsu's foundation of *Mingei* (folkcrafts) theory. Their co-operation in developing the *Mingei* movement in its later stages, particularly in the 1950s in Japan, Britain and the US, is also well known. Leach was an important source of information for Yanagi on modern aesthetic ideas from Euro-America, including Orientalism, primitivism, medievalism and Arts and Crafts aesthetic ideas. *Mingei* theory, which took its final shape in the 1920s, is about the supreme beauty of Japanese common household objects hand-made by unknown craftsmen. It theorized the 'criterion of beauty'. This included such principles as the innate beauty of handicrafts, of intimacy, of use/ function, of health, of naturalness, of simplicity, of tradition, of irregularity, of inexpensiveness, of plurality, of sincerity and honest sweat, of selflessness and the unknown. Although *Mingei* theory has long been regarded as an 'authentic and traditional' Japanese aesthetic theory, it is a modern invention and a 'hybrid' of Euro-American modern aesthetic ideas, which was localized in Japan by Yanagi's original application. *Mingei* theory was created as the mirror image of Orientalism, which was historically projected by Euro-America on to the Orient. In the complex cultural politics between the Occident and the Orient, *Mingei* theory created the discourse of 'authenticity' outside Japan and 'neo-traditionalism' within Japan.[46] Yanagi and Leach's collaborations produced interesting 'hybrid' craft theories which vitalized both Japanese and British modern craft and design. While Yanagi transplanted and applied Euro-American ideas to Japan, Leach in return took an 'Orientalized' ethical and spiritual discourse back to Britain. Leach created his version of 'hybrid' *Mingei* theory to set the 'standard of beauty'. In Leach's version this was to be found in 'the T'ang and Sung periods in China and the best of the Ming, Korean celadons, and Ri-cho, early Japanese teamaster's wares, early Persian, Syrian Hispano-Moresque, German Bellarmines, some Delft and English slipware'[47] and Leach urged British studio potters to follow this standard. Both Yanagi and Leach were mutually nourished through their complimentary activities. Both created cutting edge modernity through the process of cultural transfer, assimilation, transformation, and innovation, but unfortunately once they became self-satisfied and content with the 'complicity relationship', they were not receptive to further innovation and lost the expression of modernity.

'Orientalism' and British studio pottery: the birth of the Leach School and the 'Leach style'

Accompanied by Hamada Shoji, Leach returned to Britain from Japan in 1920 and opened the Leach Pottery in St Ives, Cornwall. In Britain the 1920s was a time when design reform activities in industrial design began developing within the still strong environment of the Arts and Crafts Movement. It was characterized by cross-fertilized design activities by fine artists, industrial designers and craft makers in the interrelated but not yet differentiated fields of architecture, interior and product design and crafts.[48] Bernard Leach and William Staite Murray are generally regarded as pioneers of British studio pottery, a concept developed during this period. Studio pottery forms a part of studio crafts and, in contrast to crafts in general made by artisans, studio crafts are made by individual artists who have chosen craft media to express their art and conceptual ideas.

It was the time of the resurgence of 'Orientalism' in the world of art and design, the time of Roger Fry's words 'the East presents the hope of discovering a more spiritual, more expressive idea of design'.[49] In the world of studio pottery, there was a great enthusiasm for Oriental pottery, and in particular Chinese 'Sung' pots. Murray and Leach were two intense rivals who both chose ceramics as their means of artistic expression, inspired by Oriental pottery.[50] But, while Murray worked as an artist, separating himself from craft workers who worked under the influence of Arts and Crafts ideas,

Leach worked as just such a craft artist. Whatever the difference, their significance lies in their roles in bringing intellectual and critical perspectives on design into the world of studio pottery through their mediating of 'Oriental' discourses.

This was also the time when Britain was in search of 'Englishness' in its culture. Awash with the radical European Modernism, Britain took its own path in searching for modernity in national character in industrial design in the environment. This was still strongly influenced by the hand-made Arts and Crafts Movement. Coinciding with the archaeological study of Celtic, Anglo-Saxon and Romanesque art in Britain, a highly charged discourse on the Englishness of English art in connection with ancient and medieval English history was developed in the 1930s by such notable art critics as Nikolaus Pevsner, Herbert Read and such artists as Paul Nash, John Piper and William Johnstone.[51] Leach's enthusiasm for English medieval slipwares, particularly in Thomas Toft's style, shares Arts and Crafts ideals, but also the contemporary trend for modernity in the discovery of English identity.

Leach's *A Potter's Book*, first published in 1940, became the Bible for studio potters, presenting a ground-breaking intellectual approach to pottery as well as practical technical information. His belief in true handicrafts as a means of creating new pottery by combining the standard of fine old crafts from the Orient and the Occident also became an extremely stimulating project for modern artists. During the Second World War, Leach began the production of his 'Standard Ware', functional tableware at affordable prices for ordinary people, embodying 'Englishness' in its forms but with the quality of Oriental pottery, as he indicated in *A Potter's Book* (Figure 8.5). Soon, Leach's teaching developed to form the so-called 'Leach style' which attracted hundreds of young potters from all over the world. Leach's disciples who trained at St Ives in the 1920s became the important second generation of British studio potters and the first generation of American studio potters. They include such figures as Michael Cardew, Nora Braden and Katherine Pleydell-Bouverie in Britain and Warren and Alix Mackenzie in the USA.[52] They propagated the Leach School's 'ethical pot' tradition in an Anglo-Oriental Leach style.

After the Second World War, Yanagi, Leach and Hamada frequently travelled all over Euro-America and Japan lecturing and demonstrating. Their craft theories were disseminated to an even wider audience. In 1952, they had a particularly profound impact on craft makers at the legendary International Conference of Craftsmen in Pottery and Textiles at Dartington Hall in England. The perfect combination of Yanagi's 'Buddhist aesthetics' in folkcraft, and its adaptation by Leach and Hamada's demonstration which literally made *Mingei theory* visible, virtually created its own cult movement.

Figure 8.5   Catalogue of Standard Ware, Leach Pottery, 1951

Conclusion: Beyond the 'Leach Tradition'

The hybrid English and Oriental 'ethical aesthetic' discourse created by Bernard Leach has been enormously significant in the history of studio pottery. The Leach tradition of 'brown ethical pots' was so dominantly persuasive in Britain that many potters followed it as their ideal until recently, when contemporary potters have begun a reinterpretation and deconstruction of Leach's discourse and have tried to go beyond the Leach tradition. Since the establishment of the Crafts Advisory Committee in 1971 (from 1979 the Craft Council) studies on and the creation of crafts have been activated. The diversity of contemporary crafts ranging from tableware to sculptural vessels has given studio pottery in Britain increased vitality.

For example, the sculptural 'Vessel school' led by crafts artists such as Liz Fritsch and Alison Britton since the 1980s has been powerful in relativizing the Leach tradition. While at the same time a new interest in reworking the vernacular tradition in line with the Leach School and English Arts and Crafts ideas can be found in John Leach, Michael Casson, Richard Batterham, Clive Bowen, Svend Bayer and Patrick Sergent. A deeper reinterpretation of the intellectual aspect of Leach's ideas can also be observed among such ex-Leach/*Mingei* school contemporary British potters as Edmund de Waal, Takeshi Yasuda and Rupert Spira. The latter have refused to sell the 'Orientalness' inherited from the Leach tradition in an obvious way, but have retained his innovative and intellectual spirit. They have also joined forces with such potters as Julian Stair and Joanna Constantinidis, who are more in line with the European Modernist tradition, rather than with the direct inheritance from the Leach tradition.

They are the most innovative potters at present in Britain making usable tableware, constantly questioning the meaning of their pottery and crafts in general. They are all expanding the horizon of the artistic creation of crafts into new concepts, new forms and new functions suited to urban British life. At the same time they are also commercially successful, integrated into the popular culture of consumption stimulated by the design and food revolution created by Terence Conran. Modernism in design and crafts, which arrived late in Britain, seems to be flowering at the start of the twenty-first century and the contemporary craft artists and designers have been creating works of cutting-edge style resulting from continuous questioning. But, the questions 'What are crafts? What is studio pottery?' have not yet been answered since first posed by Bernard Leach.

Notes

1. John Irwin, 'A Jacobean Vogue for Oriental Lacquer-ware', *Burlington Magazine*, vol. XCVI (June 1953), pp. 192–5.

2. John Stalker and George Parker, *A Treatise of Japanning and Varnishing* (reprint of 1688 edn), (London: Academy Editions, 1971), p. xv.
3. See Toshio Watanabe, *High Victorian Japonisme* (Berne: Peter Lang, 1991), pp. 113–29 for a more detailed discussion.
4. See Toshio Watanabe, 'Owen Jones' The Grammar of Ornament: "Orientalism" subverted?', *Aachener Kunstblätter*, vol. 60, pp. 439–42.
5. William Burges, 'The Japanese Court in the International Exhibition', *Gentleman's Magazine*, September 1862, pp. 234–54 (p. 254).
6. William Burges, 'The International Exhibition', *Gentleman's Magazine*, July 1862, pp. 3–12 (p. 11).
7. John Leighton, 'On Japanese Art', *Journal of the Society of Arts*, 24 July 1863, pp. 596–9 (p. 597).
8. Anon., 'Japanese Ornamentation', *The Builder*, 2 May, pp. 308–9, 23 May, pp. 364–6, 13 June, pp. 423–4, 1863; p. 364.
9. James Abbott McNeill Whistler, *The Gentle Art of Making Enemies* (New York: Dover, 1967) (reprint of 1892 edn), pp. 127–8.
10. Ibid., p. 159.
11. William Michael Rossetti (ed.), *Rossetti Papers* (London: Sands, 1903), p. 138.
12. Marcus Huish, 'England's Appreciation of Japanese Art', *Transactions and Proceedings of the Japan Society*, 7, 1906, pp. 120–39 (p. 138).
13. According to the late Basil Gray the 1939 Kelmscott sale included two Japanese paintings.
14. William Morris, 'Textiles', *Arts and Crafts Essays* (London, 1893), pp. 22–38 (p. 35).
15. His views on Japanese architecture could have been influenced by Alcock who also pronounced that the Japanese 'have no architecture' (Rutherford Alcock, *The Capital of the Tycoon. A Narrative of a Three Years' Residence in Japan*, two vols (London: Longman, Green, Longman, Roberts & Green, 1863), p. 279 and whose publications Morris was familiar with.
16. John Lowry, 'The Rise of the Japanese Vogue', *Country Life*, 10 April 1958, pp. 752–3 (p. 753).
17. See Murakado Noriko, 'Shinbi Shoin no bijutsu zenshu ni miru "Nihon Bijutsushi" no keisei' (The establishment of 'Japanese Art History' in the case of the art book series published by Shinbi Shoin), *Kindai Gasetsu*, Journal of Meiji Bijutsu Gakkai (Society for the study of Meiji art), vol. 8 (1999), pp. 33–51.
18. Ibid., p. 34.
19. Edward Barrington de Fonblanque, *Niphon and Pe-che-li* (London, 1862), p. 52.
20. Toda Masahiro, *Daiei Teikoku no Ajia Imeji* (The British Image of Asia) (Tokyo: Minerva Shobo, 1996), pp. 190–2.
21. R. H. Scott, 'Foreword', in L. R. Marchant (ed.), *The Siege of the Peking Legations: A Diary of Lancelot Giles* (Nedlands: University of Western Australia Press, 1970), pp. xx quoted from Colin Mackerras, *Western Images of China* (Hong Kong: Oxford University, 1991), pp. 70–1.
22. Louis Gonse, *L'Art Japonais* (Paris: Maison Quantin, 1883), pp. 231–2, quoted from Timothy Clark, ' "The Intuition and the Genius of Decoration": Critical Reactions to Rimpa art in Europe and the USA during the late nineteenth and early twentieth centuries', in Yuzo Yamane, Masato Naito and Timothy Clark, *Rimpa Art from the Idemitsu Collection, Tokyo* (London: British Museum Press, 1998), pp. 68–82 (pp. 72, 76).
23. William Anderson, *Pictorial Arts of Japan* (London: Sampson Low, 1886), p. 251, quoted from Clark, *Rimpa Art*, p. 70.

24. William Anderson, 'A History of Japanese [Pictorial] Art', *Transactions of the Asiatic Society of Japan*, vol. 7 (1879), pp. 339–74 (p. 356).
25. An article on Rimpa and modernism by the present writer is in preparation.
26. I owe thanks to John Hatcher for the details of this trip, as discussed in his *Laurence Binyon: Poet, Scholar of East and West* (Oxford: Clarendon Press, 1995), pp. 244–52.
27. I am grateful to Dr Tim Clark for pointing out the existence of this catalogue and to Nagashima Meiko for helping me to gain access to a copy at the Kyoto National Museum.
28. Philip James, 'Foreword', *Art Treasures from Japan*, exhibition catalogue, The Victoria and Albert Museum (London: The Arts Council, 1958), pp. 3–5 (p. 3).
29. The school of writers including Mushanokoji Saneatsu, Shiga Naoya, the three Arishima brothers: Arishima Takeo, Arishima Ikuma and Satomi Ton, Yanagi Soetsu Muneyoshi, Kinoshita Rigen, Sonoike Kinyuki, Kojima Kikuo, Nagayo Yoshiro and Kori Torahiko who were all from the Gakushuin Kotoka school. They published the magazine *Shirakaba* which widely introduced Euro-American art, particularly the Post-Impressionists, and various modern ideas from 1910 to 1923.
30. Edmund de Waal, *Bernard Leach* (London: Tate Gallery Publishing, 1997), p. 15.
31. *Bijutsu Shashin Gaho*, vol. 1, no. 1, 1920.
32. Bernard Leach, 'Nihon no Gakai ni Ecchingu o Shokaisu' (The introduction of etching to the Japanese art world), *Shumi*, 1 June 1909. English translation by Kikuchi from Morita Meireishi's Japanese translation from Leach's original English. Leach's original English text has not survived.
33. Bernard Leach, 'Nihon ni arishi Junen kan' (Ten Years in Japan), *Bijutsu Geppo*, 17 February 1921, p. 93.
34. Edmund de Waal, 'Towards a Double Standard?', *Crafts*, 149, p. 33; *Bernard Leach* (London: Tate Gallery Publishing, 1997), p. 72. Lafcadio Hearn (1850–1904), a British writer who came to Japan. He wrote fairy tales and various essays on Japanese culture with an emphasis on the exotic, aesthetic, primitive, medieval and spiritual.
35. Bernard Leach, 'Nihon ni arishi Junen kan' (Ten Years in Japan), *Bijutsu Geppo*, 17 February, 1921, p. 56. The English translation from Leach's broken Japanese is by Kikuchi.
36. Bernard Leach, *Beyond East and West* (London: Faber & Faber, 1985), (1978), p. 32.
37. For further information about Tomimoto Kenkichi and his involvement with the *Mingei* movement, see Yuko Kikuchi, 'Tomimoto Kenkichi', *Crafts*, 143, pp. 22–3, 1997 and 'The Myth of Yanagi's Originality: Formation of the *Mingei* Movement in its Social and Historical Context', *Journal of Design History*, vol. 7, no. 4 (1994), pp. 247–66.
38. Tomimoto Kenkichi, 'Takushoku Hakurankai no Ichinichi' (One Day in the Colonial Exhibition), *Bijutsu Shinpo*, vol. 12, no. 2 (1912), pp. 19–21.
39. Fry organized the first 'Manet and Post-Impressionists' exhibition in 1910 and the second 'Post-Impressionist Exhibition' in 1912 in London.
40. C. Lewis Hind, *The Post-Impressionists* (London: Methuen & Co., 1911).
41. Frank Rutter, *Revolution in Art* (London: The Art News Press, 1910).
42. Yuko Kikuchi and Toshio Watanabe, *Ruskin in Japan 1890–1940: Nature for Art, Art for Life* (Tokyo: Cogito, 1997).
43. Bernard Leach, *Beyond East and West*, p. 66.
44. Bernard Leach, *Hamada Potter* (Tokyo, New York and San Francisco: Kodansha International Ltd, 1981), p. 26.

45. Ibid., p. 24.
46. For the issue of 'hybridity' and 'Orientalism in the *Mingei* theory, see Yuko Kikuchi, 'Hybridity and Oriental Orientalism of *Mingei* Theory', *Journal of Design History*, vol. 10, no. 4 (1997), pp. 343–54.
47. Bernard Leach, *A Potter's Book* (London: Faber & Faber, 1976; first published 1940).
48. James Peto and Donna Loveday (eds), *Modern Britain 1929–1939* (London: Design Museum, 1999).
49. Cited in Julian Stair, 'Genius and Circumstance: Early Criticsm of Hamada's Pottery in England', in Timothy Wilcox (ed.), *Shoji Hamada: Master Potter* (London: Lund Humphries, 1998), p. 16.
50. Ibid., p. 17.
51. Judith Collins, 'The Englishness of English Art', in James Peto and Donna Loveday (eds), *Modern Britain 1929–1939* (London: Design Museum, 1999).
52. For Leach's wide influence in the world of pottery, see Marion Whybrow, *The Leach Legacy: St. Ives Pottery and its Influence* (Bristol: Sansom & Company, 1996).

Part III
Twentieth-Century Themes

9
The Modernist Inheritance in Japanese Social Studies: Fukuzawa, Marxists and Otsuka Hisao[1]

Kazuhiko Kondo

Fukuzawa's concern and inheritance

In 1862 the first Japanese government mission was sent to London and was despatched to other European cities to negotiate diplomatic issues with Britain and other western powers. Fukuzawa Yukichi (1834–1901), a 27-year-old interpreter attached to the mission, took advantage of this opportunity to meet well informed persons in order to discuss the British parliamentary system, political parties, freedom of the press and other matters. Recalling these discussions, Fukuzawa wrote:

> I raised queries about what constituted common sense for them [Britons] . . . and they might have thought my questions foolish. However, these were about the facts that I could not understand at all by reading. For instance, it was a capital crime in Japan for more than three people to group into a political association. But in Britain there exist political parties in bright sunshine [excuse the poetic licence!] and they contend for power. British citizens are at liberty to comment on and even to blame the government's policy. It is more than a thousand wonders and beyond comprehension that they permit such licentious outrage and keep the country in order.[2]

Fukuzawa's queries were not about the steam engine, telegraph or electricity all of which were already familiar to him through his studies of schoolbooks and encyclopedias. But his queries extended from parliamentary democracy to habeas corpus, the legal profession, insurance and the postal service. What he sought to understand by interviewing Britons was what he could not comprehend by reading – that is, modern civilization and democracy at work. Thus he gleaned the essence of parliamentary democracy and human rights in a civilized society – this in 1862, six years before the Meiji Restoration.

Fukuzawa spent four years of deliberate preparation before publishing 'Conditions in the West' in three parts in ten books, over the period 1867–70.[3] 150000 copies were sold and another 100000 appeared in pirate editions.[4] The pith and marrow of Fukuzawa's thoughts was concern for the destiny of his beloved nation in the troubled world of the late nineteenth century: the period of the Second Opium War (1856–60), the Indian Mutiny (1857–58) and Japan's own civil war (1868). Inseparable from this concern was his optimistic faith in the universal and teleological progress of history and civilization. Fukuzawa felt that Japan should learn valuable lessons from the examples of Britain and Europe:

> The aim of us, scholars of the west, . . . is clear and simple: to introduce western things to Japan and let the nation adapt to the conditions and enter the gate of civilization as soon as possible . . . We may look as if we were importing traders of cultural artifacts . . . However, there is a natural law that the knowledge of oneself develops in direct proportion to the knowledge of others: the more we know about them [the west], the more we care about our own destiny.[5]

Confidence sustained Fukuzawa's endeavours for the enlightenment of the nation. Significantly, the history books he referred to most were H. T. Buckle's *History of Civilization in England*, F. P. G. Guizot's *General History of Civilization in Europe*, and a number of schoolbooks in the whiggish mould.[6]

Of course, Fukuzawa was not the only contemporary Japanese to stay in a western country and care about the destiny of the nation. Professor Ishizuki Minoru has counted 153 mostly young Japanese who studied/stayed abroad between 1853 and 1867. Of these, 49 (or 32 per cent) stayed in Britain.[7] Ito Hirobumi, the future first prime minister, and Mori Arinori, the future first minister of education, were among them. But Fukuzawa stood out as a champion of modernizing Japan, a prolific writer as well as a remarkable educator of the Meiji enlightenment.[8] Fukuzawa was concerned about the future constitution of the new state in Japan, and he offered a summary of national options to the reading public. Thus his project was more pragmatic than academic, more committed than merely erudite. He writes in his introduction to 'Conditions in the West' that:

> In order to understand the political culture of nations of the world, it is best to read their history. Most Japanese scholars who are keen to learn western things have been too rash to take serious regard of history. I have studied and summarized in each section history, politics, the military and finance of [the] western powers. And by reading the four points you will understand the conditions of each nation and will not miss which nation to make friends with, and which nation to be on guard against. Hence the publication of this book.[9]

My essay seeks to interpret Fukuzawa's inheritance in Japanese historical studies in the twentieth century, with special reference to Otsuka Hisao (1907–96) and Maruyama Masao (1914–96) who formed the core of the modernist camp of post-1945 historical studies (Sengo shigaku). I am going to emphasize these writers' concern for the destiny of the nation, their belief in the universal development of civilization as headed by Britain, and their high academic standards and pragmatism. Britain was perceived not only as a leading figure in modern civilization, but as an exemplar of liberal reform in contrast to continental Europe. The differences between European countries were well known, but at the same time Europe as a whole was taken as forming one civilization. The Japanese modernists were learned regarding history and conditions in the West, but they did not study for study's sake. As enlightened patriots, they wanted to contribute to the cause of national reform.[10] These were the characteristics of those modernist/progressive historians who could be called the heirs of Fukuzawa, though perhaps their analysis was more sophisticated than that of their great ancestor as a result of their knowledge of Marxist history, the study of which flourished in the middle of the twentieth century.

Historical studies in Meiji Japan

Fukuzawa was the founder and president of the Keio School of British Studies,[11] and after the Meiji Restoration a number of other schools and academies also flourished. But it was not until 1877 that a modern university was established in Japan: the University of Tokyo, which first consisted of the Law School and the School of Medicine, to which were soon added the schools of Engineering and Letters. The University of Tokyo, later renamed the Imperial University, began to produce the elite cadres of the new state: until 1918 first-class graduates *cum laude* of the University (323 in all) were awarded a silver watch from the Emperor.[12]

It was a decade before the government decided to found a Department of History. Suematsu Kencho (1855–1920), the son-in-law of Ito Hirobumi, the future first prime minister, was a member of the Japanese legation in London. Suematsu met Gustav Zerffi (1820–92), an enigmatic Hungarian refugee and fellow of the Royal Historical Society (RHS), and asked him to write *The Science of History* by the commission of the Japanese government. The book, published in 1879, gave a comprehensive survey of European historical writings and studies since the 'pre-Homeric period', and described a 'European model of the appropriate union of fact and philosophy'. Zerffi paid due respect to historiography in Western Europe since the sixteenth century up to Macaulay, Seeley and Lecky, as well as to Guizot, Hegel and Humboldt, but few mentions were made of contemporary historical developments in German universities. He would become president of the RHS the following year.[13]

Table 9.1   First publication dates of major historical journals

Historische Zeitschrift	1859
*(Transactions of the Royal Historical Society)**	1875
Revue Historique	1876
Rivista Storica Italiana	1884
English Historical Review	1886
Shigaku Zasshi	1889
American Historical Review	1895
Vierteljahrschrift fur Sozial- und Wirtschaftsgeschichte	1903
Revue d'histoire economique et sociale	1908
Economic History Review	1927
Annales d'histoire economique et sociale	1929
Shakaikeizaishi-gaku	1931
Rekishigaku Kenkyu	1933

Note:
* Some reservations should be made about the early *TRHS* which printed 'the more important papers read at . . . the society'. Cf. A. T. Milne, *A Centenary Guide to the Publications of the Royal Historical Society and of the Former Camden Society* (London: RHS, 1968). The *Transactions* differed in character from other modern historical journals.

One hundred copies of *The Science of History* were sent to Tokyo, and after some delay in translation and decision the Meiji government decided to invite Ludwig Riess (1866–1928), a young German disciple of Leopold von Ranke, to Tokyo in 1887. In due course the Department of History was established at the Imperial University. The next year the Department of National History was added, and Riess urged his Japanese colleagues to found a historical society (Shigakkai) and also to publish a journal of the society based on the model of the *Historische Zeitschrift* in his fatherland. The first general meeting inaugurated the Society in November 1889 along with the Japanese monthly *Shigaku Zasshi* (Historical Journal), which continues today.[14]

The inauguration of Japanese *Shigaku Zasshi* in 1889 may be put in its international context by comparing the founding dates of other major historical journals of Europe and United States (see Table 9.1). The German *Historische Zeitschrift* heads the list, and is followed by those of France, Italy, England, Japan and the USA. By the end of the nineteenth century all the leading national journals of historical studies which thrive today had appeared.

The long history of *Shigaku Zasshi* would have been unblemished but for an early scandal, which related to the resignation in 1892 of one of the first professors of National History, Kume Kunitake (1839–1931). Kume had accompanied the government mission headed by the ambassador plenipotentiary Iwakura Tomomi round the world in 1871–73. The Iwakura mission had a dual function (i) as a diplomatic delegation to probe into a possible

revision of the unequal treaties of the 1850s; and (ii) as a kind of royal commission of investigation into the state of the Western Powers.[15] A keen
observer and writer as well as an able historian,[16] Kume was responsible for
the latter investigation and compiled five thick volumes entitled 'Observations during the Round Visits to USA and Europe' (1878). This is now
counted among the classic literature of East–West encounters.[17] In volume
II, of some 400 pages dedicated to Britain, Kume began his general survey
of the British Isles thus:

> The United Kingdom is 121 362 square miles wide with a population of
> 31 817 108 according to the census of 1871. Both the area of the islands
> and the population are comparable to ours, and the Britons flatter us by
> saying that Japan is 'Britain in the East'. However, if one refers to eco-
> nomic power, the difference is beyond comparison.[18]

At the end of the volume Kume concluded his observations of the British
national economy, industry, standard of living, and facilities at museums
and libraries with high praise. And throughout the five volumes he often
contrasts the rough and ready westernization of Japan with what he
observed in Britain and Europe: 'True progress and improvement do not
mean throwing away the old and rushing for the new . . . The reason why
the west has successfully made progress and improvement lies in their love
for the old.'[19]

The publication of Kume's lengthy account was a success, and 3500 sets
or more were completely sold out by 1883.[20] But Kume did not continue his
study of western countries; instead, he turned his interest to Japan's national
history and Shintoism. This was dangerous. After the demise of the Freedom
and People's Rights movement the Meiji state was consolidating itself along
authoritarian lines. The Imperial Constitution was promulgated in 1889,
and the Imperial Rescript on Education (a code of imperial ethics to be
recited at all schools) was proclaimed in the following year. Kume's academic and liberal-leaning article, 'Shinto, an Ancient Folklore of Worshipping
Heaven', appeared in *Shigaku Zasshi* in October 1891. The liberal-minded
journalist Taguchi Ukichi welcomed this but Shintoists and right-wingers
accused Kume of blasphemy.[21] The imperial government urged the 52-year-
old Professor Kume to tender his resignation the next year. He was not dismissed, but was forced to resign.

Thus the Imperial University lost a liberal, experienced historian. After
Kume was removed from his chair, Riess remained a constant champion of
Rankean academism. Meanwhile the school of history (now comprising
three departments: western, national and Asian history) continued its
routine work of compiling historical manuscripts and teaching young,
prospective members of the elite of the state, the history of wars and
diplomacy, dynasties and administration of Western Powers.[22] Freethinking

discussion was driven from the academy, and would only find its expression in civic journalism.

Historical studies and writing on the modernizing of Japan have been discussed in terms of two separate traditions.[23] First, civic history-writing carried out by non-academics: *Minkan shiron*. Newspapers and magazines flourished in the Meiji and Taisho periods, and they provided a public sphere for the 'country party' (*Minkan Zaiya*), who aired independent and literary opinions based upon wide historical reading, but had little interest in the specialized activities of universities. Second, were academic historical studies which were influenced by Germany before 1945, but not overwhelmingly so. The Japanese and Chinese tradition of orthodox historiography (*seishi*) had long taken root and continued in the University of Tokyo, though in a somewhat different manner. Orthodox historiography and Rankean *Wissenschaft* found each other good companions in establishing a new academic specialism detached from the contemporary political situation. The two streams, civic and academic, had separated by 1891, and would not come together again until the 1920s. By this time Kyoto, Tohoku and Kyushu Imperial universities had been founded, as well as Keio, Waseda and other private universities.

Developmental history and national characteristics

In the European academic world the German Historical School of national economy, that is the historical study of social and economic policy, had gained ground by the end of the nineteenth century. Led by Gustav Schmoller and Lujo Brentano, the school was an academic development in Bismarck's Germany to provide a defence against the free-trade imperialism of Pax Britannica. It was an intellectual reaction against the ahistorical criteria of classical political economy that thrived in Britain. The *problematique* of Frederich List *versus* Adam Smith, that is of German protection of its national economy and history *versus* British propagation of free trade and the market, provided Japanese scholars with their frame of reference. The second motive of the German School was, domestically, to deal with the *Sozialfrage* (social problems of an industrializing country) and to forestall the growing influence of social democrats. This new wave of academic engagement in policy making would not take root in the Rankean history departments of Japan's Imperial University, but in the Faculty of Law and Political Science (the Faculty of Economics was not independent either in Tokyo or Kyoto until 1919). Kanai Noburu (1865–1933) and Takano Iwasaburo (1871–1949) were among the first professors to doubt the universal progress of civilization and to propagate the teachings of the German Historical School. They were instrumental in the promotion of *Staatswissenschaft* (the study of statecraft and social policy)[24] and the establishment in 1896 of the Shakai Seisaku Gakkai (the Society for Social Policy) to deal with the social problems of industrialization: poverty, class antagonism and social democracy.

However, it was at the Tokyo College of Commerce (now Hitotsubashi University) that economic history of the German mould took firm root. Fukuda Tokuzo (1874–1930), who had studied with Brentano in Munich, returned to teach at his old College of Commerce and Keio University.[25] The theory of developmental stages of an economy began to flourish and there was also increased academic confidence in the evolution of economics and historical progress. British, French and American scholars had been visiting Berlin, Munich and other German universities in order to learn the burgeoning subjects of economic history and policy studies as well as modern teaching methods. This became a great intellectual wave in the West: for instance, the journal *Vierteljahrsschrift fuer Sozialund Wirtschaftsgeschichte* included papers not only in German but also in French and English in order, explicitly, to be an international journal. The second half of Table 9.1 shows yet another global cycle of journals, for social and economic history: German initiative leading other countries, and Japan closing the cycle in the early 1930s. More interestingly, from my viewpoint, the German Historical School, despite its original defensive objectives, helped prepare a seedbed in Japan for the Marxist developmental history that was to come.

The Russian Revolution, or more precisely the Communist International of 1919 and the founding of the Japanese Communist Party in 1922, changed the intellectual atmosphere in Japan. By this, I do not mean that Japan suddenly became communist or even social democrat, but that, at least, some knowledge of communism gradually penetrated the young, urban reading public. By 1930 it even became fashionable among students to talk about Marx and communism, as it was about to discuss modern art and literature.[26] Marxism was not just introduced and received as a revolutionary theory and determinist interpretation of history, but, as Maruyama puts it, it also provided 'a startling freshness of vision as an integrating, systematic science that offered to unite the [hitherto] specialized and compartmentalized sciences in a comprehensive *Weltanschauung*'.[27] 'Marxism as a grand theory' combined not only several specialized fields of study, but also the hitherto divided traditions of civic history-writing and academic historical studies.

This combination also gained momentum from the debate about the nature of Japanese capitalism, and the heated controversy over the characteristics of the modern Japanese economy and state viewed in historical perspective. Since this controversy was inseparable from the strategy for the coming reform and social revolution, the debate could not end as a mere show of learning. A remarkable publication followed: *Nihon Shihonshugi Hattatsu-shi Koza*, the seven-volume series of the 'Developmental History of Japanese Capitalism' (1932–33). It was a collective project intended to denounce the Rono group of Marxists who emphasized the modernity of the Japanese economy, the universal crisis of capitalism in the interwar period, and hence the inevitable socialist revolution to come. The Koza writers, on the other hand, emphasized not only Japan's backwardness but also the peculiar symbiosis of the Emperor system, hasty industrialization and poverty-stricken agriculture, which characterized Japanese capitalism. Hence the need first of all for democratic revolution.[28]

The prospectus of the Koza prepared by Iwanami Publishers declared:

> The characteristic merits of the publication included among others . . . the rejection of the hitherto common style of pedantry, compartmentalized specialism and idealism, as well as a mere analogy from foreign history . . . And the style of the series will not be too vulgar nor lose scientific exactness, but will be straightforward, clear and easy to understand.[29]

In fact the series was the result of a collaboration between Hani Goro (a prodigious freelance historian), Hattori Shiso (another freelancer), Noro Eitaro (secretary of the illegal Communist Party), Yamada Moritaro (former associate professor of economics at the Imperial University of Tokyo, recently dismissed), and others. The series came to be regarded as the manifesto of the Koza-group Marxist historians. From the viewpoint of Japanese historical studies the publication was important, in the long run, since it combined several specialized fields of study as well as the two separate streams of civic and academic history.

Among the contributors to this work, Yamada Moritaro (1897–1981) was outstanding. He revised chapters in the Koza and published his book 'Analysis of Japanese Capitalism' (1934), which would become a classic among students. The methodological preface to Yamada's work became very famous and influential. In fact the succinct text was crammed with esoteric expressions and idiosyncratic words.[30] Translated literally, Yamada's writing will make little sense. Let me break down my quotation and render it, at least, accessible. He emphasized the significance of the historical process in the formation of a national economy, stating that the peculiarities of a nation's economy were determined by its history. He did not neglect the international conditions of a nation's development, but he was more interested in the comparative study of national type/structure/characteristics in which he believed the agrarian basis was definitive, in order to discover the proper strategy of reform/revolution.

> First of all, [writes Yamada], the English absolutism from the end of the fifteenth century was terminated by the great revolution of 1648 [*sic*]. The precisely defined age of manufacturing (mid-sixteenth to mid-eighteenth centuries) was followed by the industrial revolution from 1760. Thus the classical structure of British capitalism based upon modern great land ownership is established. Next comes French capital-

ism which started with its great revolution of 1789 . . . and in relation to its tiny peasant ownership . . . In contrast to such formations, [in Britain, France Germany, Russia and the US], the characteristics of Japanese capitalism had its pre-history in the Tokugawa feudal despotism from the seventeenth century. Forced to begin again in 1868 under the pressure of advanced capitalist countries, the basis of Japanese capitalism remains peasant agriculture of semi-serfdom; yet the wars of 1894 and 1904 transformed Japan into an industrialized and imperialistic power. Hence the military and semi-servile type/formation of Japanese capitalism has been finally defined, which is peculiar, top-heavy and one of the meanest [worst] in world history . . .[31]

Yamada went on to mention the general crisis of world capitalism in the 1930s and implies its impending downfall. Yamada's analysis was particularly powerful when he placed the history and characteristics of the Japanese economy in a world perspective, and focused on several epochs of national history which determined the type/structure of a national economy. The recent history of Japan defined the 'military and semi-feudal structure' of its capitalism. At the same time, he presumes that every country must experience a bourgeois revolution as England and France did, before enjoying a fully-fledged civil society. Although his ultimate argument was reductionist and Marxist, his frame of mind had something in common with Fukuzawa's: commitment to the nation's transformation and his keen interest in the nation's destiny in the developmental stages of civilization. In fact his writing was strategic as well as academic.

The Koza group's schema provided a more determinist view of stages of development than the German Historical School did. Their 'scientific' appearance appealed not only to students of Japanese capitalism but also to many historians and social scientists in the mid-twentieth century. The other merit of Yamada's achievement was the encouragement it gave to further comparative study of histories of capitalism, especially Japan, Britain, France, Germany and the United States. Historical studies of several nations which had been isolated hitherto were provided with a common forum. For instance, two historical journals were launched in 1931 and 1933 (Table 9.1); Otsuka Hisao, Takahashi Kohachiro,[32] Matsuda Tomo and other young social and economic historians gathered to hold a small seminar on comparative history in 1937. This became an embryo for the Tochi Seido Shigakkai (Agrarian History Society), a Marxist economic history society which was established in 1948.

Otsuka Hisao and Maruyama Masao

Otsuka Hisao and Maruyama Masao were leading figures among the modernist, enlightened intelligentsia in mid-twentieth-century Japan. They shared patriotic concerns and confidence in progress, and were also well acquainted with the literary classics of East and West. As committed intellectuals they functioned as a dual bridge first between the ivory tower and the public sphere, and second between the scholarly achievements of the 1930s and the social responsibilities in the post-1945 period: at the end of the Second World War, Otsuka was 38 years old and Maruyama 31. They were professors at the University of Tokyo until their respective retirements in 1968 and 1971 and were frequent contributors to progressive magazines and academic journals.[33]

Maruyama, no economic historian, learned much about recent historical studies and debates from Otsuka, who was seven years his senior and had been a colleague at the Imperial University of Tokyo since 1939. It was Otsuka who influenced Maruyama's historical overview before and during the Second World War. For instance, the terms modern (*kindai-teki*) and premodern (*zenki-teki*) were borrowed from Otsuka as critical distinguishing concepts of a nation's history. Though the two might differ in interpreting the critical divide in human history – one looking to the Reformation and the other to the democratic revolutions at the end of the eighteenth century – they were both frank modernists.[34] Admittedly, Maruyama was to become more ambitious and wider in his interests after 1945, when he returned having survived both service in the army and the atomic bomb at Hiroshima. However, my point is that the very basis of his historical view and values had been formed since the 1930s under the mixed influence of Koza-ha Marxists and the modernist Otsuka. Maruyama would boast of himself as a Fukuzawa of the Showa period. Certainly he deserves to be viewed as the champion of Japanese enlightenment and permanent democratic revolution after 1945; however, his erudite knowledge of Marxism, history and the political theorists of the first half of the twentieth century (Laski, Mannheim and Schmitt) separates him from Fukuzawa.

The debate between the Koza-ha and Rono-ha of the 1930s revived with greater vigour in historical studies after 1945. The former group emphasized the peculiarities and typology of national histories, and the latter the structure of the worldwide economy. However, a more particular feature of the intellectual world of post-war Japan is that communists, socialists, progressivists and Christians went hand in hand to propagate and establish democracy and civilization throughout the country. Despite some serious inner struggles for leadership, they were all involved in a competitive alliance for democracy in the decades after 1945. Japan had not just been backward and poor, but unpardonable in committing itself to militarism and the invasion of its Asian neighbours up to 1945. Let the nation repent and civilize themselves again! Progressive and democratic, pacifist and industrious, the nation welcomed the Constitution of 1947 and supported the party of modernist alliance, the Socialist Party of Japan.

Otsuka's most important and influential book, 'Introduction to the Economic History of Modern Europe,'[35] was published in 1944; however, soon after this the publishing house and the copies in stock were destroyed in US air raids in spring 1945. The reissue of the book by another publishing house in 1946 was welcomed with enthusiasm, and it was awarded the book of the year prize (Shuppan Bunka Sho) by the Mainichi Shimbun. The book began with the age of the great European navigators in the fifteenth and sixteenth centuries and described the shift of the centre of economic activities (the commercial revolution) from the Mediterranean cities to northern Europe, and then further to England. Its title was 'The Economic History of Modern Europe', but it would be more accurately translated as 'The Social and Economic History of Early Modern Europe and the Beginning of the Hegemony of Modern England'. The development of English woollen and worsted industries was described, with an emphasis placed on the freedom and industrial/industrious spirit of rural men of middle rank and comparisons drawn with the early modern Dutch and French experience. As for documents he made good use of Historical Manuscripts Commission *Reports* and publications of local record societies, as well as *The Journals of the House of Commons*. They had been donated by Britain to the Library of the Imperial University of Tokyo after the devastating earthquake of 1923, and Otsuka made full use of these published documents, as well as recently published works by R. H. Tawney, G. Unwin, A. P. Wadsworth, and H. Heaton *plus* Weber and Marx. The interwar and wartime decades were a period of reaping and ruminating over the fruits of recent academic developments in history and the social sciences.

It may be surprising to present Otsuka Hisao (and not Kinnosuke) as the most important academic heir of Yamada and the Koza-ha Marxists. Otsuka was not a Marxist but a devout Christian of the 'no-church' group, a true puritan. He was a close pupil in faith of Yanaihara Tadao,[36] and politically he was a social democrat. However, in his historical studies Otsuka followed the analysis of Yamada and the Koza-ha, and focused his attention on the type/specificum of the national economy, and he regarded the bourgeois revolution as the divide in a nation's history. Japan, according to Otsuka, remained unsuccessful in its bourgeois/civic revolution, and so undoubtedly was a backward nation that desperately needed modernization. He and his followers did not interpret the social and political problems of the age as arising from modernity. Any problem which the nation suffered came from its backwardness and its immature civil society; history would provide the right escape. This frame of reference, that is an obsession with the backwardness/peculiarities of Japanese society, and faith in the universal development of civilization to come, derives from Fukuzawa, and shares with Marxists (the Koza group) its basic interpretation of history, though it is not necessarily committed to the same revolutionary strategy. This frame of reference has been bequeathed to the democratic citizens and historians of the post-1945 period.

Students and schoolteachers were keen to read Otsuka's books and articles on early modern English history (which dealt more with the social and cultural rather than the merely economic aspects). Readers welcomed Otsuka's work not just from an academic viewpoint, but also as a kind of historical compass to determine the destiny of the nation. England, as it was believed, offered historical lessons for modernizing Japan. Otsuka was more academic than Fukuzawa, but he knew his historical role as a protagonist of the nation's industry and reform. He was in fact another Fukuzawa in twentieth-century Japan. Otsuka's collected works were published in 13 volumes, and in 1992 he was belatedly awarded the highest national decoration, the Bunka Kunsho, for his historical studies and cultural merit by the Quaker-educated Emperor Akihito.

Conclusion

This chapter seeks to provide a broad perspective on the Japanese intellectual experience, as well as on the relationship between Britain and Japan. Stuart Hughes' account of French social thought in the years of desperation 1930–60[37] suggests parallels to the historical and theoretical pursuits of Japanese scholars of the same period. Japanese scholars absorbed and digested the scholarly achievements of interwar Britain and Europe, and constructed something distinctively Japanese. These young intellectuals considered themselves to be the 'cream of the intelligence of the age'.[38] However, their achievements remained largely unknown to the rest of the world because of the political and linguistic isolation of Japan, being transmitted only by a few academics, such as the Canadian historian and diplomat E. H. Norman. It was a tragedy of many twentieth-century Japanese intellectuals that their original achievements have been developed and published merely in their own language.

The deaths of Otsuka and Maruyama in the summer of 1996 were much lamented, because their loss meant not just the end of their intellectual contributions, but also the undermining of one of the central pillars of Japan's 'civil society' camp. Nationalism and national consciousness in twentieth-century Japan have been critically analysed by Sakai Naoki, Kan Sanjung, Victor Koschmann and Yamanouchi Yasushi who pointed to the narrowness, that is the lack of cosmopolitanism, among Japanese post-1945 democrats led by Otsuka and Maruyama.[39] I can agree with their criticism on most points, except for their criticism of Otsuka and Maruyama for searching for the peculiarities of the Japanese experience. Comparable trajectories of other nations who were not only latecomers to industrial capitalism, but also positive agents of their own nation-building since the late nineteenth century,[40] would be another rewarding topic for comparative analysis. Finally one should note that British influences on Japanese historical scholarship were not simply elements in a complex bilateral relationship, they were often part of a far broader interflow of European and Japanese ideas.

Notes

1. Some parallels can be noticed between my contribution to this volume and those of Tamotsu Nishizawa and Susan Townsend. This corroborates rather than weakens my argument that Britain and British studies have contributed to the modernist/progressive aspect of Japanese intellectual life.
2. Fukuzawa Yukichi, 'Introduction' to his five-volume *Works* (Tokyo, 1897). Cf. Fukuzawa's *Autobiography*, revised translation by E. Kiyooka (New York: Columbia University Press, 1966). Both are included in his complete works, *Fukuzawa Yukichi Zenshu*, 21 vols (Tokyo: Iwanami Shoten, 1958–71). The quote is from vol. I, pp. 27–8 (the author's translations are used throughout the chapter).
3. Because Japan used the lunar calendar until 1872, the end of the second year of the Keio era, which saw the appearance of the first part of *Seiyo Jijo* ('Conditions in the West'), corresponded to February 1867. (A difference of 34 days at the beginning of 1867.)
4. The sale of 250000 copies is more remarkable if we take into account that the population of the country then stood at slightly above 30 million. Cf. Miyaji Masato's editorial note in *Rekishi Ninshiki* (Historical Perceptions)*: Nihon Kindai Shiso Taikei* (Tokyo: Iwanami Shoten, 1991), p. 73; A. Hayami, 'Population changes', in M. Jansen and G. Rozman (eds), *Japan in Transition from Tokugawa to Meiji* (Princeton, NJ: Princeton University Press, 1986).
5. *Fukuzawa Yukichi Zenshu*, vol. I, p. 23.
6. Henry Thomas Buckle, *History of Civilization in England*, 2 vols (London: J. W. Parker and Son, 1857–61); François P. G. Guizot, *General History of Civilisation in Europe* (English translation) (Oxford, 1837); Fukuzawa Yukichi, *Bunmeiron no Gairyaku* (translated by D. Dilworth and C. Hurst as *An Outline of a Theory of Civilization* (Tokyo: Monumenta Nipponica Monograph, Sophia University, 1973)).
7. Ishizuki Minoru, *Kindai Nihon no Kaigai Ryugaku-shi* (History of study abroad in modern Japan) (Kyoto: Minerva, 1972); Ishizuki Minoru, 'Overseas Study by Japanese in the Early Meiji Period', in A. W. Burks (ed.), *The Modernizers: Overseas Students, Foreign Employers, and Meiji Japan* (Boulder: Westview, Press, 1985).
8. Carmen Blacker, *The Japanese Enlightenment: Study of the Writings of Fukuzawa Yukichi* (Cambridge: Cambridge University Press, 1964). On the other hand, Blacker's studies on the shadowy side of modernizing Japan include *The Catalpa Bow: a Study of Shamanistic Practices in Japan* (London: Allen & Unwin, 1975).
9. *Fukuzawa Yukichi Zenshu*, vol. I, p. 285.
10. Patriotism and concern for the destiny of the nation were shared both by the modernist/progressive camp and by those of the nationalist/romanticist camp. The former believed in the universal progress of civilization, the latter rejected the idea and stuck to the peculiarities of the Japanese/East. But both were alternative intellectual reactions against the military expansionism, overwhelming industrial capitalism and civilization of Western Europe in the late nineteenth

and early twentieth centuries. The logical consequence of this is that we may not be dealing with the peculiarities of the Japanese experience, but with some comparable trajectory of latecomer nations in the industrializing and modernizing world. Compare with Kondo Kazuhiko, *Bunmei no Hyosho Eikoku* (Civilized Britain as Represented in Modernizing Japan) (Tokyo: Yamakawa Shuppansha, 1998).

11. Since 1858 Keio School has been an independent and non-denominational institution, and it is now one of the most established private educational foundations, with educational institutions ranging from kindergarten to university (founded 1890).

12. University of Tokyo (ed.), *Tokyo Daigaku Hyakunen Shi* (100 Years of the University of Tokyo), 10 vols (Tokyo: Tokyo Daigaku Shuppankai, 1984–87).

13. G. G. Zerffi, *The Science of History, with an introductory letter by K. Suyematz* (London: privately printed, 1879), 773pp; G. G. Zerffi, 'The Historical Development of Idealism and Realism', *Transactions of the Royal Historical Society*, Old Series, V (1877)–VIII (1880); Frank Tibor, *Egy Emigrans Alakvaltasai: Zerffi Gusztav Palyakepe 1820–92* (1985); Japanese translation *Aru bomeisha no henshin* by Nishizawa Ryusei (Tokyo: Sairyusha, 1994); Margaret Mehl, 'Suematsu Kencho in Britain, 1878–86', *Japan Forum*, vol. 5, iss. 2 (1993), pp. 173–93.

14. Shigakkai (ed.), *Shigakkai Hyakunen Shoshi 1889–1989* (A Short History of the Shigakkai) (Tokyo, 1989).

15. Cf. I. Nish, *Japanese Foreign Policy 1869–1942: Kasumigaseki to Miyakezaka* (London: Routledge & Kegan Paul, 1977), p. 19.

16. Kume Kunitake's collected historical works in five volumes, which do not include *Beio Kairan Jikki*, were published by Yoshikawa Kobunkan (Tokyo: Yoshikawa Kobunkan, 1988–91). A museum has been established to commemorate him in Tokyo.

17. Tanaka Akira has compiled the definitive edition of Kume Kunitake, *Beio Kairan Jikki* ('Observations during the Round Visits to America and Europe') (originally *waso* 100 vols, 1878; Iwanami Bunko edition in 5 vols, Tokyo: Iwanami Shoten, 1978).

18. Kume Kunitake, *Beio Kairan Jikki* (Iwanami Bunko), vol. II, p. 22.

19. Ibid., vol. III, p. 72.

20. Ibid., vol. I, pp. 415–18, Tanaka's calculation.

21. *Shigaku Zasshi*, Nos 23–5 (1891); reprinted in *Shikai*, Volume 8 (1892).

22. Ludwig Riess continued to criticize the 'high-flown' arguments of some Japanese historians/intellectuals, and encouraged 'uncommitted' compilations of documents and fact-based research. He contributed to *Shigaku Zasshi* from 1889 to 1902. The pursuit of fact-based documentation bore fruit: *Dai Nippon Ishin Shiryo Kohon* (DNISK) was compiled and published by the Department of National History and later the Institute of Historiography (established 1929) of Tokyo Imperial University. For DNISK, or 'one of the greatest historiographical triumphs of mankind', see C. D. Totman, *The Collapse of the Tokugawa Bakufu* (Honolulu: Hawaii University Press, 1980), pp. 549–52.

23. Shibata Michio, 'Nihon ni okeru Yoroppa rekishigaku no juyo' (The Reception of European Historical Studies in Japan), in *Iwanami-koza Sekai-rekishi*, vol. 30 (Tokyo: Iwanami Shoten, 1971); Yamanouchi Yasushi, 'The Reorientation of Historical Studies: Japan', in G. C. Iggers and H. T. Parker (eds), *International Handbook of Historical Studies, Contemporary Research and Theory* (Westport, CT: Greenwood Press, 1980).

24. This phase of Shakai Seisaku Gaku (social policy studies) is described in K. B. Pyle, 'Meiji conservatism' in M. B. Jansen (ed.), *The Cambridge History of Japan, Volume 5 The Nineteenth Century* (Cambridge: Cambridge University Press, 1989), pp. 705–10.

25. On Fukuda and the German Historical School in Japan, see Nishizawa. 'Rekishi gaku-ha no juyo to hen'yo', *Shogaku Ronsan*, vol. XXXVIII (1997).

26. The decade after the First World War saw a rapid expansion of higher education: in 1920 students at high schools and universities comprised 1.6 per cent of the age group, in 1930 3.0 per cent, and in 1940 3.7 per cent. They still represented the cream of the nation. Tsutsui Kiyotada, *Nihon gata 'Kyoyo' no Unmei* (The demise of Japanese 'humanities') (Tokyo: Iwanami Shoten, 1995), p. 111.

27. Maruyama Masao, author's introduction to the English edition of *Studies in the Intellectual History of Tokugawa Japan* (Princeton: Princeton University Press, 1974), especially p. xxiv; Maruyama Masao, *Nihon no Shiso* [Japanese Thought] (Tokyo: Iwanami Shoten, 1961).

28. M. B. Jansen, in his introduction to *The Cambridge History of Japan, Volume 5*, pp. 41–3, epitomizes the arguments of the opposing two groups. But I emphasize that the Rono-ha predated the Koza-ha and the latter emerged against the once prevalent former group. See P. Duus and I. Scheiner, 'Socialism, liberalism and Marxism 1901–1931', in P. Duus (ed.), *The Cambridge History of Japan, Volume 6, The Twentieth Century* (Cambridge: Cambridge University Press, 1988), pp. 654–710; Nini Jensen, 'The debate over Japanese capitalism', in I. Nish (ed.), *Contemporary European Writing on Japan* (Ashford: Paul Norbury, 1988), pp. 68–76.

29. *Nihon Shihonshugi Hattatsu-shi Koza, Naiyo Mihon* (Prospectus) (Tokyo: Iwanami Shoten, 1932).

30. Yamada Moritaro did this intending to astound the imperial censor: see his preface to the Iwanami Bunko edition (1977) of *Nihon Shihonshugi Bunseki* (Analysis of Japanese Capitalism). The difficulties of another Marxist economist, Otsuka Kinnosuke, who was among the Koza-ha collaborators, between 1933 and 1945, is described by Tsuzuki Chushichi, 'Tenko or Teiko: The dilemma of a Japanese Marxist between the wars', in S. Henny and J. P. Lehmann (eds), *Themes and Theories in Modern Japanese History* (London: The Athlone Press, 1988).

31. Yamada, *Nihon Shihonshugi Bunseki*, pp. 7–9.

32. Takahashi Kohachiro (1912–82), or K. H. Takahashi as he liked to represent himself, was a friend of Otsuka and was among the founding members of *Past & Present: Journal of Historical Science* in Oxford in 1952.

33. Their collected works are each published by Iwanami Shoten (Tokyo): *Otsuka Hisao Chosakushu*, 13 vols (1969–86) and *Maruyama Masao Shu*, 17 vols (1995–97). All articles except the Introduction in Maruyama's *Thought and Behaviour in Modern Japanese Politics*, edited by I. I. Morris (Oxford: Oxford University Press, 1963) were written between 1945 and 1956.

34. See Maruyama's obituary of Otsuka, that is to say his last public remark in July 1996: *Asahi Shinbun*, Evening edition, 25 July 1996; *Maruyama Masao Shu*, Volume XVI (1996), pp. 259–60.

35. *Kindai Oshu Keizaishi Josetsu*, Part I (Tokyo: Nihon Hyoronsha/Jichosha, 1944); second revised edition in 1946.

36. Cf. Susan Townsend's essay in this volume.

37. H. S. Hughes, *The Obstructed Path* (New York: Harper and Row, 1968).

38. *Yamada Moritaro Chosakushu, Geppo 5* (Tokyo: Iwanami Shoten, 1984), p. 4.

39. The collaboration of the four and others see Yamanouchi Yasushi, Narita Ryuichi and J. Victor Koschmann, *Soryokusen to Gendaika* (Total War and Modernization) (Tokyo: Hakushobo, 1995); Sakai Naoki, Brett de Barry Nee and Iyotani Toshio, *Nashonariti no Datsu-kochiku* (Nationality Deconstructed) (Tokyo: Hakushobo, 1996).
40. There is something in common here with the debates over the German *Sonderweg* and over 'the peculiarities of the English'. Cf. Perry Anderson, *English Questions* (London: Verso, 1992).

10
Japanese Feminism and British Influences: The Case of Yamakawa Kikue (1890–1980)

Kei Imai

Preface

Yamakawa Kikue (née Aoyama, 1890–1980), the first socialist feminist in Japan, devoted her life to the liberation of Japanese women and the improvement of their domestic and social status, mainly as 'a warrior of the pen'.[1] At the time that she began writing, women's rights movements or liberal feminism had already been established in Britain for more than a century. Furthermore, news of British suffragettes and their demonstrations in London had been reported in the Japanese press as early as 1911.[2]

Yamakawa Kikue participated in the first Japanese women's movement, the Seito (Bluestocking) group, in which she was a prominent critic of its liberal wing. Through her broad study of women's movements in Europe, particularly Britain, she came to realize the difficulties which would be faced by women's movements in Japan, a country which retained much of its old feudalistic structure, producing social features which helped to strengthen the exploitative aspects of capitalist society.

Current research by Japanese and foreign scholars has concentrated on Kikue's insistence on women's sexual independence in reproductive matters, her socialist feminism,[3] and her work as the first director of the Women and Minors Bureau in the Ministry of Labour (after 1947). However, little has yet been written about how her pioneering ideas were formed, and why and how her views and attitudes changed from those of a 'socialist' to those of a 'rational democrat'.[4] In the evolution of her ideas, it is easy to discern numerous British influences. Her broad knowledge of research carried out by British scholars, and her deep insight into and analysis of diverse problems enabled her to form a definite socialist feminist view (which she had already encountered in her early days) which, according to Inumaru Giichi, was unsurpassed at the time.[5] In her appreciation of democratic or parliamentary socialism she was greatly assisted by her husband Yamakawa Hitoshi (1880–1958) whom she married in 1916 and who (in 1922) advocated greater contact with the Japanese masses.[6]

The Japanese 'Bluestocking' (Seito) and the beginning of Japanese feminism

The discussion of equal rights between men and women in Japan was begun by the Freedom and People's Rights advocates in the early Meiji period. Men such as Fukuzawa Yukichi (1834–1901), Ueki Emori (1857–1902) and others are renowned for their calls for women's education and female suffrage. Kishida Toshi (1863–1902) was the first woman activist and writer on equal rights. In fact, Yamakawa Kikue called her the 'Joan of Arc of Japan'. But the pioneering calls of these individuals for women's rights were blocked by the Imperial Constitution of 1889, the Imperial Rescript on Education of 1890 and the Meiji Civil Code of 1898. All these measures sought the construction of the *ie* (family) system according to which women were confined to the home without any meaningful rights. Women were required to be 'good wives and wise mothers'. For women, the last decade of the nineteenth century saw a return to the feudalism which the new Meiji government, in attempting to build a modern nation, had initially tried to overcome.

Yet at the beginning of the twentieth century, in the small circle of socialists who began their campaign against the Russo-Japanese War (1904–05), and then moved on to press for socialism, a faint light was lit for feminism by such women as Fukuda Hideko (1867–1927) and Kanno Suga (1881–1991). Fukuda had joined the Freedom and People's Rights movement and Kanno the Kyofukai (the Women's Reform Society, 1886–) and both women were active as feminists and socialists.

It was, however, in 1911 that feminism began in earnest in Japan with the foundation of the Seito (Bluestocking) group by Hiratsuka Raicho (1886–1971) and her followers. These women took the name Seito from the literary and intellectual circle called the 'Bluestockings' in eighteenth-century Britain, since, like their British sisters, they expected to achieve freedom and independence through literature and art.

In September 1911 the Seito group published Japan's first feminist journal *Seito* (Bluestocking). This contained Hiratsuka Raicho's famous opening lines: 'In the beginning, woman was the sun, an authentic person. Today she is the moon, living through others . . .'. This journal was published solely by women and in the first issue there were contributions from such renowned women as the poet Yosano Akiko (1878–1942) and the writer Tamura Toshiko (1884–1945). As a result *Seito* was widely publicized and gained a broad response from women who sought an outlet for their literary talent. In the beginning Raicho had only vague ideas about women's issues, but *Seito* gradually changed from being primarily a literary journal to being an avowedly feminist one. It placed an increased emphasis on those social and political issues which were important to women. Moreover, because it respected passion, love and freedom, it came into conflict with patriarchal ideas, and the maxim of 'good wife and wise mother'. As a result from 1912 *Seito* was kept under close surveillance by the police.

Yamakawa Kikue summed up the four-and-a-half years of activity of the Seito group by saying that they continued to erode the old patriarchal (family) system and made women aware of their oppression and the need to find ways to liberate themselves. She wrote that 'They succeeded in touching young hearts and kindling there the aspiration for liberty and independence.'[7] According to Kikue, the *Seito* society did not discover any geniuses among its unknown contributors, but it did allow members to discover their own discontents, which had hitherto lain dormant within themselves. She added that the reason *Seito* concentrated on the issue of 'self', particularly regarding love and marriage, was that these personal issues were the most important ones for middle- and upper-class Japanese women.

Yamakawa Kikue as a pioneer of modern feminism

Both Hiratsuka Raicho and Yamakawa Kikue opposed the old *ie* system to which all women were closely tied at that time. However, the remedies which they sought to apply in order to remedy this situation varied. Raicho wanted women to be mentally and, if possible, economically independent from their families. In other words she advocated an 'inner' solution whereas Kikue sought an 'outer' solution, seeking changes in the political and economic system. They also differed from each other as Raicho looked to middle-class women while Kikue looked to working-class women, though later the gap between these two leaders narrowed.

At an early stage in Kikue's development as a feminist, she referred to Edward Carpenter as well as Mary Wollstonecraft as pioneers of modern feminism. But soon Beatrice Webb and other British thinkers became more relevant to her interests.

Born into an intellectual family in 1890, Kikue became conscious of social issues at an early age. Her mother, a daughter of a Confucian scholar of the Mito domain, was one of the first graduates of Tokyo Women's Teachers' College (later Ochanomizu Women's University) which was founded in 1874, and as an enlightened woman she never neglected her daughters in favour of her son. Before her enrolment in 1908 at Joshi Eigaku Juku (the present-day Tsuda College), which was the first English-language academy, Kikue belonged to a literary group run by Baba Kocho (1869–1940). Because Baba was sympathetic towards radicals she took the presence of radicals for granted. Kikue's father sometimes bought the daily *Heimin-shinbun* (Common People's Newspaper), an early socialist paper, first published in 1907, saying that before long society would be changed into something more equal and just. But the experience which really awakened Kikue to social problems was a visit with the Salvation Army in 1908 to a spinning factory in the suburbs of Tokyo to preach and give Christmas presents. Girls of twelve to fifteen years of age gathered for the event and Kikue wrote:

> All during the ceremony I was seated on the platform but hated being there. I was filled with shame and anger. The girls had worked all night beside roaring machines. They were pale and bloodless. How could they be told that the life they led was due to God's blessings and that they should view this kind of slave labour as sacred and holy?[8]

When the Taisho era began in 1912 democracy was again discussed, more than twenty years after the failure of the Freedom and People's Rights Movement. At this time socialist journals were published and through them Kikue came across works on women by August Bebel and Edward Carpenter.[9]

Edward Carpenter (1844–1929) was perhaps the first English socialist to be introduced into Japan, his *Civilisation: Its Cause and Cure* being translated into Japanese in 1893.[10] Carpenter started his career as a fellow at Cambridge University, but he soon found the conventional atmosphere of the university vain and hypocritical. By the 1880s Carpenter was involved in socialist activities, and his brand of socialism attracted a broad range of people who accepted the Fabian Society and the Labour Party as well as syndicalism; indicating that his socialism was ethical rather than practical. He attacked existing class and property relationships and pleaded for a complete emancipation from class and sex.[11]

Carpenter's *Love's Coming-of-Age* (1896) reflected his views on the sexes and some sections of it were translated by Sakai Toshihiko (1870–1933) in 1905.[12] In this work Carpenter argued that 'the coming-of-age of Love (which harmonizes all the faculties in the human being) may take place early in the woman, while in the man it is long delayed and is, perhaps never completely effected'.[13] For 'its reasonable development and growth' he maintained that the following were necessary: (1) the furtherance of the freedom and self-dependence of women; (2) the provision of some rational sex education during the period of youth; (3) a more companionable and less exclusive relationship in marriage; (4) the abrogation or modification of the present odious law which binds people together for life in the most ill-assorted unions.[14]

Kikue herself had made an abridged translation into Japanese of Carpenter's *The Intermediate Sex* (1908) in 1914.[15] In his book Carpenter asserted that there are some 'Transitional Types of Men and Women', such as the feminine man and the masculine woman, or the non-warlike man and the non-domestic woman, and described homosexuality as 'healthy' and 'normal'. In her translation Kikue did not attempt any evaluation of this work. Later she portrayed Carpenter as a nineteenth-century utopian socialist and bachelor, and drew attention to his views on the contribution to society and humanity of bachelors like Leonardo da Vinci and Michelangelo.

She wanted Sakai Toshihiko to read Carpenter's writings more carefully, as they were fair and interesting, because she knew that Sakai despised spinsters.[16] Sakai was less interested in sexual issues than in contemporary social problems.[17] Yet for Kikue, a woman of rational intellect, but one who hated sewing and cooking, Carpenter's unorthodox views on sex must have been full of revelations. She also appreciated his support for birth control and the women's movement, both of which were being introduced into Japan at the time. She was critical of Ishikawa Sanshiro (1876–1956), a Japanese disciple of Carpenter's who was opposed to birth control, and she advised him to try to understand Carpenter's ideas more fully.[18]

It was under these circumstances that Kikue made her first contribution to the journal *Seito* in 1916.[19] In her first article she criticized Ito Noe (1895–1923), the common-law wife of the anarchist Osugi Sakae (1885–1923), for her views on prostitution. Noe was critical of the opposition of the Kyofukai to the licensed prostitution system, and her argument amounted to an approval of licensed prostitution. Indeed, Noe felt that prostitution, an age-old practice, had been established so firmly by male instinct that the system could not be abolished, whereas Kikue thought this was incorrect because she saw prostitution as the result of unnatural relations between men and women. Noe expressed preference for licensed, as opposed to private, prostitution, whereas Kikue supported the latter as a lesser evil. Licensed prostitution took a specially cruel form in Japan and Kikue felt that this had a deep link with women's poverty, which was exacerbated by patriarchy and feudal relationships, issues in which she was profoundly interested. Women, or often girls, were sold like goods to the licensed quarters (or industrial factories – to be discussed later) by their poor families, and they could not leave licensed quarters or even the brothel until all their debts had been cleared.

Noe's arguments, based on passion and desire, were no match for the rational analysis presented by Kikue, who pointed out the double standard in morals which was applied differently to men and women. Kikue also informed the readers that in Britain, even compulsory medical examinations to prevent the spread of venereal disease were ended in 1886 to accord with the human rights of prostitutes which had been recognized, after the long and indefatigable struggles of Josephine Butler and her followers.

In her next article, entitled 'Modern Life and Prostitutes', Kikue concluded:

What is necessary in future relations between men and women is not idolatry based on obsolete and hollow 'chastity' but self-control based on the consciousness of being a human being and a member of society. This is equally necessary for men and women, and essential to the happiness of both sexes and their descendants. With the development of free association between the sexes and the consciousness of self-control, we can for the first time afford to choose our own partners. If like today, men and women are isolated and total indulgence is given to the one and absolute asceticism to the other, there would be no understanding or sympathy between the two, and such a society would be very vulnerable.[20]

Here we can see Kikue's brave challenge to the taboo of sex and her balanced understanding of the sexual instinct which was neither too moralistic nor too liberal or libertarian. This was the lesson she learnt from Edward Carpenter, whose *The Intermediate Sex* she admired. Kikue also completed her translation of Carpenter's *Love's Coming-of-Age* in 1921.

The key points in Kikue's analysis of prostitution rested on her contention that prostitution had economic as well as educational roots, which were designed to force women into obedience. Therefore for the solution of the problem, she felt that one would have to wait for an economic revolution which would overcome poverty, and for the emancipation of women and women's educational improvement. She regretted that an influential socialist like Sakai Toshihiko expressed no opinion regarding licensed prostitution though her own husband Yamakawa Hitoshi, Osugi Sakae and Arahata Kanson (1887–1981) all strongly objected to it.[21]

The second figure whose life and writings had a profound impact on Kikue was Mary Wollstonecraft (1759–97). It was Kikue who introduced Wollstonecraft's work to Japan for the first time in her essay *The History of Women's Movements* in 1916. Kikue had read Wollstonecraft's *Vindication of the Rights of Women* while a student at Joshi Eigaku Juku, and when the women's suffrage movement was at its height in Britain. In her essay she refers to Wollstonecraft's *Vindication* as 'one of the most original books of the eighteenth century and even now a treasury of the women's movement'.[22] In this work Wollstonecraft had cursed unjust discrimination against women and women's non-education, and she had also expressed her disbelief in the so-called 'virtues' of women – namely, submission, shame, flattery and meanness.

Wollstonecraft was again cited by Kikue two years later when she plunged into the famous debate between Yosano Akiko, the equal rights feminist, and Hiratsuka Raicho, the mothers' rights feminist, around the subject of the economic independence of women and the protection of motherhood.[23] Kikue compared Yosano to Wollstonecraft and Hiratsuka to the Swedish feminist Ellen Key and paid due respect to both sides of the argument. But at the same time she predicted that even if both policies were to be adopted this would still be insufficient, as had been shown in Britain.

In Britain from 1909 to 1910 the same issue had been discussed by the Fabian Women's Group and resulted in the pamphlet *The Endowment of Motherhood*. Later, in 1916, Eleanor Rathbone took up this issue again and campaigned for many years for the introduction of the 'Family Allowance' which was finally granted in 1945. In reality this was intended to help mothers bring up their children, not to ensure women's economic independence which feminists, like Rathbone, had originally demanded. Kikue commented:

> Women are not animals with no ability other than bringing up children, nor are they obliged to end their lives by staying at home; in addition they have no right to live off society while doing nothing. Therefore women must be allowed to work in accordance with their abilities and desires. They must also be allowed the right of life in reward for their work . . . [Yet each have their defects:] 'women's rights' [advocates] only advocate the right to work, forgetting the right of life, while the 'mother's rights' movement requested the right of life only for mothers, but not for everyone.[24]

Kikue also noted the time lag of about a century between Wollstonecraft and Key. She stated that it was to be expected that in the time of the former (that is, the early period of capitalism) women, and especially middle-class women, would have argued for the identity of women, freedom of education, expansion of occupational opportunities, economic independence and votes for women. But in Key's time (the later period of capitalism), when many women worked outside the home, it was natural that social and economic problems such as low pay, overwork and the destruction of the family would become major concerns. Wollstonecraft and Key had both reflected on the plight of women and warned them of various pitfalls in their own respective times, but they had not necessarily contributed to any fundamental solutions of these problems.[25] Thus Kikue highlighted what she took to be weak points in the arguments presented by such outstanding feminist writers as Wollstonecraft, Yosano, Key and Hiratsuka while honouring them for the role which each played in their own time.

The controversy over 'the protection of motherhood' among three such distinguished feminist writers as Yosano, Hiratsuka and Yamakawa had a profound impact on the history of women's liberation in modern Japan, and in the course of this controversy Kikue's feminism reached a mature stage in which she began to advocate a change in society for women, and embraced the cause of socialist feminism.

Yamakawa's perception of women workers in Britain and Japan

In Britain the First World War helped to give women the vote in 1918 and opened up the professions to them in the following year. Kikue now felt that the first phase of women's movements in Britain, which had begun in the mid-nineteenth century – to secure freedom of education and employment, and to achieve women's suffrage – was now ended.[26] These had been the demands of middle-class women and had been largely realized. Therefore, according to Kikue, the second period was now beginning and it was time for the awakening of working women. She became more interested in the conditions of women workers in Britain in order to anticipate the problems of their Japanese sisters. In 1918, when she was invited to read a paper on 'Women and Occupations'[27] to the Japan Academy of Social Policy, a male-established and male-dominated society, she outlined five issues which constituted the problems facing working women, and which were based on research by B. L. Hutchins, Beatrice Webb and others. These issues were: protection of women workers, women's low wages, women's organizations, harmony between work and marriage, and infant mortality. Then Kikue cited the proposals made by Clementina Black, the editor of *Married Women's Work*: the establishment of a minimum wage, the introduction of improved methods of child nurture, a demand for the endowment of mothers, and the right of wives to a fixed share of their husbands' incomes. Kikue agreed with these measures and added that the question of how well children were brought up was more important than who brought them up, and that there would be no problem in their being brought up by professionals.[28] In her own conclusions she predicted a bright future for women's work:

> Whatever harmful effects and misery women's occupations entail in this process, they have clearly an evolutionary meaning in terms of the changes they will bring to women's views, and the social reforms that evils and misery will accelerate. I believe that in the end when work loses the character of compulsory toil for the benefit of others . . . work will, regardless of sex, be pleasant work for [the workers'] satisfaction and for social service . . . , [something] now only some of the privileged are enjoying.[29]

What then was the situation of women workers in Japan? Kikue found similar problems to those existing in Britain, but in addition she noticed sufferings peculiar to Japan, caused by the remains of feudal relationships which provided a base for the sweated labour system. However, she believed that the 'economic and social foundations' of feudalism had already passed away after the Meiji Restoration.

In 1922 Kikue published an English-language article entitled 'Women in Modern Japan'[30] in serial form from January to September (excluding May and August). Kikue's article was highly acclaimed as 'the first comprehensive Marxist history of Japanese women and women's issues' covering the whole period from the Meiji Restoration to 1922.[31] It described a rapid increase in the number of women workers, which stood at 13 million in 1922, of whom four million had independent jobs. She analysed the working life of the women engaged in agriculture, home industries, the silk and cotton industries, mining and others, referring to the government statistics of 1918 and the first report of factory inspectors in the same year. Working conditions in every trade and industry were appalling because many workplaces were not covered by the factory law which had been enacted in 1916 (a hundred years after the first British act). Even in those Japanese workplaces that were covered by the law, it was often ignored. Women and girls were so poorly organized that they were unable to revolt against these conditions except in a few cases. Feudalistic ideology and attitudes obstructed the improvement of their lives.

Concerning the relationship between capitalism and feudalism, Kikue noted that the *ie* (family) system and the customs based upon it provided a cheap and docile workforce of girls[32] which formed a large proportion of the female labour employed in the textile industry. Kikue analysed in detail how these girls had been taken from very poor villages with advance payments of their wages being handed to their parents. These workers accounted for around 70 per cent of young women or girls of around twelve years old, and most of them lived in factory dormitories. In these dormitories, they looked upon the manager as their father, thus bringing the custom of feudalistic *ie* dependence from home into the factory. Therefore, the young women thought it natural that under this patriarchal system their wages were lower than men's and that the personal freedom given to men was not granted to them. As a result attending a union meeting was impossible.[33] Kikue concluded that the education and organization of women were urgently needed.

In this setting Kikue was involved in forming the Sekirankai (Red Wave Society), the first women's socialist group, in the spring of 1921. However, because of repression by the police, its members could not act freely, but simply held small lecture meetings until 1925 when the society was dissolved. Kikue's writing in those years was very sharp and critical of the activities of 'bourgeois women', in particular those of the Shinfujin Kyokai (New Women's Society, 1920–22), the first nationwide women's organization, founded by Hiratsuka Raicho, Ichikawa Fusae (1893–1987) and Oku Mumeo (1895–1997). These groups were composed largely of middle-class women, who had been encouraged by the granting of women's suffrage in other countries. They felt it necessary to unite women in Japan regardless of class distinction and attacked 'class-war' theories. They actively lobbied Diet members for the vote and succeeded in obtaining the reform of the Peace Police Law in 1922. As a result the right to hold or attend political meetings was granted to women – but not the right to join political organizations or to vote. Sharon L. Sievers, the American historian, has said, 'It seemed that at last the connection between Meiji feminism with its stress on equality and political rights, and Taisho feminism with its emphasis on the spiritual and creative strengths of women, had been made.'[34] Yet Kikue insisted that 'it would be wrong for them to waste the energy of women workers in lobbying, for an improvement of the working conditions, . . . [the overthrow] (blank in the original to escape censorship) of capitalism would have relieved them'.[35] She also asserted that Hiratsuka's current ideas were nothing but a charitable pastime – added to the playful instinct of the Seito period.[36] Sometimes Kikue seemed to be very partisan and hasty, in her views of possible changes that might soon have occurred in Japan. But her impetuosity gradually changed and during these years the Yamakawas were active in spreading information about Russia after the 1917 revolution. Kikue also translated western publications on women and labour, such as Beatrice Webb's 'The Wages of Man and Woman' in 1920, Carpenter's *Love's Coming-of-Age* in 1921 as mentioned above, and August Bebel's *Women and Socialism* in 1923. Her husband Yamakawa Hitoshi, in collaboration with Arahata Kanson, translated and published the Webbs' *History of Trade Unionism* in 1920.

Through these and similar activities, including discussions with young activists, and with the prospect of the enactment of universal suffrage in the near future Yamakawa Hitoshi formed a new strategy, and published an article entitled 'A Change of Direction in the Proletarian Class Movement'[37] in 1922. In this article he proposed that the leaders of the movement should 'go to the masses', because up to this time the campaign had been led by a handful of intellectuals and workers, with few followers. He wrote 'our movement should be based on the real demands of people not on ideal socialism, and should put more emphasis than now on the improvement of their present day lives'. Under his influence Kikue became more cooperative with middle-class women in their campaigns for the abolition of licensed prostitution and for 'universal women's suffrage'.[38] At the same time, she increased her attempts to approach 'the working woman' and 'the professional woman' who formed part of 'the masses' whom Hitoshi appealed to.

At this time Kikue's main concern had become how to address 'women's questions' properly in the context of the working-class movement. She believed that three measures could be taken to benefit working and working-class women: First, to present a concrete proposal in the form of 'Women's Special Demands' to the Seiji Mondai Kenkyukai (Political Issues Research Association) which might have developed into a united working-class (legal Marxist) party; second to establish a 'women's section' in the Hyogikai Chuo Honbu,[39] and third to form a women's council which would consist of the representatives of various working women's organizations.[40] In formulating these proposals, Kikue was influenced by British experience which she found in the research carried out by Barbara Drake on women workers' special demands to the Labour Party, the women's section of the Trades Union Congress[41] and the Joint Standing Committee of Women's Industrial Organizations.[42] In 'Women's Special Demands', Kikue claimed that 'to the extent that the important mission of a proletarian party, which is now going to be formed, is the establishment of political and social democracy, . . . it would be a just duty to represent the demand for democracy for all women'.[43]

In the 'Programme for the Women's Section' Kikue also emphasized that because of the huge increase in women workers (who constituted 58 per cent of all factory workers in Japan), they played an important role in the labour movement. Furthermore, the feudalistic relationship between men and women, and the latter's position of dependence, were both evils in the world of labour. She listed concrete demands which concerned, in particular, the everyday lives of women such as six hours' work per day; the abolition of night work, the dormitory system and compulsory savings.[44]

However, the proposal for a women's section was rejected in 1925 and again in 1926. Kikue repeatedly pointed out the need for immediate unionization, as in Japan less than one per cent of all female factory workers were members of a union, while in Britain in 1925, around 20 per cent were unionized.[45] Even the British figure of 20 per cent was far below that of men, and there had been an ongoing discussion on how to increase the number of women union members.

As the Hyogikai seemed reluctant to encumber trade unions with political issues such as the abolition of feudalism, Kikue maintained that it would be difficult to separate feudalism from capitalism in Japan, as these were so closely intertwined. The Hyogikai's declared intention to form a Women's (Political) League, which would include 'petit bourgeois women', outside the Hyogikai,[46] was contradictory to international trends and also to Comintern policy.[47] Kikue believed that since women had no political rights in Japan, and the number of women activists was so limited, trade unions and their women's sections were the only places where women could be trained and educated.

Kikue's proposal, which was based upon a thorough study of the elaborate network of women workers' organizations existing in Britain, was finally approved in 1927. Surprisingly the Hyogikai's plan for a Women's League was accepted – at the cost of the women's section, because women activists in the section (there were never many) were required to work for the League. Later two more women's leagues were founded. Each was affiliated to its respective political party (centrist and rightist), which is what Kikue had feared. Meanwhile the Kanto Women's League (communist) was disbanded in the following year, the reason given being that it was sex-based. Again, this decision was made by the male leaders, without consulting its women leaders.

As Tanaka Sumiko has commented, the controversy over the 'women's section' was not merely a simple dispute between Kikue and the unsympathetic, undemocratic male leaders of the Hyogikai. It was also caused by differences in ideas and policies, and the disparity of political approaches between the Comintern communists and the *Rono* group to which the Yamakawas belonged.[48] In June 1923 the clandestine Communist Party of Japan was severely suppressed and disbanded itself in the following year. For these reasons neither Hitoshi nor Kikue joined the second Communist Party, which was re-established in 1926, but instead founded their own political journal *Rono* (Labour-Farmer) with Sakai Toshihiko in December 1927. This led to a complete split in the socialist movement in Japan, leaving the *Rono* group as a minority. Kikue was responsible for the 'Women's Edition' of *Rono* from May to November 1928.

Controversy over the 'women's section' occurred at a time of confusion and immaturity[49] in the left-wing movement in Japan. This immaturity had much influence on the outcome of the debate about 'women's questions'. The cutting edge of Kikue's arguments was exceedingly sharp and clear, but she retired from the front line of socialist journalism in 1928, because of her son's illness. However, she continued to write on more general topics in such journals as *Chuo Koron, Fujin Koron, Kaizo* and others. The real reasons for her retirement seem to have been twofold: divisions in the left wing on the one hand, and the rise of militarism on the other. It was also said that she might have lost her vision of the rapid development of women's movements.[50] What is clear is that in March and April 1928, many active communists were rounded up and arrested by the government.

Kikue, as well as Hitoshi, came to believe more and more in an independent path to socialism, accepting the concepts of 'social democracy' and sometimes even 'bourgeois democracy' within a legal framework, which would help the gradual awakening of working women. By then they seemed to have become a type of social democrat who regarded 'enlightenment, gradualism and anti-radicalism' as more relevant to society, though they did not describe themselves in these terms.[51] However, even such a modest approach to action was closed to them due to the totalitarian forces of militarism and the war. In this period they were forced to maintain a long political silence, which Kikue later reflected upon: 'Now, when I remember, I feel as if there has been no history of the people's activities but only the history of persecution by the government since the Meiji era, because there has been such a long, blank period in political and social movements in Japan.'[52]

Yamakawa Kikue and Britain after the Second World War

There is some debate concerning the roles played by Yamakawa Kikue prior to and during the Second World War.[53] However, the democratization of Japan imposed by the American forces (1945–52), especially in the early occupation period, supplied her with opportunities to put her long cherished aims into practice.

Firstly, in 1947, she assumed the office of the first director of the Women and Minors Bureau, in the Ministry of Labour, under the first socialist government of Katayama Tetsu (1887–1978). She began by appointing as many women civil servants and private citizens as possible as heads of women and minors sections in local government, and made efforts to spread equality between the sexes and to develop democracy among local people.[54]

She conducted research on women workers and framed regulations for better working conditions for them. She ensured that labour laws and trade union laws, which would protect women workers, were widely known. Furthermore, she established a 'women's week' in April to call for the advancement of the position of women in Japan, which is observed even today.[55]

She also distributed a great deal of information on the life of working women in Britain, the welfare state and the policies of the Labour Party which she had gathered while staying in Britain from 1951 to 1952. She was initially invited by the British government with four other women for a month, but she stayed longer. Kikue observed two things in particular: first the everyday life of working people in the industrialized North; their educational, social and recreational institutions; trade unions and co-operatives. She noticed that all of these institutions and facilities were run by working people; it was noteworthy that in Britain workers themselves planned measures for their life and work, and that their generosity arose from their self-confidence which derived from their independence and stable life. She observed that more than half of the women working in the cotton mills were married, 'tall, full-bosomed and of good complexion'. She wrote:

What I was struck with whenever I visited a mill, was the difference in the age and physique of women workers. In Japan each time I visited a textile factory, I was sorry to see that small girls, like peas, were pressed by the machines, roaring and turning round at full speed . . . If they had visitors to the factory, they became much too nervous to reply [to an enquiry], . . . whereas here [in Britain] they nodded with a smile.[56]

Secondly Kikue was interested in the activities and organization of the British Labour Party. She reappraised the fact that by adopting its constitution of 1918, the Party had proclaimed a socialist platform and expanded its membership to include ordinary citizens and intellectuals as individual members, being based upon local parties. Kikue admired the activities of rank-and-file members of the party and the unions. These included the 'collectors' – mostly women who collected fees while reminding workers of the importance of unions – and thus supported the Labour Party financially.[57] But she was rather critical of the union leaders, most of whom were on the right wing of the Party.

In her article entitled 'Why was the Labour Party Defeated?' (1955) and other writings,[58] Kikue commented on the domination of the Party by right-wing members from the big trade unions. In many unions the chief secretary and the paid staff appointed by him had too much power and wouldn't listen to the voices of ordinary union members. On women's issues within the Party, she commented on demands from the left,[59] including those of Aneurin Bevan, who wanted to reform the way women were represented on the National Executive Committee.

Kikue valued highly the progress of the welfare system and the stable life of working-class people in Britain. However, she recognized that class differences still remained noticeable because only the most extreme evils had been removed from the system of production for profit. She concluded her account of her journey by saying that 'Britain is not yet a socialist paradise', but that paradise 'would be attained by the power of many people who dedicate themselves to their beliefs without seeking recognition'.[60]

In 1953 she began publishing *Fujin no Koe* (The Voice of Women) in cooperation with the left-wing members of the Japan Socialist Party. This small monthly organ was called Kikue's 'souvenir of Britain', because she had been inspired to educate and organize women, by *The Labour Woman*, the vehicle of the Women's Section of the British Labour Party.

Then, in 1961, at the age of seventy she established the Fujin Mondai Konwakai (its English name has been Japan Women's Forum since 1985) when the publication of 'The Voice of Women' ended. The purpose of the Forum is to conduct general research into women's issues regardless of ideology and belief. Its 'News', a quarterly publication, has been issued on a regular basis since 1965.

Conclusion

Yamakawa Kikue played a distinguished role in introducing western ideas and experience of women's emancipation to Japan – in particular, those of the British women's movement. She was also a distinguished publicist and a promoter of labour policies for women in Japan. Above all, she was equipped with great knowledge of the history and conditions of women both in Japan and Britain.

Now, when we re-examine her work over the entire span of her life, her 'narrow minded, sectarian, impatient' criticism of 'bourgeois feminism' in her early period can be seen in its proper perspective. In her later years she approached middle-class feminism with more tolerance and understanding.

Regarding extreme leftists (the communists of those days), she found that they lacked a sense of democracy, illustrated by their unsympathetic treatment of women's demands. Against the criticism that she was not a woman of deeds,[61] it can be asserted that she played a pioneering role as a woman of the 'intelligentsia' in an international mould, working under the powerful hostile pressures of prewar and wartime Japanese nationalism and militarism. Perhaps her intellectual and international character created barriers between ordinary men and women and herself. However, she sought to put her ideas into practice in order to achieve the liberation of ordinary citizens. However we view Kikue, it is clear that in more recent times the situation of Japanese women has certainly changed due to a significant increase in the number of Japanese women who, like Yamakawa Kikue, are well educated and endowed with an international outlook.

Notes

1. Tanaka Sumiko, 'Kaidai 1, Fujinbu Ronso to Sono Shuhen', in Tanaka Sumiko and Yamakawa Shinsaku (eds), *Yamakawa Kikue Shu* (The Selected Works of Yamakawa Kikue), 10 vols and a supplementary volume (Tokyo: Iwanami Shoten, 1981–82), vol. 4, p. 309. Hereafter cited as YKS.
2. Hasegawa Nyozekan, *Rondon! Rondon?* (1912. repr. Tokyo: Iwanami Bunko, 1996), pp. 279–390.
3. 'Yamakawa Kikue Seitan Hyakunen Kinen Symposium: Gendai Feminizumu to Yamakawa Kikue', *Nihon Fujin Mondai Konwakai Kaiho*, vol. 51 (1991), pp. 59–77.
4. Tanaka Sumiko, 'Fujinshonen Kyokucho Jidai no Yamakawa Kikue Sensei', *Nihon Fujin Mondai Konwakai Kaiho: Yamakawa Kikue Sensei Tsuito Go*, vol. 34 (1981), p. 7.
5. Inumaru Giichi et al. (interview), 'Yamakawa Kikue-shi ni Kiku: Nihon ni okeru Marukusushugi Fujinron no Keisei Katei', *Rekishi Hyoron*, no. 335 (March 1978), p. 17.
6. Yamakawa Hitoshi, 'Musan Kaikyu Undo no Hokotenkan', *Zen'ei* (1922), vol. 2, no. 1, pp. 20–9.
7. Yamakawa Kikue, 'Women in Modern Japan', *Shakaishugi Kenkyu*, vol. VI, no. 2 (September 1922), p. 2.
8. 'Rodo Shinsei', YKS, vol. 9, p. 159. Translated by Mikiso Hane, *Reflections of the Way to the Gallows* (Berkeley: University of California Press, 1988), p. 167.
9. Yamakawa Kikue, *Nijusseiki o Ayumu: Aru Onna no Ashiato* (Tokyo: Yamato Shobo, 1978), p. 150.
10. See Chushichi Tsuzuki, 'My Dear Sanshiro: Edward Carpenter and His Japanese Disciple', *Journal of Hitotsubashi Academy* (Hitotsubashi University, 1972).
11. Chushichi Tsuzuki, *Edward Carpenter 1844–1929: Prophet of Human Fellowship* (Cambridge: Cambridge University Press, 1980). Also J. M. Bellamy and J. Saville *Dictionary of Labour Biography*, vol. II (London: MacMillan, 1974), pp. 85–92.
12. Edward Carpenter, *Love's Coming-of-Age*, translated by Sakai as *Seijuku no Koi*. Published in 1915 as a book entitled *Jiyushakai no Danjokankei* (Tokyo: Toundo Shoten, 1915).
13. Carpenter, *Love's Coming-of-Age*, p. 27. Translated by Yamakawa Kikue, *Ren'airon* (Tokyo: Daitokaku, 1921, repr. Sanko Shorin, 1946), pp. 33–4.
14. Ibid., p. 100.
15. E. Carpenter, *The Intermediate Sex: Study of Some Transitional Types of Men and Women* (1908, repr. London: George Allen & Unwin Ltd., 1952), Translated by Aoyama Kikue, 'Chuseiron', *Safuran* (May–July 1914), May, pp. 1–22, June, pp. 130–53 and July, pp. 55–76.
16. 'Yamakawa Kikue-shi ni Kiku', p. 12.
17. Sakai Toshihiko, 'Kutsumi-kun e', *Shin Shakai*, no. 5 (January 1916), p. 3.
18. 'Ishikawa Sanshiro-shi to Hininron' and 'Hinin Zehi nitsuite Futatabi Ishikawa Sanshiro-shi ni Atau', *Onna no Sekai* (March/June 1921), UKS, 2, pp. 244, 290–2.
19. Aoyama Kikue, 'Nihon Fujin no Shakai Jigyso ni tsuite Ito Noe-shi ni Atau', *Seito* (January 1916), YKS, vol. 1, pp. 2–12. For criticism of Kikue, see Fujime Yuki, *Sei no Rekishigaku* (Tokyo: Fuji Shuppan, 1998), p. 168.
20. Aoyama Kikue, 'Gendai Seikatsu to Baishunfu', *Shin Shakai* (July 1916), YKS, vol. 1, pp. 61–2.
21. YKS, vol. 9, p. 203.
22. Aoyama Kikue, 'Fujin Undo no Enkaku', *Sekaijin* (May 1916), YKS, vol. 1, p. 29.

23. 'Bosei Hogo to Keizaiteki Dokuritsu: Yosano/Hiratsuka Nishi no Ronso', *Fujin Koron* (September 1918), YKS, vol. 1, pp. 176–84.
24. Ibid., pp. 193–4.
25. Ibid., p. 194.
26. 'Fujin Undo ni Arawaretaru Shin Keiko', *Chugai* (December 1918), YKS, vol. 1, p. 201.
27. 'Fujin to Shokugyo Mondai', *Kokka Gakkai Zasshi* (February/March 1919), YKS, vol. 2, pp. 2–39. Yamakawa owed her opinion to B. L. Hutchins, *Women in Modern Industry* (London, 1915, repr. Garland Publishing, Inc. 1980); Beatrice Webb, *The Wages of Men and Women: Should They be Equal?* (The Fabian Society, 1919). Abridged translation by Kikue, *Kaizo* (August 1920), repr., *Josei Kaiho-e* (Tokyo: Nihon Fujin Kaigi, 1977), and Clementina Black (ed.), *Married Women's Work: Being the Report of an Inquiry Undertaken by the Women's Industrial Council* (London, 1915, repr. London: Virago, 1983).
28. Black, *Married Women's Work*, p. 14.
29. 'Fujin to Shokugyo Mondai', YKS, vol. 2, p. 38.
30. Kikue, 'Women in Modern Japan' (January to September 1922, exc. May and August).
31. 'Yamakawa Kikue-shi ni Kiku', pp. 19–20.
32. For criticism of the docile and submissive image of textile mill workers, see E. Patricia Tsurumi, 'Female Textile Workers and the Failure of Early Trade Unionism in Japan', *History Workshop Journal* (Autumn 1984), pp. 3–27.
33. 'Musankaikyuundo ni okeru Fujin no Mondai,' *Kaizo* (January 1926), YKS, vol. 4, pp. 134–6.
34. Sharon L. Sievers, *Flowers in Salt: the Beginnings of Feminist Consciousness in Modern Japan* (Stanford: Stanford University Press, 1983), p. 187.
35. 'Shin Fujin-Kyokai to Sekiran-kai', *Taiyo* (July 1921), repr, Maruoka Hideko (ed.), *Nihon Fujin Mondai Shiryo Shusei* (Tokyo: Domesu Shuppan, 1976), vol. 8, p. 266.
36. Ibid., p. 267.
37. Yamakawa Hitoshi, 'Musankaikyuundo no Hokotenkan', *Zen'ei* (August 1922), pp. 16–25. For the significance of this article, see Koyama Hirotake and Kishimoto Eitaro (eds), *Nihon no Hi-kyosanto Marukusushugisha: Yamakawa Hitoshi No Shogai to Shiso* (Tokyo: San'ichi Shobo, 1962), pp. 90–4. Also Stephen S. Large, *Organized Workers and Socialist Politics in Interwar Japan* (Cambridge: Cambridge University Press, 1981), pp. 45–50.
38. 'Musan Fujin Undo no Ninmu to Sono Hihan', *Rono* (March/May 1928), YKS, vol. 5, pp. 107–8.
39. The Nihon Rodo Kumiai Hyogikai (the left-wing trade union federation) was formed in 1925 after the split of the Nihon Rodo Sodomei founded in 1912.
40. 'Musan Fujin Undo no Ninmu to Sono Hihan', YKS, vol. 5, pp. 115–16. See also Vera Mackie, *Creating Socialist Women in Japan* (Cambridge: Cambridge University Press, 1997), pp. 105–8.
41. Barbara Drake, *Women in Trade Unions* (London: Virago, 1984; 1st edn 1920). Abridged translation by Yamakawa Kikue, 'Eikoku Fujin Rodo Kumiai Undoshi', *Fujin to Rodo* (August 1925) and *Fujin Undo* (September 1925; the title was changed from this issue onwards). See also 'Fujin Rodosha to Rodo Kumiai', *Kaizo* (October 1926, repr. *Josei Kaiho-e*.), pp. 95–104; 'Eikoku Rodo Fujin no Seijiteki Katsudo', *Fujin Koron* (December 1925).
42. 'Eikoku no Josei Rodo-sha', *Josei no Hangyaku* (Tokyo: Santokusha, 1922), pp. 199–202.

43. ' "Fujin no Tokushu Yokyu" ni tsuite', *Hochi Shimbun* (5 to 16 October 1925), YKS, vol. 4, p. 78.
44. 'Fujinbu Teze', *Nihon Rodo Kumiai Hyogikai Zenkoku Fujinbu Kyogikai* (25 December 1925), YKS, vol. 4, pp. 102–22.
45. 'Musan Kaikyu Undo ni okeru Fujin no Mondai', *Kaizo* (January 1926), YKS, vol. 4, pp. 141–2.
46. Tanaka Sumiko, 'Kaidai 1: Fujinbu Ronso to Sono Shuhen', ibid., p. 90; 'Musan Fujin Undo no Ninmu to Sono Hihan', YKS, 5, pp. 111–16.
47. YKS, vol. 5, p. 126.
48. Tanaka Sumiko, 'Kaidai 1', YKS, vol. 4, p. 289.
49. Inumaru Giichi, 'Nohon ni okeru Marukusushugi Fujinron no Ayumi', in Joseishi Sogo Kenkyukai (ed.), *Nihon Josei Shi*, vol. 5, *Gendai* (Tokyo: Tokyo Daigaku Shuppankai, 1982), p. 167.
50. Yamada Ko, *Josei Kaiho no Shisokatachi* (Tokyo: Aoki Shoten, 1987), p. 171.
51. Hanzawa Hiroshi, 'Ronoha to Jinminsensen: Yamakawa Hitoshi o megutte', in Shiso no Kagaku Kenkyukai (ed.), *Kyodo Kenkyu: Tenko, Chu* (Tokyo: Heibonsha, 1978, 1st edn, 1960), pp. 409–13.
52. *Nijusseiki o Ayumu: Aru Onna no Ashiato* (Tokyo: Yamato Shobo, 1978), p. 26.
53. See, for example, Sotozaki Mitsuhiro, 'Yamakawa Kikue Ron: Shakaishugi Josei Kaiho Ron no Taito', *Josei Kyoiku Mondai* (Autumn 1981), p. 114. Suzuki Yuko, *Joseishi o Hiraku 1, Haha to Onna: Hiratsuka Raicho, Ichikawa Fusae o Jiku ni* (Tokyo: Miraisha, 1989), pp. 161–2.
54. For the recollections of the heads of the women and minors sections in local governments, see Yamakawa Kikue Seitan Hyakunen o Kinen suru Kai (ed.), *Gendai Feminizumu to Yamakawa Kikue no Kouhansei* (Tokyo: Yamato Shobo, 1990), pp. 63–93.
55. Sugaya Naoko, *Fukutsu no Josei: Yamakawa Kikue no Kouhansei* (Tokyo: Kaien Shobo, 1988), pp. 37–8.
56. Kikue, *Heiwa Kakumei no Kuni* (Tokyo: Keiyusha, 1955), p. 39.
57. Ibid., pp. 34–5.
58. 'Rodoto wa Naze Maketa ka', *Shakai Shugi* (July 1955); 'Eikoku Rodo Undo to Minshuka no Mondai', ibid. (September 1955); 'Igirisu Rodo Undo no Yukidoke: TUC to Rodoto no Taikai', ibid. (November 1956); 'Sangyo Kokuyuka to Igirisu Rodo Undo', ibid. (December 1957); 'Rodoto Saha wa Ikiteiru', ibid. (February 1958).
59. Kikue translated the publications by leftists of the Labour Party into Japanese: for example, Aneurin Bevan, *Kyofu ni Kaete* (Tokyo: Iwanami Shoten, 1953), and G. D. H. Cole, *Kore ga Shakaishugi ka* (Tokyo: Kawade Shinsho, 1955).
60. Kikue, *Heiwa Kakumei no Kuni*, p. 245.
61. Jennifer Shapcott, 'The Red Chrysanthemum: Yamakawa Kikue and the Socialist Women's Movement in Pre-war Japan', *Papers on Far Eastern History*, no. 35 (Canberra, Australia, March 1987), p. 30.

1. Illustration of the Emperor's reception of the Dutch Minister at the Shishinden, Kyoto, 26 March 1868, by Hirashima Koho, 1931.

2 A foldout reproduction of Hiroshige, *Yodogawa* (c. 1834), Francis Hawks, *Narrative of an Expedition of an American Squadron to the China Seas and Japan*, Washington DC 1856. Reproduced with the kind permission of the British Library.

3. A reproduction of Hiroshige, *Hoki* from his series *Rokujuyoshu meisho zue* (Famous places from more than 60 provinces) (1853–1856), Sherard Osborn, *Japanese Fragments*, London, 1861. Reproduced with the kind permission of the British Library.

4. J. B. Waring (ed.), *Masterpieces of Industrial Art & Sculpture at the International Exhibition*, London, 1862. Reproduced by permission of Roy W. Norman of Timefame LSC International.

5 Walter Crane, *One, Two, Buckle my Shoe* from the *Sixpenny Toy Series*, London: George Routledge & Sons, 1869. Reproduced with the kind permission of Routledge, London.

6. *The Geisha*, 1896, sheet music cover, John Culme Collection. Reproduced with the kind permission of the British Library.

7. Theodore Roussel, *A Girl Reading*, 1886–7, oil painting. Reproduced with the kind permission of Tate, London, 2000.

8. Front cover of the exhibition catalogue, *Art Treasures of Japan*, The Victoria and Albert Museum, London: The Arts Council, 1958. Reproduced with the kind permission of The Arts Council of England.

9. Yusaka Kamekura, poster for the Tokyo Olympics, 1964. Reproduced with the kind permission of the IOC/Olympic Museum Collections, Lausanne, Switzerland.

Part IV
The Inter-War Years

11
New Liberalism and Welfare Economics: British Influences and Japanese Intellectuals Between the Wars – Fukuda Tokuzo and Ueda Teijiro

Tamotsu Nishizawa

Introduction

This essay focuses on two Japanese intellectual leaders of the Taisho and early Showa periods, a time when a form of 'English Renaissance' flourished among Japanese intellectuals. In these years a significant number of British intellectuals visited Japan: the Webbs in 1911, Lowes Dickinson in 1913, Bertrand Russell in 1921, and Seebohm Rowntree in 1924. During the years of so-called 'Taisho democracy' the works of William Morris and John Ruskin were widely read, and in 1923 the 150th anniversary of Adam Smith's birth was enthusiastically celebrated in Japanese academic circles. In 1924 the birth of the first Labour government in Britain was warmly welcomed in Japan, and the Japanese Fabian Society was founded in the same year. During this time British influences were increasingly replacing the German influences which had been dominant in the Meiji period. Ueda Teijiro, who advocated the policies of 'new liberalism' and 'practical idealism', and Fukuda Tokuzo, who attempted to create 'welfare economics', were probably the outstanding academic figures, together with Kawai Eijiro (1891–1944), who represented British intellectual influence in this period.

Fukuda Tokuzo (1874–1930) and Ueda Teijiro (1879–1940) were the great pioneers of modern economic and business thought in Japan. They both taught at Tokyo Higher Commercial School, later the Tokyo University of Commerce (and now Hitotsubashi University), where a strong tradition of liberalism had been nurtured in opposition to the traditions of Tokyo Imperial University. These scholars' studies of economics and business embraced broad areas, as can be seen from the contents of Fukuda's *Keizaigaku Zenshu* (Collected Works on Economics) and Ueda's *Zenshu* (Collected Works).[1] But their focuses and intellectual destinations differed – in Fukuda's case welfare economics-cum-social policy; and in Ueda's business economics-cum-new liberalism. They appear to have sought a new path at a time of rising Marxist influence in Japanese economic circles, particularly at Tokyo Imperial University.

Two intellectual leaders

Ueda Teijiro

> Scholars are detached from reality, practitioners are unaware of scholarship, politics have become alienated from industry, and industry disregards society – this is the primary agony of Japan, buffeted by the billows of the industrial revolution. In this state of confusion, corporations should recognise society, society should recognise corporations. We should search for principles for the construction of a new global Japan . . .

This frequently quoted statement was the manifesto of *Kigyo to Shakai* (The Enterprise and Society), a monthly journal established in 1926 by Ueda Teijiro, then at the peak of his career. The journal was published for two years – with great help from Ueda's students and former students, in particular Itani Zen-ichi of the Tokyo University of Commerce. It attracted a large readership at a time when 'new middling ranks of people' were becoming more numerous. The journal's principal message was 'new liberalism'. Ueda contributed articles to every issue and published them as a collection, *Shin Jiyushugi* (New Liberalism), in 1927. He also wrote *Shin Jiyushugi to Jiyu Tsusho* (New Liberalism and Free Trade) in 1928.

This programme of new liberalism reflected Ueda's social philosophy. He had already published *Shakai Kaizo to Kigyo* (Social Reconstruction and the Enterprise) in 1922 and *Eikoku Sangyo Kakumeishi Ron* (A History of the British Industrial Revolution) in 1923 as well as *Eikoku Sangyo Kakumeishi Kenkyu* (Studies on the British Industrial Revolution) in 1924, which sold extremely well at the time of Japan's rapid industrialization, the Russian Revolution and the rise of the Japanese labour movement after the First World War. Ueda taught, and wrote these books after returning from the first meeting of the International Labour Organization (ILO), held in Washington, DC in 1919. He attended the meeting as an adviser, with Muto Sanji of the Kanegafuchi Cotton Spinning Company and other Japanese representatives.[2]

Ueda was greatly influenced by British intellectuals, more specifically the intellectual tradition of the Oxford Economists. At the beginning of his 'History of the British Industrial Revolution' he made a particular reference to the 'enthusiastic social reformer at Oxford, Arnold Toynbee'. Ueda was also influenced by W. J. Ashley, the Webbs and R. H. Tawney. In a review article on Tawney's *The Acquisitive Society* (1921), which was included in 'Social Reconstruction and the Enterprise', Ueda stated that although numerous works on social reform had appeared since the 1914–18 war, none had engaged his sympathies as profoundly as Tawney's work. He believed that this book – although written in a foreign language – best expressed what he himself had wanted to say or had already said.[3]

Fukuda Tokuzo

Fukuda published his final work *Kosei Keizai Kenkyu* (Studies in Welfare Economics) in 1930, just two months before he died aged 56. In this he wrote:

> It is said that economics has reached a deadlock. Often we hear voices declaiming the ruin of the German Historical School, or the bankruptcy of the marginal utility theory. But among my fellow scholars a good number have looked towards the quickly taken escape route of Marxism, or especially historical materialism.

Fukuda could take little interest in any of these, nor did he hold out any great hope for mathematical research. Consequently he concluded: 'The only course left to me is to move forward on the theoretical path of welfare economics created by our teachers Hobson, Pigou and Cannan.'[4] Although Fukuda studied the works of Alfred Marshall and A. C. Pigou it was perhaps from J. A. Hobson (who inherited John Ruskin's ethics) that he learnt most about welfare economics. His reaction to Hobson's *Wealth and Life* (1929) and Edwin Cannan's *A Review of Economic Theory* (1929) was a feeling of great delight – that these two Oxford economists were moving in the same direction as his own recent work.[5]

Background: from the German Historical School to new liberalism

Ueda Teijiro enrolled at the Tokyo Higher Commercial School in 1896. Three years later he wrote in his diary

> The two approaches to research, British and German, have become the two main schools, and their various strengths and weaknesses are clear . . . in economics in particular, these schools stand out; and because there exist the British and German schools, Mill's liberalism and Wagner's national socialism form a duality, the two great influences.[6]

The years from the late 1880s to the mid-1890s were the era when Japanese economics moved towards the German Historical School. In 1896, following the example of the German Society for Social Policy, the Japanese Association for the Study of Social Policy was created with Kanai

Noboru, Yamazaki Kakujiro and Kuwata Kumazo as its leading figures. All were on the staff of Tokyo Imperial University and had studied in Germany. It has been said that the Russo-Japanese War (1904–05) was the 'springboard for historicism'; and that 'upon this springboard, Japan's historical school economics, also known as the German social policy school, established itself'.[7]

Although the latter decades of the Meiji period were dominated by the historical – social policy school, the economic approaches which were developed at the Higher Commercial Schools and Tokyo Imperial University were significantly different. In 1906, shortly after the Russo-Japanese War the *Keizaigaku, Shogyogaku, Kokumin Keizai Zasshi* (Journal for National Political Economy: Economics and Commercial Studies), co-edited by the Higher Commercial Schools in Tokyo and Kobe, first appeared as a form of in-house magazine of the Japanese Society for Social Policy. While Kanai and his followers were proud to be 'Socialists of the Chair' (at Tokyo Imperial University – which inclined towards Wagner-style state socialism), Fukuda and his followers at the Higher Commercial Schools were sympathetic to 'reform liberalism' and were closer to the British tradition of political economy.

In the later 1910s and the 1920s Marxism emerged and flourished in Japanese intellectual circles, quickly replacing the German Historical School. The Society for Social Policy soon lost its vitality and its membership declined. It virtually stagnated and disbanded in 1924, partly due to the ideological conflict with Marxism.

During the transition from the authoritarian Meiji state to the parliamentary politics of the Taisho period, intellectuals participated in democratic movements in their own individual ways. In 1918 Fukuda, along with Yoshino Sakuzo, established the Reimei-kai. Fukuda, as a declared leader of Taisho democracy, strove to create a new economics which would consolidate the well-being of the nation. Following his growing interest in Cambridge economics, Fukuda gradually became more sceptical about the German Historical School. He opposed the statist concept of social policy propounded by theorists such as Adolf Wagner. Above all, Fukuda stood for liberalism in social policies. Indeed he embraced the task of taking over the social-liberal tradition and creating his own system of welfare economics. By this means Fukuda sought to provide an alternative to Marxism.

Fukuda, Marshall and welfare economics

In 1905 when Fukuda began lecturing at Keio Gijuku (later Keio University) the German translation of Marshall's *Principles of Economics* was published with an introduction by Lujo Brentano. Brentano's introduction was also translated and included in the first Japanese translation of the *Principles* (by Otsuka Kinnosuke). Fukuda attached a 'reviser's supplementary introduction' to Otsuka's translation in which he wrote that Marshall's *Principles of*

Economics were 'the pinnacle of contemporary economics, as my mentor Brentano wrote in his introduction to the German translated edition'.[8] Fukuda used Marshall's *Principles of Economics* as his textbook for his lectures at Keio. He compiled commentaries on the first four books of the *Principles* for his lectures and published them as *Keizaigaku Kogi* (Lectures on Economics). Fukuda began this volume with the first passage from Marshall's work, 'Economics is a study of mankind in the ordinary business of life'. The problems of poverty and ignorance cannot be totally eradicated by economics alone, but 'the greater part of the facts and reasoning necessary to resolve these problems are encompassed within the sphere of economic research'.[9]

Criticizing the German Historical School, Fukuda wrote that the most distinguished doyen of economics was Britain's Alfred Marshall. Marshall had mastered the recent research of German scholars but not neglected the purely theoretical studies of British scholars.

> Marshall's idea that economics is the study of the relationship between human beings and wealth should be regarded as fulfilling its true nature . . . this relationship is not simply to speak of the degree of wealth, but of whether or not the necessary material base can be created on an equal basis to achieve a higher level of development and a richer level of human activity . . . the historical school and the ethical school achieve no more than this basic concept.

According to Fukuda, Marshall's able disciple Pigou was continuing his work and becoming a leading figure among contemporary scholars.[10]

Fukuda also sought to compare Marshall's ideas and his own in 'From Price Struggle to Welfare Struggle: Especially Labour Struggle as Welfare Struggle'. This work appeared in *Kaizo* (Reconstruction) in 1921 and was also included in the collection *Shakai Seisaku to Kaikyu Toso* (Social Policy and Class Struggle, 1922). In this Fukuda argued that social policy rather than socialism provided the best means of remedying the defects of capitalism.

As already noted, Fukuda had praised Marshall in *Keizaigaku Kogi* as 'the greatest authority among contemporary economists'. However, he criticized Marshall in 'From Price Struggle to Welfare Struggle.' According to Fukuda, in the first edition of the *Principles of Economics* Marshall had presented the clearest and boldest statement of welfare economics but

> starting with the second edition he gradually follows the conventional beliefs of price economics, and at the end he falls to the lowest viewpoint, one that is no different from that of his fellows. In particular, Book V and Book VI which deal with distribution theory are the worst of all . . . the criticism that Marshall is wandering at the crossroads between old price economics and the new welfare economics is not a reckless slander.[11]

Fukuda sought to absorb the vision of welfare economics of Marshall and Pigou. However, although he was strongly influenced by Pigou, his own belief was that welfare economics could not be fully understood from Pigou's definitions and analysis alone. Fukuda's welfare economics is said to be a form of economics based on income theory – influenced by such thinkers as Hobson, Pigou and Cannan – but he believed that economics' most important role was to deal with concrete labour issues. These included issues of income distribution – such as whether the workers' share was equitable, whether the labour movement or labour disputes had achieved a fair distribution, in terms of welfare, for workers, or whether socially reasonable working hours were guaranteed. Fukuda's welfare economics went beyond the neoclassical economics of Marshall and Pigou and concerned itself with policy issues. In other words, Fukuda diverged from the Cambridge school and returned to the tradition of the English Historical School or the School for Social Policy which emanated from Oxford and was represented by such thinkers as J. A. Hobson and Edwin Cannan, William Beveridge, G. D. H. Cole, and the economic and social policies of the British Labour Party.

Fukuda's tentative conclusion was 'the development of communal principles for capitalist society' which he stated in 'Surplus Production–Exchange–Distribution'. According to Fukuda, the communal principles of 'from each according to his ability' and 'to each according to his need' were 'woven into the texture of contemporary capitalist society, like the thread of fate, through the entirety of production, exchange and distribution'. He believed that the development of communal principles had to be demonstrated in the progress of capitalist society, and that the advance of communal principles had to be seen as occurring in the progress of the British welfare state.[12]

On 10 June 1929, immediately following the establishment of the second Labour government in Britain, Fukuda wrote,

[I] learned from this morning's newspaper that Mr. MacDonald, in his installation speech . . . stated that the major tasks of his new cabinet would be to reform the industrial system and solve the unemployment problem. The formation of this cabinet may even constitute a major 'development of communal principles' in Britain, and it may have a close connection with the future of British capitalism.

In September 1929 he wrote in *Kaizo*:

In this chaotic arena, now like the thread of fate, I must admit that the correct principle has raised its head . . . I must see this as a further example of 'the development of communal principles in capitalist society'. Most of all I acknowledge its remarkable development among people in the Labour Party who have formed Britain's new cabinet. How this cabinet will advance and what kinds of things it will do in the future cannot be foreseen at present. However its 'Economic General Staff' plan doesn't seize my attention at all. [In contrast] I find that *The Next Ten Years in British Social and Economic Policy*, a recent book by a former guild socialist [G. D. H.] Cole, to be powerful . . . This work will probably be issued as the intellectual ledger for the new cabinet.[13]

Ueda and new liberalism

Ueda Teijiro left for England in 1905 to study 'Business Policy' under W. J. Ashley in Birmingham. Ashley, a talented disciple of Arnold Toynbee, was an Oxford historical economist, who had taught at Toronto and Harvard before returning to England in 1901. There he organized the newly established Faculty of Commerce at Birmingham.

Before leaving Japan, Ueda wrote a 'Proposal regarding Business Economics' and presented it to the principal of Tokyo Higher Commercial School. In this he stated that Ashley was one of the earliest advocates of business economics, the very subject that was developing and taking shape in the new century. In his proposal Ueda also referred to L. R. Dicksee, who was Professor of Accounting. Ueda had already written two articles on Sir Josiah Mason, the founder of Mason College, which developed into Birmingham University.[14]

The Faculty of Commerce at Birmingham attracted a significant number of Japanese students in its early decades. One of a total of five graduates in 1906 was Tazaki Shinji (later the first President of Kobe University of Commerce) who had studied at Tokyo Higher Commercial School and the London School of Economics before studying at Birmingham. On 20 January 1906, when Ueda attended Ashley's commerce seminar, Tazaki read a paper on 'war risks'. Two other Japanese students, Akimoto and Mitsui, were also present. Mitsui Takakiyo was probably the first Japanese who registered at the Birmingham Faculty of Commerce. G. C. Allen, who studied under Ashley and who was appointed in 1922 to be a lecturer at Nagoya Higher Commercial School, later wrote in his memoir *Appointment in Japan*: 'It is symptomatic of national attitudes towards innovation that, while British firms regarded the venture with coolness, if not suspicion, the Mitsui family of Japan . . . should send one of its members to become an early pupil.'[15]

After three years' study in Birmingham, Manchester, Bonn and Berlin, Ueda returned to Japan in 1909 and began to lecture on *Shoko-Keiei* (Commercial and Industrial Administration) from September 1909. This marked the very beginning of lectures on Business Administration at any school, college or university in Japan. Being inspired by Ashley's views of business policy, particularly his article 'The Enlargement of Economics' in the *Economic Journal* in 1908, Ueda wrote an article 'What is Business Economics?' for the *Kokumin Keizai Zasshi* in 1909.

As the scale of businesses increased it had become impossible to discuss the national political economy without having knowledge of management and administration within businesses. As studies of the internal organization of businesses had progressed, Ashley had begun to lecture on business policy at Birmingham. In his article 'The Enlargement of Economics' he argued that studies of business administration developed a new area of business economics, in contrast to the existing field 'political economy'.

Ashley's 'Enlargement of Economics' appeared in the *Economic Journal* in June 1908. It was translated and published in an abridged version in *Kokumin Keizai Zasshi* as early as January 1909. Since Ueda felt deeply indebted to Ashley, he believed that people wishing to study business economics should not overlook this article. Ashley intended to create a science not by studying business economics from a practical book-keeping approach – as in the Berlin Handelshochschule – but by advancing the study of business administration *within* economics. Naturally Ueda did not formulate a plan to create an independent private science of economics. At the end of his article he wrote: 'I can't help hoping that young students of economics here [in Japan] would be excited by engaging in this original and creative field of study – and turn their hands to "the enlargement of economics".'[16]

Ueda then published 'Theories of the Joint Stock Company' in 1913 which established his reputation as an academic scholar. In this work he developed his ideas on the separation of management from ownership, and began a theoretical recognition of management as an important social function of duty. He readily shared the view of Heinrich Nicklisch at Berlin that business economics aims at high efficiency, not high profits. Ueda also tried to separate commercial science and administrative science from profit making – to make them sciences of socially efficient management – which would be equally necessary in a private business or a public corporation – in a profit-making business or a non-profit organization.[17]

After publishing this work Ueda went to study abroad again. He attended the Webbs' lectures in London, studied with Lowes Dickinson in Cambridge, and met Keynes and Foxwell. During October and November 1913 he attended Sidney Webb's lectures at the London School of Economics. On 13 November he wrote to Webb on the subject of socialism, stating that 'Socialism must be the outcome of the development of democracy and a socialistic measure without democratic spirit will only lead to bureaucracy and paternalism.' Ueda asked: 'Is it not advisable to encourage the development of joint stock enterprises as a stepping stone to socialistic organization?' On 19 November 1913 Webb replied in a long letter:

> In Japan, the most important thing is to encourage and develop the feeling of democracy. Therefore, all voluntary associations ought to be supported and assisted by the Government and public opinion. But I should try to get them started on a mutual basis (like cooperation) rather

than on a basis of profit for capitalist shareholders. The Cooperative movement in Great Britain is (with our local government) best worth your study – not our capitalist manufacturers and trading.[18]

In May 1920, the year when Tokyo Higher Commercial School was elevated to become Tokyo University of Commerce, Ueda gave a lecture before the Alumni Association in Osaka. This was entitled 'The Theory of Social Reconstruction and the Role of Managers'. He stressed the important role of managerial personnel in real business. They were neither proletarian workers nor bourgeois capitalists. Ueda praised the future role of middle-management classes, men who were largely graduates of Higher Commercial Schools and the University of Commerce. He felt that these would be the middle-class intellectuals of a company.

According to Ueda, capital might be gradually nationalized and the social system transformed, but productive organizations which had established efficient production by using machinery, and the division of labour, could not be abolished for ever. Even if all profit-making enterprises and capital were socialized, production and trade and their administration and management must continue, otherwise society could not exist. Those who would run administration and management would be the middle-class managers. Ueda placed great emphasis on, and later wrote about, 'The Social Significance of New Middle Classes' in 'Enterprise and Society'. In 1920 Ueda wrote 'Socialism and the Duty-Role of Managers', stating that 'as the age of socialism would come, the capability of managers and their "duty-role" would be increasingly important'. 'Even if we could remove profit-making and enterprise, as long as production would be necessary, we could never remove administration or management', which was shown by the fact that even Lenin had started to study American scientific management.[19]

In 1919 and 1920 Ueda lectured on business enterprise and the role of managerial personnel in social reconstruction. These were epoch-making years, a time of transition for the labour movement and also one of broad intellectual development, a time when socialism, Marxism and Taisho democracy increased in influence. Ueda gave lectures to the *Kyocho-kai* (Labour-Management Cooperation Society), which was created in December 1919 following an initiative by the minister of the Interior, Tokunami Takejiro. Ueda wrote in 'Socialism and the Duty-Role of Managers' that business corporations had already become major structures handling domestic production and that their success or failure would have a great impact on the lives of thousands of people. Therefore, the role of managerial personnel was not that of mere men of commerce; rather, they must become 'public men of the country' (*Tenka no Kojin*). Ueda praised their high administrative and managerial efficiency and expressed his opposition of nationalization and bureaucratic statism. Ueda's ideas constituted the 'bold opposition of liberalism to the tide of socialism', 'well socialized liberalism' or 'new liberalism', and this became his prescription for the age of social reconstruction.[20]

In 1923, the year when Ueda published 'A History of the British Industrial Revolution', he also wrote 'The Economic Policy of Adam Smith' for a special issue of the university journal published to celebrate the 150th anniversary of Smith's birth. Ueda argued in support of Adam Smith's criticism of mercantilism, a system which had defended the merchants' and manufacturers' monopoly of trade and industry. At around the same time, Ueda also wrote in support of Muto Sanji and his 'Commercial and Industrial Party' – a structure which opposed those monopolistic and privileged classes who colluded with politicians – and called for a rallying of the 'middle' business classes. Ueda wrote that in Japan the industrial revolution and mercantilism had converged at the same time.[21]

In 1926 Ueda began to publish 'Enterprise and Society', a journal which advocated 'new liberalism', in opposition to mercantilism, statism and socialism. In this, Ueda was critical of state-run corporations and emphasized the importance of private business, even arguing for the privatization of higher education. Reviewing *The End of Laissez-Faire* by Keynes (1926), Ueda wrote on 'Mr. Keynes on Social Reconstruction' for 'Enterprise and Society'. In this article, he praised Keynes' argument for rationalizing the capitalist market economy without following escape routes to socialism. In a review of Norman Angell's *Must Britain Travel the Moscow Road?*, Ueda confirmed his view that Marxism did not pay adequate attention to the significance of the managerial middle classes and their role in the process of social reconstruction.[22]

It is clear from this brief exploration of the ideas of Fukuda and Ueda that contemporary British economic thought was a major creative influence in the pluralistic intellectual world of Taisho Japan. Furthermore, the thought of these major economists was more relevant to the solution of Japan's major social and economic problems than the authoritarian proposals of its military leaders.

Notes

1. Fukuda Tokuzo, *Keizaigaku Zenshu* (Collected Works on Economics), 6 vols (Tokyo: Dobunkan, 1925–6); Ueda Teijiro, *Zenshu* (Collected Works), 7 vols, Ueda Teijiro Zenshu Kanko-kai, 1975–6.
2. See Nishizawa Tamotsu, *Ueda Teijiro no keizai shiso* (Economic Thought of Ueda Teijiro), in S. Sugihara (ed.), *Kindai Nihon to Igirisu shiso* (Modern Japan and British Thought) (Tokyo: Nihon Keizai Hyoronsha, 1995), pp. 144–75.
3. Ueda, *Zenshu*, vol. 4, *Shakai keizai to kigyo* (Social Reconstruction and Enterprise), p. 101.

4. Fukuda, *Kosei keizai kenkyu* (Studies in Welfare Economics) (Tokyo: Tokoshoin, 1930), pp. 5–6.

5. Ibid., pp. 3–4.

6. *Ueda Teijiro Nikki, Meiji 25–Meiji 37* (The Dairy of Ueda Teijiro, 1892–1904) (Tokyo: Keio Tsushinsha, 1965), pp. 400–1.

7. Ouchi Hyoe, 'The Formation of an Old Liberal', in his *Zenshu*, vol. 1 (Tokyo: Iwanami Shoten, 1975), pp. 3–4.

8. Otsuka Kinnosuke (trans), *Keizaigaku Genri* (Principles of Economics), vol. 1 (Tokyo: Sato Shuppanbu, 1919).

9. Fukuda, *Keizaigaku kogi* (Lectures on Economics), in *Keizaigaku Zenshu*, vol. 1, pp. 1, 5–6.

10. Fukuda, *Keizaigaku Zenshu*, pp. 17–18, 21–5, 31.

11. Fukuda, *Shakai seisaku to kaikyu toso* (Social Policy and Class Struggle) (Tokyo: Okura Shoten, 1922), pp. 5–6, 182–3.

12. Fukuda, 'Yojo no seisan – kokan – bunpai: shihonshugi shakai ni okeru kyosan gensoku no hatten' ('Surplus Production–Exchange–Distribution: the Development of Communal Principles in Capitalist Society'), in *Kosei keizai kenkyu*, pp. 178–9.

13. Fukuda, 'Shitsugyo no hitsuzen-fuhitsuzen to shitsugyo taisaku no kano-fukano' ('The Inevitability or Not of Unemployment and the Possibility or Not of an Unemployment Policy'), in *Kosei keizai kenkyu* (Welfare Economic Studies), pp. 215–16.

14. *Ueda Teijiro Nikki Meiji 38 – Taisho 7* (The Diary of Ueda Teijiro, 1905–1918), pp. 45–54; Ueda, 'Sir Josiah Mason', *Shogyo sekai* (Commercial World), vol. 4, nos 2, 3, 1900.

15. Nishizawa, 'The Making of Japan's Business Elites', in T. Yuzawa (ed.), *Japanese Business Success* (London: Routledge, 1994), p. 206.

16. Ueda, 'Shoji keizaigaku to wa nanzoya' ('What is Business Economics?'), in *Zenshu*, vol. 1, pp. 388, 394, 397.

17. Ueda, 'Keiei keizaigaku soron' (Introduction to Business Economics), in *Zenshu*, vol. 1, pp. 45, 429–30.

18. *The Diary of Ueda Teijiro, 1905–1918*, p. 437; letter from Ueda to Webb, 13 November 1913. This correspondence is kept in the Documents Room at Hitotsubashi University History Department.

19. Ueda, 'Shakai kaizo no riron to kigyoka no ichi' ('The Theory of Social Reconstruction and the Role of Managers'), *Alumni Journal of Josuikai*, no. 1, 1920, pp. 40–6; Ueda, 'Shakaishugi to kigyosha no shokubun' ('Socialism and the Duty-role of Managers'), in *Zenshu*, pp. 13, 20.

20. Ibid., pp. 25, 28. Ueda Tatsunosuke, 'On the Entrepreneur's Duty-role by Dr. Ueda Teijiro', in *Keiei keizai no shomondai* (The Issues of Business Economics), Festschriften for Dr Ueda Teijiro, vol. 1 (Tokyo: Kagakushugi Kogyosha, –), p. 32.

21. *The Diary of Ueda Teijiro, 1919–1940*, pp. 81–2.

22. In Ueda's *Zenshu*, vol. 7, pp. 279–5.

12

Yanagi Muneyoshi (1889–1961) and the British Medievalist Tradition

Toshio Kusamitsu

1995 was the centenary of the death of William Morris – designer, poet, publisher, socialist and owner of a firm which specialized in interior decoration. At that time there were many commemorative exhibitions and conferences both in Britain and overseas. In fact exhibitions were held across the world, including Japan. In 1996, following a successful exhibition held in 1995 at the Victoria and Albert Museum in London, a giant exhibition opened in Tokyo at the National Museum of Modern Art.

Japanese translations now exist of major biographies of Morris and of books on his designs and ideas. There is now worldwide understanding and appreciation of Morris. His lifelong concern about the preservation of the environment and ancient buildings is now a very topical issue, as we witness a new growing interest in the heritage industry. Although socialism in Russia and East European countries ultimately declined and collapsed, Morris' earthly utopian ideal of socialist endeavour still has the power to fire our imagination. However, when the hundredth anniversary of the birth of Morris was celebrated in Japan, in 1934, according to a Morris scholar, Ono Jiro, 'it represented neither the peak nor the full understanding of William Morris' influence, but . . . revealed the general trend of the perception of his thoughts: to assemble his ideas in a superficial way, and reforge them into a matter of mere taste'.[1] But Ono noted some writers who were exceptions to this tendency: notably Okuma Nobuyuki and Yanagi Muneyoshi. When socialism was introduced into Japan as a by-product of Taisho democracy, Okuma interpreted William Morris as providing a theory of socialism which included questions of art within socialist ideas. Yanagi Muneyoshi was, on the other hand, not under Morris' influence, rather he was in a kind of blood relationship with Morris, in that his ideas of art and society closely resembled those of Morris. Both tried to organize artistic movements to transform society into a community without the separation of artistic and social principles. This essay will *not* discuss the one-way flow of the influence of British thought into Japan. Rather, it will discuss how one Japanese thinker perceived the ideas of a certain group of British thinkers, and integrated them into his original ideas, establishing one of the most remarkable art movements in Japan and, indeed, the world.

Yanagi Muneyoshi was born in 1889, seven years before Morris' death. He is now remembered as the founder of the folk craft movement (*Mingei Undo*), but we should remember that he studied psychology at the Imperial University of Tokyo when he was young, and at the age of 24, he wrote a voluminous book on William Blake. He was a younger member of the '*Shirakaba*' (silver birch) group which occupies a unique position in the history of arts and literature in Japan. The group was formed by students of the Imperial University and pupils of Gakushuin High School. All were from upper- and upper-middle-class families of that time. (Some people liken them to the Bloomsbury Group on account of the similarity of the members' elitism and family backgrounds.) Through the friendship of this group Yanagi came to know the works of Kropotokin and Blake. (He read the former's *Mutual Aid* when he was twenty years old.) According to Nakami Mari of the Keisen Women's College, Yanagi might have been influenced by Arishima Takeo, also a *Shirakaba* member, who had actually met Kropotokin and attempted to create a utopian cooperative farm in Hokkaido.[2] Yanagi was fascinated by Kropotokin's concept of 'mutual aid' which, Nakami argues, remained as one of the most important guiding principles of Yanagi's thought and practice throughout his life. Kropotokin's book is a critique of a society in which free competition and Darwinian social evolution dogmas prevail. He proposed an orderly and balanced society where the strong always protect the weak. His medievalist ideals are no doubt derived from John Ruskin and William Morris, and Yanagi was particularly interested in the social system of the Middle Ages, above all the guild system that was indispensable for realizing 'mutual aid' in society.

The idea of reviving guilds was already present in the activities of Ruskin and Morris. Ruskin's guild of St George, although it ended in failure, was an attempt to create a workers' commune in the country where all could share the joy of labour. In the nineteenth century there were many attempts to establish communal villages based on the idea of mutual aid – (however paternalistic they might have been): for example, Robert Owen's Lanark factory, Titus Salt's Saltaire near Bradford and the soap tycoon Lever's Port Sunlight in Cheshire. These did not constitute a revival of the guild system exactly, but these enlightened employers tried to combine the work and lives of their employees; and their enterprises were innovative in including the welfare of the workforce within their concept of business management. Workers themselves also felt the necessity of returning to a medieval system. For instance, building workers in the 1830s founded the National Guild of Builders. The Arts and Crafts Movement, inspired by William Morris and initiated by his followers such as Walter Crane, began as the Arts and Crafts Exhibitions Society in 1888; but in 1885 the disciples of Richard Norman Shaw, the Gothic Revival architect, founded the Art Worker's Guild. Many of the Guild's members later joined the Arts and Crafts Movement. It was in the 1880s and 1890s that many artists and craftsmen began to think that the guild was the most suitable form to achieve their ideals. Charles Robert Ashbee, once a member of the Art Workers' Guild, founded the Guild and School of Handicrafts and moved into a village in the Cotswolds to establish a utopian community. Organizations such as Arthur Mackmurdo's Century Guild, the Independent Labour Party's Clarion Guild of Handicrafts and the Women's Bookbinders' Guild all show the intimate relationship between arts and crafts *and* medieval corporations.

At the beginning of the twentieth century, Ruskin and Morris' ideals from the Middle Ages had a further impact on British socialism. Arthur Joseph Penty and Alfred Richard Orage, both from the north of England and admirers of William Morris and the Arts and Crafts Movement, became regular contributors to the *New Age*, which was then edited by a Christian Socialist Joseph Crayton. This journal was originally established in 1894, and attracted a wide range of writers – for example, Ramsay MacDonald, Holbrook Jackson and G. K. Chesterton. Many who supported the *New Age* were also members of the Fabian Society. Penty was born in York in 1875. His father was an architect, and Penty worked with his father before he went to London in 1902. In that year he began writing *The Revival of Guild Socialism* which became the Bible of guild socialism in Britain.

British socialism has two sources: one of utilitarian origin and the other utopian. Within the Fabian Society one can also observe this tendency. Raymond Williams points out that the Fabians had two pillars – Sidney Webb and George Bernard Shaw – the latter being inspired by Ruskin and Thomas Carlyle. Webbian Fabian Socialism aimed at the gradual development of society into socialism through the intervention of the state. William Morris and his followers were critical of this strategy as it overestimated the significance of the social system with its lawmaking and administrative mechanisms. According to Penty, modern society had destroyed the simple state of medieval society, and modern knowledge could no longer control the details necessary for properly organizing society. In order to reform that condition it was impossible to rely on a civilization which divides people into classes and groups, and segments them further into isolated individuals. People must be combined and united as the great medieval culture combined them. But this should not be done by the intervention of state collectivism, rather it should be created by a community in which guilds occupy a central position. Penty believed that socialism needs humanity, and industry needs the arts. Nationalization of industry would merely reproduce capitalist industry whose purpose is the pursuit of profit. The alienation of workers would never be removed by nationalization. He thought that trade unions would play a central role in the process of creating a modern guild society. In 1922, Penty published another influential book, *Post-Industrialism*, in which he argued that the basic problem of modern society was caused by mechanization and pleaded for the control of machines and the revival of handicrafts. It was this book by Penty which Yanagi read in 1927 when he was contemplating the foundation of the Kamigamo Handicrafts Commune in Kyoto. But before discussing Yanagi's reactions to reading Penty, let us examine the development of Yanagi's thought and its relationship with the English medievalist tradition.

Yanagi 'discovered' the Middle Ages through his interest in religion. Towards the end of his life he wrote an essay 'Return to Buddhism' in which he confessed that Japan, especially after the Meiji period, was greatly surprised by western science and technology, and became an admirer of the West, and he himself was no exception to this. He wrote 'I thought that the eastern civilisation of the past was anachronistic and western civilisation alone could provide useful aids to modern society. I also believed that western religion, philosophy and arts were the forces to lead Japan into the new age.'[3] As mentioned previously, Yanagi joined the *Shirakaba* group whilst he was at Gakushuin High School when his main interests were literature, arts and sculpture, and Christianity attracted him a great deal since it was, to him, a *new* religion. He 'read new books on Christianity, studied theology and went to church to listen to many sermons with pleasure'.[4] At university he earnestly studied philosophy, especially the relationship between religion and science, and religion and philosophy. Firstly, he began studying Protestant theology, but he soon realized that the further one went back in history, the richer the depth of thought became. He also discovered that the Middle Ages, and Catholic rather than Protestant religion, held more interest for him. In other words a youth who was enthusiastic for the creation of modern civilization in Japan (*Bunmeikaika*) here encountered the mystic thoughts of the European Middle Ages. For Yanagi this was also the period when he discovered William Blake, mystic poet and artist of modern England. Yanagi wrote many essays in which he expressed his admiration for the medieval tradition. In 1934, for instance, he wrote an essay entitled 'Medieval Arts' in which he argued, 'I would prefer the medieval arts to Greek and Roman ones: Romanesque arts in particular are wonderful. It is generally asserted that the middle ages were the period of darkness, but I would argue that it was the most glittering period in history'.[5] He argued this because of the centrality of religion at this time, and thought medieval culture was also much more profound. Then he defended Ruskin and Morris against those who had labelled them anachronistic medievalists. If people discredited the handicrafts of the Middle Ages as something which has passed away, they would not understand new handicrafts either. Intuitive insight, which Yanagi called 'temperament', could not be achieved by the simple criteria of judging whether things were old or new.

It is difficult to speculate exactly when Yanagi first became familiar with the works of Ruskin and Morris. In *The Path of Handicrafts* (1928), he confessed that he first learned about them when he had read Okuma's book

Ruskin and Morris as Social Thinkers, published in 1927. By this time, Yanagi had already published his book on Blake, become interested in Korean arts and crafts, discovered the beauty of 'lesser arts' (*getamono*), and, with friends like Bernard Leach, Hamada Shoji and Kawai Kanjiro, had conceived the idea of a new folk arts movement. Indeed, by providing the theoretical foundations for such a movement, he had become its leader.

Although Yanagi Muneyoshi was enthusiastic about the discovery of Ruskin and Morris as the precursors of the theory of craft arts, he had at the same time one strong reservation about them. This was that although both Ruskin and Morris understood the problem of the division between artists and craftsmen (artisans), they were trying to solve this problem of separation by elevating craftsmen to the level of artists. Yanagi's idea was not to raise the lower position of craftsmen, but rather that handicrafts should be returned to the common people, since the real problem as he saw it was the separation of beauty from the people. The beauty of handicrafts was no longer serving the pleasure and daily uses of ordinary people. The radical dimension of Yanagi's concept of handicrafts stems precisely from this point.

Yanagi's critical perception of Ruskin and Morris is also found in his commentaries on Penty's *Post-Industrialism*. After reading it he wrote in the margin of the book:

Excellent book! The author is undoubtedly the best and most correct thinker of the present age regarding the problem of industrialism. I agree with nearly all his viewpoints, except one point which is very radical. He begins from the question of social organisation, but not from 'beauty'. I think he fails to see three important things:

1) He does not seem to have a clear notion of the difference between fine arts and handicrafts, the former is individualistic, while the latter is communal. The Guild is a matter of the latter.

2) He speaks much of handicrafts, but never touches the question of handicrafts proper. Machinery is wrong, but we cannot say all handicrafts are good. If we want to have a revival of handicrafts, we must firstly understand what is right and proper, and what are wrong and unjust crafts.

3) He never speaks of the nature and meaning of the beauty of democratic crafts. If we do not understand this it is idle to speak of their revival.

He would assert that 'It seems that the author of this book, along with Ruskin and Morris, fails to understand the difference of art and craft . . . Morris' was artistic and individualistic, hence he failed. Ruskin and Morris may have been good art critics and artists, but not craftsmen, nor processors of an understanding of craft.

Yanagi had sympathy for as well as a profound understanding of Ruskin, Morris and Penty, and yet had reservations towards their notions of craft.

He once clarified what he thought was distinctive about craft. The Japanese words *'bijutsu'*, *'kogei'*, *'gigei'*, are in English 'art' and 'craft', but they were originally expressions of the same thing: skill or skills. The words 'artist' and 'craftsman' also meant artisan and artificer. It was only in modern society that we began distinguishing between these words. Yanagi's argument preceded Raymond Williams' study by thirty years. But Yanagi was not merely playing an etymological game. It was a crucial question for the revival of true crafts in modern times.

Unlike many intellectuals of his time Yanagi Muneyoshi was a rare and original thinker. He did not remain a mere interpreter or translator of western culture. He did not simply introduce the ideas of western thinkers; his reading of Blake, Ruskin, Morris and Penty was not passive, but simultaneously critical and creative. He tried to place what he thought important in the West, and for that matter in the East, in a much wider perspective. Perhaps Yanagi was an exception to the general trends of Japanese perception or misperception of Britain or Europe, but surely he was a happy exception.

In the preparation of this essay, I was able to use Yanagi's library in the Japanese Folk Craft Museum, in Tokyo. I am grateful to its Director, Mr Yanagi Souri and the principal curator, Mr Sugiyama Ryoji for their help.

Notes

1. Ono Jiro, *Uiriamu Morisu* (William Morris) (Tokyo: Chuo Koronsha, 1973), pp. 10–11.
2. Nakami Mari, 'Yanagi Muneyoshi, Kuropotokin Girudo Shakaishugi', *Mingei*, nos 9, 11, 12 (1993) and no. 1 (1994), passim.
3. 'Bukkyo ni kaeru', *Yanagi Muneyosh Zenshu* (Tokyo: Chikuma Shobo), vol. 19, p. 485.
4. Ibid., p. 486.
5. 'Chusei no geijutsu', *Yanagi Muneyosh Zenshu*, vol. 8, p. 586.

Bibliography

Association for the Commemoration of the Hundredth Anniversary of the Birth of Morris, *Morris Kinen Ronshu* (Essays in Commemoration of Morris) (Tokyo: Kawase Shoten, 1934).
Chandler, Alis, *A Dream of Order* (Lincoln, NE: University of Nebraska Press, 1970).

Kropotokin, P. A., *Mutual Aid* (London, 1908).

Kusamitsu Toshio, 'Artist to Artisan (Artist and Artisan)', in Kusamitsu Toshio, Kondo, Kazuhiko. Matsumura Takao, Saito Osamu (eds), *Eikoku wo Miru: Rekishi to Shakai (Looking at Britain)* (Tokyo: Libroport, 1991).

Matthews, Frank, 'The Ladder of Becoming: A. R. Orage, A. J. Penty and the Origins of Guild Socialism in England', in David E. Martin and David Rubenstein (eds), *Ideology and the Labour Movement* (London: Croom Helm, 1927).

Mizuo Hiroshi, *Hyoden Yanagi Muneyoshi* (Biography of Yanagi Muneyoshi) (Tokyo: Chikuma Shobo, 1982).

Nakami Mari, *Yanagi Muneyoshi, Kropotokin, girudo shakaishugi* (Yanagi Muneyoshi, Kropotokin and Guild Socialism), vols 1–4, *Mingei*, nos 9, 11, 12 (1993) and no. 1 (1994).

Okuma Nobuyuki, *Shakaishisoka to shite no Ruskin to Morris* (Ruskin and Morris as Social Thinkers) (Tokyo: Shinchosha, 1927).

Ono Jiro, *William Morris* (Tokyo: Chuo Koronsha, 1973).

Penty, A. J., *Post Industrialism* (London: George Allen & Unwin, 1927).

Pevsner, Nicolaus, *Pioneers of Modern Design: From William Morris to Walter Gropius*, revised edition (London: Pelican, 1975).

Tsurumi Shunsuke, *Yanagi Muneyoshi* (Tokyo: Heibonsha, 1976).

Williams, Raymond, *Culture and Society* (London: Pelican, 1963).

Yanagi Muneyoshi Zenshu (The Complete Works of Yanagi Muneyoshi) (Tokyo: Chikuma Shobo, 1980–92).

13
Yanaihara Tadao and the British Empire as a Model for Colonial Reform

Susan C. Townsend

When the Japanese acquired their first formal colony, Taiwan, in 1895 (though they were no strangers to domestic colonization), it was only natural that they should turn to the examples of the European empires for guidance on colonial policy. The British Empire, with its highly flexible approach, was held up as a model of colonial rule by some Japanese colonial administrators and condemned by others. As Kibata Yoichi has pointed out, however, the Japanese were more keen to foster the image of British rule than to employ its techniques.[1]

In terms of social and cultural policy the Japanese leaned more towards the French example of *l'assimilation* in the belief that the peoples of East Asia, with their apparent racial and cultural affinities, could be turned into Japanese. Whilst the French made a pragmatic adjustment to the principle of 'association' in the early twentieth century, however, the Japanese intensified their policy of assimilation in the early decades of colonial rule and *bunka seiji* (cultural rule) became a crude type of Japanization, which in Korea amounted to no less than an attempt to eliminate Korean identity.[2] Assimilation reached its apotheosis in the ruthless policy of *kominka* (the transformation of colonial peoples into loyal imperial subjects) in the 1930s and sought to remove every last vestige of the indigenous populations' cultural identity.[3]

One of the fiercest critics of Japanese assimilation policy was Yanaihara Tadao (1893–1961). He used the example of the British Empire both to demonstrate the abject failure of assimilation policy as well as to construct a model of colonial reform based on Britain's relationship with her self-governing colonies, particularly Canada, Australia and New Zealand. Yanaihara occupied the Chair of Colonial Policy at Tokyo Imperial University from 1923 until his enforced resignation in December 1937 after he openly criticized Japan's undeclared war on China. Whilst a student at Tokyo Imperial University he converted to *Mukyokai* ('No-church') Christianity under the tutelage of Uchimura Kanzo. Yanaihara was a student of the well-known internationalist Nitobe Inazo and was his successor to the Chair of

Colonial Policy which had been founded in 1908 by the colonial adminis-
trator Goto Shimpei. Yanaihara was arguably the most knowledgeable
Japanese commentator on British colonial policy in the period before the
Pacific War. In the early 1920s he studied in Britain and Europe for a little
over two years and he visited Ireland and the Middle East before returning
to Japan via the United States.

He published his first two major works, *Shokumin oyobi Shokumin Seisaku*
(Colonization and Colonial Policy) and *Seisaku Shinkicho* (The New
Foundations of Colonial Policy), in 1926 and 1928 respectively.[4] He also
published a series of articles on British policies in India and Ireland. The
basis of his theory of colonization was Adam Smith's *Wealth of Nations*
(1776). Writing on the eve of the American War of Independence, Smith
urged Britain to relinquish her hold on the colonies and instead draw up
commercial treaties that would guarantee free trade. He believed that if the
colonists were able to separate on good terms from the mother country, this
might dispose them not only to respect the mother country but to become
valuable allies in both trade and war.[5]

In *Shokumin oyobi Shokumin Seisaku* (Colonization and Colonial Policy)
Yanaihara pointed out that the loss of the American colonies was a salutary
lesson to the British on how the failure to grant autonomy could lead to
disaster forcing Britain to find a way of granting autonomy through 'responsible government' to the colonies of white settlement. After the trauma of
the First World War, the British had also been forced to extend areas of
autonomy in India and even a small measure of autonomy to Nigeria and
other parts of Africa. Yanaihara evidently approved of Sir Frederick Lugard's
theory of 'Indirect Rule' in Nigeria and believed that Lugard's policies were
responsible for the gradual prosperity of trade in the region.[6] Though
Yanaihara was a firm and consistent believer in the positive effects of capitalist development within the colonies, as long as the benefits were shared
by all, he was wary of fully endorsing Lugard's concept of the 'dual
mandate'. He asked, 'is this "dual mandate", that is to say mutual benefit
for both colonisers and indigenous peoples, really realisable?' A 'civilized'
metropolis, he argued, can pursue policies which cause it to prosper whilst
at the same time benefiting the indigenous people. He pointed out that as
a result of 'capitalization', however, the indigenous society 'accidentally'
undergoes progressive development and begins to assert its own autonomy
and independence. At the very least capitalist development leads to a desire
to participate in the political process and the real test of the 'civilizing
process' in Africa, he argued, was the recognition and facilitation of this
desire. If, on the other hand,

> freedom is not granted then the indigenous peoples are deceived. It goes
> under the name of exploitation. The weak are squeezed and the foolish
> are deceived. If they are not to be deceived they must be strong, they

must be wise. Their strength; their wisdom; the indigenous peoples are granted even these by the colonizers. What is that but an irony of fate?[7]

Britain's self-governing colonies, however, proved that granting autonomy to colonies need not be at the expense of the metropolis:

> The principle of autonomy respects the special characteristics of the colony and because it aims towards autonomous development, the logical end result is the disappearance of the relationship of possession and domination between the mother country and the colony. The principle of autonomy, however, does not necessarily mean sacrificing the interests of the metropolis. Rather . . . it can strengthen the unity between the metropolis and the colony and is a route to the continued mainte-nance of a large empire.[8]

With the British self-governing colonies in mind, therefore, Yanaihara proposed a change in Japanese policy, seeking to turn it away from military suppression and assimilation and towards autonomy. For Korea and Taiwan he advocated 'responsible cabinet government' along the lines drawn up in Lord Durham's *Report on the Affairs of British North America* (1839). Durham believed that the rebellion in Lower Canada in 1837 had been caused not only by racial tensions between the French- and English-speaking settlers but also by the arbitrary use of power by a small clique of the governor's advisors. He advised that the British constitutional practice of 'cabinet government' or what contemporaries called 'responsible government', should be extended to the colonies.[9]

Yanaihara argued that the adoption of policies of autonomy and the recog-nition of the right of Taiwanese and Koreans to participate in the political system through the establishment of colonial assemblies, was a 'requirement of justice'.[10] It must be pointed out, however, that at this stage in his intel-lectual development Yanaihara did not argue for complete independence, since the granting of responsible government was designed to strengthen imperial unity. Though he foresaw and welcomed the eventual peaceful separation of the colonies from the mother country this was to be in the distant future.

Though he obviously approved of the principle of dominion status within the British Empire, Yanaihara realized that in practice the emerging British Commonwealth of Nations was far from being the ideal sphere of coopera-tion, mutual benefit and free trade that he envisaged for Japan. He was pro-foundly disillusioned by the proliferation of racially motivated immigration restrictions within the self-governing colonies and outraged by the policy of forbidding non-whites, including Japanese, from entering Australia. He saw the term 'White Australian Faith' as nothing more than an exhibition of 'national egoism'.[11]

The 'White Australia' policy began to be formulated during the second half of the nineteenth century, beginning with isolated and temporary measures to check Chinese immigration during the gold rush. This was followed in the 1880s by attempts to broaden restrictions and by 1888 they were fairly uniformly adopted.[12] These measures appeared to conflict with the Anglo-Japanese Commercial Treaty of 1894 which granted the subjects of either empire the liberty to enter, travel and live in any part of the other's territories. Article 19, however, allowed the self-governing colonies to opt out of the treaty if they intimated their wish to do so within two years from the date of ratification. At the Sydney Conference held in March 1896 the premiers of the various self-governing colonies decided unanimously not to adhere to the treaty and resolved to exclude all Asian immigration.[13] At the Commonwealth of Australia inauguration in 1901 the Immigration Restriction Bill became law. One member of the new Federal Parliament asked that the new nation retain 'the noble ideal of a White Australia – Let it be pure and spotless.'[14] This was a matter of some embarrassment for the British government since, with the conclusion of the Anglo-Japanese Alliance in 1902, the British were particularly anxious to remain on friendly terms. After considerable Japanese pressure, however, the Restriction Act did undergo some minor changes.[15]

Yanaihara regarded these racially motivated restrictions on immigration within the British Empire as a threat to its continuing peace and unity. Moreover, economic relations between the self-governing colonies were far from friendly and it was obvious that 'the interests and freedoms of the indigenous peoples of those colonies which do not have dominion status rest on the goodwill of the peoples of the autonomous regions of the British Empire'.[16] He analysed the report on the First British Commonwealth Labour Conference held in 1925[17] and concluded that relationships between the dominions hinged on the principle of mutual benefits for the working classes.[18] The conference was small with all the main nations being represented, except for New Zealand, which was in the throes of a political crisis. The delegates were primarily concerned with the contrast in the standards of living between European and non-European races. The South African delegates stated that the argument was an economic one; white labour could not compete with Indian labour because Indian workers accepted a lower standard of living. The object of labour organization, they declared, was to raise rather than lower standards of living. The Indian delegates replied that this 'economic' argument did not justify refusal of the vote and other political rights, and they clearly believed that racial hostility lay behind the attitudes of some labour groups in certain dominions.[19] In the light of such difficulties, Yanaihara concluded that all regulations, whether designed by capitalists or socialists, required a certain amount of sacrifice of self-interest and co-operation:

If the working classes of other countries request that they be allowed to emigrate due to conditions of poverty or unemployment then Australia with its huge amount of space should accept them. If the living standards of Indians in South Africa are low then the white workers of South Africa should help them to advance.[20]

Yanaihara argued that neither socialism nor laissez-faire capitalism could guarantee the peaceful unity of the empire, but could the British Labour Party and the short-lived Labour government of 1923–24 steer a middle course? He was particularly interested in the views of Labour leaders such as Philip Snowden, the Wesleyan Methodist from the Pennines who became a major figure in the Labour Party and eventually the first Labour Chancellor of the Exchequer,[21] and J. H. Thomas, the railwayman's leader who became Colonial Secretary in 1923. Though Yanaihara regarded the Labour Party as the true inheritors of the Liberal tradition, he disagreed with T. F. Tsiang's thesis which argued that the Labour Party had assumed the mantle of Cobden and Bright and that Labour's ideals were essentially the ideals of 'Little-Englanders'.[22] Yanaihara stated that though some members of the Labour Party regarded the colonies as white elephants, they also saw the existence of the empire as a fait accompli and could not be regarded as 'Little-Englanders'. He cited Philip Snowden who, in his pamphlet *If Labour Rules* (1923), argued that the empire was a fact, and though the Labour Party had reservations about the way in which it had been established, it had a responsibility towards it and could not countenance abandoning it. Yanaihara compared the views of Snowden to those of Adam Smith:

> The idea of one large 'homeland', the advocacy of free trade between the constituent parts, the policy of protecting and educating the residents of the territories closely resembles Smith's theory of colonisation. However, Smith had doubts with regard to the value of the colonial possessions but there is no trace of this in Snowden.[23]

Yanaihara also quoted extensively from J. H. Thomas's *When Labour Rules* (1920) which promised that a Labour government would aim towards making India a 'self-governing dominion'.[24] Thomas criticized that fact that 28 million Africans were 'without the power of raising a voice' and were dictated to by 'little gentlemen' in Whitehall. He declared that 'Labour's aim will be to civilise, not to exploit the African.'[25] Yanaihara stated that despite all these promises, however, when Labour actually came to power, its colonial policies were a profound disappointment for the 'nationalist patriots' of India and Egypt.[26] He cited the Indian activist M. N. Roy who described the Labour Party's refusal to oppose the annexation of Sudan as 'frankly imperialist'.[27] Yanaihara also concurred with another critic who stated that despite the great hope that the Labour Party had given to Indian nationalists it 'was only when the time for giving at least an earnest of their good wishes that they as a government failed. They failed India and they failed their own principles'.[28] Once the Labour Party had come to power and were in a position of responsibility, Yanaihara concluded, they 'departed from the castle of the critics'.[29]

In his study of the British Empire and the labour movement, Partha Sarathi Gupta spoke of the 'tension between ideology and pragmatism' in the Labour Party.[30] It is evident, however, that though Yanaihara was critical of Labour Party policy, this same tension is also present in his works on Korea and Taiwan. Like Snowden and Thomas, he regarded the Japanese empire as a fait accompli and his approach to colonial reform was essentially gradualist. Where he differed from many other colonial reformers either in Japan or in Britain, however, was in the fact that he looked forward to the inevitable, complete and peaceful cessation of the colonial relationship in the distant future. Time and again he warned that if concessions were not made to nationalist demands within either the British or the Japanese empires this inevitable separation would occur through violence.

If Britain's self-governing colonies, even with their problems of race and class, could be held up as models of enlightened colonial policy, conversely, the examples of British India and Ireland could be held up as models of everything that was wrong with British rule and by analogy everything that was wrong with Japanese rule. In the late 1920s and early 1930s Yanaihara published a series of articles which severely criticized British colonial policies in India and Ireland.[31] He held Ireland up as an example of the violent separation of colony from metropolis since in 1921–22 it had acquired dominion status through force, and warned that India was showing signs of repeating Ireland's history of violent secession.[32] These essays were collected together, revised and reprinted in 1936 under the title *Teikokushugi-ka no Indo* (India Under Imperialism)[33] at a time when increasing restrictions on freedom of speech in Japan meant that open condemnation of Japanese colonial policy was no longer possible. Yanaihara recommended that *Teikokushugi-ka no Indo* be compared to its sister publication *Teikokushugi-ka no Taiwan* (Taiwan Under Imperialism) because 'although the methods of handling the problems are not necessarily the same, there are similarities in the characteristics of the problems themselves'.[34]

Teikokushugi-ka no Indo is divided into four chapters, 'A General Outline of the Indian Problem', 'The Indian Monetary System and its Significance in Terms of Colonial Policy', 'Indian Industry and Colonial Policy' and finally 'Indian Agriculture and Colonial Policy'. Yanaihara stated that the premise for his study was that 'all social development of colonies, being based on the colonial policies of the ruling country, tends towards a fixed direction which may either cause them to progress or, conversely, may actually hinder their development.' He chose to study India because at the time it was 'the largest colony in the world under the rule of the greatest colonial power' and it offered a wide range of materials to aid in the research of this topic. His aim was to analyse the way in which British policies caused changes in India's economy and society. As the resultant new land and class relationships placed strains on the relationship between metropolis and colony, and the Indian nationalist movement grew increasingly more powerful, Britain was forced to make political compromises and change its industrial and agricultural strategies.[35]

His analysis was influenced by the classical Marxist theories of imperialism but, trained in Rankean methodology, he was scrupulous with regard to his sources. Approximately half of these were published by Indian economists, such as R. Mukerjee and R. C. Dutt's[36] multi-volume *Economic History of India* published around 1906. For his tables and statistics he relied upon government reports and other sources such as B. Narain's *Source Book for the Study of Indian Economic Problems* (1922). Another important source with reference to India's financial system was P. A. Wadia and G. N. Joshi's[37] *Money and the Money Market in India* (1926). He also drew on the slightly earlier works of William Digby[38] who, together with Dutt, formulated the classic contemporary analysis of the Indian economy. These so-called 'nationalist' interpretations tended to attack colonialism as an inhibiting, distorting influence on India's economic growth.[39] They borrowed from latter-day Marxist theories which stress the parasitic role of colonialism, its political alliance with 'feudal' landlord elements and the comprador character of the national bourgeoisie. They generally support Bipan Chandra's argument that the impact of colonialism in the nineteenth century resulted in 'an aborted modernization'.[40] Soon after the Second World War, these interpretations came under increasing criticism. For example, Sir Percival Griffiths, in *The British Impact on India* (1952), argued that British policy actually had a positive impact on Indian modernization and D. M. Morris in the early 1960s also stressed the positive aspects of British rule in India and in so doing invited considerable criticism from other academics.[41]

On the other hand, Yanaihara seemed to make a genuine attempt to seek a balance in his sources for he also consulted the blatantly pro-British M. de P. Webb, who praised British rule as a model of benevolence, sympathy and justice.[42] Though Yanaihara was a critic of the pro-British views of economists such as Lilian Knowles and Vera Anstey, he was equally critical of the more extreme views of Indian nationalists such as M. N. Roy, the Indian revolutionary communist.

Yanaihara began his analysis of British rule in India by examining the roots of poverty and ignorance which, he stated, were as much a feature of 1930s India as it they were in the past. In support of his arguments he used statistics published in *The Indian Year Book* for 1936–7 which suggested that one of the main causes of Indian poverty was the still largely agrarian nature of India's economy, and the fact that 90 per cent of the population still lived in villages and 71 per cent of the population still depended on agriculture for a living. Of the 25 million or so factory labourers, not more than $8\frac{1}{2}$ million people worked in what could be called factories organized along modern lines. He pointed out that this was despite the fact that India could be counted as one of the eight industrialized countries of the world.[43] The poverty of farmers, he wrote, was a well-known story and in the Punjab, 'farmers are born into debt, live in debt and die in debt' and even factory workers suffered from low pay whilst owners made large profits. As for the large tea plantations of Assam, he cited V. H. Rutherford who, in *Modern India*, commented that Mrs Harriet Beecher Stowe, author of *Uncle Tom's Cabin*, would have plenty of material with which to arouse world indignation should she write a story based on the tea plantations of British India.[44]

According to Yanaihara, in rural areas land taxes and rent owed to the government and to landlords were high, farming methods were crude and the harvest could be counted as one of the lowest among civilized countries, with the incidence of famine in some areas being extremely high. For example, between 1876 and 1900 there were 18 famines resulting in 26 million deaths. He cited a report issued by the Labour Bureau in Bombay in 1922, which claimed that the amount of cereals consumed by the local population was below the amount stipulated in prison regulations. For the poor, problems of overcrowding and high infant mortality rates were added to the problem of hunger. The poor distribution of institutions for health care and 'social hygiene' meant a high death rate compared with other countries. Added to extreme conditions of poverty was a low level of education. Yanaihara cited a survey of 1921 which stated that 91.8 per cent of the population was illiterate. The question was: did British rule help to alleviate these problems of hunger, poverty, ignorance and high death rates, or did it actually exacerbate them?[45]

Much of Yanaihara's book is concerned with India's monetary system which he believed was highly unsuitable for a relatively 'backward country' (*koshinkoku*) with a 90 per cent illiteracy rate. The British government, he argued, had been unwise to forge ahead with a sophisticated monetary system which, centred on the world economy, required a high degree of confidence in its operation. He declared that the Indian financial system had been foisted on India by her British masters in the teeth of Indian public opinion and in the absence of any analysis of the social relations which currency exchange brings into existence. As a result, it had been introduced without a true comprehension of its nature and function within a colonial relationship.[46] The monetary system displayed an utter disregard for the interests of Indians and had been pursued only with the interests of Britain in mind. He gave the example of the period between 1873 and 1892 when Britain had kept India on the silver standard even though silver's falling value caused problems within the Indian economy. Not only had Indian companies been accustomed to dealing with gold, he argued, but a gold currency was more appropriate for an undeveloped economy with a small amount of industrial output.[47] In her recent economic history of India, however, Deitmar Rothermund has pointed out that silver had always played a role in the Indian economy and the Mughals at one time collected land revenues in silver.[48] The point Yanaihara was making, however, was that keeping India on the silver standard benefited Britain which remained on the gold standard at India's expense: 'Necessarily, Britain in order to have her flowers of gold gave flowers of silver to India. India was Britain's dark-skinned handmaiden. A white-faced currency for a dark-faced handmaiden. What a beautiful colour scheme!'[49]

As B. R. Tomlinson has recently pointed out, however, though the world gold price of silver fell by around 40 per cent during this period it fell no faster than any other gold price. He argued that it is difficult, therefore, to sustain the argument that the 'world was somehow acquiring India's exports cheap by paying for them with a devalued commodity'.[50]

In conclusion, Yanaihara argued that quite clearly the Indian public were not satisfied with the financial system: 'In India's financial system, there exists the culmination of the colonial question. It is not a question of results but a question of principle. It is not a question of benefits but of justice. It is not a question of good government but a question of autonomy.'[51] Recent interpretations, however, suggest that overall the policy of retaining the silver standard was largely successful before the First World War as it avoided unnecessary movements of bullion. They also absolve the Indian Office of deliberately manipulating India's currency affairs for Britain's benefit, although the system demonstrated that the British government was determined to maintain control. The fundamental problem with the system was that it did not produce a central bank which might have solved the problem of the inflexibility of the system during fluctuations in currency values.[52]

Following this analysis of the monetary system Yanaihara turned to the slow pace of industrial development in India. The 1918 *Report of the Indian Industrial Commission*, he stated, had also criticized the unevenness and inadequacy of India's industrial development. Reforms were biased towards trade rather than industry, and many features of an underdeveloped economy remained.[53] Yanaihara argued that these characteristics owed much to the domination of foreign capital, but he was careful to point out that these did not comprise the whole picture of industry in India and that a traditional handicraft sector persisted, though it was in relative decline. This relative decline, he argued, had a major impact on structural changes in the Indian economy. One of the main problems was that the slow development of modern capitalist enterprises meant that unemployed handicraft workers could not all be absorbed into the cities and modern industries. As a result these former artisans returned to the land, where increased population pressure resulted in the further impoverishment of the Indian farmer. He compared this situation with an early period during the industrial revolution in Britain where declining standards were not unusual for artisans. However, the faster development of capitalist social organization in Britain had resulted in a migration to the towns from the villages and thus, to some extent, the British and Indian populations had moved in opposite directions. Whereas Britain's industrial revolution had been regulated by her own capitalist development India's industrial development was based not so much on her own requirements but on Britain's demands for agricultural produce and raw materials.[54]

Yanaihara criticized both Vera Anstey's and Lilian Knowles' accounts of the development of Indian industry. Anstey had claimed that in India, whilst the potential for large-scale development existed, there was nothing that could be equated with an industrial revolution.[55] Yanaihara disagreed and argued that the beginnings of an industrial revolution had existed for a long time in India, though he admitted that the rate of progress and diffusion was extremely slow. Lilian Knowles, on the other hand, argued that India in the 1920s was in a similar state to England in the early sixteenth century.[56] Again Yanaihara challenged this comparison and argued that on the contrary Indian society in the 1920s and 1930s was a pre-capitalist society where a few large-scale manufacturing industries, such as Tata Iron and Steel, had been superimposed on top of an ancient agricultural village-type structure. India's capitalistic organization was, therefore, essentially foreign and even though capital ownership in industries such as coal and steel was gradually being transferred to India, the management of these enterprises still remained largely in the hands of the British and tied to Britain's financial institutions.[57]

He concluded that the whole question of whether British industrial policy in the 1930s was good or bad for India was difficult to answer. Whilst it is undeniable that in the 1930s poverty and ignorance was still rife among the Indian people, Yanaihara warned against arguments which attempted to place the blame entirely at the door of British rule. British rule could even be regarded as providing a stimulus to the modernization of the Indian economy through maintaining the Pax Britannica. Neither could it be argued, he wrote, that there was some kind of 'Golden Age' in India before British rule. Nevertheless, the fact that conditions of poverty still existed after 150 years of British rule must mean that British policy was in some way culpable for this continuing state of affairs.[58]

With regard to the Indian nationalist movement, whilst he acknowledged its role in pushing through reforms, he was critical of Gandhi whose policies, he claimed, appealed mainly to artisans and farmers whilst the Congress Party in fact embraced elements of every class. Gandhi's *Satyagraha* campaign, he argued, appealed essentially to the religious sentiments of pre-capitalist Indian farmers rather than to the emergent bourgeoisie. The failure of Gandhi's non-violent, non-cooperation campaign and his alienation from the political mainstream in the nationalist movement demonstrated the fact that after the First World War the power of both the capitalist class and the working class had become more organized.[59] Yanaihara was perhaps too dismissive of Gandhi's importance. The non-cooperation campaign, which lasted from 1 August 1920 until February 1922, when Gandhi called it off because of a violent attack on a police station, had proved easy for the government to manage. The British authorities' combination of firmness at the local level and restraint at the national level did not drastically affect revenue nor did it disrupt collaborative structures. However, as Judith Brown has pointed out, never before had the government faced continent-wide opposition and in this respect the campaign marked a change in the depth and scale of political attacks on the Raj. Moreover in the imagination of the people of India, Gandhi's vision offered something to all men, whether they were Congressmen, traditional idealists or peasants, and at the time he filled an important vacuum in the all-India political leadership.[60]

Turning finally to agricultural conditions, Yanaihara pointed out that the 1921 national census of India showed that 72.8 per cent of the total Indian population was supported by agriculture. This contrasted starkly with Britain, where approximately 60 per cent of the population was engaged in industry and only about 10 per cent employed in the primary production sectors of agriculture and fisheries. A comparison in the process of urbanization showed a similar tendency. In India in 1931 only 11 per cent of the population lived in cities compared to over 80 per cent in Britain. According to Yanaihara, these two trends, one taking place in Britain and the other in India, existed in an inseparable relationship as two dimensions of a single social development. He felt that Britain's industrialization depended upon India's 'agriculturalization'. India had become 'Britain's village and Lancashire's farm'.[61]

India's export surplus, wrote Yanaihara, was a 'social and political bridge of rainbows'[62] spanning capitalist Britain and her colony. Seen from Britain it presented the 'splendid sight' of Indian agricultural development but the rainbow ended in feudal methods of production, very slow improvements in farming methods and extremely poor standards of living for 220 million Indian farmers.[63] India's increasing exports were, he concluded, 'a whited sepulchre' (*shiroku nurareta haka*)[64] built on the increasing poverty of the Indian farmer.[65] He stated that from the last half of the nineteenth century the opening up of previously unexploited regions of Canada and America, together with improved methods of production in other countries, had resulted in increased competition and falling prices. Due to their low levels of investment and technology, Indian farmers were only able to increase production through bringing a greater area of land into cultivation. Whilst the First World War provided an opportunity for increasing exports, it was soon followed by the crisis of the post-war agricultural depression when the tension between capitalistic exports and feudal methods of production was exposed.[66] Yanaihara allowed that natural causes, such as prolonged drought, also contributed to the problem of famine but the construction of railways and irrigation systems were supposed to alleviate or even prevent its ravages. The immediate impact of irrigation and railways on farming, however, differed from region to region. Irrigation systems, he argued, should have developed land productivity, diversification and improvements in the methods of production, and thus its importance to farming was immediate. Despite this, however, the government's expenditure on railways between 1882 and 1889 was seven times more than expenditure on irrigation and from 1898 to the 1930s, Yanaihara claimed, the construction of irrigation systems went into relative decline.[67] Not until after the 1901 Famine Commission did irrigation receive more attention from the Indian government. Yanaihara concluded that these policies showed that markets for British exports, the suppression of rebellions and the military subjugation of frontiers were all considered to be far more important than improvements in farming methods. Moreover, the commoditization of food production had destroyed traditional systems of famine relief in the villages[68] and the building of railways may even have exacerbated famine conditions because it took food out of the villages.[69]

The point Yanaihara was making was that whilst British policies freed Indian agricultural production from mere subsistence farming they had nevertheless resulted in 'medieval systems' of production being retained. This meant that:

> The export of raw cotton from India is carried out on the basis of the decline of cotton handicrafts and the underdevelopment of the modern textile industry. The export of leather items is highest during years of high death rates of domestic animals through neglect, drought, pestilence and poisoning, all of which could have been avoided. This reflects the underdevelopment and famine conditions of cattle raising and the death of cattle means the loss of the means of production. The export of cereals is carried out on top of a dearth of foodstuffs ... India, in creating these huge export surpluses is not obeying the laws of wisdom of an international division of labour, rather she is meeting the costs of imported goods, international lending, payment of interest profits on investment capital and payment of so-called home charges.[70]

Yanaihara was thus incensed by Lilian Knowles' suggestion that the Indian nationalist movement ignored the 'blessings' of progressive rule[71] and quipped: 'British imperialism has as much right to expect gratitude from the nationalist movement as a man has to expect gratitude from someone he has just succeeded in enraging by hitting him on the head with a stick.'[72]

He was critical of British academics who, whilst recognizing the fact that the development of Indian methods of farming production was slow and farmers were poor, failed to consider the influence of British colonial policy on the conservatism of the Indian farmer, which they gave as a pretext for refusing aid. He criticized both Lilian Knowles, who was a firm believer in self-help and regarded Indian apathy as the main cause of poverty, and Vera Anstey, another 'self-helper' who doubted the ability of the government to aid farming communities.[73] He concluded that 'what these British researchers have in common is a complete disregard for the detrimental effects of British rule on Indian agriculture'.[74]

Though undoubtedly conditions for Indian agriculturists during the nineteenth century were grim, recent interpretations stress that many of the problems, such as high rural populations relative to land availability, were common in Asian economies at the time. The large cattle population was of poor quality and traditionally dung was used as fuel rather than fertilizer. Moreover, Yanaihara relied on statistical evidence which has been shown to be notoriously unreliable. The statistical returns relied on the mass of illiterate and probably corrupt village officials and farmers who wished to evade land revenue and who thus consistently underestimated their crop. Moreover, recent accounts which rely on an assessment of surplus benefits to the economy as a whole have argued that the agricultural sector was not, as critics have implied, stagnant during the nineteenth century.[75]

Did expansion in commercial agriculture threaten the peasantry's supply of food, as Yanaihara has suggested? In his research on rice and jute cultivation in Bengal, Chaudhuri has suggested that there was no separation or conflict between 'commercial' and 'food-grain' products – the two often complemented each other.[76] In general, recent studies suggest that the peasantry was able to protect its supply of food grains, except in a few isolated areas where cash crop expansion created an absolute decline in acreage available for food grains.[77] Judith Brown has also argued that the expansion of commercial crops did not occur at the expense of basic food-grains thanks to the success of irrigation projects, especially in areas such as the Punjab. These recent interpretations appear to contradict Yanaihara's thesis about the government's reluctance to back irrigation projects. However, there is some disagreement among historians with regard to the effectiveness of irrigation schemes. Whereas Brown cited the 'spectacular' success of irrigation schemes in the Punjab and northern India,[78] Tomlinson, on the other hand, was less convinced of the success of irrigation schemes and, like Yanaihara, pointed to their patchy distribution.[79]

Yanaihara's analysis of the Indian economy does appear to be slightly biased (though not always uncritically) towards Indian sources, but this bias reflects the availability of sources at the time and the lack of detailed local studies. Within these older sources, the debate, as Tomlinson has pointed out, was political, revolving as it did around the question of whether India benefited or suffered under British rule. Its focus was on the evident poverty of the Indian masses in the late nineteenth century and the prevalence of famine in the latter half of the century which suggested that Indian agriculture could not support its population.[80] Recent regional studies, however, challenge the picture of a monolithic, all-pervasive imperialism.[81] The conclusion appears to be that even in India imperialism was too weak to transform completely the economy and society and may even have had the effect of actually bolstering traditional systems.[82]

The point that Yanaihara was making with regard to India was also political rather than economic and it extended far beyond the boundaries of Britain's relationship with India. When he compiled and updated his essays on India for his 1936 publication he had yet to witness the full consequences of the India Act of 1935, which was designed in part to grant more autonomy to the provinces in a type of federal system. For Yanaihara the act did not go far enough down the road to granting full autonomy and he was aware of its unpopularity among Indian politicians and some British MPs. It was in effect a case of 'Too little, too late' and he stated that Britain should take heed from its experiences in Ireland.[83] During a time when open criticism of Japanese imperialism in Japan was impossible Yanaihara's writings on India and Ireland were by analogy a warning and a plea to Japanese policy makers to extend genuine autonomy to the Japanese formal empire. The case of India, moreover, demonstrated the fallacy of assimilation policy, since 'in the case of Indians most elements who are in opposition to the English are the best versed in the English language'. Even if native tongues are forgotten or eradicated, warned Yanaihara, this does not mean that their national identity will be forgotten.[84]

Other Japanese intellectuals also criticized the British Empire, but sometimes for very different reasons' as in the case of those right-wing nationalists and militarists who sought to justify further Japanese expansion on the Asian continent. Okawa Shumei (1886–1957) was a scholar of Islamic studies who trained at the newly established Institute for Oriental Studies (*Toyokenkyujo*) at Tokyo Imperial University. He was also an ultra-nationalist and was heavily involved in right-wing paramilitary organizations.[85] In 1913 he began a PhD thesis on the Indian nationalist movement and claimed, when it was originally published in 1916, that it was the first book in Japan to discuss the political situation in modern India.[86] Most of his sources were early classic 'wealth drain' interpretations such as William Digby's *'Prosperous' British India* (1901). In a lengthy work remarkable for its eloquence, emotive power and devastating critique Digby had set out to prove that British rule, by its very nature, made impoverishment inevitable. Digby set out to 'bring to a definite issue two contrary views regarding India', the first claiming that India's increasing prosperity was due to British rule and the second which stated that British rule made impoverishment inevitable.

Based on sources such as these, Okawa concluded that the awful poverty of India, regardless of its historical and social causes, and 'seeing that it is the natural obligation of statesmen to reform these', was mainly due to

British policies in India. He cited the businessman and politician Dadabhai Naoroji and J. T. Sunderland, author of *Indian Famines and their Cause*, as 'impartial researchers' who laid the blame for chronic famine firmly at the door of British rule.[87] Another source used by Okawa to challenge Britain's fitness to govern India was Archibald R. Colquhoun's *Russia Against India* (1900) which warned that discontent among Indians meant that Britain may not be able to count on their loyal support should circumstances require it. Colquhoun argued that a discontented and dissatisfied peasantry, especially on the Northwest frontiers, may even regard Russia as a deliverer.[88] Okawa was much less critical of his sources than Yanaihara because his motive in painting such a relentlessly grim picture of British rule in India before the First World War was to suggest that Japan would be a more suitable leader in Asia. To justify his arguments further he seized upon Rabindranath Tagore's vision of Japan as a natural leader in the East.[89] But by 1929 Tagore was clearly disillusioned and he wrote:

> May I be frank with you and say that when I chance to hear of some instances of ill-treatment to Koreans and to others who are less fortunate than yourselves, it hurts me very deeply causing keen disappointment. . . . And therefore I appeal to you as representatives of your people, win their love whom you can be foolish enough to bully into a sullen subjection, make them trustworthy by trusting them and by respecting them, train them into self-respect which is for your own good.[90]

No doubt Tagore would have been dismayed to witness Okawa using his words to justify aggressive Japanese expansion on the Asian continent during the late 1930s and early 1940s.[91] Yanaihara, on the other hand, had made very similar appeals to Tagore on behalf of the Korean and Taiwanese people. His critique of the British Empire is unique not only in terms of the sheer breadth of his knowledge and his scrupulous attention to sources, but also in as much as both the worst and the best aspects of British colonial policy were held up as a mirror to the Japanese empire.

Yanaihara stated that in researching what he called 'actual colonial policies' he had seen 'how powerful are the pivotal interests of the colonizers and consequently how the indigenous peoples cannot help but resist'.[92] With regard to colonies or former colonies of settlement such as the United States, Canada, Australia and New Zealand, he believed that 'colonisation is in fact nothing other than a manifestation of civilisation'. In the case of India and Africa, however, colonial policy had a long way to go before it could be proclaimed as a civilizing influence. However, the trend towards autonomy shown by the British Empire, he declared, was 'not the sole, logical basis of the connections between colony and metropolis' – there must also be justice and respect for the nobility of groups of individuals. He echoed Tagore when he stated that 'without respect for the individual there is no justice and without justice neither will there be peace'.[93] A fellow Mukyokai Christian, Nakamura Katsumi, has pointed out the profound impact that Christianity had on Yanaihara's colonial writing.[94] Nowhere is the strength of his faith more apparent than in the moving last lines of *Shokumin oyobi Shokumin Seisaku*:

> One thing is certain, that mankind desires this; the liberation of the oppressed, the raising up of the fallen and the peaceful unity of the independent. Man has wished for these things in the past, he wishes for them today and will wish for them in the future. Hope! Faith! I believe that the guarantee for peace lies in 'Strong Son of God, immortal Love.'[95]

The tragedy is that in Japan the more enlightened intellectuals such as Yanaihara were totally isolated from the 'official mind' of colonial practice. Whilst some young academics such as Yanaihara's colleagues Nambara Shigeru and Ouchi Hyoe turned to political movements in order to try and influence policy, Yanaihara remained aloof from politics. In contrast, British critics of colonialism, partly because they had more opportunities, were far more politically active and, as a rule, far more influential than their Japanese counterparts in effecting changes in colonial policy. In the end Yanaihara's warnings and his pleas for colonial policy to be tempered with humanity and justice went unheeded with tragic consequences for both Japan and Asia.

Notes

1. Kibata Yoichi, 'British and Japanese Colonial Rule in Comparison', offprint from *The Proceeding of the Department of Foreign Languages and Literature, College of Arts and Sciences, The University of Tokyo*, vol. XLII, no. 3 (1994), p. 57.
2. Michael Weiner, *Race and Migration in Imperial Japan* (London: Routledge, 1994), p. 90.
3. For further details see Wan-yao Chou, 'The Kominka Movement in Taiwan and Korea: Comparisons and Interpretations', in Peter Duus, Ramon H. Myers and Mark R. Peattie (eds), *The Japanese Wartime Empire, 1931–1945* (Princeton: Princeton University Press, 1996), pp. 40–68.
4. Both these publications appear in their entirety in Nambara Shigeru et al. (eds), *Yanaihara Tadao Zenshu* (The Collected Works of Yanaihara Tadao – cited hereafter as YTZ), 29 vols (Tokyo: Iwanami Shoten, 1963–5), vol. I.
5. Adam Smith, *The Wealth of Nations* (London: Everyman, 1991), p. 113.
6. *Shokumin oyobi Shokumin Seisaku*, YTZ, vol. I, p. 249.
7. Ibid., p. 227.
8. Ibid., p. 250.
9. Peter Burroughs, 'Colonial Self-government', in C. C. Eldridge (ed.), *British Imperialism in the Nineteenth Century* (London and Basingstoke: Macmillan – now Palgrave Macmillan, 1984), pp. 55–6.

10. *Shokumin oyobi Shokumin Seisaku*, YTZ, vol. I, pp. 282–3.
11. 'Nikki' (Diaries), YTZ, vol. XIXX, p. 553.
12. Myra Willard, *History of the White Australia Policy to 1920* (London: Frank Cass, 1967), p. 17.
13. Ibid., pp. 110, 114.
14. Cited in H. I. London, *Non-White Immigration and the 'White Australia Policy'* (New York: New York University Press, 1970), p. 12.
15. Ibid., p. 14.
16. *Shokumin oyobi Shokumin Seisaku*, YTZ, vol. I, p. 478.
17. 'Labour and Empire', in *The Round Table: a Quarterly Review of the Politics of the British Commonwealth*, vol. XVII, no. 61, Dec. 1925–Sep. 1926 (London: Macmillan).
18. *Shokumin oyobi Shokumin Seisaku*, YTZ, vol. I, p. 479.
19. 'Labour and Empire', p. 119.
20. Ibid., YTZ, vol. I, p. 481.
21. Keith Laybourn, *Philip Snowden: a Biography 1864–1937* (Aldershot: Temple Smith, 1988), p. 37.
22. Tingfu F. Tsiang, *Labour and Empire: a Study of the Reaction of British Labour, Mainly as Represented in Parliament, to British Imperialism Since 1880* (New York: Faculty of Political Science Columbia University, 1923), pp. 171, 215.
23. *Shokumin oyobi Shokumin Seisaku*, YTZ, vol. I, pp. 241–3.
24. J. H. Thomas, *When Labour Rules* (London: W. Collins Sons & Co., 1920), p. 138.
25. Ibid., p. 134 cited in *Shokumin oyobi Shokumin Seisaku*, YTZ, vol. I, p. 244.
26. *Shokumin oyobi Shokumin Seisaku*, YTZ, vol. I, p. 244.
27. M. N. Roy, 'The Empire and the Proletariat', in *The Labour Monthly*, vol. 7, no. 1 (January 1925), pp. 13–22 (p. 18).
28. M. Abdullah, 'The Trust of Empire and Mr. MacDonald A Trustee', in *The Labour Monthly*, vol. 7, no. 4 (April 1925), pp. 222–6 (p. 225).
29. *Shokumin oyobi Shokumin Seisaku*, YTZ, vol. I, p. 244.
30. P. S. Gupta, *Imperialism and the British Labour Movement 1914–1964* (London: Macmillan, 1974), p. 7.
31. For an analysis of Yanaihara's essay on Ireland see Susan C. Townsend, 'Yanaihara Tadao and the Irish Question: a Comparative Analysis of the Irish and Korean Questions, 1919–36', in *Irish Historical Studies*, vol. XXX, no. 118 (November 1996), pp. 195–205.
32. *Teikokushugi-ka no Indo*, YTZ, vol. III, p. 462.
33. The essay on Ireland, 'Airurando Mondai no Enkaku', is an appendix to this publication.
34. *Teikokushugi-ka no Indo*, YTZ, vol. III, p. 462.
35. Ibid., p. 461.
36. R. C. Dutt joined the Indian Civil Service in 1871 and became a Division Commissioner in 1894. He was a lecturer on Indian History at University College London and the author of a series of historical works and novels; *Dictionary of Indian Biography*, edited by C. E. Buckland (Varanasi, Delhi: Indological Book House, 1971).
37. Wadia was founder of the Madras Labour Union and had close associations with the British labour movement. Joshi was an Indian social worker and trade union leader. Gupta, *Imperialism and the British Labour Movement*, pp. 46, 405.
38. William Digby (1849–1904) was editor of the *Madras Times* (1877–9) and *India* (1890–2). He was connected with the Indian National Congress. Buckland, *Dictionary of Indian Biography*, p. 119.

39. Neil Charlesworth, *British Rule and the Indian Economy 1800–1914* (Basingstoke: Macmillan – now Palgrave Macmillan, 1985), p. 12.
40. Eric Stokes, *The Peasant and the Raj: Studies in Agrarian Society and Peasant Rebellion in Colonial India* (Cambridge: Cambridge University Press, 1978), p. 37.
41. Charlesworth, *British Rule* p. 12.
42. M. de P. Webb, *Advance India!* (London: P. S. King & Son, 1913), p. 5.
43. *Teikokushugi-ka no Indo*, YTZ, vol. III, p. 465.
44. Ibid., p. 466.
45. Ibid., pp. 467–9.
46. Ibid., p. 493.
47. Ibid., p. 493.
48. Deitmar Rothermund, *An Economic History of India* (London: Routledge, second edition, 1993), p. 42.
49. *Teikokushugi-ka no Indo*, YTZ, vol. III, p. 501.
50. B. R. Tomlinson, *The New Cambridge History of Modern India, vol. III: The Economy of Modern India, 1860–1970* (Cambridge: Cambridge University Press, 1993), p. 14.
51. *Teikokushugi-ka no Indo*, YTZ, vol. III, p. 557.
52. Charlesworth, *British Rule*, p. 65.
53. *Teikokushugi-ka no Indo*, YTZ, vol. III, p. 577.
54. Ibid., pp. 580–2.
55. Vera Anstey, *The Economic Development of India* (London: Longman's, Green and Co., 1929), p. 227.
56. L. C. A. Knowles, *The Economic Development of the British Overseas Empire* (London: George Routledge & Sons Ltd., 1924), p. 266.
57. *Teikokushugi-ka no Indo*, YTZ, vol. III, pp. 583–8.
58. Ibid., p. 590.
59. Ibid., pp. 597–600.
60. Judith Brown, *Modern India: the Making of an Asian Democracy* (Oxford: Oxford University Press, 1994), pp. 223–5.
61. *Teikokushugi-ka no Indo*, YTZ, vol. III, p. 604.
62. Yanaihara's metaphor of the rainbow was based on the superstitions of the South Sea Islanders who believe that the rainbow is an ill omen.
63. Ibid., p. 616.
64. Lit. 'white painted grave'.
65. Ibid., p. 622.
66. Ibid., pp. 629–30.
67. Ibid., p. 470.
68. Ibid., p. 625.
69. Ibid., pp. 614–15.
70. Ibid., p. 615.
71. Knowles, *Economic Development of the British Overseas Empire*, pp. 274, 312 and 393.
72. *Teikokushugi-ka no Indo*, YTZ, vol. III, pp. 596–7.
73. See Vera Anstey, *The Economic Development of India* (London: Longman's, Green and Co. 1929). Along with Lilian Knowles, Vera Anstey was one of the first economic historians to challenge the 'drain of wealth' interpretation posited by nationalist historians such as William Digby.
74. *Teikokushugi-ka no Indo*, YTZ, vol. III, p. 649.
75. Charlesworth, *British Rule*, pp. 22–4.

76. B. B. Chaudhuri, 'The Growth of Commercial Agriculture and its Impact on the Peasant Economy', in *The Indian Economic and Social History Review*, vol. 7, no. 2 (June 1970), 211–51 (pp. 250–1).

77. Charlesworth, *British Rule*, p. 25.

78. Brown, *Modern India*, p. 117.

79. Tomlinson, *The Economy of Modern India*, pp. 85–6.

80. Ibid., pp. 11–12.

81. C. A. Bayly, 'English-Language Historiography on British Expansion in India and Indian Reactions Since 1945', in *Reappraisals in Overseas History: Essays in Post-War Historiography about European Expansion* (Comparative Studies in Overseas History no. 2) edited by P. C. Emmer and H. L. Wesseling (Leiden: Leiden University Press, 1979), pp. 21–53 (p. 30).

82. Charlesworth, *British Rule*, p. 13.

83. *Teikokushugi-ka no Indo*, YTZ, vol. III, p. 489.

84. *Minzoku to Kokka* (Ethnic-nation and State), YTZ, vol. XVIII, p. 282.

85. Tetsuo Najita 'Japanese Revolt against the West: Political and Cultural Criticism in the Twentieth Century', in *The Cambridge History of Japan, vol. VI*, edited by Peter Duus (Cambridge: Cambridge University Press, 1988), p. 730.

86. Okawa Shumei, *Indo ni okeru Kokumin Undo no Genjo oyobi sono Yurai* (The Current Situation of the Nationalist Movement in India and its Origins), reprinted in Okawa Shumei, *Zenshu*, vol. II (Tokyo: Iwasaki Shoten, 1962), p. 533.

87. Ibid., p. 591.

88. Archibald R. Colquhoun, *Russia Against India: the Struggle for Asia* (London: Harper & Brothers, 1900), p. 135, cited in Okawa, *Indo ni okeru*, p. 594.

89. Rabindranath Tagore, 'Wide World', in *The Manchester Guardian*, 12 August 1916, cited in Okawa, *Indo ni okeru*, p. 587.

90. Rabindranath Tagore, 'On Oriental Culture and Japan's Mission', in *The English Writings*, pp. 608–9.

91. See Okawa Shumei, 'The Establishment of the Greater East Asia Order', in Joyce Lebra (ed.), *Japan's Greater East Asia Co-Prosperity Sphere in World War II: Selected Readings and Documents* (Kuala Lumpur: Oxford University Press, 1975), pp. 36–40.

92. *Shokumin oyobi Shokumin Seisaku*, YTZ, vol. I, p. 482.

93. Ibid.

94. For more details see Nakamura Katsuma, *Uchimira Kanzo to Yanaihara Tadao* (Tokyo: Libro, 1981), pp. 197–211.

95. The last line is taken from Tennyson's *In Memoriam*: 'Strong son of God, immortal Love / Who we, that have not seen thy face / By faith and faith alone, embrace / Believing where we cannot prove.'

14

'Nation Shall Speak Peace Unto Nation':[1] The BBC and Japan, 1929–1939

Gordon Daniels and Philip Charrier

Introduction

During the inter-war years the rapid development of British broadcasting coincided with Japan's expanding role as a political, economic and military power. When the British Broadcasting Company (later Corporation) was established in 1925, Japan was already a well-established member of the Council of the League of Nations. Four years later the Wall Street Crash intensified Japan's search for export markets and provoked economic friction with the British Commonwealth. In September 1931 Japanese military action in Manchuria provoked further diplomatic conflict, and Australian and Canadian barriers to Japanese immigration also brought indirect tensions to relations between London and Tokyo.

Against this complex background the BBC sought to interpret developments in Japan and East Asia to an audience which had little direct experience or knowledge of the non-European world. This essay will explore the BBC's perspectives on Japanese politics, trade and diplomacy between 1929 (the year of the first BBC 'talk' on Japan's international relations) and 1939, when the outbreak of the Second World War and wartime censorship changed the content and intentions of BBC broadcasts. As no scripts of news bulletins for these years have survived, this study will primarily examine radio 'talks' (a distinct genre of spoken journalism), many of which were published in the BBC's weekly magazine *The Listener*.

The transition of radio broadcasting from small-scale amateur activity to large-scale commercial and governmental transmissions followed different paths in different societies. In Britain, Japan and continental Europe governments saw radio as a powerful social and political weapon and established state broadcasting authorities. In the United States geographical isolation and major commercial interests created a system in which non-political advertising held sway. In countries as diverse as Germany, Britain and the Soviet Union, radio served various of governmental purposes. These could embrace totalitarian or liberal principles, but among liberal broadcasting regimes Britain's was distinctive and perhaps eccentric. The BBC was not the simple tool of a propaganda ministry, it was, and remains, a quasi-independent public corporation.[2] Moreover, its early leaders saw it as a cultural agency – designed to promote social and educational advancement – rather than frivolous pleasures, associated with commercial stations such as Radio Luxembourg.

For the BBC the development of public understanding of the non-European world, and international relations, was a major objective during the interwar years. Indeed such objectives were pursued with a distinct post-war urgency and idealism. The BBC maintained a strong bias towards 'peace' throughout these years, and saw education, and cooperation with foreign broadcasting institutions, as significant parts of its mission. Broadcasting was often seen as a means of uniting peoples, and the BBC was happy to cooperate with its sister service in Japan. A number of Japanese radio technicians served apprenticeships at the BBC in the 1930s, and the BBC contributed a congratulatory message, which was broadcast from Tokyo, when NHK's new broadcasting centre was opened in 1938.

This outlook was generally in harmony with the attitudes of British governments and of the wider public. BBC talks were often given by opinion leaders who had the ability to communicate effectively over the radio. In several cases these were personalities committed to international understanding and social progress. However, amid the increasingly complex political problems of the 1930s it is not surprising that BBC talks and news broadcasts precipitated frictions with government. News bulletins were occasionally a source of conflict on account of inaccuracies. In fact the BBC did not always consult the news department of the Foreign Office before broadcasting an international item. These problems arose from the domestic and foreign news services upon which news bulletins were based. Regarding radio 'talks', difficulties arose due to perceptions inside and particularly *outside* Britain that the BBC was the 'official' voice of the British government. In the 1930s a number of incidents concerning European political issues prompted Whitehall to attempt to bring BBC 'talks' under a greater degree of official control. However, the government was unwilling to weaken the ideal of independent public service broadcasting championed by the BBC's powerful director-general John (later Lord) Reith. However, there were no examples of disputes between the Foreign Office and the BBC concerning broadcasts covering Japan. In 1938 a Foreign Office official suggested that Reith be asked whether the BBC would broadcast critical reports on Japanese trade competition in the Far East. However, the suggestion was not pursued as it was believed that Reith was unlikely to cooperate.[3] The BBC's philosophy regarding 'talks' it appears to have been to increase public awareness of international issues by allowing different views to compete openly. The Foreign Office did not share this view but, by 1935, it appears to have accepted that there was insufficient political will to muzzle the BBC on international issues. The best that could be achieved would be consultation before the transmission of potentially controversial talks.

Because of the specialist nature of Japan as a subject for BBC talks a relatively small number of commentators had tremendous influence in conveying a view of contemporary Japan to radio audiences. One such commentator, Vernon Bartlett, was profoundly influenced by the casualties of the First World War and sought to encourage the social and political improvement of mankind. In the early years of British broadcasting Bartlett dominated coverage of international affairs and hence of Japan's role in world politics.[4]

Bartlett had himself been wounded in the First World War and was a passionate advocate of peace and the newly created League of Nations. After the Paris Peace Conference Bartlett worked for *The Times* and in 1922 he became the director of the London office of the League of Nations, a position he occupied until October 1933, when he briefly became an employee of the BBC. Bartlett never visited Japan or China, but his stance on Asian issues was invariably internationalist. He always saw negotiation as the best means of resolving international disputes. Other significant commentators on Japan at this time were the writer and public servant Sir Frederick Whyte, the traveller and *Times* journalist Peter Fleming and the Shanghai-based journalist O. M. Green.

1929–1931: Japan, China and the Soviet Union

Between 1929 and 1931, Vernon Bartlett was the only BBC voice to provide analyses of East Asian politics. In commenting on the deterioration in Sino-Japanese relations he remained remarkably even-handed. Whilst he sympathized with China, which was beset by poverty and disorder, he also recognized that these instabilities created difficulties for more organized states, including Japan, a respected member of the League of Nations. Although Bartlett did not state this openly he believed that in special circumstances it was legitimate for Japan to employ force in order to ensure the protection of its citizens and commercial interests. His even-handedness was evident in his broadcast 'The Far East and the League of Nations' which was transmitted on 31 January 1929. In this he stated:

> There are certainly times when countries can be too touchy where patriotism and prestige are concerned . . . If the Nanking Government could come to terms with Japan, it would then be able to say that it had been recognised by all the important Governments in the world. If the Japanese could come to terms with the Nanking Government, the Chinese boycott of Japanese goods, which must already have cost Japan millions of pounds, would stop. It is now reported that on nearly every point agreement has been reached, only Japan demands that Nanking should

apologise for the behaviour of Chinese forces concerned in the Tsinan-fu incident last May, and China demands that Tokio should apologise for sending troops to Tsinan-fu at all. If some process could be devised whereby both Governments apologised at exactly the same moment their patriotic feelings might be allayed, and all would be well.[5]

In May 1931, Bartlett moved away from issues in Sino-Japanese relations to discuss the then current fishing dispute between Japan and the Soviet Union. This had already developed into a wider crisis. After the Soviet Union had closed the Vladivostok branch of the Japanese-owned Chosen Bank, a Japanese citizen had shot and seriously wounded the Soviet trade agent in Tokyo. Subsequently the Japanese government had expressed its regret but, according to Bartlett, 'the Russians ... took the matter much more seriously than seems reasonable'. He concluded 'that Russo-Japanese relations were dangerously strained'. Once again Bartlett perceived 'reasonable' conduct as the measure by which international conduct should be judged. He expected both sides to be sufficiently enlightened and find an equitable basis for a settlement. Whatever the details of the dispute, Bartlett insisted on portraying the parties as equals. He concluded on a characteristically optimistic note, claiming that the dispute 'was well on the way to being settled by negotiation since it is hard to see how Russia would gain by taking more drastic steps to push the Japanese fishing fleet out of Soviet seas'.[6]

In the same broadcast Bartlett touched briefly on the Sino-Russian dispute over the Chinese Eastern Railway in Manchuria. Once again he revealed a sympathy for the interests and position of Japan. Of Tokyo's neutrality in the dispute he commented 'she may not want Russian interests strengthened in Manchuria' but 'she also knows that if the Chinese destroy Russian influence one day they would destroy Japanese influence next'.[7]

The Manchurian crisis, 1931–1933

In July 1929, two years before the outbreak of the Manchurian crisis, Vernon Bartlett had already noted, sympathetically, the immense importance of Manchuria to Japan's future. In a talk focusing on Sino–Soviet rivalry he stated:

> The difficulties placed in the way of Japanese immigrants in Australia and the United States, for example, makes it more important than ever before for Japan at least to maintain her position in a country to which so many of her nationals and so much of her money have gone – I believe that there are over seven hundred and fifty thousand Japanese subjects in Manchuria, and over twelve hundred miles of Japanese railways to be protected.[8]

With prophetic insight he concluded: 'the ultimate struggle for Manchuria is likely to be between Japan and China, so that the Chinese, if they are sensible will hesitate to do anything . . . to increase Japanese influence North of the Great Wall'.[9]

In the aftermath of Japanese attacks on Chinese forces at Mukden on 18 September 1931 Bartlett quickly appreciated the seriousness of the situation. He saw the crisis as one which might 'very easily lead to,' war but only when 'the Chinese feel strong enough to fight'. Furthermore he saw the League's response to Japanese action as crucial to its own future. After the League's first discussions Bartlett retained a measure of confidence in its workings, concluding that 'the international machinery to restore confidence *does* work, if a little creakily'. He also recalled Japan's constructive role in earlier disputes at Geneva, noting: 'the representative of Japan had himself warmly supported M. Briand when, in 1925, he made it clear that Greece had been wrong in taking the law into its own hands by reoccupying Bulgarian territory, instead of appealing to the League'.[10]

As before Bartlett emphasized Japan's diverse interests in Manchuria, mentioning her 'many rights confirmed by treaty or by custom'. In these circumstances he declared 'a complete and dramatic withdrawal . . . would of course be out of the question'. Even at this early stage in the crisis Bartlett was aware of the differences dividing civilian and military leaders in Tokyo. In view of this situation he held that avoidance of 'drastic action' by the League was the best course. This might ultimately remind the Japanese 'that less warlike methods of righting their wrongs were advisable'.[11]

By late October 1931 there was little sign that Japanese forces were responding to League of Nations calls for restraint. Nevertheless a new radio commentator O. M. Green, the *Times* correspondent in China, also showed a profound sympathy for Japan. In a broadcast entitled 'War Clouds in the Far East' he acknowledged China's aspirations but also criticized Chinese haste and tactlessness.[12] He echoed Bartlett in seeing Manchuria as Japan's economic lifeline. He continued:

> For Japan, Manchuria is really a question of life and death, she must have an outlet for her population . . . she must have markets and raw materials . . . it must be remembered that before the Japanese the Chinese had never done anything much to develop Manchuria. Japan has invested in it over £225 millions . . . and in doing so has provided work for millions of Chinese and created at least as much wealth for them as for herself.[13]

Noting the links between British and Japanese experiences in China he continued, 'The Japanese say that their treaty rights have been consistently violated by the [Chinese] Nationalists . . . Japan is not the only country that had complaints of the same sort against China.' In fact Green was more fearful of communism, the Soviet Union and left-wing Chinese politicians than he was of the threat from Japan. His final thoughts were as follows: 'What is specially serious – for all the world – is the rise in power of . . . the Left Wing of the Nationalists. The chief influence in Canton is Eugene Chen who was closely associated with the Russian agent Borodin.'[14] For Green the focus of the Manchurian crisis was not the League of Nations but the preservation of British trade and prestige in China.

In early November Bartlett returned to the microphone to analyse a clearly worsening situation. Japanese troops showed no sign of withdrawing from newly conquered territory, as the League had requested. Nevertheless this commentator desperately tried to mix commitment to the League with even-handedness. He emphasized that the Council was 'in no way taking the side of China against Japan in the matter of treaty rights', but was merely seeking to remind Japan of her obligations under the League Covenant and other international agreements. He sadly concluded 'However much sympathy other members of the Council have with [Japan] they feel that the rules which she has helped to draw up since the Armistice must be respected . . . Japan realises the need for international organization just as much as any other power.'[15]

Two weeks later, Bartlett attempted to square the increasingly complex circle of Japanese, Chinese and British interests and the League Covenant. He demonstrated sympathy for Japan by noting that

> everybody, diplomat or businessman who has had dealings with China feels a certain sympathy for the Japanese, quite apart from any particular feelings of friendship that results from the old Anglo-Japanese alliance . . . For years the lives of foreigners in China have been made difficult by civil war and rival administrations.[16]

He also acknowledged that 'that part of Manchuria which has come under [Japanese] control has been much better governed than large areas of China proper'. But clearly Bartlett preferred negotiation to Japanese military methods in resolving frictions between Chinese aspirations and foreign commercial interests.

Despite Japan's failure to withdraw her forces, and the spread of Sino-Japanese hostilities to Shanghai, Bartlett continued to find shreds of internationalist hope in Japanese conduct. He interpreted Tokyo's active campaign of self-justification at Geneva as evidence of her 'international conscience', rather than simple public relations activity.[17] Furthermore, he saw the ending of fighting at Shanghai in 1932 as evidence of Japan's conciliatory spirit. Even when Bartlett made critical observations these were usually balanced by his sensitive appreciation of Japan's economic difficulties, and the need to take international steps to ameliorate them. Some months after Japan's creation of the puppet state of Manchukuo he declared:

I do not think it is generally realised how serious the economic position of Japan has become. According to official reports the rice harvest last year only reached 40 per cent of the normal harvest, and this at a time when prices have fallen so disastrously that they are lower than the actual cost of production. Raw silk, the other great product of Japan is only selling for about one half of the amount it costs to produce. A result of this is that the peasants, who still form the great majority of the population, are terribly in debt. The interest on their debts is said to amount very nearly to the total annual value, at present prices, of the agricultural production of Japan . . . And now the taxpayer has to find heavy additional sums to fight the famine at home and the Chinese in Manchuria.[18]

The BBC's commitment to political balance, which Bartlett epitomized, was strikingly apparent on 11 March 1933 when Japanese and Chinese diplomatic representatives were given the microphone to present their respective cases on the Manchurian question. Neither Matsuoka Yosuke nor Quo Tai-chi voiced novel or surprising arguments but the BBC's magazine *The Listener* hailed this as:

the first occasion upon which the representatives of two nations engaged in a dispute have come to the microphone to take into their confidence the vast listening public . . . Last Saturday's broadcast was a fine example of the spirit behind the BBC's motto, 'Nation Shall Speak Peace Unto Nation'.[19]

Manchukuo, 1934–35

Even after Japan had withdrawn from the League of Nations, the BBC continued to give Japanese actions in Manchuria significant and sympathetic coverage. In February 1934 the conservative traveller, author and *Times* journalist Peter Fleming followed a visit to Manchuria with a talk on 'The Meaning of Manchukuo'. In his talk Fleming justified Japan's invasion as a measure taken 'under a good deal of provocation', but he admitted that the new state's nominal head ex-Emperor Pu Yi possessed only minimal authority. Yet Fleming appeared reluctant to criticize Japanese domination. He rejected the notion that Japan was 'overdoing the part of fairy godmother', noting that Japanese officials ran Manchukuo 'with a skeleton staff'. More significantly he asked: 'Do they run it well and do they do it in such a way that the thirty million inhabitants will benefit from Japanese control?'[20] Fleming's answer was clear:

I think on the whole they do. The Japanese are very progressive and efficient people: the Chinese, though I have the very greatest respect and liking for them, and though I think as individuals they can be greater than the Japanese, are not good at governing themselves. The Japanese are out to develop Manchuria: they will develop it better than the Chinese ever could have, and in the process of development the thirty million inhabitants are bound to benefit. They will not of course benefit as much as the Japanese, but the Japanese, after all, are doing most of the work, and may reasonably claim a lion's share of the profits. Last summer I was taken to task by a Japanese official . . . for sending back a despatch to the *Times* in which I said that Japanese policy in Manchuria might be summed up as enlightened exploitation . . . in the end he . . . admitted that enlightened exploitation was a fair way of describing it.[21]

Among Japanese achievements Fleming singled out currency stabilization as especially important, declaring 'every dollar is worth a dollar. You can imagine what a blessing that is to the people!'[22] He also enjoyed joining Japanese troops on a bandit hunting foray and observed: 'When the troops come through the wretched people have a brief respite from being terrorised – when the troops have gone the reign of terror is resumed.'[23] Despite his praise for Japanese achievements Fleming admitted that banditry remained a serious problem. Nevertheless his closing words were positive if somewhat facetious: 'Japan is a very powerful ally; and unless she overrates her own power and challenges Russia; Manchukuo is going to be a very important place: and not only to stamp collectors.'[24]

In 1935 Dame Rachel Crowdy, a former chief of the Social Questions and Opium Traffic Section of the League of Nations, visited Manchukuo for two months. Despite Japan's withdrawal from the League Dame Rachel generously lauded Japanese achievements. Like Fleming she recognized that Manchukuo was effectively a Japanese puppet state, and that banditry remained an unresolved problem, but her responses were surprisingly favourable. She described Japanese pioneers as follows:

There is something of a crusading spirit among the young Japanese one meets here. They may not have to die for Manchukuo, but they have to live in Manchukuo, something which to them is infinitely harder – something which means uncongenial exile.

The Japanese have something to show for all their efforts. Roads and railways are knitting the country together . . . Everywhere in the capital Government buildings are being built . . . which would not shame the greatest cities of the world and in the town planning nothing seems to have been forgotten.[25]

While aware that local farmers and traders had probably suffered from the arrival of Japanese and Korean immigrants, Dame Rachel was particularly impressed by the changes which the Japanese had instituted in the recently annexed province of Jehol:

> I asked a good many people who knew the situation in Manchuria far better than I do whether the Japanese had brought any sort of order out of the chaos in . . . Jehol, and found that even the people who had been most opposed to the Japanese action in 1933 had to own that, the people in the province of Jehol are in a better situation today than they were two years ago. This is partly because the War Lord who ran the Province before the Japanese came in happened to be a particularly bad specimen . . . It was a rule of terror. Today the people are at least sure that their crops will be paid for, they know what their taxes will be, they are protected by and not from soldiers, their currency is stable, and a great deal has been done to reduce the epidemics of cholera, dysentery and plague. Added to that . . . they are safer from bandits today than they have been for a very long time.[26]

Clearly Fleming and Crowdy could not have travelled freely or independently in Japanese-controlled territory, but their sympathetic attitudes may well have expressed paternal imperial reflexes – as well as a desire to avert Anglo-Japanese controversy.

Economic issues, 1933–35

Although Japanese textile exports to Britain and the Dominions seriously threatened British and Indian manufacturers, BBC commentators attempted to deal with economic issues in a surprisingly broad-minded way. One example of this came from Barnard Ellinger who, in 1933, used the current textile negotiations in Simla as an occasion to review the textile trade in its broadest terms. Like Bartlett, Ellinger showed considerable sympathy for Japan's economic position, commenting:

> Japan's greatest difficulty is her population problem. Her population increases at the rate of about a million persons per year, and practically every available yard of land is already cultivated . . . Japan is still an agricultural country . . . yet she cannot feed her people without importing food. Nor can she clothe her people without importing cotton and wool.[27]

Ellinger noted that Australia, Canada and the United States were closed to Japanese immigrants and declared: 'The only other possibility which Japan has to enable her to feed and clothe her people is to absorb her surplus population into industry, and to export goods in order to import those commodities which a people must have in order to live.'[28]

The logical conclusion of Ellinger's argument was that if Japan's cotton cloth exports were restricted 'we may expect to have to face increased competition in our wool, iron and steel and shipbuilding industries'. Ellinger was also surprisingly objective in answering the frequent charge that Japanese competition was 'unfair because she has a lower standard of living than our own'. He pointed out that Canada and the United States similarly 'complain of our competition which they say is based on a standard of living which is less than theirs'. He also rejected the notion that Japan's key advantage lay in the employment of 'sweated labour'. Not only was this an ill-defined term, but he pointed out that many girls in Britain earned less than Japanese girls working in textile factories.[29]

In March 1934 the distinguished British scholar-diplomat George Sansom also spoke sympathetically, and surprisingly positively, about Japan's economic responses to the depression. In Sansom's words, 'she had to cut down her imports of foreign manufactures so that . . . she began to manufacture articles for export on a large scale, and in great variety'. He concluded: 'there is no doubt about it – the *quality* of these articles is good and is improving all the time. This is because sensible Japanese manufacturers, in the lean years before Japan went off gold, took drastic steps to increase their technical efficiency.'[30]

This admiring view of Japan's economic vitality was also echoed in N. K. Roscoe's 1934 talk 'The Japanese Farmer'. In what was a well-informed tribute to the Japanese peasantry, Roscoe proclaimed:

> I doubt if there is any body of farmers anywhere in the world more skilful than the Japanese. Not only have they the traditional experience of countless generations of farmers behind them, but they have the benefits of modern up-to-date research, for there is an agricultural experiment station in every one of the forty-seven prefectures into which the country is divided.[31]

He continued: 'The Japanese farmer is remarkably keen to learn. During the winter months . . . he will come miles, often through the snow, and sit on a hard floor for as much as five or six hours in the day, listening to lectures and taking notes.'[32] Roscoe concluded: 'that's the Japanese farmer – intelligent, hard-working, honest, courteous and patient – the backbone of the Japanese nation.'[33]

In May 1935 Sir Frederick Whyte, former advisor to the Chinese Nationalist government, extended admiration for Japanese economic achievements to the China trade. Commenting on the situation in Shanghai he declared:

> Ask anyone what the situation now is and he will tell you that the progress made by Japan in every direction is amazing. He will tell you that he admires Japan and recognises that her achievement is the reward

of a great effort in which merchant, manufacturer and Government alike all unite to push the national interest forward.[34]

Yet Whyte's increasingly frequent 'Foreign Affairs' commentaries also revealed a measure of unease at the broad direction of Japanese commercial and military policies. Nevertheless his measured criticisms were usually counterbalanced by expressions of goodwill toward Foreign Minister Hirota, and mention of more congenial Japanese statements. Typical of this approach was a broadcast entitled 'What is Japan Driving At?', in which Whyte noted increasing trade restrictions in Manchukuo, but also referred to the Japanese foreign minister's expressed desire for warmer relations with Britain.[35]

The 26 February incident, 1936

Perhaps the tendency to present unpleasant aspects of Japan as favourably as possible was most apparent in 1936, following the abortive military coup of 26 February. Shortly after the rebels had murdered three leading statesmen, ex-Ambassador Sir Francis Lindley broadcast an analysis of 'Recent Events in Japan'. This called for an attempt at sympathetic understanding. Lindley admitted that political assassination was 'the greatest blot on Japanese civilization at the present time' but pointed out the moral basis of Japanese political violence. The ex-ambassador noted:

> It has always been a tradition in Japan from the earliest times that violence is not to be condemned when a man or a body of men have a grievance, or see an injustice which they think so serious that they are ready to sacrifice their lives in order to put it right. In the past there have been numerous instances of men who have deliberately committed some act of violence with the determination either of committing suicide themselves . . . or of giving themselves up to justice and being executed out of hand.[36]

More remarkable was Lindley's explanation of the lenient treatment which the rebellious officers had received; namely 'that the Japanese are temperamentally opposed to pushing things to extremes'. He continued: 'it is one of the most striking features of the Japanese character that they always attempt to find a compromise in any dispute or struggle which arises in the country whether it is a private quarrel or over a political or industrial question'.[37] Particularly surprising was Lindley's conclusion that 'In this the Japanese, for all their differences of civilization and history and religion, resemble our own island people which for so long was allied with them to our mutual advantage'.[38]

The Anti-Comintern Pact, 1936–37

When Japan signed the Anti-Comintern Pact with Nazi Germany in November 1936, the BBC's East Asia commentator O. M. Green optimistically noted the many weaknesses of the Japanese government's position rather than the potential threat of the new alignment to Britain. Not only was the new link with Germany the object of 'strong disapproval . . . shown by practically all the Japanese newspapers, who say . . . that its disadvantages are likely to far outweigh its advantages', but the rising military budget was also highly unpopular. In addition Green believed that 'the condition of the farmers . . . is truly deplorable, their rents, taxation and what they have to spend on fertilisers . . . an almost unendurable burden'.[39] According to this broadcaster, Japanese–Soviet relations had improved in recent months so it was foolhardy for Japan to jeopardize possible agreements with Moscow on oil and fisheries for the sake of links with Berlin. Yet Green saw some potential for good in 'the internal condition and ferment in Japan'. He concluded:

> after the Great War the Japanese military tried to seize the Russian dominions of Eastern Siberia. The adventure ultimately became thoroughly unpopular in Japan and the military were obliged to drop it. So may it be again as regards the Japanese forward movement in North China.[40]

In other words public opinion might prefer peace and undermine the power of the Japanese military.

Italy's adherence to the pact in 1937 produced a further BBC analysis. This time the commentator was F. A. Voigt, an authority on European dictatorships. Perhaps this speaker's non-Asian expertise readily explains his mistaken belief that Japanese forces were likely to achieve major victories in China; before challenging the European colonial powers in South-East Asia. For Voigt the pact was ultimately directed against Britain and the Netherlands rather than the Soviet Union.[41]

Domestic politics and the China War, 1937–39

The combined drama of the 26 February incident and the creation of the Anti-Comintern Pact led the BBC to devote increasing attention to the complexities of Japanese domestic politics. Perhaps a shortage of Japanese experts led to O. M. Green, being given chief responsibility for analysing this particularly complex situation. Green did succeed in conveying the complexity of the Japanese scene, though he probably overstated the significance of Imperial 'divinity' and 'tradition' in the events he described. Green saw Japanese society as divided between the Army and the people, though he admitted to confusion as to where the locus of power lay within the Imperial Army and its controlling Ministry. Whatever Green's misunderstandings, he praised such Japanese leaders as General Ugaki ('a man of the highest character and ability'), General Hayashi ('a man of ability and high character') and Admiral Yonai ('a much respected man').[42] Furthermore he saw public opinion and parliamentarians as significant positive forces. Not only was the Diet hostile to the establishment of a new quasi-fascist regime but one of its members Dr Hamada had openly criticized the Army's appetite for power.[43]

This led Green to a measure of optimism regarding future trends. He believed that popular elections might well produce an even more self-confident Diet, more resistant to army demands. Like most BBC commentators Green ended this talk with words which suggested hope, rather than disaster: 'The Diet today is probably stronger and more insistent than for many years past. The Japanese, like all Orientals, are very clever at compromise. One cannot despair of wiser counsels yet taking effect in the "land of the Rising Sun".'[44] A month later, in early March 1937, Green cited new grounds for optimism regarding Japan's future. He claimed that:

> the whole balance of power has altered in the Far East. Four or five years ago, Japan was supreme . . . Now Russia is a formidable factor . . . China has raised her head . . . and is ready to bargain as an equal . . . There begins to be an equipoise of forces which should be the foundation of peace. And the Japanese are far too clever not to realise it.[45]

In the immediate aftermath of fighting between Japanese and Chinese forces at the Marco Polo Bridge Green still retained a belief in 'a certain silver lining in these dark clouds'.[46] He noted the overwhelming defeat of the government in the General Election and a 'very strong feeling among leading men in Japan that . . . Japan and China, and Japan and Russia must get on better terms'. The possibility of new talks between Britain and Japan also added to Green's optimism. He thought 'there was good reason to believe that Japan is very anxious . . . that these should have good result . . . and she is certainly well aware that anything like ruthlessness on her part towards China would gravely prejudice her chances with Great Britain'.[47]

Five days later Green broadcast again in more sombre mood, now focusing on the continuing fighting in North China. In a masterly analysis of the broad and immediate historical background of the conflict he noted both Japan's ambitions in North China and the strengthening of Chinese solidarity. Green described the outlook as 'very gloomy' but finally mobilized an unreal degree of rationality to extract some hope from the situation. He concluded:

> War must be equally ruinous for both parties. It would wreck all the splendid schemes of development with which China has latterly been

making so much progress, and set her back a quarter of a century. And on the Japanese side it is self-evident that nobody can conquer China ... The Japanese may win some battles, take some towns, nip off a bit of territory ... but neither they nor anybody else could ever conquer China. Their military expenses would be colossal and their valuable trade with the Chinese would vanish into thin air. It may safely be assumed that both the Japanese and Chinese Governments are fully aware of these facts; and so it may be hoped that common sense and the inexhaustible Oriental ingenuity in devising formulas and compromises may yet find a way out of the present crisis.[48]

The first time a BBC broadcaster clearly condemned any Japanese action was in October 1937 in a talk entitled 'War and Law in the Far East'. In this the distinguished international lawyer Sir John Fischer Williams declared that 'Events in the far East have shocked the civilised world', and affirmed that the undeclared war in China was as subject to international law as legally declared conflicts.[49] He admitted that the Japanese government made no claim to immunity from the restraints of international law; but, implicitly, Williams found Japan's explanation of many of her actions unconvincing. He asked, rhetorically, whether Japan had treated civilians as legitimate targets and replied:

Observers on the spot believe that she has. Public opinion in this country and ... at the Assembly of the League of Nations accepts this view. Certainly Japan has caused horrors to which I can remember no parallel in the Great War. The whole sympathy of this country is with her victims.[50]

However, rather than proceeding from this condemnation to a climactic attack on Japan, or a call for hostile action, this speaker devoted his final minutes to a generalized discussion of the need to abolish all war.

In much of 1938, broadcasting was dominated by events in Central Europe, which culminated in the Munich Agreement. However, the war in China remained a theme of serious radio comment. Much analysis focused on the economic impact of the conflict, and the capacity of the belligerents to withstand a protracted struggle.

In late January, N. Skene Smith, who had taught for six years at the Tokyo University of Commerce, warned that whatever British views of the 'wrongs and rights' of the war might be it was possible for Japan to continue fighting for at least a further year. To confirm this he noted that:

Following in the footsteps of the Japanese soldiers is a small army of businessmen and officials belonging mainly to the two or three chartered companies which have been set up to develop North China. These hope to increase the production of Chinese cotton, coal, iron, gold and foodstuffs which will be exchanged for Japanese and Western manufactures.[51]

Skene Smith believed that Sino-Japanese economic cooperation, or its success, could not be taken for granted, but he suggested that, for Japan, transition to a peacetime economy would now be very difficult; furthermore a Japanese economic collapse would hardly benefit the depressed world economy.

Despite a growing tendency for speakers to lament the destructiveness of the Sino-Japanese conflict, it is notable that none spoke, even indirectly, of the Nanking massacre, or directly of Japanese atrocities. Instead much comment concentrated on military developments, with particular emphasis on Chinese resistance. By March 1938 O. M. Green's pro-Chinese stance was increasingly apparent. Even more striking, considering his opinions in 1931, was his positive view of Chinese Communist forces, now described as a 'picturesque and very useful element'.[52] Green was not only aware of the iron resolve of the Chinese and Japanese governments, but also of the grave economic losses that both countries were suffering. These extended far beyond direct damage resulting from military action. In this harsh situation the almost obligatory coda of optimism of BBC talks was difficult to compose. Confronted by 'mad destruction' in East Asia and threatening crises in Europe Green could only conclude 'If only Europe could be brought to a state of better mutual understanding and peacefulness it could hardly be doubted that the reactions would also make for peace in the Far East.'[53]

Perhaps the frequent tendency to use economic arguments to advocate peace in Asia was most apparent in comments by the respected historian and advocate of the League of Nations, Sir Alfred Zimmern, in a discussion in June 1938 entitled 'Youth has its Say'. In answer to a young discussant Zimmern declared:

> The demands made by Japan on China seem . . . unreal because they do not correspond to any of the essential needs of Japan. The real interests of Japan would be much better served by constructive cooperation between the two countries. This would improve her economic position and would serve her vital strategic interests through the maintenance of a stable balance of power in the Far East. The present position has arisen either because we have not listened to the Japanese when they made their demands in a reasonable way, or because the rulers of Japan themselves preferred to pursue a policy of violent aggrandisement even when this ran counter to their real needs and interests.[54]

However, such lofty analysis was far removed from the harsh realities of Japanese military operations. More realistically, two new commentators now addressed the issue of China's capacity to battle on. In June 1938 Colonel

Steward, who had 'served for many years in China', asserted that Japan could 'endure longer than China' but raised the interlinked question 'Can Japan allow China's prolonged resistance to undermine the financial support on which her world position rests?' He answered 'Not if she values that position and intends to remain the strongest power in the East'. He continued 'Japan must try to finish the war this year or be prepared to compromise in an unsatisfactory peace'.[55] Two months later, Edwin Haward, ex-editor of the *North China Daily News*, also chronicled Japan's military successes, but similarly noted the economic strains she would suffer after a lengthening campaign, or a military stalemate. Such a situation would not 'necessarily jeopardise her position as a great Power but it may compel her to cut her diplomatic coat more closely to her economic cloth, as is already shown by her earnest attempts to compose the awkward face-imperilling dispute with Russia'.[56] At the end of this broadcast the notion of 'friendly mediation', presumably British, was mentioned as the only possible exit from 'a senseless and devastating war'.

Throughout two years of broadcasts on the Sino-Japanese conflict the main preoccupation of commentators had been the complex interaction of military and economic power. In 1939, in an ambitious series entitled 'The Pacific', the BBC turned to academic authorities to place current events in a much broader geographical and historical perspective. Within this series one programme, 'Japan as Empire Builder', enabled two distinguished historians, Geoffrey Hudson and Charles Webster, to present a sophisticated and sympathetic view of modern Japan's development. In their highly academic analysis these speakers attempted to create 'balance' at a time when anti-Japanese feeling was understandably widespread. Hudson suggested that much in the Japanese past was at variance with its military present. He wryly commented that in the mid-nineteenth century 'the Japanese had not made a war outside their own country since 1598, in the time of Queen Elizabeth, and they had not had a serious civil war since 1615'. He added 'No European nation can approach Japan's record of internal and external peace for the seventeenth and eighteenth centuries.'[57] In discussing Japan's recent trading difficulties Hudson commented:

> the conditions of international trade since the Great War have made her commerce specially insecure. Japan's chief raw material export, raw silk, is specially subject to great fluctuations of price, as it depends so much for its demand on a high level of prosperity in the world as a whole, while her manufactured goods have been affected to an increasing degree by the tariffs and quotas of other countries. Like a number of other nations therefore she has been very short of foreign exchange.[58]

Suggesting the deep ironies of foreign protectionism he observed 'it was at a time when the Government of Japan was more liberal than it has ever been before or since that the highest . . . American tariffs were clamped on'.[59] Affirming the link between Japan's economic difficulties and the rise of authoritarianism, Hudson stated: 'in 1930 and 1931 Japan's export trade was nearly halved . . . and because Japan had so little margin of safety in her economic system the situation rapidly became desperate. In the depths of the crisis they turned to the army'.[60]

Charles Webster also showed remarkable empathy in his analysis of Japan's economic plight. 'All impartial critics', he noted, 'have sympathised with the difficult position in which Japan was placed by the necessity of finding markets for her goods when economic nationalism was closing them, Britain and the United States have some responsibility here.'[61] Although Webster did not acquit Japan of aggressive acts he skilfully turned to Japanese tradition as offering more peaceful models of conduct – namely Ieyasu's legendary patience which helped to deliver centuries of Tokugawa peace. In the final programme of 'The Pacific' series Webster concluded by hoping for 'a new Japan . . . with whom other nations can live in peace and cooperation' – an objective later to be espoused by American and British planners during the Pacific War.[62]

Conclusion

Despite the deterioration of Anglo-Japanese relations during the interwar years, the BBC pursued a restrained and 'balanced' policy in its interpretation of Japanese politics and diplomacy. During the Manchurian crisis much understanding was shown of Japan's position. Later, Japan's commercial challenge was viewed with remarkable detachment. Even Japan's excesses during the China War were presented in surprisingly diplomatic language. After the Anti-Comintern Pact and Japan's alignment with Nazi Germany her difficulties were still evaluated with impressive analytical depth. The BBC's broadcasting for understanding and peace may be interpreted as the natural expression of the needs of a satisfied, status quo power, but it is undeniable that peace building was a novel and complex objective, an objective which the BBC pioneered with originality and intelligence during this period.

Notes

1. The BBC adopted this quasi-biblical motto in 1927.
2. For the origins of the British Broadcasting Company – later the British Broadcasting Corporation – see A. Briggs, *The History of Broadcasting in the United Kingdom. Volume I. The Birth of Broadcasting* (Oxford: Oxford University Press, 1961).

3. Dr Charrier's extensive research in the Foreign Office files has revealed no government intervention shaping broadcasts on Japan in the years 1929–39.

4. For a brief outline of Bartlett's career, see Lord Blake and C. S. Nicholls (eds), *The Dictionary of National Biography 1981–1985* (Oxford: Oxford University Press, 1990), pp. 29–30.

5. Vernon Bartlett, 'The Far East and the League of Nations', *The Listener*, 6 February 1929, p. 137.

6. Vernon Bartlett, 'Troubled Waters', *The Listener*, 6 May 1931, p. 760.

7. Ibid., p. 760.

8. Vernon Bartlett, 'The Russo-Chinese Dispute', *The Listener*, 31 July 1929 (talk broadcast on 25 July 1931), p. 153.

9. Ibid., p. 153.

10. Vernon Bartlett, 'The Way of the World – Unrest in Manchuria', *The Listener*, 30 September 1931, p. 544.

11. Ibid., p. 554.

12. O. M. Green's writings include *Discovering China* (1938), *China's Struggles with the Dictators* (1941), *The Foreigners in China* (1933) and *The Story of China's Revolution* (1945). O. M. Green, 'War Clouds in the Far East', *The Listener*, 28 October 1931, pp. 714–15.

13. Ibid., p. 714.

14. Ibid., p. 715.

15. Vernon Bartlett, 'The Way of the World – Other People's Crises', *The Listener*, 4 November 1931, p. 764.

16. Vernon Bartlett, 'The Way of the World – Manchuria the Danger Spot', *The Listener*, 18 November 1931, p. 854.

17. Vernon Bartlett, 'The Way of the World – Tokyo, Nanking and Geneva', *The Listener*, 9 December 1931, p. 996.

18. Vernon Bartlett, 'The Way of the World – Back to Asia', *The Listener*, 21 December 1932, p. 402.

19. 'Week by Week', *The Listener*, 15 March 1933, p. 400.

20. Peter Fleming, 'The Far East – VI, The Meaning of Manchukuo', *The Listener*, 14 February 1934, p. 262.

21. Ibid., p. 262.

22. Ibid., p. 262.

23. Ibid., p. 264.

24. Ibid., p. 264.

25. For Dame Rachel Eleanor Crowdy's career, see E. T. Williams and C. S. Nicholls (eds), *The Dictionary of National Biography, 1961–1978* (Oxford: Oxford University Press, 1981), pp. 250–1. Dame Rachel Crowdy, 'The Making of Manchukuo', *The Listener*, 6 February 1935, pp. 218–19.

26. Ibid., p. 219.

27. For Ellinger's career, see *Who Was Who, Vol. 4, 1941–1960* (London: A and C. Black, 1962), p. 354. Barnard Ellinger, 'Japan and Lancashire Negotiate', *The Listener*, 1 November 1933, p. 652.

28. Ibid., p. 652.

29. Ibid., p. 653.

30. A correspondent from Tokyo (George Sansom), 'The Far East – XI, Japan is Changing', *The Listener*, 21 March 1934, p. 480.

31. N. K. Roscoe, 'The Far East – VIII, The Japanese Farmer', *The Listener*, 28 February 1934, p. 357.

32. Ibid., p. 358.
33. Ibid., p. 359.
34. For Whyte's career (1883–1970), see *Who Was Who, Vol. 6, 1961–1970* (London: A. and C. Black, 1972), pp. 1197–8. Sir Frederick Whyte, 'British Interests in the Far East', *The Listener*, 29 May 1935 (Broadcast 30 May 1935), p. 908.
35. Sir Frederick Whyte, 'What is Japan Driving At?', *The Listener*, 30 January 1935, p. 185.
36. Sir Francis Lindley, 'Recent Events in Japan', *The Listener*, 11 March 1936, p. 475.
37. Ibid., p. 475.
38. Ibid., p. 475.
39. O. M. Green, 'World Affairs – Reactions to the German–Japanese Agreement', *The Listener*, 9 December 1936 (Broadcast on 30 November 1936), p. 1086.
40. Ibid., p. 1086.
41. F. A. Voigt, 'World Affairs – Significance of the Anti-Comintern Pact', *The Listener*, 1 December 1937, p. 1182.
42. O. M. Green, 'World Affairs – Army or People in Japan?', *The Listener*, 10 February 1937 (Broadcast on 1 February 1937), p. 250.
43. Ibid., p. 252.
44. Ibid., p. 253.
45. O. M. Green, 'Balance of Power in the East', *The Listener*, 10 March 1937 (Broadcast on 2 March 1937), p. 468.
46. O. M. Green, 'War Clouds in the Far East', *The Listener*, 21 July 1937, (Broadcast on 14 July 1937), p. 152.
47. Ibid., p. 152.
48. O. M. Green, 'World Affairs – Peace or War in North China?', *The Listener*, 28 July 1937 (Broadcast on 19 July 1937), p. 194.
49. For Sir John Fischer Williams' career, see L. G. Wickham Legg and E. T. Williams (eds), *The Dictionary of National Biography 1941–50* (Oxford: Oxford University Press, 1959), p. 959. Sir John Fischer Williams, 'War and Law in the Far East', *The Listener*, 13 October 1937, p. 755.
50. Ibid., p. 766.
51. N. Skene Smith, 'How Long Can Japan Go On?', *The Listener*, 9 February 1938 (Broadcast on 25 January 1938), p. 287.
52. O. M. Green, 'World Affairs – Sino-Japanese Struggle', *The Listener*, 9 March 1938, p. 500.
53. Ibid., p. 501.
54. A Discussion between John Howard and Sir Alfred Zimmern, 'The Way of Peace – Youth Has its Say', *The Listener*, 18 June 1938, p. 1283.
55. Colonel G. R. V. Steward, 'Can China be Beaten?', *The Listener*, 30 June 1938, p. 1406.
56. Edwin Haward, 'Stalemate in the Far East?', *The Listener*, 18 August 1938, p. 318.
57. G. F. Hudson, Interlocuter: Professor C. K. Webster, 'The Pacific – Japan as Empire Builder', *The Listener*, 9 February 1939, p. 291.
58. Ibid., pp. 292–3.
59. Ibid., p. 293.
60. Ibid., p. 294.
61. Ibid., p. 294.
62. Professor C. K. Webster, 'The Pacific – The Present Situation', *The Listener*, 13 April 1939, p. 785.

15
Anglo-Japanese Trade Union Relations Between the Wars

Takao Matsumura

Awkward beginnings through the International Transport workers' Federation

Although Japan enjoyed a variety of links with Britain in the late nineteenth and early twentieth centuries, there were virtually no relations between Japanese and British trade unions before 1945. One exception was contacts between the Trades Union Congress (TUC) and the Japanese Seamen's Union (JSU) during the early 1930s. However, following the outbreak of Japan's war with China in July 1937 relations between trade unions disintegrated and there followed a boycott of Japanese goods in Britain.

The Japanese Seamen's Union was exceptional among Japanese trade unions in the 1920s in being centralized and united. In 1920 some fifty different seamen's unions had amalgamated into one – the JSU. The Union's official journal, *Kaiin* (Seamen), devoted a considerable part of its contents to the work of the International Transport Workers' Federation (ITF) and promoted internationalist ideas.[1] The ITF had been established in 1893 and was reorganized after the First World War. It recruited among seamen, railwaymen and other transport workers in the 1920s, when its membership rose from $1\frac{1}{2}$ million in 25 countries to $2\frac{1}{4}$ million in 35 countries. Its headquarters were located in Amsterdam and Edo Fimmen, a Dutch trade union leader, became its general secretary in 1924.[2]

On 27 September 1930 the General Council of the ITF appointed its president, C. T. Cramp (the general secretary of the British National Union of Railwaymen) and Fimmen as delegates to be sent to East Asia to establish a regional secretariat. Ernest Bevin, C. T. Cramp and M. Daud (the president of the Indian Seamen's Union) attended a meeting to consider this step.[3]

However, in June 1931 it became clear that Cramp's own union work prevented him travelling to East Asia. As a result, in July, the General Council of the ITF decided that Fimmen should travel to Japan, China, the Dutch East Indies and India on his own. Of these countries Japan and India were seen as the most important in terms of establishing a Far East Secretariat.[4]

The 'delegation' had planned to spend four to six weeks in India. However, shortly before it was due to leave, the British Labour government refused to grant a visa for its visit to India. Similarly the Netherlands government was unwilling to permit the ITF representative to travel to the Dutch East Indies. The British government explained its refusal by stating that a Royal Commission had recently undertaken an inquiry into working conditions in India, and that therefore a further inquiry, particularly by a foreigner, was neither necessary nor desirable. The real reason for these refusals was that the British and Dutch governments and their officials in India and the Dutch East Indies feared and wished to prevent the creation of a sub-secretariat in the Far East, because such an organization might threaten closer relations and cooperation between workers in various colonial territories.

On 22 August 1931 Fimmen left Amsterdam for Japan and he arrived at Yokohama on 26 September. The *Tokyo Nichi Nichi* reported that he was greeted by Yonekubo Mitsunori (the international secretary of the JSU) and Matsuoka Komakichi (the principal secretary of the General Federation of Japanese Labour) and others.[5] Fimmen went straight to the headquarters of the General Federation at Shibazonobashi in Tokyo, to be greeted by the flags of their unions and of the IFT. Leftists opposed Fimmen's visit and the *Chugai Shimbun* commented that 'The real purpose of Mr Fimmen's visit is to extend the influence of the Second International to the Orient.'[6]

On the following day Fimmen was invited to the opening ceremony of Nihon Rodo Kaikan (Japanese Labour Hall) at Mita, Tokyo, where he addressed 500 people. The General Federation of Japanese Labour had spent 55 000 yen on the building as a symbol of the growing strength of Japanese trade unionism. Other activists present at the ceremony included Abe Isoo, the head of the Social Democratic Party, two liberal academics – Nitobe Inazo and Yoshino Sakuzo, as well as Suzuki Bunji, Nishio Suehiro, Katayama Tetsu and Hamada. One leftist critic' suggested that they constituted the 'headquarters of the foul right-wing world of labour'.[7]

On 28 September Fimmen, Hamada and Yonekubo visited the Ministry of the Interior. Once again 'many people gathered outside and made a demonstration against the visitor, calling him a traitor to the working class'.[8] Later Fimmen visited Tokyo, Yokohama, Nagoya, Osaka, Kobe and Moji, all the towns in which the JSU had branches. He used the opportunity to collect data about the conditions of many different types of workers.

Fimmen remained in Japan until 30 October when he left Shimonoseki for China. He could not have anticipated that the Japanese invasion of Manchuria, which had begun on 18 September, would completely undermine his attempt to establish a sub-secretariat in the Far East.

After Fimmen had left Europe, Walter Citrine, the secretary of the TUC, and Mogi Sobei (the London representative of the JSU) had tried to obtain permission for Fimmen to visit India. In 1931, however, the Labour Party was in crisis and figures such as Tom Shaw and George Lansbury were 'now election mad and have not time to spend on anything else.' Mogi approached several Labour MPs in connection with Fimmen's visa problem but, he reported, 'they say that their efforts would be useless because in the present political crisis in this country their questions would not be heard'.[9] Mogi met Citrine on 29 September 1931 to try to resolve this problem. Citrine informed him that, according to unofficial information which he had received, Fimmen was suspected of sympathizing with the communist movement.[10]

After obtaining details of Fimmen's career from Nathans (assistant secretary to the ITF),[11] Citrine met Sir Malcom Seton, deputy under secretary at the India Office, on 12 October 1931, and explained that Fimmen had never been a communist and was 'going there [to India] solely and purely for the work of his Federation, the International Transportworkers' Federation'. Seton asked, 'Was it not a fact that Mr Fimmen belonged or used to belong to the League Against Imperialism?' Citrine responded: 'Mr Fimmen has been formally expelled on 5th June this year at a meeting of that League, but he had resigned long before that. . . . Mr Fimmen himself, it must be remembered has never been a Communist'.[12]

However, on 25 November 1931 Citrine received the final rejection of his request from Samuel Hoare (the minister for India).[13] Three weeks before, Mogi had already sent a telegram to Fimmen when the latter was en route from Japan to China: 'DEEPLY REGRET IMPOSSIBLE PROCURE VISA MOGI'.[14] As a result it was quite impossible to hold an international transport workers' conference in India.

After travelling in Korea and Manchuria with Yonekubo, Fimmen reached Shanghai on 6 November. Yonekubo remained with Fimmen for only eight days, and he returned to Japan when telegrams made it clear that the British government's refusal to allow Fimmen and Yonekubo to enter India was final.

Being shocked by 'Terrorism' in Shanghai, on 8 December 1931 Fimmen sent an open letter in the name of the ITF criticizing 'the fascist Kuomintang government's regime of terror and bloodshed' referring to Chiang Kai-shek's recent coup d'état, and demanding the assurance of basic rights for Chinese workers.[15] He urged the release of the imprisoned workers, the repeal of the emergency laws and demanded that all terror should cease.

Under these circumstances, alongside the conflict between China and Japan in Manchuria, it became very difficult for Fimmen to contact Chinese workers or to obtain reliable information about their conditions. As he could not visit India, he returned to Amsterdam via the Philippines. In a letter to Mogi from Amsterdam dated 30 January 1932, he wrote: 'As it is, the fact that I was unable to arrange for the international conference in India has made the results of my trip to the Far East to a certain effect problematic.'[16] It was, in fact, more than 'problematic'. It had been an awkward, futile mission.

This was the last real chance for a western trade union leader to visit Japan, as Fimmen acknowledged in a letter to Cramp on 1 February 1932: 'things have so developed in the Far East that I just go there – into China and Japan, at least – before the door was closed. For the next few years . . . I fear it is going to be very difficult for a delegation of European trade unionists to go to the Far East and do anything useful there'.[17]

The next day Fimmen wrote pessimistically to Yonekubo: 'I am rather afraid that much, if not all, of what we have discussed, prepared and achieved during my stay in the Far East, will be brought to nothing by this Chino-Japanese conflict.'[18] As a result the plan to hold an international conference between representatives of East Asiatic organizations in order to establish a sub-secretariat of the ITF could not be realized.

Before Fimmen visited Japan, the sending of a second delegation to the Far East had been planned by the International Federation of Trade Unions (IFTU). On 21 July 1931 the Executive Meeting of the IFTU decided to send both its president, Citrine, and its general secretary, Schevenels, to Japan, India and China.[19] On 21 August Schevenels asked the TUC General Council 'to grant Comrade Citrine the necessary leave of absence', though this would be 'a great sacrifice of the British Trade Union Movement'.[20] On 2 December 1931 the International Committee of the IFTU formally appointed Citrine and Schevenels as delegates.[21] Two days later, Matsuoka Komakichi wrote to Citrine and suggested 'a visit to the Prime Minister, Minister of Home Affairs and Foreign Affairs, the Minister of the Railways and the Head of the Social Bureau, also the Mayors of Tokyo and Osaka'.[22] On 13 January 1932 Mogi met Citrine and Bolton to suggest the route to Japan, the places to visit and the persons to meet, and stated that 'he would endeavour to travel to Japan with Mr Shevenels and Citrine in October'.[23] On the following day Mogi expressed his strong hope for the success of Citrine's visit to Japan: 'I think your visit to Japan will arouse more interest among the trade unionists and the public than that of Mr Fimmen.'[24]

Despite these preparations and expectations, the Executive Meeting of the IFTU held in Berlin on 9–10 June 1932 decided to postpone sending the delegation, for three reasons: first, 'the political position, both in Germany and elsewhere. . . . would hardly allow for the absence of Citrine and Schevenels'; second, 'the military dictatorship of Japan would make it impossible to carry out an impartial enquiry'; and third, 'the trouble in British India and the suppression of the right of public assembly'[25] made this an inopportune time to visit India.

Japanese seamen's ambivalence towards Japanese expansion in China

As Japan invaded Manchuria and then China, a delicate difference developed between the JSU and Fimmen. In October 1931 Mogi insisted that 'undoubtedly the anti-Japanese boycott movement and the anti-Japanese educational policy in China from the purely international and socialist point of view is just as wrong as the militarist intervention in Manchuria'.[26] While staying in Japan Fimmen heard that Hamada had publicly declared that he was in favour of the move into Manchuria, though Yonekubo had opposed it in public. Fimmen was worried and wrote to Mogi on 30 January 1932:

> The attitude of Imperialist Japan towards China will make it very difficult for the Japanese Seamen's Union to secure acceptance as the pioneer of workers' internationalism amongst the Eastern peoples, the more so as I am a little uneasy about the attitude of the Japanese Seamen's Union towards the conflict.[27]

On 1 March 1932 the puppet state of Manchukuo was established and the differences between the JSU and Fimmen deepened, as a letter from Yonekubo indicates:

> Thankful to say that a new nation is now to be created in Manchuria and also a new movement to restore peace in The Shanghai Conflict is likely to be realized which will serve us in our effort to get the good understanding of the Chinese proletariat to join to our task in future, though it might not be very near.[28]

On 1 April 1932 Fimmen replied that 'the work for the ITF in the Far East ... will be very difficult on account of the attitude taken up by the Japanese militarist clique'. The workers in other Far Eastern countries 'will regard Japan as a "danger", and will be as suspicious of Japanese labour in the international field as they have hitherto been of the white workers'.[29]

When the Japanese Trade Union Congress (Nihon Rodo Kumiai Kaigi) was established in September 1932, the TUC General Council in Britain saw it as a valuable movement for it reported that the Japanese TUC was

> established ... on the following principles – anti-capitalism, anticommunism and anti-fascism. It has now a membership of 278 000 from ten organizations ... This is the latest step in the work of centralising the Japanese Trade Unions ... The Japanese Seamen's Union played an outstanding part in paving the way for the unification of the country's labour movement. This Union is the most important in the country, which finds expression in the fact that the Congress elected K. Hamada, President of that Union, as its President, and M. Yonekubo, General Secretary, as its Secretary and Treasurer.[30]

Despite the continuing rise of militarism in Japan, some portion of the trade union movement continued to exist. Matsuoka wrote to Citrine on 15 April 1935:

I am pleased to be able to report to you that in spite of the ascendancy of nationalism in Japan, in the same way as in most European countries, and in spite of the difficulties arising therefrom, we have been able to maintain the position of the trade union organization with even a slight increase in membership, and the Japanese Trade Union Congress, of which I am vice-president, still maintains the policy of close collaboration with the International Labour Office and will continue to strive for international solidarity of the working classes.[31]

When Mogi died soon afterwards, Citrine wrote to Matsuoka on 15 July 1935, regretting the passing away of such a valuable informant concerning trade union movements in the Far East.[32]

Since our late esteemed colleague Mogi passed away, we have had to be content here mainly with the information given in newspapers and the occasional reports which reach us from time to time . . . this can never be so useful and accurate as the statements we can get verbally from you [Matsuoka] or your colleagues.

I am very pleased to learn that in spite of the ascendancy of militarism in your country your Trade Unions are maintaining their strength, and even increasing their membership. This is extremely gratifying when we bear in mind that in other countries in Europe Trade Unions have been suppressed for the time being, and the principle of freedom of association no longer prevails.[33]

In these difficult circumstances both British and Japanese trade union leaders continued to exchange information and to try to establish a united international organization between East and West until the outbreak of the full Sino-Japanese conflict in July 1937.

Japan's war with China and the British movement to boycott Japanese goods

The Marco Polo Bridge Incident took place on the night of 7–8 July 1937 and the Japanese forces began their attack on Shanghai on 9 August. When the National Council of Labour (NCL – a joint body of the Labour Party, the TUC and the Co-operative Union) discussed the matter on 14 August Japanese armies had already penetrated North China and bitter fighting was raging in the Shanghai area. On 28 August the International Federation of Trade Unions declared that 'The IFTU regards it as its duty, at this time of great distress for the Chinese people, to express its deep sympathy and assure them of the solidarity of the workers of the whole world.'[34]

At a meeting of the General Council of the TUC held at Norwich on 9 September 1937, an emergency resolution was approved and submitted to the Congress the following day. This stated that the TUC:

> views with horror the indiscriminate murder of the civilian population of Chinese towns and cities by Japan's naval, military and air forces and expresses profound sympathy with the sufferings of the Chinese people whose homes have been so ruthlessly destroyed by the invaders.[35]

On 24 September a deputation from the TUC General Council and the Labour Party Executive met Anthony Eden, the foreign secretary, to submit the resolution to him. 'It was suggested to him that action should be taken by the British and other Governments banning the import of Japanese goods, or by the application of financial and economic sanctions by the League of Nations.'[36] As 'the Foreign Secretary gave only a non-committal reply', the NCL held a special meeting on 29 September and decided to issue a declaration to

> call upon the British Government to prohibit British citizens from selling war material or lending money to Japan, and to urge through the League of Nations that all other Members of the League should take similar action and also co-operate in an embargo on imports from Japan, at the same time taking into serious consideration the wider economic measures involved in bringing Japanese aggression to an end.[37]

By the end of September Japanese bombing had spread to Nanking and Canton. The bombing and indiscriminate murder of civilians moved many British people to seek to aid the victims in China. As a result the boycott of Japanese goods began.

However, the NCL had to take cognizance of the limitations of any boycott of Japanese goods implemented by Britain alone. Only 5 per cent of Japanese exports were bought by Britain. Even the whole of Europe absorbed no more than 12 per cent of Japanese exports. In contrast more than 50 per cent of Japan's exports were purchased by the British Dominions, British Colonies and the United States.[38] Thus it was clear that a boycott of Japanese goods could only be effective if it was simultaneously implemented in many countries, including the British Dominions and Colonies. The policies of the United States were also crucially important. The 29 September resolution was communicated by cable on the following day to the National Trade Union Centres in the United States, New Zealand, India, Australia, South Africa and Canada. It was also dispatched by letter to the IFTU, the Labour and Socialist International and the Irish Free State. Replies were received from the American Federation of Labour, Canada, New Zealand, Australia, Mexico, India, Belgium, Holland, France, Switzerland, Scandinavia, Czechoslovakia, Austria and Ireland, indicating 'a determination to carry out the boycott policy to the utmost'.[39] On 6 October President Roosevelt had declared in Chicago that 'the peace-loving nations must make a concerted effort in opposition to those violations of treaties and those ignorings of human instincts which are today creating the international anarchy and instability from which there is no escape through mere isolation of neutrality'.[40] However, Citrine and other TUC leaders were doubtful whether the United States would take part in the boycott movement. On 28 September the League of Nations condemned Japan for arousing horror and indignation around the world but decided that no specific action could be taken. This passivity was largely due to British caution. Nevertheless, the leaders of the TUC continued to invest their hopes in the League.

The 1937 Labour Party Conference, which was held at Bournemouth from 4 October, adopted an emergency resolution that 'this conference views with horror the massacre of helpless Chinese people pursuing their peaceful callings on land and sea'.[41] On 17 October the London Labour Party and the London Trades Council organized 'a very successful mass demonstration in Trafalgar Square for China'. On 22–4 October the British Council of the International Peace Campaign had its first national congress, attended by 783 delegates. The organizers had invited Madame Sun Yat-sen (Ching Ling), but she was forced to cancel her visit at the last minute. Chiang Kai-shek was not pleased with the prospect of his sister-in-law receiving a enthusiastic reception in London.[42]

The NCL considered the situation on 26 October when attention was given to practical steps to put the 29 September resolution into effect. The difficulty in enforcing a boycott of Japanese goods lay principally in problems of identification. As a result it was decided that

> the principal Japanese commodities sold in the shops and stores (tinned salmon, peas, fruit) to be identified with their brands. These brands to be itemized in an illustrated leaflet and distributed in sufficient quantities to all sections of the NCL with circular. Substitutes to be suggested, and warning uttered against German and Italian goods.[43]

The boycott of Japanese goods began to spread. Many large co-operative societies, including those in London, Royal Arsenal, Leicester, Nottingham, Oxford, Hull, Peterborough, Chester and Blackburn, decided to support the boycott.

Many British firms in China were more reluctant than the churches to support communists in China. Nevertheless they wished to encourage Chinese resistance, since they knew that Japanese offensives were directed against them as well as against the Chinese. As a response to church and business concern, the Lord Mayor's Fund was launched on 1 October, aiming at the relief of human distress in China. It was founded by the British Red Cross Society, the China Association (of British firms engaged in the China trade) and the Conference of British Missionary Societies.[44]

Several citizens' groups, of which the China Campaign Committee (CCC) was the most important, played an important role in the boycott movement. Within a few days of the outbreak of war in China the Union of Democratic Control held a meeting out of which the CCC was formed. When the CCC gathered, Victor Gollancz took the chair and Ben Bradley, Ben Tillett and Peggy Moxon attended as individuals rather than representatives. The Earl of Listowel, who had been chairman of the Friends of the Chinese People, was now appointed president of the CCC.[45] Listowel had already written a letter entitled 'A Danger to World Peace' in the *Manchester Guardian* on 5 August 1937, insisting that 'the Japanese militarists intend to pursue a policy of indefinite expansion, which clearly promotes a world war'.[46]

The first public meeting of the CCC was held on 30 September at Whitfield's Tabernacle in Tottenham Court Road, London. The speakers included Lady Dorothea Hosie, Professor Harold Laski, Pat Koo and Professor Chan Peng-chun of Nankai University, Tientsin, with messages from Madame Chiang Kai-shek, Lord Cecil and the Chinese ambassador. The meeting called for an embargo on all supplies to Japan and a boycott of all Japanese goods.[47] The support of members of the Left Book Club was invaluable. There were no official links between the Club and the CCC, but members of the Club often took the initiative in establishing local China Committees.

A boycott of the goods of any foreign country could take the following forms: (1) a government embargo; (2) a boycott by importers and wholesalers; (3) a boycott by retail consumers; (4) a boycott by the workers handling foreign goods at the docks or in the country. According to the NCL, 'Form 4) is primarily the concern of the individual union, and is a matter which can only be decided by the union directly concerned.'[48] This meant that from the beginning the NCL would not support the dockers' refusal to unload war materials for Japan. That is to say,

> Forms 2) and 3) could be organized and encouraged by the National Council of Labour, or an *ad hoc* boycott organization. But it should be noted as far as raw materials are concerned unless there is available an alternative source of supply at little or no increased cost, a boycott of goods from any foreign country will have adverse effects on employment of workers in this country.[49]

The case of Japanese raw silk was particularly significant since it was 'the main raw material of the processors of Macclesfield, and [one] for which there is practically no alternative source of supply'.[50]

By far the most significant news at the end of 1937 was the refusal of Southampton dockers to unload some Japanese goods onto trucks or trains.[51]

In pursuing the war of aggression against China Japan is importing large quantities of materials which are essential of war. These include: petroleum, iron, coal, rubber, cotton, copper, lead, tin, zinc, aluminium, automobiles and parts thereof, metal and woodworking machinery and internal combustion engines. Without these materials, the Japanese war mechanism would be paralyzed. In 1936, the British empire supplied Japan with 30 per cent of the latter's imports of these materials. This shows the significance of an embargo by British workers.[52]

The China Bulletin, published fortnightly by the CCC, reported the Southampton dockers' activities in detail. An article entitled 'What the Dockers did in Southampton' reported that

On Thursday last [2 December] the Canadian Pacific Liner 'Duchess of Richmond' docked at berth 106, Southampton, with 200 tons of Japanese cargo, chiefly silks and fancy goods for the Christmas market. On Saturday the 'Duchess of Richmond' was on her way back to Canada with the 200 tons still in her hold. On every case the Dockers stencilled in bold blue lettering THIS CARGO Refused by Southampton Dockers. At a meeting held on the docks, members of branch No. 2 2/28 TGWU passed a resolution to the effect that no future Japanese cargo could be touched, as a protest against Japanese invasion of China.[53]

This action alarmed many manufacturers. On 4 December Gary Locock of the FBI (Federation of British Industries) tried to ring Citrine but Citrine had already left for Paris. So Locock told Miss MacDonald that

a very difficult situation had arisen. Some of the dockers and stevedores at Southampton refused to unload Japanese goods and they went back to Canada! 'The Silk Association had approached Mr Bevin about this. He quite appreciated the gravity of the situation but felt chary of speaking to the Press. The Silk Association want the 'Daily Herald' to be informed, in view of certain comments they might make. They did not want to take work away from British workers and give it to Swiss or French.[54]

The dockers' action embarrassed the leaders of the TUC. Bevin, General Secretary of the TGWU, was 'dead against' dockers' action. Bevin was ready to support government action but not union action.[55]

In the middle of December Thomas Tchou (the national representative of the Chinese Labour Unions) returned to London after participating in a series of conferences with leaders of transport workers' organizations in

Belgium, France, Holland, Denmark, Sweden and Norway. All of these organizations seemed prepared to take part in a boycott of Japanese goods and a transport blockade of goods to and from Japan. All wanted an assurance that Britain would follow suit.[56] To clarify the situation, the British Section of the ITWF convened a meeting in London on 22 December which was attended by representatives of the TGWU, the Associated Society of Locomotive Engineers and Firemen, the National Union of Railwaymen, the National Union of Seamen, and the Railway Clerks' and Coal Trimmers' Unions. Tchou and Fimmen also attended. However, it was decided to leave 'the decision as to what further action should be taken'[57] to the joint meeting of the TUC General Council, the Executive Committee of the Labour Party and the Parliamentary Labour Party.

At the joint meeting held on 7 January in London, a memorandum entitled 'a Note on Proposals for economic Action against Japan' was circulated and discussed. Citrine made a long speech stating that:

> So far as I can see the war . . . is likely to go on for at least a period of fifteen to eighteen months before this policy could come to be effective . . . I come to the conclusion that we cannot hope to succeed by this policy . . . I consider the maximum we can do in this situation is to make a moral gesture . . . We can strengthen our own consumer's boycott, that is what we should be doing and turning our energies on to.[58]

As a result the responsibility for the decision on an embargo was passed on to the IFTU and LST to be held at Brussels on 15 January.

This resolution disappointed the Liverpool dockers who refused to unload a Japanese cargo on 7 January 1938. The *China Bulletin* stated

> at a time when a positive line is urgently demanded, this negative result has created widespread disappointment, more especially as the refusal of the dockers to unload the Japanese ship 'Lisbon Maru' which docked at Liverpool on January 7th following the example of the Southampton and Glasgow dockers, showed what the feeling of the British dockers themselves is.

The NCL which met on 10 January was faced with the opposition of the Liverpool branch of the TGWU but it opposed the dockers' action. The Liverpool branch was reminded that they would 'receive no union support'.[59] Unloading of the Japanese cargo which had been held up by the dockers began.

When the Japanese steamship *Haruna Maru* docked at the Teesside port of Middlesbrough on 21 January, the dockers and stevedores were asked to load her with 400 tons of pig iron and 100 tons of steel sheets. They refused to load them saying 'She'll go as she came'. On 30 January in Middlesborough the CCC convened a mass meeting 'to prepare for the expected return of the *Haruna Maru* to London'. A thousand people attended. Two dockers – one from Middlesborough and one from Southampton – expressed the wish that the London dockers would follow their example when the *Haruna Maru* put into London to pick up a further cargo. 'A message of congratulation was read from Ben Tillett, the veteran dockers leader, on the sympathy with Chinese people expressed by the action of the dockers at Middlesborough and Southampton.'[60]

On 31 January the *Haruna Maru* arrived at the Royal Albert Docks. The Thames dockers, following the example of Middlesborough, refused to load iron on the ship. 'The East and West Ham Trades Councils had passed a resolution urging the TUC General Council to support all transport workers who take action by refusing to handle Japanese cargoes and boats.'[61] However, the TUC's response was negative.

The embargo on war materials for Japan was becoming an international issue. In Marseilles French dockers refused to load the *Haruna Maru*. In Sydney workers 'refused to handle cargo for the Japanese liner "Atsuta Maru" declaring that the tinplate and scrap iron would be used for bullets against Chinese'.[62]

Against this background the Japanese government sent propagandists to the West. The CCC's *Bulletin* published an article on the matter:

> One of these propagandists was Bunji Suzuki, a member of Parliament and former leader of the 'Social Mass Party' which has now split over the question of war . . . The Japanese Government considered that he was the right man to send to America, where the boycott movement started by the Trade Unions was causing them alarm. Suzuki reported from San Francisco: The mood of American workers in coastal districts is quite different from that imagined in Japan. I simply thought I could easily convince them of our sacred mission to China once I talked to them. The negotiation was difficult because they are already prejudiced . . . I told and will further tell the Trade Union Leaders in the name of the Japanese people that, if Trade unions of American seamen would boycott Japanese boats, Japan might resort to retaliatory measures.[63]

Suzuki's report effectively expressed the attitudes of the Japanese trade unionists to the international boycott movement.

On 15 January a joint meeting of the Labour and Socialist International and the IFTU in Brussels called on all workers to protest against Japan's attack, boycott Japanese goods and press their governments 'to perform their international duties to China'.[64] But the British NCL, under the influence of Bevin and Citrine, brushed this recommendation aside and contented itself with a demand to the British government that it should 'urge' the British people to refrain from buying Japanese goods.

On 25 January the NCL deputation, led by Attlee and Citrine, met the prime minister at 10 Downing Street to discuss Japan's aggression in China. Sixteen representatives from the NCL attended, including Citrine, H. S. Lindsay and George Dallas. Neville Chamberlain represented the government. The foreign secretary, Eden, could not attend. The NCL's views were presented by Citrine, Dallas and Noel-Baker. At the meeting, Citrine:

> referred to the action of the Southampton dockers in refusing to unload Japanese goods from a CPR steamer, and of the Middlesbrough dockers refusing to load a Japanese steamer with a cargo of iron and steel. It might be, therefore, that unless something was done to show that Japan was not to be allowed to continue her aggression without any effective protest by the Powers that the British Trade Union Movement, against its better opinion, might be driven into action of that kind.

Citrine continued: 'The Movement was asking that the British Government should take the lead and get concerted action between the Powers.'[65]

However, Chamberlain's response was negative. On the question of an embargo of exports and imports to and from Japan, Chamberlain said that

> this, it would be recognized, was a double edged weapon. The boycott was being operated very strenuously in America, and already it was being found that as a result American labour was being displaced – particularly in those industries which were dependant upon Japanese raw silk.[66]

Regarding oil supplies to Japan, the cooperation of the USA and the Dutch East Indies was required. But 'that was not a practicable proposition in the present circumstances' because

> Holland might be prepared to operate such an embargo if she were offered guarantees of assistance in the event of the Dutch East Indies being attacked by Japan as a consequence. Who was to give those guarantees? The only Powers in a position to give guarantees of such a character were the USA and Great Britain.

In that case 'capital ships and all the smaller craft would have to be withdrawn from Western waters and concentrated in the Far East. That was not a practicable proposition in the present circumstances.' Chamberlain 'concluded by repeating that the key to the situation lay in the securing of American co-operation'.[67] The prime minister's view was shared by Citrine and other trade union leaders, since they were also afraid that the workers in the silk industry would become unemployed. Consequently the boycott movement which had been initiated by the NCL rapidly declined though the CCC continued its activities. This major change was evident by July 1939 when Chu Hsueh-fan spoke at the Eighth International Trade Union Congress which was held in Zurich. Chu stated

> I wish to call your attention to the apparent utter inactivity on the part of the IFTU in respect to the Sino-Japanese war since January 1938. As it is, 18 months have been allowed to elapse without the IFTU having done anything concrete to help the Chinese people to ward off aggression and to uphold social justice and world peace. The boycott movement seems to have cooled down; financial aid ceased; while the plan for economic sanctions against Japan was shelved and . . . forgotten.[68]

Notes*

* Reports, letters and other sources quoted here are kept at the Modern Records Centre, Warwick University (MSS. 159/1–4, MS. 292/951)
1. Zennihon Kaiin Kumiai (ed.), *Zennihon Kaiin Kumiai Katsudo Shiryoshu*, Part I, 1986, pp. 90–2. Regarding the JSU see Numata Inejiro and Sasaki Hiroshi, *Kaiin Kumiai no Soshiki to Dantai Kosho*, (Tokyo: Nihon Hyoronsha, 1966), pp. 1–34.
2. Edo Fimmen, The Transport Workers' International (typescript, 7 pp., 1932). Regarding the early history of the ITF, see K. A. Golding, 'Transport Workers' International: the History of the International Transport Workers' Federation', Part I: 1896–1916 (unpublished proof, 205 pp.), Modern Records Centre, Warwick University, MSS. 154/4/526. Fimmen's CV attached to a letter from Edo Fimmen to S. Mogi, 23 July 1931.
3. Report on Activities and Financial Report of the ITF for the years 1930 and 1931, and Proceedings of the International Transport Workers' Congress and Sectional Conferences held in Connection therewith, at the Municipal Reception House, Prague, 7–13 August (Amsterdam), 1932.
4. Report on Activities and Financial Report of the ITF for the years 1930 and 1931, p. 48.
5. *Tokyo Nichinichi*, 27 September 1931.
6. *Chugai*, 27 September 1931.
7. *Miyako*, 28 September 1931.
8. *Tokyo Mainichi*, 29 September 1931.
9. A letter from S. Mogi to Edo Fimmen, 22 October 1931.
10. A letter from S. Mogi to Edo Fimmen, 30 September 1931.
11. A letter from W. M. Citrine to N. Nathans, assistant secretary to the ITF, 30 September 1931.
12. Memorandum of the interview with Sir Malcom Seton, Deputy Under Secretary, on 12 October 1931 at the India Office. Subject: Refusal to grant visa enabling Mr Edo Fimmen, General Secretary of the ITF to enter India. Present: Mr Walter M. Citrine, General Secretary of the TUC and Mr W. J. Bolton.
13. A letter from Samuel Hoare to W. M. Citrine, 25 November 1931.
14. A telegram from S. Mogi to Edo Fimmen (Nihon Kaiinkumiai, Dairen), 3 November 1931.

15. Fimmen despatched a report on 'Terrorism in China' from Shanghai on 8 December 1931. *The International Transportworkers' Federation*, vol. X, no. 3, March 1932.
16. A letter from Edo Fimmen to S. Mogi, 30 January 1932.
17. A letter from Edo Fimmen to C. T. Cramp, 1 February 1932.
18. A letter from Edo Fimmen to M. Yonekubo, 2 February 1932.
19. Report on Activities and Financial Report of the ITF for the years 1930 and 1931, p. 203.
20. A letter from Schevenels to the TUC General Council, 21 August 1931.
21. Extracts from Minutes of the International Committee Meeting held on 2 December 1931.
22. A letter from K. Matsuoka to W. M. Citrine, 8 November 1931 (MS in Japanese).
23. A letter from S. Mogi to W. M. Citrine, 14 January 1932.
24. Ibid.
25. Extracts from the Minutes of the IFTU Executive Meeting, held on 9–10 June 1932 in Berlin.
26. A letter from S. Mogi to Edo Fimmen, 22 October 1931.
27. A letter from Edo Fimmen to S. Mogi, 30 January 1932.
28. A letter from M. Yonekubo to Edo Fimmen, 1 March 1932.
29. A letter from Edo Fimmen to M. Yonekubo, 1 April 1932.
30. The TUC General Council, Trade Unionism in Japan, 3 November 1932 (typescript, 3 pp.).
31. A letter from K. Matsuoka to W. M. Citrine, 15 April 1935.
32. A letter from W. M. Citrine to K. Matsuoka, 15 April 1935.
33. Ibid.
34. Declaration by the IFTU on the Japanese Invasion of China (typescript), p. 1.
35. Norwich TUC 1937, 10 September 1937 (typescript), p. 1.
36. Sino-Japanese Conflict. Action Taken In British Labour Movement and IFTU, 2 December 1937 (typescript), pp. 3–4.
37. Japan's War in China, NCL Declaration, 29 September 1937 (typescript), p. 1.
38. NCL, International Solidarity Fund. An Appeal For Help, 30 September 1937.
39. Sino-Japanese Conflict, p. 5.
40. Roosevelt speech in *Proposals for Economic Action against Japan*.
41. Sino-Japanese Conflict, p. 6.
42. Arthur Clegg, *Aid China 1937–1949: a Memoir of a Forgotten Campaign* (Beijing: New World Press, 1989), p. 35.
43. NCL, Boycott of Japanese Goods: Decisions of the NCL, 26 October 1937 (typescript), p. 1, items 3 and 4.
44. Clegg, *Aid China*, p. 26.
45. Ibid., p. 22.
46. Ibid., p. 27.
47. Ibid., pp. 28–9.
48. NCL, Boycott of Japanese Goods, 21 March 1938 (typescript), p. 1.
49. Ibid.
50. Ibid.
51. *The Daily Herald*, 6 December 1937.
52. Memorandum on Action for Checking Japanese Aggression in China, Submitted to Annual Congress, TUC, 1938, by Chu Hsue-fan, Chinese Workers' Delegate to the International Labour Conference (typescript), p. 7.
53. CCC, *China Bulletin* (Bodleian Library, Oxford), No. 3.
54. Telephone conversation between Mr G. Locock (FBI) and Miss MacDonald. Subject: Boycotting of Japanese Goods, 4.10 p.m., 6 December 1937.

55. Clegg, *Aid China* pp. 39–40.
56. CCC, *China Bulletin*, No. 4, 8 January 1938, p. 1.
57. Ibid., p. 2.
58. Joint Meeting of TUCGC, Labour Party Executive and Parliamentary Labour Party held at Transport House on 7 January 1938, regarding Japanese Aggression in China (strictly private typescript), pp. 5–9: NCL, Memorandum by Sir Walter Citrine, 10 January 1938.
59. *China Bulletin*, No. 4, 8 January 1938, p. 3.
60. Ibid., No. 5, 1 February 1938, p. 2.
61. Ibid.
62. Regarding the boycott movement in Australia, see Derek MacDougall, 'The Australian Labour Movement and the Sino-Japanese War, 1937–1939', in *Labour History* (Australia), no. 33, November 1977.
63. *China Bulletin*, No. 5, pp. 2–3.
64. TUC, Japanese Aggression in China, Resolution Passed at Joint Meeting of the IFTU and LSI held in Brussels, 15 January 1938.
65. NCL, Deputation to Prime Minister at 3.30 p.m. on 25 January 1938 at 10 Downing Street regarding Japanese Aggression in China (typescript, strictly private and confidential), pp. 2–3.
66. Ibid., pp. 4–5.
67. Ibid., p. 5.
68. Eighth International Trade Union Congress, Speech by Chu Hsuen-fan (China), 5 July 1939, Zurich (typescript), p. 1.

16
British Writing on Contemporary Japan, 1924–1941: Newspapers, Books, Reviews and Propaganda

Jon Pardoe

Introduction

British writing on contemporary Japan in the interwar years is of interest for the insights it offers into: the changing perceptions of Japan from the end of the Anglo-Japanese Alliance to the eve of the Pacific War; the opinions of Japan held by the conservative Establishment, the liberal Anti-Establishment and the small pro-Japanese group; the battle between pro-Japanese and pro-Chinese writers; and the impact of global communications.

Newspapers

The impact of global communications

Mass communications in the twentieth century have proceeded by a series of overlapping waves, each partly subsuming and building on its predecessors: newspapers, cinema and radio, television and the Internet. The interwar years marked the high-water mark of newspapers, but it was a period also distinguished by the surging tide of cinema.

In step with the development of communications was social change. A progression can be seen in the course of the nineteenth and twentieth centuries: from elites addressing themselves primarily through the medium of books, to elites broadcasting to the public through mass media, and finally to individuals speaking to each other through the non-hierarchical medium of the Internet. Each phase overlaps, but in the interwar period the mass media predominated. Ordinary men and women read mainly newspapers and more of them than ever before. Serious reading took up little time. The cinema was the essential social habit, with newsreels part of every programme.[1]

Earlier ideas of nationalism and realpolitik were increasingly challenged by support for supranational bodies and debates about moral values in domestic and international politics. Although the former appeared to prevail with the demise of the League of Nations, as ideas they became more and more discredited. Many of the above trends appear to have escaped the Japanese government in its 'public relations' communications to Britain which focused on elites and largely neglected public opinion.

Establishment and Anti-Establishment

The deterioration in British opinion of Japan can be followed in the editorials of *The Times*, associated with 'the Establishment', and the 'anti-Establishment' *Manchester Guardian*, which was to prove the most markedly anti-Japanese and pro-Chinese newspaper.[2]

The foremost concern in the Far East of the British Establishment, as represented by leading articles in *The Times*, was British financial interests and trade in China. In the 1920s and the first half of the 1930s they saw Chinese Nationalism (at times in association with communism) as the main threat. The Establishment remained broadly neutral as regards the Japanese seizure of Manchuria in 1931 – because Britain had no major financial interests there. It was to take fighting in Shanghai in 1932 and the 1934 Amau Statement (dubbed 'a Japanese Monroe Doctrine') to make the leader writers waver from the hitherto broadly pro-Japanese and anti-Chinese stance. Overt hostility to Japan was not to develop until after the outbreak of war between Japan and China in 1937 as a result of Japanese forces moving into areas such as the Yangtze Valley where Britain's financial and trade interests were concentrated.

In the 1920s *The Times* leader writers admired Japan as a 'great nation' whose capital was 'rising gallantly' from the ruins of the 1923 earthquake. Japan was 'maintaining its poise' in spite of provocations from the Chinese. Although it was acknowledged that no one quite knew what the Japanese were thinking, it was felt that the country was little changed from the one that had been Britain's ally in the first two decades of the century. Although the Anglo-Japanese Alliance was now ended, British sympathy for Japan remained.[3] The ending of the Alliance, however, had left Japan internationally isolated. At her doors were a 'Bolshevist Russia and a China in anarchy'. Her relations with Britain and America were friendly, but 'cool, correct and distant'. Japan's future was uncertain, but she had endured the difficulties of the 1923 earthquake and a banking crisis in 1928 'gallantly and patiently', inspiring 'respect and sympathy'. Her statesmen had shown 'great sagacity' and had been able to draw upon the 'marvellous resource' of a strong and tenacious national character.[4]

At the time of the enthronement of Emperor Hirohito in November 1928, *The Times* wrote that 'the substitution for [the Anglo-Japanese Alliance] of a broader arrangement has not in any way modified the strong sympathy with and respect for the Japanese character and spirit'.[5] The *Manchester Guardian* noted that Japan's 'friendship with Great Britain is of long standing, and did not end when the Anglo-Japanese Alliance ended' but complained that Japan had been called 'a hell for proletarians'.[6]

In contrast, according to *The Times*, China was a country where American, European and Japanese subjects were 'as liable to attack by soldiers as much as by brigands'. Since the Chinese government was incapable of protecting foreigners, caution should be exercised in making concessions to Chinese demands for the ending of foreign privileges. On land, roving armies looted and terrorized large areas. Along the coast of Southern China pirates, allowed to flourish unchecked by the Chinese authorities, mounted raids on both Chinese and foreign shipping.[7] It was not surprising that a leader in *The Times* assessing the background to the Manchurian incident of September 1931 showed no sympathy for the Chinese:

> During the last year or two conditions in Manchuria have deteriorated. ... [The administration of Manchurian warlord Chang Hsueh-liang] became more extortionate as it became feebler, and even more anti-Japanese. Administrative obstruction received tacit and even open approbation; acts of sabotage against perfectly legitimate undertakings became frequent; brigandage grew; the railways were damaged ... The Japanese military authorities, whose treaty rights covered the defence of the railways, could restrain their impatience no longer; and, on whatever pretexts and by whatever stratagems they advanced their claims, none can deny the extreme efficiency with which they have now expelled from the whole of Southern Manchuria the Chinese troops and the hostile Chinese administration. The Tokyo Government ended by supporting the actions of their generals ... and they have authorized the installation of new Chinese officials, favourable to Japan, in all the principal administrative posts of the province.[8]

With the outbreak of the 'Manchurian incident' *The Times* and the *Manchester Guardian* drew different conclusions. *The Times* acknowledged that the Japanese garrison in Manchuria had 'taken the law into its own hands' but pointed out that the Japanese had 'endured with remarkable patience a series of affronts'.[9] The *Manchester Guardian* commented that it was for foreign governments to protect their nationals by warning of the dangers of travel in China, and not by 'punitive expeditions and military demonstrations'.[10]

By early 1932 the *Manchester Guardian* was complaining that the most serious aspect of the war in China was that the system of collective security had broken down and that the 'old diplomacy, from which the civilized world turned in disgust in 1918 when its consequences were only too apparent' would again prevail.[11] A year later the paper was being sarcastically critical of Japan's action in northern China: 'The stoat, attacked by the cruel rabbit, again defends itself. ... Jehol is to Manchuria what Wales would be to England if the Japanese decided to take us over for our own good and, of course, at our insistence.'[12] In the following year it attacked British foreign policy towards Japan and China as 'one long retreat from plain morality under a legalistic cover'.[13]

The Japanese seizure of Manchuria was neither welcomed nor condemned by the Establishment – Britain had no major financial interests there. What was important was that Japan should uphold the Nine Power Pact, with its emphasis on Great Power cooperation in China and the 'Open Door' to foreign trade. It was to take fighting in Shanghai in 1932 and the Amau Statement of April 1934 to make *The Times*, leader writers deviate from their hitherto pro-Japanese and anti-Chinese stance.

The Times's response to the statement came in a leader on 26 April 1934:

> The political and economic importance to Japan of her relations with China, and the needs of her geographical position, are universally recognized. They entitle her to a foremost place in any international conference that may deal with Chinese affairs. But they do not justify the claim to a monopoly of influence, and it is because recent Japanese statements seemed to make this claim, with an arrogance that recalled the days of the Shoguns . . . , that they caused such widespread uneasiness. The Japanese Government seem now to wish to allay the anxieties which their spokesmen have aroused. Surely they can best achieve this end, and obtain a hearing for their views on Chinese affairs, by co-operation rather than friction with other civilised nations . . .[14]

British priorities – trade and investment in China – were made perfectly clear in another leader which appeared five days later:

> A long series of delicate adjustments is necessary before foreign activities can be completely reconciled with the new spirit of nationalism in the Eastern nations. If any one country tries the discarded method of domination, then the smooth development of Chinese prosperity must be indefinitely retarded.
>
> As greater security is established and the peaceful organization of the country progresses, the Chinese market is seen to be almost illimitable. The British interest . . . lies in promoting . . . peace, security and economic development.[15]

Thus, by May 1934, *The Times* leader writers had changed in their attitude towards Japan and China. With Japan now perceived as the major threat to British financial interests in China, the Chiang Kai-shek government was seen in a more favourable light. Chiang had improved his standing with the British business community by consolidating the stability of his regime, by suppressing communism and by demonstrating an increased willingness to negotiate with the Western Powers. All of these actions were seen to offer an improved environment for British business interests. Both Chiang and *The Times* had shifted their positions since the late 1920s: they had a certain shared interest in the suppression of communism and in resisting Japanese attempts to dominate China.

However, *The Times*, even in August 1936, would proclaim that Britain 'would welcome the friendship of Japan, a proud and gallant young nation for whom we have always had respect', but added that 'the foundations of such a friendship must include a genuine ... regard for the sovereign rights of the Chinese Republic'.[16]

By January 1935 the deterioration in the public opinion of Japan had come to the attention of Captain Malcolm Kennedy, the former Reuters correspondent in Tokyo, who had lost little of the pro-Japanese attitudes associated with the Anglo-Japanese Alliance. In the conservative *Daily Telegraph* he wrote: 'it comes somewhat as a surprise, on returning to England, to find how strangely distorted are many of the beliefs current in this country regarding the alleged aggressive intentions of the Japanese'.[17]

Overt hostility to Japan did not appear in *The Times* until after the outbreak of full-scale war between Japan and China in 1937, and the movement of Japanese forces into areas such as the Yangtze Valley, where Britain's financial and trade interests were focused. The serious wounding of the British ambassador to China, Knatchbull-Hugessen, on 25 August 1937, when his official car was attacked by a Japanese plane, provoked both official and public protest. Captain Kennedy noted in his diary:

> As expected, Sir Knatchbull-Hugessen's wounding has called forth a terrific scream and *The Times* has come out with an absolute snorter on what it calls 'an outrage for which there is no parallel'. That it is a thoroughly bad show is not to be gainsaid, but it certainly will not help matters to have a responsible paper like *The Times* losing its sense of proportion and going into hysterics about it.[18]

Ever since the attack on the British ambassador to China the Japanese Embassy in London had been inundated with abusive and threatening letters and telephone calls. Individual Japanese were being insulted in the streets. On several occasions anonymous callers rang up the Embassy and demanded to speak to the 'murderers' department'. There were a number of demonstrations outside the Embassy. Such treatment alienated previously pro-British diplomats: 'Terasaki [2nd Secretary] remarked bitterly that he himself had always been a friend and admirer of England's, but he has nothing but contempt for her now and regards her as Japan's principal enemy and thinks Japan was well rid of her as an ally.'

A major contributing factor in this deterioration in relations was the graphic reporting of the war in China, particularly the Japanese bombing of civilians. Press articles brought the horrors of war in China home to the

British public by using 'human interest' angles such as British humanitarian aid, the work of British missionaries in China and the sufferings of ordinary Chinese civilians:

> There are now some 10 000 000 destitute in China . . . They have nothing to look forward to and many nothing to exist on but what can be provided from the Lord Mayor's Fund . . .[19]

> The British missionaries in Canton have telegraphed to the Archbishop of Canterbury appealing to him to draw the British public's attention to the bombing of civilians and to do all he can to secure a protest from the British Government . . . During a tour this afternoon I witnessed some ghastly sights . . . The woman sat sobbing on a tree-stump looking down at the little blasted body of her only child, whose tiny chest had been blown away.[20]

In June 1938, a *Times* editorial noted that the British ambassador in Tokyo, Sir Robert Craigie, had drawn the attention of the Japanese government to 'the unfortunate effect upon British public sentiment, and hence upon Anglo-Japanese relations, of the indiscriminate aerial attacks upon populous Chinese cities'.[21]

Meanwhile, anti-Japanese campaigners in Britain were working on the fears of the British public. According to a speaker at a demonstration in Trafalgar Square organized by the China Campaign Committee, 'The air raids in China and Spain are only dress rehearsals for air-raids we may expect on London . . . Every day the war [in China] goes on increases your chance of being killed if war spreads as it is spreading now.'[22]

The Committee also had an effect on the Japanese Embassy. On 14 August 1938 a demonstration which passed close to the Japanese Embassy led to the temporary arrest of the Japanese assistant military attaché, Major T. Takahashi, when he seized one of the booklets being distributed by a protester, tore it up and threw some of the pieces in her face.[23]

By the late 1930s Establishment and Anti-Establishment opinion were again as united in their opinions of Japan as they had been in the late 1920s, but on this occasion they were united in opposition. As noted by G. C. Allen: 'Many circles not otherwise congruent in this country are united in viewing the Japanese with suspicion and dislike.'[24] The 'conservative-imperialists' feared Japanese territorial expansion in Asia and 'liberally minded people' acquiesced in the condemnation of Japan's economic development because of their abhorrence of Japan's political actions.[25]

By 1939 *The Times* had given up on Japan: 'Two years, even one year, ago several nations still thought it worth while remonstrating with Japan, in the name of humanity and civilization, against deliberately barbarous conduct towards non-combatants. The world knows better today.'[26]

The outbreak of war with Germany in 1939 and of full-scale fighting in 1940 served to shift the attention of the British public and newspapers from events in the Far East. The *Manchester Guardian* reminded its readers that: 'In the Far East another war, which has already been in progress over two years, is still going on even though forgotten by the West.'[27] *The Times* commented that 'even the grave predicament of Europe cannot altogether obscure the drama that is being played out in the Far East'.[28] Both papers took a sanguine view of any threat that Japan might pose to British interests in the Far East. *The Times* stated that Japanese armies remained 'embedded in the Chinese morass'. The *Manchester Guardian* observed that 'Japan could not really undertake any move against the Western Powers until she had first settled with China, and for this purpose the European war is of little use.'

Such editorial comment as there was about Japan tended to focus on British policy rather than Japan itself. In March 1940 the liberal *News Chronicle* criticized the government for appeasing Japan:

> We don't at all like the way British policy is developing towards Japan. . . . Sir Robert Craigie, the British Ambassador in Tokyo, has just made a soft-soaping 'good-will' speech, in which he talks a little about 'thorny questions', but sets aside as absurd the idea that . . . Britain and Japan should be on bad terms merely because of a war of aggression.[29]

> [The people of Britain] are not prepared to condone Japan's aggression and to sell China in return for Japan's friendship. While the effect of any such retreat would be bad enough in this country, it would be even worse in America. Nothing would do more harm to Anglo-American relations than the acceptance of Japan's claims and the betrayal of the Chinese people.[30]

In July 1940, the British government, under pressure from Japan, reluctantly agreed to a temporary closure of the Burma Road which was used to supply the Chinese Nationalist government. The *News Chronicle* again saw signs of appeasement in this action: 'Nothing that Mr Churchill said yesterday about the closing of the Burma Road reconciles us to the action. On the contrary, many of the expressions he used were painfully reminiscent of Mr Chamberlain's language in September 1938 . . .'.[31] The *Manchester Guardian* described the closure as a three months' default from Britain's obligations.[32] The paper had previously blamed such appeasement as the cause of the war.[33]

By contrast, the Establishment was defended by the *Daily Telegraph*, which pointed out that: 'In practical as apart from moral effect, however, the concession itself is of little importance, since during the next three months the value of the Burma road will in any case be substantially reduced owing to the seasonal rains.'[34] *The Times* defended the government's decision:

[the Government desire to improve our relations with Japan] could not be approached, much less reached, while the transport of war material through Burma was placing an increasing strain on our relations with Japan. There are very good reasons for attempting to improve those relations. The fact that we are involved in a life-and-death struggle in Europe is one of them.[35]

Only after the start of the Pacific War in December 1941 did Japan move up the British news agenda. But now the focus of attention was on British armed forces as exemplified by the *Daily Telegraph*'s headlines on an article reporting the Japanese capture of Hong Kong: 'Hong Kong's fall during Christmas – Seven-Day Fight Against Odds – Water Supply Ran Out – Troops' Morale Unshaken'.[36]

Books

Pro-Japanese writers

Only a very small number of serious studies of contemporary Japan were written by British authors in the 1920s and 1930s. Captain Malcolm Kennedy[37] with his books on the Japanese Army (*The Military Side of Japanese Life* (1924), *Some Aspects of Japan and Her Defence Forces* (1928)), on Japanese society (*The Changing Fabric of Japan* (1930)), and on Japan's international position in the 1930s (*The Problem of Japan* (1935)), was probably the most prolific writer of such studies. Kennedy was broadly pro-Japanese in his views, but always endeavoured to give a detached account of his subject in the light of the information available to him. In this he was no different from other serious authors such as G. C. Allen and Vere Redman.

The difficulties that such authors faced lay in the political emotions aroused in sections of the British public by the issues of Chinese nationalism and Japanese imperialism. As the *Times Literary Supplement* review of *The Military Side of Japanese Life* on 18 December 1924 pointed out:

Most Englishmen are undoubtedly much more 'pro' the gentler Chinese than 'pro' Japanese, but it would be difficult to find one who is 'pro' both yellow races. And so Captain Kennedy's friendship with the men who received him so hospitably has naturally tended to colour his views on the Chinese, among whom he spent a comparatively short time, and of whom he has little good to say.[38]

The difficulties of the serious writers was further complicated by the appearance of books on Japan which made no effort to disguise their blatant anti-Japanese or pro-Japanese prejudice. Vere Redman referred to such publications in the chapter on 'Recent Japan Books' in his *Japan in Crisis*:

In another realm that one hesitates to define, two Britons have distinguished themselves on opposite sides of an emotional fence, Mr Conroy
with 'The Menace of Japan' and Major Bodley with 'The Japanese
Omelette' and 'The Drama of the Pacific'. It has been suggested that those
desirous of getting a balanced picture of the Japanese scene should read
the works of both these authors. Personally, I would recommend another
course, which, while leaving the balance unaffected, would save considerable time.[39]

Captain Kennedy, G. C. Allen and Vere Redman had much in common:
several years' residence in Japan, a general admiration of the Japanese and
a belief in the importance of good Anglo-Japanese relations.

In 1928 G. C. Allen wrote admiringly of Japan in *Modern Japan and its
Problems*:

This is the only country in the world where cleanliness is found together
with the picturesque; where a love of beauty and a high standard of artistic taste live on good terms with practical achievement; and where local
and public loyalties are reconciled with a sense of social responsibility.

. . . Alone of the Asiatic peoples she has offered an effective resistance to
the encroachment of Western Powers. Alone she has assumed their material equipment without sacrificing her own forms of social and political
life. Alone she appears likely to be able to work out some compromise
between the West and the East, and, by her comprehension of both civil-
isations, to bring the two great branches of the human family together.[40]

By 1938 Allen was far less optimistic. Nevertheless he endeavoured to
make the conclusion of *Japan: the Hungry Guest* as confident as honestly
possible:

Up to now Japan has been skilful in avoiding extremes in her social, political and cultural life, and experience should warn us against the assumption that the present disastrous trends will continue indefinitely. Her
future course will depend in some measure on the policy of the Western
Powers, and it must be remembered that the clumsy treatment which she
received from them in the past has helped to foster the present national
temper. Abhorrence of Japan's current policy ought not to cause us to
withhold sympathy from her in the difficult problems with which she is
faced.[41]

One of the less sophisticated pro-Japanese writers was Ernest Pickering.[42]
However, Pickering's advice on the future course of British policy in the Far
East in his book, *Japan's Place in the Modern World*, was relatively restrained:

[Great Britain, American and Japan] must somehow succeed in reconciling their interests and aspirations. A ménage à trois is always a serious problem, and it usually falls on one of the three to make possible peace for all. Here it is Great Britain's responsibility. She is on good terms with America, and Japan admires and respects her more than any other Western power.[43]

By contrast, Vere Redman, in his *Japan in Crisis*, adopted a much more extreme stance:

We can offer [Japan] partnership in maintaining the peace of the world, recognising a Japanese Monroe Doctrine in the Far East . . . In the meantime, we protect those interests which are really vital to us: the route to India and to Australia. This can be done without danger. We shall have no trouble with Great Asia if only we will recognize Great Japan. After all, the policy here proposed amounts simply to a revival in a new form of our policy preceding the Washington Conference. Till then we were in partnership with Japan on the understanding that we were the senior partner. We should now renew that partnership on the basis of equality. To do that represents common sense, and at the same time a method of enlisting the generous sympathies of a people among the most warm-hearted in the world.[44]

Major Bodley's book, *A Japanese Omelette*, had certain unfortunate similarities with Kennedy's *The Problem of Japan*. The former was little more than a travel book based on a visit to Japan: the latter was based on Kennedy's 18 years of close association with Japan. Nevertheless, both authors were former army officers who had turned to writing, and their admiration for Japan was strongly influenced by a contempt for the Chinese – a contempt which at times became loathing. This contempt was the Achilles' heel of Kennedy's analysis of the Far East in *The Problem of Japan*.

Bodley's views of the Chinese, the Bolshevik menace to the British Empire and the importance of good Anglo-Japanese relations, were remarkably similar to those held by Kennedy. In his book Bodley wrote:

I came to China with no other feelings about its people than interest but I left disillusioned . . .

How . . . can people talk of unity and patriotism in a country which not only collapses at the first show of force [Manchurian Incident] but actually lives in a state of civil war when the future of the nation is at stake. How can anyone sympathize when one sees China's would be rulers taking refuge in foreign concessions, which they have done their utmost to abolish, and seek the protection of those people who they would have no hesitation in massacring if the opportunity presented itself.

. . . On how many occasions did I see foreign women being hustled and insulted by ricksha coolies within the confines of large cities and hear of worse outrages in remoter districts, to none of which was there any redress.[45]

Kennedy's experiences in China had led him to form exactly the same opinions as Bodley. Both former army officers were appalled by the disorder and ill-discipline of Chinese armies. Both were enthusiastic at the prospect of the disorderly and disrespectful Chinese being 'taught a lesson' by the well-disciplined and well-organized Japanese. Bodley appreciated that China was not the only problem:

There is the attitude of the European and American governments, whose policies, though probably dictated by some excellent motives, are obscure to anyone who has lived for any length of time in China and Japan. And there is also . . . the Russian peril which none can visualize until, as I, they have travelled in the interior of China and been in the midst of its seething population, or come into contact with its hordes of ill-disciplined soldiery who, if led and organized, could do what they liked with the rest of the world.

Japan's role in the shaping of the future of the Far East in the twentieth century is as clear as Rome's was in Europe and Africa two thousand years ago, and though the process may cause a certain amount of unavoidable pain, the ultimate result will benefit everyone.[46]

Although Kennedy never shared Bodley's uncritical admiration for Japan and would never have indulged in such excesses as to compare Japan with the Roman Empire, he was vulnerable to accusations of bias on account of his intolerant views of the Chinese. In *The Problem of Japan*, a balanced analysis of Japan's international position, he toned down his views of China, but nevertheless left himself open to criticism.

In the *Changing Fabric of Japan* (1931), Kennedy's subject was the rapid social, economic and political changes in Japan since the end of the First World War and, more especially, since the Great Earthquake of 1923. Kennedy admired Japan's old 'feudal system' in which the warrior class were at the top of the social scale and the merchants at the bottom – Such a system would naturally appeal to a former army officer. However, he believed that in the years since the war, industrialization, increasing commercialism and Bolshevik propaganda were undermining the 'fine old traditions' of discipline, self-sacrifice and social harmony. These unwelcome intruders had brought labour unrest, disrespect for authority and a selfish, money-grubbing attitude. Foreign films were also undermining morals generally. Only the armed forces were maintaining the lofty principles of loyalty, patriotism, and the spirit of self-sacrifice for the good of the community.

Corruption in politics as a result of the close links between politicians and big business had created a vicious circle which would have to be broken if Japanese politics were to be 'purified'. There was also the problem of student unrest caused by 'long-haired visionaries'. Kennedy believed that the only antidote to the spread of radical ideas in the student body was the growing popularity of outdoor sport. Kennedy saw the basis of the social unrest in Japan, Britain and elsewhere as lying in the undue emphasis on citizens' rights rather than their duties.

According to Kennedy, prior to 1921 Japan had committed a number of minor acts of aggression on the Asian mainland. These had been wildly exaggerated by skilful Chinese propaganda. But at the Washington Conference of 1921–2 Japan had shown a broad-minded willingness to reach agreements with the other powers. Japan had continued to be reasonable and cooperative ever since, primarily due to economic considerations – such as saving money by curbing defence expenditure. In such calculations Japan was no better nor any worse than the other powers.[47]

Kennedy saw serious difficulties ahead for Japan resulting from the rapid process of industrialization. At present many industrial workers who had been drawn to the towns from the countryside could return to their families if laid off in a recession. But what would happen in terms of social unrest when, after two or three generations, a recession would find urbanized descendants of these workers without jobs or close relatives in villages who might take care of them?

Despite these reservations, Kennedy acknowledged that there was much that was positive in the recent developments in Japanese society: 'Lovers of Old Japan, with its atmosphere of medieval enchantment, will regret its passing; but it is inevitable and, though some of the changes may be for the worse, there is much that is commendable in the New Japan now springing up.'[48]

A review of the book in the *Times Literary Supplement* suggested that Kennedy was exaggerating the extent of social change in Japan – Kennedy was too close to the ' "cafe civilisation" and jazz music of present-day Tokyo' to place it in its proper context. The reviewer took a more sanguine view of Japan's future – 'the courage, loyalty and patriotism of her people, those qualities which brought her in fifty years from obscurity to the rank of a Great Power, may confidently be expected to survive the demoralising influences of cafe civilisation, yellow journalism, and jazz'.[49] When a copy of the book was sent to the Foreign Office, Mr Charles of the Far Eastern Department noted that the author was 'very painstaking but somewhat dry to read'.[50]

In May 1935 the publishers Nisbets had requested Kennedy to write a book on Japan and her problems. But Bertram Christian, the director of Nisbets, became unhappy about the effect Kennedy's pro-Japanese views would have on sales of the book. As Kennedy noted in his diary:

Friday 1st November 1935

Am getting very annoyed with him, as he tries to dictate to me what I ought to do and what I ought not to do, and he wants large chunks of the book cut out as he dislikes my views and says they will cause offence to the Lothian-Cecil crowd. Be blowed to them, I say . . . as I told Christian, the tragedy is that the views of doctrinaire pacifists like Lothian and Cecil, who have no first-hand knowledge of the situation, are accepted like Holy Writ.[51]

Saturday 2nd November 1935

Had a heated talk over the 'phone with Christian on the subject of my comparison between our own position vis-à-vis Egypt and Japan's towards Manchuria. He maintains that there is no comparison and wants me to cut out all my references to Egypt and he as good as called me a liar when I assured him I had checked up my assertions about Britain making herself responsible for the protection of foreign interests in Egypt, though it should not have been necessary to check up such well-established facts . . . He is now threatening to take action against me on the grounds of my alleged failure to live up to the terms of my signed agreement, though there is nothing in the agreement about my ' writing to order' in the matter of views expressed in the book. It is obviously pure bluff on his part and I have written to say that I am perfectly willing to have the matter put up to arbitration . . .[52]

In *The Problem of Japan* (1935), Kennedy stated that the underlying causes of Japanese military action in China were: (1) economic necessity arising from the pressure of a rapidly growing population and a lack of indigenous raw materials, a problem aggravated by restrictions imposed by the western countries on Japanese immigrants and the import of Japanese manufactured goods; (2) anxiety regarding Japan's security in the face of instability in China, the perceived threat from the Soviet Union and from American intervention against Japan in China. According to Kennedy, Japan's actions had been dictated by vital considerations of strategy and economics; she had no aggressive intentions against either the American mainland or Australasia, but was determined to build up her navy so as to prevent American interference with her policy in China. Her aim in China was to ensure peace and stability so that she could develop her trade and industry there. By establishing Manchukuo she had set up a model for the relationship she was seeking with China as a whole. It was a 'rough-and-ready sort of wooing', but if she succeeded she would be able to prevent the Soviet Union exploiting Chinese instability. Kennedy claimed that although Japan had no territorial ambitions south of the Great Wall she was convinced that the power which controlled Mongolia and Turkestan would control China. Since the Soviet Union was dominant in both those regions, Japan might very possibly try to oust the Soviets.

Although acknowledging the widespread scepticism over Manchukuo's degree of independence, Kennedy believed that similar questions could be raised over China where extraterritorial rights were still widespread, and over Egypt, controlled by Britain, and Central America, controlled by the United States.[53]

According to Kennedy, the main point of friction in relations between Japan and the United States lay in the question of the 'Open Door' in China. Similarly the main problem in Anglo-Japanese relations was that of trade rivalry. Japan was never likely to resort to war with either Britain or the United States unless she was attacked or threatened with encirclement, which would force her to give way to 'pressure'. In other words there could be nothing more harmful than an Anglo-American front against Japan. Britain should assume the role of mediator between the United States and Japan, but should on no account attempt to court the friendship of one at the expense of the other. Indeed, had it not been for British readiness, in the post-war years, to sacrifice almost anything for the sake of American friendship, Anglo-Japanese relations would have developed on a far firmer basis.

Kennedy believed that if adequate guarantees regarding the protection of their legitimate interests could be obtained, Britain and America might find it to their ultimate advantage to agree to some kind of Monroe Doctrine for East Asia as desired by Japan. Although Japan would be the chief beneficiary, the resultant stability in China would be to the benefit of British and American trade. If matters were allowed to drift, however, the steady advance of Japanese control over large areas of North China was likely to continue and foreign interests would inevitably suffer. In time, western resentment at Japanese expansionism might lead to an armed clash. Alternatively Japan, in a fit of desperation at western opposition to its expansionism in China, might decide to act for herself, and take by force very much more than the Western Powers might be prepared to concede by negotiation. The powers would then be faced with the alternatives of war or an inglorious climbdown. In any war between Japan and the United States, with or without Britain on America's side, the initial advantage would go to Japan. Thanks to superior British and American financial resources, Japan might eventually be defeated, but only after a long and bloody struggle. The only country standing to gain from such a struggle would be the Soviet Union. The Soviets would 'sit on the fence', watching the capitalist powers destroying each other. Then, in her own good time, the USSR would step in to carry out her long-cherished plans to 'sovietize' Asia. Japan, the only power in East Asia able and willing to check the extension of the Soviet system, would probably be plunged into revolution in the aftermath of defeat.

Kennedy believed that a revision of the League of Nations' Covenant was required in order to bring it in line with the realities in the Far East. The

Nine-Power Pact (on the integrity of China) might also be revised. It ought to be made clear to China that she could expect no help from the League and should enter into direct negotiations with Japan. According to Kennedy, much responsibility for the consequences of the Manchurian incident could be laid at the door of the League for encouraging China by false hopes to resist Japan's insistence on direct negotiations.[54]

The 'Haves', Britain with its empire and the United States, both rich in territory and raw materials, should recognize the rights of the 'Have Nots', Japan, Germany and Italy, each short of land and raw materials, to have guaranteed access to sources of raw materials and emigration outlets for their surplus population. Despite his general sympathy for Japan, Kennedy believed that it should be impressed on the Japanese that it takes two to make a quarrel.

For the safety and protection of British interests in China, friendly relations between Britain and Japan were perhaps more important than those between Britain and China. Nothing was more conducive to 'more respectful and correct conduct' on the part of China than the knowledge that Britain and Japan were prepared to cooperate in defending their interests in China. To Britain, anxious to hold on to India, the growth of Soviet influence in Central Asia must inevitably be a matter of concern. Japan and Britain thus had a mutual interest in resisting Soviet ambitions in Central Asia and the Far East.

In view of their shared interests, London and Tokyo should come to an agreement over trade and investment in China. North China might be recognized as Japan's special field for commercial and industrial exploitation, and South China as Britain's, while joint undertakings might be carried out in the Yangtze regions, which would form the dividing line between the two. Guarantees, however, would have to be given for the protection of the other powers' interests and those of China itself. Such an agreement would eliminate cut-throat competition between Britain and Japan and their interests in China would interlock in such a way as to ensure mutual cooperation. Japan could rest assured of British assistance against Soviet encroachments in China, while Britain could depend on Japan to defend their mutual interests there. If, in conjunction with this agreement, Britain and the other powers were prepared to recognize a modified form of Monroe Doctrine for East Asia, the international rivalries, which had done so much to disturb the peace and stability of the Far East, would largely be eliminated.[55]

Kennedy's book was strongly criticized in a review in *Punch*:

BRAVE NEW BANZAI

The Japanese nation, it seems, is grossly misjudged. It really consists of innocent children, forced to stand on the defensive against the threatening tyranny of those sinister bullies, China, Russia, America and Great Britain. We must therefore be sympathetic and helpful whilst the Yamato race proceeds with its benevolent expansion. Such, at any rate, is the view maintained by Captain M. D. Kennedy in 'The Problem of Japan'. It is an astonishing piece of propaganda, for in order to make his contentions even plausible the author is compelled to impute the basest motives to all the nations and their League and to explain away some extremely stubborn facts. In this he is not uniformly successful . . .[56]

The *Times Literary Supplement* also took Kennedy to task:

When the Japanese landed troops in Shanghai in the spring of 1932 a Japanese friend of the author remarked 'The only thing for the Powers to do is to shut their eyes for a week or two while the Japanese drive back the Chinese'. The Powers did so, and Captain Kennedy commends them for their wisdom. His approval provides the keynote of the book. 'Give Japan her head' is what he says in substance, 'she deserves a free hand, and in any case you cannot stop her'.

In reaching this comfortable conclusion – for the line of least resistance is the easiest path – Captain Kennedy gives us an interpretation of Japan's military expansion and 'forward' foreign policy which amounts in the main to an apology of her actions in the last four years. Though obviously free from the taint of deliberate propaganda, the author allows his pro-Japanese sympathies to serve on occasions as blinkers . . .

The sympathetic understanding of Japan which gives its value to the book is unfortunately counterbalanced by lack of ability to see any of China's good points. She is weak but arrogant, obstructive, unreliable, and an inveterate intriguer, and as such fair and proper prey for Japan's continental ambitions'.[57]

In 1938 G. C. Allen complained that Japan had been ill-served by her friends in western countries:

A brief study of Japanese conditions within the last few years can lead to a sympathetic understanding of the causes which led to the tragic events in Manchuria and China and released the forces of fanaticism within Japan itself. To understand the springs of action is not, however, to make the action itself any less deplorable or less disastrous for the progress of civilization. Many friends of Japan pass too easily from sympathy with her problems and difficulties to support of her policy of aggression in Asia.[58]

Allen went on to criticize their arguments:

Some of those who view international relationships as a conflict between rival imperialisms for the exploitation of the weak, argued after 1932 that

Great Britain should ally herself before it was too late with the ascendant power of Japan, and should divert Japanese attention from British territories and interests on the Pacific shores by giving diplomatic support to her in her expansionist policy in North China.[59]

Japan's territorial expansion has been necessitated by the over-population of Japan Proper and the threat of Russia to her existence as a Power. Great Britain, so it is said, should sympathize with her difficulties and support her policy ... yet these arguments cannot move those who believe that it is dishonourable to sacrifice the weak to the necessities or ambitions of the strong, especially when this country has sworn to protect the integrity of the former.[60]

They repeat the official Japanese propaganda which declares that since Japanese goods are excluded from markets, the only way of occupying the growing population and supplying the necessary raw materials is by acquiring territories ... But there is a wide difference between supplying Eastern people with goods they are anxious to buy and imposing on some of them a form of government which they dislike.[61]

Morgan Young, the long-serving editor of the *Japan Chronicle*, wrote two books on Japan: *Japan under Tenno Taisho, 1912–1926* and *Imperial Japan, 1926–1938*, 'for readers who would like the facts rather than my gloss on them'.[62] He remained a critical observer. In the former he concluded that 'The chronicler of the period has to record many grave errors ...'.[63] In the latter he stated:

It was the firm belief of the rulers of Japan that the Empire could only endure if every spark of intellectual honesty was relentlessly stamped out. This dread of truth is a phenomenon found all over the world, but seldom in such strength and abundance as modern Japan.[64]

Japan has tried to destroy the culture from which she drew her own civilisation. If China resists to the end, the universities and colleges that the invader has destroyed will rise again, but the world will regret the passing of a great civilisation that cared more for the gracious arts of life than for the tarnished glories of conquest.[65]

Anti-Japanese writers

Throughout the 1930s pro-Japanese writers fought a losing battle against their pro-Chinese rivals – journalists such as Hollington K. Tong, the Australians W. H. Donald and H. J. Timperley, the American Agnes Smedley (a close associate of Soviet spy Richard Sorge) and the Englishwoman Freda Utley (who was married to a Soviet citizen).

Donald had served as an adviser to Chang Hsueh-liang, the Manchurian warlord, before and during the Japanese seizure of Manchuria. By 1934 he had become a friend and adviser to the Kuomintang leader, Chiang Kai-shek. In 1935 he recruited Hollington K. Tong, an American-trained journalist and long-standing friend of Chiang Kai-shek, to be chief censor of all outgoing foreign press messages – a task which Donald himself had performed unofficially. With the outbreak of the Sino-Japanese War in July 1937, Tong was at the forefront of the international propaganda battle. He formed an anti-Japanese committee in the Shanghai international settlement to publicize the Chinese cause. Three of its four members were Chinese, and the fourth was the *Manchester Guardian's* correspondent in China, Harold Timperley. On the fall of Shanghai to the Japanese at the end of 1937 the committee dispersed: one member remained in Shanghai (and was assassinated by Japanese agents), one went to Hong Kong, and one to the United States, while Timperley went to London to take charge of the overseas information operation under Tong's direction. At the same time Tong was appointed vice-minister of Information in the Nationalist government and set up an office at Hankow: his staff included a number of foreign journalists, including Freda Utley and Agnes Smedley. With the fall of Hankow to the Japanese at the end of 1938, the National government retreated to Chungking. It was from this base that Tong masterminded the Chinese propaganda effort throughout the Second World War.[66]

Freda Utley stood diametrically opposed to Kennedy's pro-Japanese, anti-Chinese and anti-Soviet viewpoint. She had been a correspondent for the *Manchester Guardian* in Japan in the 1920s and worked in China for the *News Chronicle* in the 1930s. In 1936 Faber & Faber published her book, *Japan's Feet of Clay*. As an idealistic liberal with socialist leanings, she was outraged at the position of women in Japan:

> The real Japan is a country of half-starved peasants; of children working long hours and always hungry as in England a century ago; of women whose status, rich or poor, is practically that of slaves and whose picturesque kimonos mock the misery and frustration of their lives . . . The Japanese woman has no legal personality, no social or political rights; she can be sold to a factory or a brothel by a legal contract signed by her father or husband or other male guardian, she can be divorced without cause at the will of her husband; a married woman has no property rights, and no rights over her children . . .[67]

Kennedy took a different view of the women's movement in Japan:

> Any attempt to slow [the movement] up unreasonably would probably only result in the appearance of militant methods on the part of a section

of the women; for Japanese women, despite their usual docility, have been lacking neither in spirit nor in courage.

On the other hand, any attempt to hasten the emancipation movement, without good reason, would result in too great a jolt to the whole social fabric of Japan. To give them the vote at this stage would be to place a weapon in the hands of the women before they were sufficiently trained, either to accept their new responsibilities or to use their new privileges in the best interests of themselves and of their country.[68]

Utley criticized the admiration for Japan, which still remained 'amongst a large number of Conservatives and most markedly at the War Office and the Admiralty'. She condemned their line of argument that Japan was already invincible in the Far East and that the wisest policy was to 'make the best of it by quickly coming to an understanding . . . to ensure [Japanese] goodwill and willingness, if not to let Britain share in the spoils, then at least to leave British interests in China intact'.[69]

According to Utley, Japan was presenting a big bluff to the world. She had started her military aggression in China with meagre economic and financial resources, but, if she was allowed to entrench herself in Manchuria and China and subsequently to develop her strength unmolested, her next step would inevitably be to turn on Singapore, the Dutch East Indies and finally on India and Australia. However, Japan's aggression could easily be checked without war:

Economic measures against [Japan] would be quite sufficient. I am aware that it is usually said in answer to this argument that economic measures must inevitably lead to war. This is, however, not the case with regard to Japan. She cannot proceed without the tacit consent of England and the USA. It is not a question of blockading Japan; it is merely a question of refusing to buy her goods or supplying her ourselves with oil, iron, cotton and machinery, and of refusing her the credits she is now still able to obtain. Refusal to buy from her for a few weeks would indeed be sufficient. Japan cannot attack England or the USA for the same strategic reason that they cannot attack her, so that there is no reason at all why economic sanctions need lead to war. True, there are parts of the British Empire which could be attacked but even Japan cannot imagine that Britain would not defend them, and even Japan would not dare to challenge the joint strength of Britain and the USA. Moreover, the seizure of Malaya or Hong Kong or Borneo would not solve Japan's raw material problems and she would still be in no position to carry on a war for long.

A brief period of collaboration between England and the USA is all that is necessary. Japan would collapse in a few weeks.[70]

The *Times Literary Supplement* criticized her views as set forth in *Japan's Feet of Clay*:

> Miss Utley sets out to shatter the Great Illusion of Japan's unassailable strength and to prove her a public danger which can be, and should be, suppressed. This she does with a religious fervour which takes one's breath away. As seen through her eyes Japan is internally 'a seething cauldron of misery and injustice', and externally a threat to civilisation which, if not arrested in her course, will inevitably end in 'tearing the British Empire to pieces'. It is to save China in the first place, and secondly in our own Imperial interests, that the author exhorts the British nation to deal with Japan while she is yet weak . . . Great Britain and the United States are called on, in combination, to check Japan's criminal career, and that by the easy method of boycotting her commercially and financially . . . She somewhat light-heartedly dismisses the possibilities of retaliatory action by Japan.[71]

In a foreword to Amleto Vespa's book *Secret Agent of Japan*, published for the Left Book Club, Timperley describes Vespa as 'the unwilling tool of the Japanese Secret Service' and expressed his conviction that 'in the main' the Vespa's story must be accepted as authentic.[72] Vespa explains that the book was written:

> . . . to expose before the conscience of the entire world the rapacious officers of the Japanese Army; to show the unfathomable abyss of infamy into which these savages in uniform are capable of descending; and, in the name of humanity, civilisation and justice, to tell of the strangling degradation to which the people of Manchuria have been subjected under their crushing rule.[73]

In his book Vespa commends *The Menace of Japan* by T. O'Conroy. *The Menace of Japan* was published in October 1933 accompanied by the following publicity notice:

THE MENACE OF JAPAN
by
T. O'CONROY
Late Professor of Keio University
TOKYO

[The author] portrays a country that is corrupt from one end to the other. He shows that the power is in the hands of a few strong men who, through their intensive patriotic propaganda, have subverted the minds of the people until they believe themselves all-powerful and divine. He tells authentic stories of the debauchery of the Buddhist priests, of unutterable cruelty, of sex orgies, of trafficking in human flesh, and of baby-brokers, of things impossible to believe without the proof supplied by the author.

The book is not mere sensationalism, it is a cold, logical thesis compiled by the author during the last fifteen years. In manuscript form it was consulted by Lord Lytton when he was about to present his report [on the Japanese seizure of Manchuria] to the Assembly of the League of Nations.[74]

The newspaper reporting surrounding *The Menace of Japan* generated further sensational adverse publicity for Japan.

In addition to anti-Japanese writing, the effectiveness of Chinese propaganda was complemented by the ineffectiveness of Japanese propaganda.

Japanese propaganda

The basis for official Japanese propaganda had been laid in 1898 when the Foreign Ministry began the systematic collection of comments about Japan in foreign newspapers and journals. Apart from attempts to buy the goodwill of journalists, the Japanese sought to justify their actions in China through radio broadcasts, pamphlets, commissioned books, goodwill missions overseas and conducted tours of Japan for foreign visitors. In 1936 the Domei news agency, the successor to Rengo, began the full-time dissemination of Japanese propaganda. The government sought to promote British and American appreciation of the cultural aspects of Japan (as a distraction from the military aspects) by sponsoring a variety of English-language publications as well as lectures, films, exhibitions and performances of Japanese arts overseas. This 'cultural propaganda' often found a natural British supporter in the Japan Society of London. Such efforts, however, made virtually no impact on either British or American public opinion.[75]

Conclusion

The failure of the pro-Japanese lobby in stemming the rising tide of anti-Japanese sentiment in the 1930s stemmed from the following causes:

Its most active adherents were those who had lived in Japan: it was thus numerically weak. Lacking resources for large-scale publicity, it concentrated on lobbying leading political figures. The battle for British public opinion was lost largely by default. It spoke through occasional books and articles in 'serious' newspapers whilst the public were watching films and newsreels, and reading the 'popular' press.

The actions of the Japanese military in China alienated both the Establishment and Anti-Establishment opinion leading to a deterioration in

Anglo-Japanese relations which left the pro-Japanese lobby in an invidious position and undermined its publicity work.

It was not necessarily that the pro-Japanese lobby had been defeated in debate. They were outnumbered by their rivals, increasingly out of step with the public mood, and overwhelmed by the march of events in the Far East.

Notes

1. A. J. P. Taylor, *English History, 1914–1945* (London: Penguin, 1977), pp. 387, 389, 391–2, 395.
2. R. Bassett, *Democracy and Foreign Policy* (London: Frank Cass & Co., 1968), pp. 28–9.
3. 'The Poise of Japan', *The Times*, 24 August 1925.
4. 'Japan in Transition', *The Times*, 25 January 1928.
5. 'Today at Kyoto', *The Times*, 10 November 1928.
6. 'A Gorgeous Ceremony', *Manchester Guardian*, 12 November 1928.
7. 'The Chinese Anarchy', *The Times*, 31 May 1927; 'Japan and China', *The Times*, 9 September 1931.
8. 'Japan and Manchuria', *The Times*, 4 February 1932.
9. 'Fighting in Manchuria', *The Times*, 21 September 1931.
10. 'The Japanese in Manchuria', *Manchester Guardian*, 21 September 1931.
11. 'The War', *Manchester Guardian*, 22 February 1932.
12. 'Always Tomorrow', *Manchester Guardian*, 16 January 1933.
13. 'China's Integrity', *Manchester Guardian*, 27 July 1934.
14. 'The Attitude Of Japan', *The Times*, 26 April 1934.
15. 'Japan and China', *The Times*, 1 May 1934.
16. 'Japan and Great Britain', *The Times*, 8 August 1936.
17. Captain M. D. Kennedy, 'Japan's Policy in Asia', *Daily Telegraph*, 15 January 1935.
18. Kennedy, Diary, 27 August 1937. The 1917–46 diaries of Captain Malcolm Duncan Kennedy are part of the Kennedy Collection (Sheffield University Library).
19. 'Ten Million Destitute: British Relief in Hankow', *The Times*, 16 April 1938.
20. '1,100 Now Dead in Canton', *Manchester Guardian*, 31 May 1938.
21. 'War on Civilians', *The Times*, 6 June 1938.
22. 'Japan's Use of Air Bombs', *Manchester Guardian*, 20 June 1938.
23. 'Japanese Attaché in Scene Near Embassy', *Manchester Guardian*, 15 August 1938.
24. G. C. Allen, *Japan: the Hungry Guest* (London: George Allen & Unwin, 1938), p. 16.
25. Ibid., pp. 16–17.
26. 'The Massacre at Chungking', *The Times*, 9 May 1939.
27. 'The Far East', *Manchester Guardian*, 21 October 1939.
28. 'The Far Eastern War', *The Times*, 25 November 1939.
29. 'No Deal with Japan', *News Chronicle*, 30 March 1940.
30. 'Britain and Japan', *News Chronicle*, 7 March 1940.
31. 'Back to Munich', *News Chronicle*, 19 July 1940.
32. 'The Burma Road', *Manchester Guardian*, 19 July 1940.

33. 'An Object Lesson', *Manchester Guardian*, 27 June 1940.
34. 'The Burma Road', *Daily Telegraph*, 19 July 1940.
35. 'Agreement with Japan', *The Times*, 19 July 1940.
36. *Daily Telegraph*, 27 December 1941.
37. Kennedy was a language Officer in Japan (1917–20); a Japan expert at the War Office (1921–22); adviser/salesman with the Rising Sun Petroleum Company (1922–24); Reuters correspondent in Tokyo (1925–34) and a freelance writer and lecturer on the Far East (1934–36).
38. *Times Literary Supplement*, 18 December 1924.
39. H. Vere Redman, *Japan in Crisis* (London: George Allen & Unwin, 1935), p. 164.
40. G. C. Allen, *Modern Japan and Its Problems* (London: George Allen & Unwin, 1928), p. 222.
41. G. C. Allen, *Japan: the Hungry Guest* (London: George Allen & Unwin, 1938), p. 245.
42. Kennedy, Diary, 25 July 1939.
43. Ernest H. Pickering, *Japan's Place in the Modern World* (London: George G. Harrap & Co., 1936), p. 322.
44. Redman, *Japan in Crisis*, pp. 217–18.
45. Major R. V. C. Bodley, *A Japanese Omelette* (Tokyo: Hokuseido Press, 1933), pp. 2–6.
46. Ibid., pp. 231–2.
47. M. D. Kennedy, *The Changing Fabric of Japan* (London: Constable, 1931).
48. Ibid., p. 14.
49. *Times Literary Supplement*, 18 December 1930.
50. Public Record Office, Kew. FO 371\15521.
51. Kennedy, Diary, 1 November 1935.
52. Ibid., 2 November 1935.
53. M. D. Kennedy, *The Problem of Japan* (London: Nisbets, 1935).
54. Ibid.
55. Ibid.
56. *Punch*, 25 December 1935.
57. *Times Literary Supplement*, 21 December 1935.
58. G. C. Allen, *Japan: the Hungry Guest* (London: George Allen & Unwin, 1938), p. 17.
59. Ibid., p. 18.
60. Ibid., p. 18.
61. Ibid., p. 19.
62. A. Morgan Young, *Imperial Japan, 1926–1938* (London: George Allen & Unwin, 1938), preface.
63. A. Morgan Young, *Japan under Taisho Tenno, 1912–1926* (London: George Allen & Unwin, 1928), p. 340.
64. Morgan Young, *Imperial Japan, 1926–1938*, p. 249.
65. Ibid., p. 300.
66. A biography of Hollington K. Tong can be found in Howard L. Boorman (ed.), *Biographical Dictionary of Republican China*, 4 vols (New York: Columbia University Press, 1967).
67. Freda Utley *Japan's Feet of Clay* (London: Faber, 1936), pp. 17–18.
68. Kennedy, *The Changing Fabric of Japan*, pp. 148–9.
69. Utley, *Japan's Feet of Clay*, pp. 24–7.
70. Ibid., pp. 35–6.

71. *Times Literary Supplement*, 26 November 1936. In 1930 George Sansom, the British commercial counsellor in Japan, had complained to the Foreign Office that Utley's Soviet affiliations, combined with her research for a book on the Japanese textile industry, had aroused the suspicions of the Japanese police and had made difficult his own work in monitoring the Japanese textile industry difficult. Public Record Office, Kew. FO 371/15521.
72. Amleto Vespa, *Secret Agent of Japan* (London: Victor Gollancz, 1938), pp. x, viii.
73. Ibid., p. 283.
74. Publisher's publicity as printed on the dust-cover of the book and on publicity leaflets. A leaflet is to be found among Foreign Office papers on O'Conroy at the Public Record Office, Kew, FO 371/16243. O'Conroy was an alias of Tim Conroy. In a cable to Reuters in November 1933 Kennedy quoted the Japanese Foreign Ministry description of Conroy as a 'well-known impostor'. For further details, see *Conroy Papers*, Kennedy Collection, 10.3/5.
75. John W. Dower, *War Without Mercy: Race and Power in the Pacific* (New York: Pantheon Books, 1986), p. 97. In 1934 the Kokusai Bunka Shinkokai (Society for International Cultural Relations) was formed. Essentially the organization was an agency of the Japanese Foreign Ministry which provided it with much of its funding: Robert S. Schwantes, 'Cultural Foreign Policies', in John W. Morley (ed.), *Japan's Foreign Policy, 1868–1941: a Research Guide* (New York: Columbia University, 1974), p. 179.

Appendix: Japan in the pages of *Punch*, 1921–1938

A ROUGH ISLAND WELCOME.

JOHN BULL *(to the CROWN PRINCE of Japan).* "IT MAY SHOCK YOU, SIR, BUT I PROPOSE
TO SAY 'HOORAY'!" *(Says it.)*

[In Japan it is the custom to greet Royalty in silence.]

Figure 16.1 'A Rough Island Welcome', *Punch*, 11 May 1921

THE WASHINGTON HATCHET.

AMERICAN DESIGN FOR A JAPANESE SCREEN.

[It is announced that the Anglo-Japanese Alliance is to be terminated in favour of an understanding between the Four Great Powers that have interests in the Pacific.]

Figure 16.2 'The Washington Hatchet', *Punch*, 14 December 1921

WHERE EAST AND WEST ARE ONE.

Figure 16.3 'Where East and West Are One', *Punch*, 12 September 1923

"AND JAPS RUSH IN WHERE DEVILS FEAR TO TREAD."

[The term "foreign devils," as used by the Chinese, is not applied to the Japanese.]

Figure 16.4   'And Japs rush in where devils fear to tread', *Punch*, 16 May 1928

THE HANDS OF THE LEAGUE;
OR, HER FIRST GREAT TEST.

Figure 16.5 'The Hands of the League', *Punch*, 18 November 1931

THE KNIGHT-ERRANT.

"UNHAPPY CREATURE! ONE BY ONE I PROPOSE TO SEVER THE BONDS OF YOUR MISERABLE ENSLAVEMENT."

Figure 16.6 'The Knight-Errant', *Punch*, 6 February 1935

DAWN OVER ASIA

Figure 16.7 'Dawn Over Asia', *Punch*, 29 September 1937

THE CLOSING DOOR

Figure 16.8   'The Closing Door', *Punch*, 9 November 1938

Part V
The Post-War Era (1945–2000)

17

British Labour and Japanese Socialists: Convergence and Divergence, 1945–1952*

James Babb

Introduction

Both the Japanese Socialist and British Labour parties formed governments in the immediate post-war period in very testing times. Wartime destruction, post-war inflation, and the repatriation of demobilized servicemen needed to be balanced against the needs of reconstruction, rehabilitation and rationing. The two parties faced similar political and economic pressures, including left-wing oppositions, which did much to bring down both governments.

With moderate stances on defence, gradual nationalization and a commitment to democracy, the two parties were relatively similar in 1947. Moreover, in these areas of common interest, the British Labour Party had an influence on the shaping of post-war Japanese socialism. However, the story of subsequent relations between these two post-war left-wing governments is one of declining British influence on Japan as the lines created by the Cold War hardened, and America's paramount position was confirmed.

Indeed, significant differences between the two parties developed as the early post-war period progressed. The British Labour Party was a model for a democratic left, willing to side with the United States in the Cold War against a Stalinist Soviet Union. In contrast the Japanese Socialists advocated unarmed neutrality in the conflict. On this issue, the two parties chose sharply different paths.

This essay has four sections. Section one will trace the assumption of power by the left in both countries, while section two surveys British influence on the issue of coal nationalization in Japan. The third section examines the overall problem of economic recovery, with similarities between the two countries being underlined by British support for the Japanese left.

* I would like to thank Professor Chushichi Tsuzuki, Dr Gordon Daniels and Professor Tim Gray for comments on earlier drafts of this essay. All translations and remaining errors are mine.

Finally, I examine the issue of defence which saw initial convergence but eventually drove both parties apart. In a brief conclusion, I discuss the reasons for these convergences and divergences focusing of the differing role of the extreme left in both countries.

The assumption of power by the left in Britain and Japan

In a sense the British Labour Party began its rise to power by ignoring the issue of Japan. In 1945, Prime Minister Winston Churchill urged Labour to continue to support the coalition cabinet, which ruled during the war with Germany, until Japan was defeated – a period expected to last as long as 18 months.[1] However, the Labour Party leadership was unable to overcome the view within the party – backed by public opinion polls – that the best opportunity for Labour to gain power was slipping away.[2] As a result, the Labour members of the Churchill Cabinet resigned on 20 May 1945. The result of the subsequent election was a Labour landslide, winning 393 seats to the Conservatives' 210 and the Liberals trailing with just 12. The percentage of the vote for the two main parties was 48 per cent for Labour and 39.6 per cent for the Conservatives. The Labour government of Clement Attlee was inaugurated on 27 July 1945. Following the dropping of atomic bombs on Hiroshima and Nagasaki, and the Soviet invasion of Manchuria, Japan surrendered on 15 August.

Japan was immediately occupied by the 'Allied Powers' though in practice, the United States played the dominant role. Indeed, as Bates notes: 'The Allied Council for Japan and the Far Eastern Commission proved to be no more than superficial devices for ineffective consultation between the Allies without altering the course – [the Supreme Commander for the Allied Powers General Douglas McArthur] had set.'[3] Nonetheless, Britain participated in the occupation not only through the Allied Council and Far Eastern Commission, but also through the British Commonwealth Occupation Force in western Honshu and the smallest of Japan's four main islands, Shikoku.

The basic objectives of the occupation were largely shared by the Allied powers. The Allied forces were in Japan to promote demilitarization and democratization; the remnants of the Japanese military forces were to be demobilized; and the perpetrators of wartime atrocities were to be tried for war crimes. At the same time, the Japanese constitutional structure was to be revised and elections held to advance the full process of democratization. On these principles, the United States and the United Kingdom were agreed.

The Japanese socialists re-emerged as a result of the liberalization of politics fostered by the Allies and were one of the earliest parties to form, as the Japan Socialist Party (JSP), on 2 November 1945, less than three months after surrender. The JSP and associated activists were to play a major role in the leadership of labour unions and tenant organizations, and had goals which were consistent with the occupation's aims – particularly the provision of rights for organized labour, and land reform.

In the first post-war Japanese elections, held in April 1946, the Socialists won 92 seats, just one seat less than the conservative Progressive Party (associated with the wartime regime) with 93 seats, but far behind the 140 seats secured by the Liberal Party, the most conservative party. The JSP's main rivals on the left, the Japan Communist Party, obtained only five seats. None of the parties secured a majority of the 466 seats in the Lower House of the Diet – largely because a significant number of independents and representatives of minor parties were elected; consequently, the Liberal Party formed an alliance with the Progressive Party to form a government under the Liberal Party leader, Yoshida Shigeru.

This coalition government was far from stable, however, because Yoshida and the 'old line' conservatives were unable to cope with the new forces created by post-war liberalization. In particular, labour unrest escalated and culminated in the call for a general strike on 1 February 1947 which was prohibited at the last moment by General MacArthur. However, MacArthur had little confidence in the Yoshida government, so the promulgation of the new post-war constitution provided an excuse for an early dissolution of the Diet and a general election.

The Socialists appeared to be the one party best able to deal with labour and tenant unrest. Unlike the Communist Party, which had played a disruptive rather than constructive role in labour and tenant movements, the Socialists were considered to be moderate reformers along the lines of the British Labour Party. Moreover, the transformation of the Progressive Party into the Democratic Party, with a new programme of reform capitalism, created an ideological centreground amenable to the Socialists.

It is hardly surprising that the JSP emerged as the largest party after the April 1947 General Election, winning 144 (30.9 per cent) out of the 466 seats in parliament, while the Liberal Party retained only 129 (27.7 per cent), the Democratic Party gained 22 and rose to 132 (28.3 per cent), and the People's Cooperative Party remained relatively steady at 31 (6.7 per cent). Given the increase of support for the Socialists and the shift in vote away from the ruling Liberal Party, the Socialist Party came to be seen as the natural leader of a new coalition government.

While a grand coalition of national unity involving all major parties, except the Communists, was considered, in the end the coalition was led by the Socialist leader Katayama Tetsu with the support of the Democratic Party and the smaller People's Cooperative Party. One result of the coalition negotiations was that the far left of the Socialist Party was excluded from the cabinet, due to their too close association with the Communist Party. Nonetheless, the far left Socialists agreed to support the coalition.

The issue of coal nationalization in Britain and Japan

One issue on which one can see an initial close link between the British Labour government and the Japanese Socialist-led government was coal nationalization. Indeed, most members of the JSP saw the British model of nationalization as the point of departure for themselves. Prime Minister Katayama seems to have requested a large quantity of Labour Party publications which were forwarded through the Foreign Office to Tokyo early in his administration.[4] Coal nationalization was the only identifiable socialist policy in the agreement which led to the formation of the coalition government, and was seen as the first step in the socialization of key industries, though these plans were only reluctantly accepted by the Socialist's coalition partners, the Democratic Party, which experienced considerable internal dissension over the issue.[5]

The most formidable obstacle to coal nationalization seemed likely to be the United States, and, specifically, the Supreme Commander for the Allied Powers (SCAP), General MacArthur. The 1946 US Congressional elections returned a conservative Republican majority hostile to the New Dealers remaining in the Truman Administration. This new conservative congressional leadership was vehemently opposed to the plans of the British Labour government to push for socialist measures in their West German Occupation Zone, and this opposition was echoed forcefully in the Truman Administration itself. Moreover, MacArthur was believed to be personally opposed in principle to such left-wing ideas.[6] However, the Japanese Socialists were encouraged to portray the coal nationalization plan as necessary to increase coal production for Japanese economic recovery, and, by doing so, they were able to secure MacArthur's approval for the scheme.[7]

One official in the occupation subsequently pointed out the importance of the British model for this Japanese policy on coal nationalization. When the new Commerce and Industry Minister, the Socialist Mizutani Chosaburo, met with Theodore Cohen in SCAP Headquarters, he pointed to the unifying effect of the coal scheme:

> The Japan Socialist party, he said, was a mixture, consisting of Fabians, Christian Socialists, Marxists, non-Marxists, revisionists, and just plain social reformers. But one thing they all had in common was an admiration for the recently victorious British Labour Party, and the latter had started its nationalization program with coal. No one in the Japanese Socialist Party, therefore, could object to nationalizing coal. It was a political, if not ideological, natural.[8]

However, the actual legislation was gradually watered down because of opposition from within the Democratic Party, and in the end, the law provided for no more than state supervision of the coal industry with continuing subsidies to mine owners. The nationalization attempt was a disaster for the Socialists and also resulted in a split among their Democratic Party colleagues. The first great socialist initiative of the Katayama government ended in failure.

The contrast with British success in nationalizing the same industry deserves comment. Coal nationalization in Britain was a much less contentious issue than in Japan. In the prewar period, there had been intense conflicts between mine owners and workers in Britain which generated considerable public sympathy for the coal miners. By 1945, coal mine owners had lost both public sympathy and the attention of the Conservatives.

Although the coal industry in Japan raised clear issues of labour rights given the widespread use of wartime forced labour, especially of conscripted Koreans and Chinese who were little more than slave labourers, post-war coal mining provided jobs at a time of high unemployment, and special pay to miners was provided to maintain production even if inflation and corrupt mine owners limited the value of such awards. As a result, the merits of coal nationalization were insufficient in the Japanese public mind to overcome the vigorous opposition of the coal industry. On this issue, therefore, the initial convergence between British Labour and the Japanese Socialists was very quickly eroded.

The issue of the cost of economic recovery

The second issue to face both left-wing governments was the severe cost of economic recovery. After the first flurry of successful legislation on the nationalization of the Bank of England, the coal industry and transport as well as the establishment of a National Health Service to provide free universal health care, Britain's Labour government was hit by a severe economic crisis in 1947, around the same time that the Japanese Socialists had come to power to grapple with similar problems. Debates over nationalization were swept aside in both countries as the governments tried to cope with the immediate crises which faced them.

In Britain, the severe winter of 1946–7 created a serious fuel shortage and the recovery of the economy led to increased demand for imports from the United States which threatened to drain valuable dollars from British reserves. The Attlee government sought to cut its overseas commitments, and decided to withdraw virtually all its occupation forces from Japan. In addition, rationing controls were maintained until the crisis subsided. The cabinet also promoted wage restraint to combat inflationary pressures.

In Japan, the shortage of food and rationing of foodstuffs was the most immediate problem.[9] A related problem was hyper-inflation, which was a result of the Japanese government continuing to pay its wartime debts, subsidies to key industries – especially coal and steel – and the wage bill for a government payroll bloated by the war. Controlling inflation was vital to economic recovery in Japan, and, as in Britain, wage controls were adopted to cope with the problem, including the concept of a base wage.

The Japanese base wage was problematic, however, because it failed to keep pace with inflation. Average manufacturing wages were 1503 yen in June 1947, the first full month of the Katayama government, when the proposed wage base was 1600 yen, but by the end of September 1948, the planned wage base of 3791 yen was far outstripped by actual manufacturing wages at 5841 yen.[10] Soon, therefore, the wage base fell seriously behind actual wages in manufacturing.

The Katayama government did insist, however, on enforcing the wage policy on public employees directly under its control. The first signs of tension between the Japanese Socialists and public employees were in part due to the wage issue, but other problems also existed. Public employees' unions were among the most militant of the period and any government would have been confronted by them. In fact, public employees' unions were affiliated to the communist-controlled Sanbetsu labour federation which opposed the Socialists. In contrast the moderate Sodomei labour federation was dominated by the Socialists.

The Central Labour Commission eventually proposed a settlement favourable to the government employees. This included a lump sum payment equivalent to 2.8 months' salary and the formation of an independent commission to determine appropriate wages for government employees. The Katayama government accepted these proposals, but the new budget only included a payment equivalent to two months' salary because the government claimed it had insufficient resources to fund the remaining eight-tenths of a month's salary.[11] As a result, this proposal was voted down by the Lower House Budget Committee because several left Socialists voted with the opposition against the bill. The bill's opponents included the chairman of the Budget Committee, the left Socialist Suzuki Mosaburo. The left Socialists knew that their party would lose support among government workers to the Communist Party if they had failed to act.

It is unclear whether Suzuki intended to bring down the government. Nonetheless, Katayama decided that he was unable to continue in power, and passed the leadership of the government to the Democratic Party president Ashida Hitoshi. One of Ashida's first initiatives was to incorporate the left Socialists into his new coalition government. Even so, the Ashida government, formed on 9 March 1948, pursued a severe austerity programme to cope with massive inflation. This led to further conflict.

The opposition of public employees' unions to layoffs was vigorous. In particular, in March 1948 the communication workers organized a 'March Offensive' – a series of strikes and other actions leading to the first nationwide strike attempt since the abortive General Strike of February 1947. It became apparent that some way had to be found to weaken the ability of public employees to resist the government.

A move was made to remove the right of public employees to strike. This right had been guaranteed by immediate post-war labour legislation which granted Japanese workers the right to organize unions. Even the Socialists, who had favoured the original legislation, were willing to consider changes in the civil service law because their left-wing opponents were firmly entrenched in the public employees' unions. The left Socialists were, of course, opposed to the changes, but even the left Socialist labour minister, Kato Kanju, decided not to resign and merely attempted to soften the impact of the law. Moreover, in the public employees unions themselves, alternatives to the militant leadership began to emerge that accepted the need for the new arrangements.[12]

Ironically, it was Britain which took the strongest stance against stripping government workers of their rights. This placed them closest to the left Socialist position:

> The Australian and British governments believed that government workers should be entitled to some form of collective bargaining or arbitration. A majority in the FEC seemed to support the Australian proposal that in effect could have given the strike right to government enterprise workers, but Australia did not press for a vote in the face of adamant US opposition.[13]

The wage control policy and increasing austerity measures had opened deep fissures in the Japanese labour movement and alienated public employees from the Socialist leadership. But, given the difficult economic situation facing Japan in 1947 and 1948, it was inevitable that sacrifices would have to be made, and Socialist frustration with union militants gave further impetus to the situation. The British foreign secretary Ernest Bevin (a one-time union leader) and his Commonwealth allies probably did not appreciate the threat to the Japanese Socialists from militant government workers.

The challenge from the Japan Communist Party, which began to make dramatic gains on the left as a result of Socialist failures in government, was felt most keenly by the left-wing Socialists. In July 1948, members of the left-wing Farmer-Labour (Rono) faction in the JSP voted against the government budget because they argued that it did not include adequate wage increases for government workers. There were many more abstentions by JSP members of parliament. When the MPs involved were ejected from the party (or, in some cases, the whip was simply removed), a number split from the Socialist Party to form the Farmer-Labour Party (Ronoto).

Once the JSP fell from power in late 1948, and after a massive defeat in the general election of 1949, it was the remnants of the left wing in the party which took control from the discredited right wing to rebuild and reinvigorate the party. The left were largely successful in their efforts, but they moved the party as a whole to the left as the conflict between the JSP and JCP developed. This had its most profound impact in the final issues to be considered: peace treaties and defence.

Now turning briefly to the role of economic recovery in the demise of the Labour government in Britain, we find it also had its origins in the opposition of the left wing to retrenchment policies, though in Britain these were concerned mainly with Cold War rearmament and the escalating cost of the new National Health Service. When the chancellor of the Exchequer, Hugh Gaitskell, decided to impose prescription charges for the National Health Service, three cabinet ministers – Aneurin Bevan, Harold Wilson and John Freeman – resigned. Attlee called an early election to renew his mandate, but instead Labour lost the election and the Conservative Party came to power.

It had been a budgetary matter which precipitated these resignations. At this point the Keep Left group, formed in 1947 to pursue a 'third way' between the United States and the Soviet Union, coalesced with the left wing of the Labour leadership under Bevan.[14] It is significant that the leading representative of the pro-defence wing of the Labour Party in the 1950s was Gaitskell. In both Britain and Japan, therefore, left-wing opposition to issues in the budget led to defections which helped to bring governments down. From this time on security issues were to shape the role of the left in both countries.

Different paths confirmed: peace treaty and defence

The issues of a peace treaty and defence are the third area which began with convergence and ended in divergence. One of the important tasks confronting the Katayama government was a peace treaty with the victorious allies, which would bring a swift end to the occupation. The presence of a cooperative administration – unlike the previous Yoshida government – meant that an early end to the occupation and a restoration of Japanese sovereignty could now be contemplated. Indeed, the Socialists seemed to relish the notion that they would be the party to regain Japanese independence.

The Socialists' stance on security was intimately tied to a peace treaty which would bring the occupation of Japan to an end. The Socialists were committed to pursuing a peace treaty as quickly as possible, and, therefore, were anxious to fulfil the conditions for peace set out by the Allies, such as trying war criminals and democratically reforming Japan. In addition, they argued that since Japan had renounced war, a United Nations or regional security scheme should be considered to provide for Japanese security.[15]

Since the occupation had effectively cut Japan off from the rest of the world, the primary task facing Foreign Minister Ashida was negotiating a peace treaty. Katayama's Foreign Minister, Ashida, was leader of the Democratic Party and was considered to be one of the few truly capable members of the cabinet.[16] Ashida undertook the most significant action of the Katayama government and one which underlines the divergent paths taken later by Labour and the Japanese Socialists. This step arose in the form of a memorandum drafted in September 1947 on Japan's military security.

In this document, which Ashida had sent to Washington through General Eichelberger, the Japanese government recognized that the United States' military forces might remain in Japan after the conclusion of a peace treaty. As Finn notes, 'Yoshida and other leaders had seen the memo and agreed with its position' before it was given to Eichelberger on 13 September 1947.[17] Finn goes on to note that 'there is no record, however, that any senior [US] officials saw it or that any use was made of it then or later'.[18]

However, there was one government which gave informal encouragement to Ashida's initiative – Attlee's Labour administration in Britain. On 24 September 1947, 11 days after submitting his memorandum to the United States government, Ashida met the head of the British liaison mission, Sir Alvary Gascoigne, to discuss the issues involved. They discussed three points with regard to a possible peace conference, of which the third is most relevant. Ashida later wrote:

> I raised the problem of Japanese security and asked him 'If you were in my position what do you think that you would do?' The British ambassador did not directly respond, but very naturally said without hestation 'We will protect you.' (emphasis in English in the original)[19]

Gascoigne admitted that ' "We cannot, however, say this publicly," [but] it is a issue which also must be seriously considered by the United States.'[20] This inability to give a public guarantee may have been out of deference to the Soviet Union which would have viewed such a statement as directed against it, or it may have been to avoid conflict with the United States. Whatever Gascoigne's reasons, the British government was the only power to reinforce the Katayama government's strategy.

In addition, Gascoigne took the view that the stationing of troops in Japan would be limited. Ashida reports that the British ambassador argued that:

After he said that 'It is probably not necessary to station troops on Japanese territory to defend Japan', 'One should think about the situation where troops are necessary on Japanese territory for airfields to defend Hokkaido from the Kuriles or Sakhalin.'[21]

The only possible enemy being considered was therefore the Soviet Union since it occupied the Kuriles and Sakhalin in August 1945.

It is significant that this acceptance of a western defence of Japan from potential threats such as the Soviet Union was an official Japanese government position – a government led by the Socialist Party – accepting a role for United States forces in Japanese security after the signing of a peace treaty. Given the fact that the Socialists and most other political leaders accepted that Japan would have no military forces, it was natural that the United States should continue to protect Japan. In fact, the prohibition of military forces was enshrined in Article 9 of the new Constitution which was passed at the same time that the Socialists rose to become the largest party in the Diet.

While Japanese conservatives, including Ashida himself, and the United States government later reinterpreted the Constitution as permitting defensive forces, no mention was made of any such ideas at the time. Yet, the need for a defence force was also obvious due to tension which seemed to be growing between the United States and its wartime ally the Soviet Union. As early as 22 July 1947 Ashida noted with concern the worsening of relations between the two largest post-war powers, and wrote in his diary that he had been told that MacArthur believed that a war between the US and the Soviet Union was possible but not probable.[22]

Similarly, the British Labour government clearly allied itself with the United States in disputes with the Soviet Union, primarily in Europe. Soviet actions in Iran seemed to persuade the Labour left to support the pro-United States position of the party leadership. Up to this point, the JSP appeared to be heading toward a similar position. After all, the JSP was not a communist party, and key party leaders, such as Nishio Suehiro, were not only suspicious of the far left in their own party but clearly anti-communist in outlook. Thus, the JSP as leader of a moderate centre-left government friendly with the US and willing to explore US security guarantees was not an anomaly. At this point, on this crucial issue, British Labour and Japanese Socialists in power adopted a similar stance.

Soon, however, the two parties' views began to diverge. It is difficult to say precisely when the shift occurred but it seems to have been gradual as communist attacks on the Socialists began to have an impact at the same time that the Cold War between the US and the Soviet Union intensified in late 1948. The first evidence we have of Socialist concerns over defence is a statement by Katayama that his government collapsed because MacArthur was pressuring him to rearm Japan.[23] Even if Katayama's memory of the significance of this pressure was faulty, the fact that the issue was confronted and that it disturbed him at the time is significant.

However, an anti-American and neutralist pacifist position only emerged clearly in the JSP after the party was in decline at the end of 1948. This position was confirmed in the 1949 general election. The two parties which gained in the election took anti-US positions: the Liberal Party, which won an absolute majority of 264 seats, and the Japan Communist Party, which jumped from 9 to 35 MPs. Socialist representation, on the other hand, fell by two-thirds, from 143 to 49, and the Democratic Party from 90 to 68. It was a repudiation of not only a centrist coalition, but of cooperation with the occupation authorities.

Significantly, the left wing of the Socialists led the fight to rebuild the party, with leftist Suzuki Mosaburo being elected as party leader in the aftermath of the election. No doubt as a reaction to the inroads of the Communist Party into the Socialist support base, the party's policy shifted sharply from leaning toward the US to a neutralist position. The Socialists adopted a position opposed to any security treaty with the United States which would retain US forces in Japan after a peace treaty, and were opposed to a peace treaty which excluded the Soviet Union and the People's Republic of China. The right wing of the Socialist Party split the party in 1951 because it wanted to support the peace treaty, though not the security treaty.

The British Labour government also tried to insist on a comprehensive peace much like that desired by the Japanese left. The Labour government's foreign secretary, Ernest Bevin, visited Washington in September 1949 to promote a new peace effort, urging the US government to produce a draft peace plan which was very close to the Japanese proposal. However, Bevin was sent away empty-handed, as Finn explains:

> Unfortunately, the new draft contained no provisions on defense or the security of Japan because the Department of Defense failed to produce any. [US] Military leaders believed that a peace treaty with Japan was premature, and they went on record that any treaty must permit the United States to retain forces and bases in Japan and include the Soviet Union and 'the de facto government of China' as signatories. The State Department was therefore not able to provide the full draft Bevin had requested, and the 1949 draft proved abortive.[24]

In contrast to the position within the US military, the dominant view in the American government was that negotiations about a peace treaty should be delayed in order to prevent the participation of the Soviet Union and the newly created People's Republic of China, which the US refused to recognize. The British government, however, recognized the PRC and wanted both communist states involved in the peace treaty. As late as May 1950,

Bevin was complaining that US stalling regarding Japan had placed the British in a ' "position of extreme difficulty," had embarrassed London in its relations with its Commonwealth partners and provided the Soviet Union with a golden opportunity to "take the initiative" and write a "peace treaty of their own".'[25]

The United States still insisted on excluding the Soviet Union and Communist China and was able to pressure the Yoshida government to accept a separate peace. In the end, the British Labour Party agreed with the United States and Japan. However, to the consternation of the new Churchill government in late 1951, the far left Labour opposition to the Japanese peace treaty persisted although the treaty had been negotiated by the Attlee government. This was part of the general disintegration and demise of the Labour government in 1951.

> At the end of November 1951, thirty-five Labour MPs had defied the party whips to vote against a Japanese peace treaty, while another 100 abstained. On 5 March 1952, an amendment put forward by Bevan and his supporters, which condemned the rearmament programme, produced 57 rebels against Attlee and the official leadership . . . From that time onwards, Labour was to be racked by prolonged civil war.[26]

At the same time, the Left Japanese Socialists confronted the conservative British Labour leadership at international fora. At the June 1951 Socialist International, Left Socialist Suzuki Mosaburo noted that,

> I participated in a sub-committee to consider resolutions on peace issues, but we were unable to put forward any proposals for consideration by the conference. A proposal that 'Without armaments, peace cannot be secured' which put military preparations first was insisted upon by the British Labour Party, so as a result no resolution was made.[27]

The left Socialists also clashed directly with the Labour leadership at the first plenary session of the Asian Socialist Conference in January 1953, when Clement Attlee represented the Socialist International which was accused of being 'divorced from Asian aspirations, especially on questions of defence'.[28]

A pro-defence leadership dominated the Labour Party despite vigorous dissent. This leadership was the face primarily shown to the Japanese Socialists. The official stance of the British Labour Party was firmly on the US side in the Cold War and opposed to the neutralism and pacifism of the Japanese Left Socialists. In Japan, in contrast, the left continued to dominate the Socialist Party even after the left and right Socialist Parties reunited in 1955. The position taken by the Socialists aroused sympathy in the public

at large so the Socialist Party tended to emphasize this aspect of its programme at the expense of its other policies. In fact, pacifism became the
dominant feature of the post-war Japanese left in sharp contrast to the official position of British Labour.

Conclusions

In the immediate aftermath of the Second World War, the British Labour
Party and Japanese Socialist Party were similar in some respects – coal
nationalization, austerity with a sensitivity to worker rights, moderate
socialism opposed to communism, and an emphasis on defence with the
United States and the allies playing a role. However, the two parties subsequently took sharply divergent paths. The process leading to this outcome
must now be analysed. Why did these differences arise? It would be a
mistake to answer this question entirely in terms of the Cold War, but it is
significant that the conflict between the Socialists and Communists in Japan
had no parallel in the weak challenge of the far left to the Labour Party
leadership in the United Kingdom.

In Britain fears over the motives of the Soviet Union were widely shared
and only a small minority of left activists sought to point out the danger of
East–West polarization. In contrast, the Japanese Socialists were preoccupied
by the Japan Communist Party inroads into their core constituencies.
Initially the Socialists tried to use their position in government to attack
the far left, but, once in opposition, they felt compelled to move to the left
and adopt a policy of neutralism and peace to regain support. The consequent split between the far left and the moderate left in Japan was sharper,
but the communists were also a much more formidable challenge in Japan
than they were in Britain.

The divergence between the British Labour Party and the Japanese
Socialists can be largely explained by the differing constituencies which the
parties faced in the context of the Cold War. It was logical for a British
Labour Party, competing against the Conservative Party, to reassure voters
that it was committed to defence against the Soviet threat while the Japanese Left Socialists found the peace issue useful to compete with both their
Communist opponents and against their Right Socialist rivals. Similarly,
austerity caused division and tension in both countries, but it was in Japan
that the policies of the government placed the Socialists in direct conflict
with a key constituency – public employees – with more significant consequences, due to the magnitude of communist competition for government
workers' support. Finally, the groundwork for coal nationalization in Britain
had been prepared in the prewar period, but there was little support for such
a move among the Japanese, many of whom viewed the ideological implications of nationalization plans with alarm. Given these conditions, it is not
surprising that the British Labour Party model quickly faded in significance

in post-war Japan. Labour's influence was yet further diminished by America's increasing determination to impose non-socialist prescriptions for Japan's economic reconstruction.

Notes

1. Roger Eatwell, *The 1945–1951 Labour Governments* (London: Batsford Academic, 1979), p. 70.
2. Kenneth Morgan, *Labour in Power, 1945–1951* (Oxford: Oxford University Press, 1984), pp. 35–6.
3. Peter Bates, *Japan and the British Commonwealth Occupation Force* (London: Brassey's, 1993), p. 218.
4. Gordon Daniels, 'Britain's View of Post–war Japan, 1945–49', in Ian Nish (ed.), *Anglo-Japanese Alienation, 1919–1952* (Cambridge: Cambridge University Press, 1982), p. 267.
5. Matsuoka Hideo, *Rengo Seiken ga Tokai shita Hi: Shakaito Katayama Naikaku kara no Kyojun* (The Day the Coalition Government Fell: Lessons from the Socialist Party's Katayama Cabinet) (Tokyo: Kyoiku Shiryo Shuppan Kai, 1990), p. 104.
6. Theodore Cohen, *Remaking Japan: The American Occupation as New Deal* (New York: Free Press, 1987), p. 316.
7. Ibid., pp. 318, 321–3.
8. Ibid., pp. 318–19.
9. Ibid., p. 143 ff.
10. Okada Akira, 'Senryo Seisaku to Nihon Kanryo Sei' (Occupation Policy and the Japanese Bureaucratic System), *Gyosei Kanri Kenkyu* [Public Administration Review Quarterly], no. 59 (September 1993), p. 24.
11. Ayusawa Iwao, *A History of Labour in Modern Japan* (Honolulu: East–West Centre Press, 1966), pp. 288–9.
12. Chuo Rodo Iinkai, *Nakamura Ichiro Sensei to Rodo Iinkai* (Nakamura Ichiro and the Labour Commission) (Tokyo: Roi Kyokai, 1981), p. 297.
13. Richard Finn, *Winners in Peace: MacArthur, Yoshida and Postwar Japan* (Berkeley: University of California Press, 1992), p. 175.
14. David Coates, *The Labour Party and the Struggle for Socialism* (Cambridge: Cambridge University Press, 1975), p. 190.
15. Nakakita Koji, *Keizai Fukko to Sengo Seiji: Nihon Shakaito, 1945–1951* (Economic Reconstruction and Postwar Politics: The Japan Socialist Party, 1945–1951) (Tokyo: University of Tokyo Press, 1998), p. 271.
16. Ashida Hitoshi, *Ashida Hitoshi Nikki* (Ashida Hitoshi Dairies), 7 vols (Tokyo: Iwanami Shoten, 1986), vol. 7, p. 4.
17. Finn, *Winners in Peace*, p. 250.
18. Ibid.
19. Ashida, *Ashida Hitashi Nikki*, vol. 7, p. 405.
20. Ibid.
21. Ibid.
22. Ibid., p. 13.
23. Takahashi Hikohiro, *Gendai Seiji to Shakai Minshushugi* (Modern Politics and Social Democracy) (Tokyo: Hosei University Press, 1985), pp. 158–63.

24. Finn, *Winners in Peace*, p. 247.
25. Michael Schaller, *The American Occupation of Japan: the Origins of the Cold War in Asia* (Oxford: Oxford University Press, 1985), p. 259.
26. Morgan, *Labour in Power*, p. 487.
27. Suzuki Mosaburo, Ouchi Hoyei and Sakisaka Itsuro (eds), *Suzuki Mosaburo Senshu* (Selected Works of Suzuki Mosaburo) (Tokyo: Rodo Daigaku Shuppankyoku, 1970), p. 260. See also J. A. A. Stockwin, *The Japanese Socialist Party and Neutralism: a Study of a Political Party and its Foreign Policy* (Carlton: Melborne University Press, 1968), p. 177; Yamazaki Hiro, *Shakaito 10-nen Shi* (Ten-Year History of the Socialist Party) (Tokyo: Taibunkan, 1956), pp. 126–7.
28. Stockwin, *The Japanese Socialist Party*, p. 51.

18
Masking or Marking Britain's Decline? The British Council and Cultural Diplomacy in Japan, 1952–1970

Christopher Aldous

In a study of German–American cultural relations in the post-war period, Manuela Aguilar defines cultural diplomacy as 'the way a government portrays its country to another country's people in order to help achieve certain foreign policy goals'.[1] Interestingly Philip Taylor, focusing on 'cultural propaganda' during the interwar period, sees its purpose in similar terms – 'the promotion and dissemination of national aims and achievements in a general rather than specifically economic or political form, although it is ultimately designed to promote economic and political interests'.[2] The establishment in 1934 of the British Committee for Relations with Other Countries, a title shortened to 'British Council' in 1936, represented the belated realization in British political circles that cultural propaganda issued by other nations, particularly fascist regimes, was weakening British influence in strategic areas. However dramatic an innovation the establishment of the British Council may have seemed to those involved, they must also have been only too aware that Britain was embracing cultural diplomacy very late in the day – long after other governments had done so – and that there were many in government circles, particularly in the Treasury, intent on judging it against very exacting criteria.

Indeed, the debate over cultural diplomacy raged throughout the 1930s. The twists and turns of policy and the inter-agency rivalry that preceded the establishment of the Council prefigured many of the problems that would bedevil it in the future, particularly in Japan. Its chief weakness was its hopelessly inadequate budget, reflecting deep divisions over the nature and purposes of cultural diplomacy. The Department of Overseas Trade, together with the economic interests it represented, emerged as the Foreign Office's chief sparring-partner for control over the new cultural relations committee, the outlines of which were beginning to take shape by 1930. It was in that year that the Treasury agreed for the first time to fund cultural activities abroad under the aegis of the Foreign Office. Philip Taylor argues that one of the chief determinants of the Treasury's conversion (if an initial grant of £2500 amounts to a conversion) was the 'recommendations of the D'Abernon trade mission to South America which repeatedly emphasised the inter-dependence of commercial and cultural propaganda'. Given the emphasis placed on economic advantage, it is perhaps surprising that the British Council was not vested with a narrower, more trade-related brief. The main reason the Foreign Office triumphed, and with it the promotion of national rather than sectional (that is to say, commercial) propaganda, was the Council's increasing dependence on its government grant which reflected a general unwillingness on the part of private industry to provide significant sums of money.

Of course, the Foreign Office argued that economic benefits would flow *indirectly* from a diplomatic approach that promoted national prestige in the broadest sense, and in any case there were industrial representatives on the Council. Still, Taylor contends, the interwar Treasury regarded cultural propaganda as 'a vague, indefinable and somewhat nebulous activity which did not hold out any promise of immediate or visible returns'. The difficulty of measuring long-term, often indirect, benefits, made it all too easy for opponents of the Council to belittle its contribution. The fact that the British Council was not really designed to generate 'immediate returns', which indeed might have compromised its status as a 'cultural' organization, did not make its future any more secure. In contrast, commercial propaganda could be seen to pay its way in the short term, and for that reason always lurked in the background as the saving grace of cultural diplomacy.[3]

Another argument deployed to justify very limited funding for the Council was the perceived need to reach the right balance between selling the country short and engaging in activities that might easily be characterized as propagandist by their intended audience. In response to the appeals of Anthony Eden (the then foreign secretary) to increase funding for the Council in 1937, Sir John Simon, the chancellor of the Exchequer, admitted to a view of 'cultural propaganda' as 'a field in which the law of diminishing returns applies, and while a moderate expenditure carefully applied can do good, there is no better propaganda than the bad and extravagant propaganda of our rivals'.[4]

In the case of Japan, however, it was the timing of British efforts at cultural propaganda, rather than their scale or intensity, that ensured that they would prove counterproductive. In a memorandum to the Foreign Office, dated 2 June 1943, Richard Ledward, 'one of those engaged in publicizing our war effort in Japan during the years 1939 and 1940', argued that 'our sudden conversion to the idea that cultural interchange might serve a useful purpose at all made it lamentably easy for malicious tongues and pens to attribute our cultural activities in Japan to propagandist motives'. By way of contrast, Ledward referred to the cultural initiatives of Germany, the foundations for which had been laid in the early 1920s, 'when Germany was in Japanese eyes politically insignificant yet culturally acceptable'. In sum, British cultural policy in Japan before the outbreak of war with the West is described as 'a heroic last minute rearguard action on unfamiliar terrain against a carefully prepared and skilfully delivered attack'.[5] Ledward's comments reveal how little Britain achieved in the cultural sphere during the 1930s. In the 1940s a ferocious war had ensnared many British residents of eastern colonies, and a US Occupation force had sponsored American-inspired reforms of Japanese institutions. Neither of these developments boded well for British interests in Japan, which were promoted from 1952 by Mr R. A. Close, the Council's first representative in Japan. His prospects were further damaged by a budget which he knew to be inadequate.

Like all representatives, Close had to justify his existence, and thus aimed to achieve a balance in his activities between facilitating sales of British products in Japan and protecting Britain's long-term political interests vis-à-vis Japan. Regarding the former, he may or may not have been aware of a letter from R. Seymour, the secretary of the British Council, which was sent out to all overseas representatives in 1950. Some of the statements made in this letter are very revealing of the pressures felt by officials in London, seemingly under sustained attack from the Beaverbrook press (chiefly the *Daily Express* and *Evening Standard*) for their alleged extravagance and cultural elitism. As a result, the British Council began to exhibit symptoms associated with a personality disorder, some of which are only too plain from Seymour's letter. It begins with the reassuring words that '[w]e all know that in many ways, directly or indirectly, the Council has been responsible for increases in the sales of British products abroad, the expenditure of foreign currency by visitors to the UK, and the appointment of British experts to posts abroad'. His prescription then leads one to suspect a 'split personality':

> It is very useful to give specific instances (of the benefits referred to above) in discussion with critics in London and with those whose main interest is the export drive . . .
>
> Representatives will, of course, recognise the need to be discreet in making any enquiries on these subjects. I should like to make clear also that our desire to be as fully informed as possible does not indicate any change of policy in regard to the Council's participation in commercial matters.

The message is clear: promote British products, but make sure that you are very subtle in your approach, and that you do not let the cultural mask slip. Whilst the overseas representatives were dealing with a foreign audience, the London-based staff were courting the political establishment, of which Seymour has this to say: 'MPs for example usually realize that stimulation of exports is not the object for which the Council exists, but none the less they are very interested in any figures that can be given.'[6]

Apart from considering the commercial effects of his activities, Mr Close as overseas representative also had to promote Britain's long-term political interests vis-à-vis Japan. One of the means by which this was done was the award of British Council scholarships to some of the most able Japanese students, the idea being that those chosen to study in Britain would then return to Japan and rise to positions of great influence, through which they would hopefully work to foster cordial and lucrative ties between the two countries. Here again, British Council activities in Japan in the early 1950s were beset by problems. In 1950, there was an adverse public reaction, particularly amongst ex-POWs of the Japanese, when it was disclosed that the British Council planned to award scholarships to five Japanese postgraduates. In its defence, the Council reminded critics of Britain's dependence on trade and its responsibilities in the emergent Cold War: 'The United Kingdom cannot maintain its present population and standard of living in isolation. Nor can it afford to ignore the importance of Japan, or to act in any way which would encourage it becoming a communist satellite or associate state.'[7] Furthermore, it was 'not considered at all desirable that Japan should fall exclusively into the American sphere . . .', a justifiable concern given the high number of Japanese 'taken to the US at the expense of that government'.[8] In short, critics of the scholarship scheme were missing the point:

> The primary purpose of these scholarships is not to help the Japanese but to further British interests . . . As far as Japan is concerned we cannot afford to ignore the importance of that country where far less is now known of our affairs than is necessary if we are to avoid harmful misrepresentation by those who are ill-disposed to Britain and the democracies in general.[9]

So in 1951 the Council had not moved far from its original mission – to protect Britain's image abroad against hostile propaganda, the chief sources of which were now the Soviet Union and the People's Republic of China. The above statements in support of the scholarships typify the British Council's impossible position in Japan in the 1950s. It had to contend with pervasive anti-Japanese feeling at home, American cultural dominance in Japan and the further prospect of corrosive communist initiatives in the future. According to Philip Taylor, 'the British Council was created partly to perpetuate the appearance of power in the minds of foreigners at a time when hostile propaganda was beginning to expose the harsh realities of British decline . . .'.[10] Those harsh realities were all too evident in the limited scale and dullness of Britain's cultural diplomacy in Japan during the 1950s.

Selling British culture short

When Mr Close arrived in Japan in October 1952 he set out to establish a cultural presence there that could stand comparison with what had been, until 1951, a very successful operation in China. His 1952–3 annual report raised a number of issues that would crop up again and again during the 1950s. He referred to 'very high costs and the equally high bidding for accommodation and services'. His sketch of the Japanese social environment highlighted problems of 'confusion' and feelings of 'rootlessness', and, more positively, 'an eager and conscious pursuit after "culture"', evidenced by 'flourishing bookshops, and the concentrated attention given to the more serious of a variety of exhibitions . . .'. Close strongly believed that there was an affinity between Japan and Britain that if skilfully exploited could only work to the Council's advantage:

> In many Japanese families there is a tradition of friendship with Britain and of study from British sources. Respect for long-established institutions and a yearning for mental and moral stability, as well as the idea that Britain is solving social problems similar to their own, make our country particularly attractive for many young Japanese.

The rather desperate argument that Britain and Japan ought to be on good terms because both countries were experiencing straitened economic circumstances was an odd one that seemed peculiarly attractive to those concerned with cultural diplomacy – in January 1951 Sir Alvary Gascoigne had remarked that Japanese felt 'that to a great extent their own economic difficulties are shared by us'.[11] This weak logic is surely indicative of the feeble position in which Britain found herself in the early 1950s.

Regarding this latter point, Close was at pains in his report to highlight the degree to which British cultural efforts were falling short of Japanese expectations. He outlined the depth, breadth and variety of American cultural programmes, implemented by 19 purely American cultural centres, each endowed with a library of 10000–20000 volumes. Fulbright and Smith-Mundt schemes produced 75 scholarships a year for Japanese graduates and around 125 grants for travel only. Close stated that these programmes generated employment for 65 Americans and 380 Japanese. In marked contrast, the British cultural presence in Japan initially consisted of two officials (one of whom, Mr Scott, resigned in March 1953) and a Japanese secretary; 13 scholarships were available for Japanese graduates; assistance was given to only six Japanese who visited the UK; and there were no concert tours or exhibitions by British artists. According to Close, the French record was considerably more impressive, and, he suggested, the efforts of Germany, Italy and India would soon surpass those of Britain. For all these reasons, many Japanese felt let down – the chief sources of disappointment were the failure to make rapid, visible progress with the expansion of the Council Library and the lack of progress made in appointing British professors and lecturers to Japanese university posts.

Close concluded his report with a warning – 'In making financial provision for this country, care must be taken to prevent our establishment falling to the near missionary level . . .'. He cautioned that 'in attempting to do things on the cheap, we shall only lose ourselves in the teeming millions'. Faced with a budget of £21 000 for 1953–4 – in his view two-thirds of the minimum required (£30 000) – this representative opted to 'concentrate on the work that can be done at a high level . . . remembering that Japan is a country where the elite is always influential'. Finally, he stated that his priorities were to foster trade in British books and periodicals ('within the British Council's terms of reference'), to reinforce the Council Library, and to improve the teaching of English in Japan so as to facilitate effective communication between the two countries.[12] The above points raised by Mr Close draw attention to a number of larger issues that merit investigation – namely, the consequences of the apparent lack of interest in Japan that was evidenced by London's failure to correct the representative's budgetary shortfall; the implications of American cultural dominance and the poor showing of Britain in comparison with other countries, a trend that became more marked as the decade progressed; and finally the degree to which the Council succeeded in promoting British interests in Japan during the 1950s.

The perception that Japan was very low on the Council's list of priorities was keenly felt by Mr Close and expressed in a long letter to the director-general shortly before he left Japan in 1956, in which he urged that 'our position vis à vis this country now be radically reviewed'. The representative then sketched out the financial backdrop to his activities in Japan, arguing that he had been hobbled by a decision early on in his term to freeze Council expenditure: '. . . a ruling was announced in Parliament that the British Council should restrict itself to the "existing level of activity". This was applied to Japan where there had of course been no time to reach a normal level of activity'.[13]

Interestingly, the Drogheda Report (1953), compiled by the Independent Committee of Enquiry into the Overseas Information Service, recommended that 'large extra funds should be made available for expansion of the British Council's work in the Far East'. However, as the controller of Overseas Division 'B' explained to Close, 'Britain's present economic position has made it impossible to get any proposals for new expenditure accepted'.[14] Thus, the representative in Japan complained that two years after the publication of a summary of the report 'a partial implementation' of its recommendations 'added some £5000 to Japan but this still kept the total below the minimum . . . considered necessary in 1952'.[15]

Close also remarked on the fact that the Council's 21st Annual Report made 'only two, quite minor references to Japan in the text' despite its being 'the largest and certainly the most dynamic highly-educated population amongst which the Council is at present able to operate'. More seriously, he drew attention to the human costs of the budgetary shortfall, which had left the Council's small staff in Japan so 'exposed' that A. C. Scott had resigned and the librarian had suffered a nervous breakdown. In addition, the failure to extend operations beyond Tokyo, the prolonged absence of British cultural representation from Kyoto and the lack of British teachers in Japanese universities all proved to be serious weaknesses. Close argued that the Council's obvious lack of commitment in Japan was 'now beginning to make us appear undignified', and he warned Sir Paul Sinker that there was a limit to the willingness of Japanese 'to pay for what they want of our culture'. His overriding point about Britain's failure to exploit the potential of Japan – 'the splendid ready-made opportunities' there – was surely a valid one, and should have elicited a proper response from London.

However, the most usual responses from the Far East Department were hollow assurances, or, worse still, expressions of regret. During the 1950s lengthy annual reports penned by the Council's representatives in Japan – Close, Dr L. R. Phillips (1956–9) and Mr F. J. Bottrall (1959–61) – do not seem to have generated much interest among the various specialist committees in London. In January 1958, Mrs Kitchingham, director of the Far East Department, wrote to Phillips stating 'how much we all appreciated your Financial Report for 1956–7'. She went on to remark on 'how difficult it must be working in such a country as Japan on an "emergency budget" but it seems we can only extend sympathy and understanding with little or no financial help'.[16] This was in response to a hard-hitting report from the representative, in which he stated that the 'desperate shortage of funds is converting us into smooth-mannered mendicants . . . We are poor relations in a country where loss of face is a disaster'.[17]

There was one consolation for Phillips, the merits of which he was only too pleased to specify in his next sentence:

> That the Council has maintained its slow advance . . . must be attributed . . . , in large part . . . , to our formal association with the Embassy. After seven months' experience of its working, I should say that it has very much in its favour. Many of the anomalies of our position disappear, whilst facilitation in a host of matters – customs, clearance, taxation, motor transport etc., save both time and money. The disadvantage . . . that we may become associated with the political ends of the Embassy, has not been felt.[18]

This close relationship between the Embassy and the British Council in Japan – referred to by Phillips as a sensible one of 'association with separateness' – was an exceptional one. When a similar link was suggested for Burma, the Council's deputy director-general cautioned that 'we must not let ourselves be so beglamoured (or chivvied) by economy as to forget the reasons for our policy of non-identification hitherto . . .'. He drew attention to the views of the Drogheda Committee and the Foreign Office, who were 'inclined to admit that there is advantage in the Council's remaining separate when political relations with the Government of a country are strained . . .'.[19] In the case of Japan, economy triumphed over all other considerations, the implication being that the British government and the Council were happy to work in tandem where Japan was concerned, and, more significantly, saw no reason to disguise their close association. Perhaps it was the natural outcome of the Council's decision, again made for financial reasons, to concentrate its efforts on the elite of Japan. Presumably, the latter were not so much wary of the representative's diplomatic status as rather impressed by it.

The converse of Britain's concentrating on the elite was to leave the masses to the Americans. After all, they had the necessary resources to take up the challenge. Meanwhile, Britain hoped to benefit from an overweening American presence. The exigencies of the Cold War and the need to improve English language training (ELT) were the two areas of common interest for Britain and the US in 1950s Japan. That is not to say, however, that they always worked in concert.

In the case of ELT, although there was no question of its urgency and the superiority of American resources, there was some impatience on the part of Britain with the US's tight control of policy. Whilst Dr Phillips remarked in 1958 that the 'main responsibility in the field of linguistics has been deemed to lie with the Americans', he hinted at the possibility of division by referring to the Council's contribution as giving 'a degree of balance, or British bias, to their efforts'.[20] In May 1957 the representative had reported the findings of the Exploratory Committee on English Language Teaching in Japan, which firmly recommended the teaching of English by oral methods.[21] The British delegate on the committee was Professor Hornby. His American counterpart, Professor Fries, was variously described as prone to 'imperialistic behaviour'[22] and 'the main influence inimical to British penetration . . .'.[23] In April 1959 Phillips warned his successor that he was 'bound to be appalled by the low standard of spoken English . . . even among Japanese professors of English', suggesting on a more positive note that Fries' virtual retirement would improve the likelihood of productive Anglo-American cooperation in this field. Still, there were some British successes to celebrate by the end of the 1950s – five British lecturers in Japanese universities subsidized by the Council, annual summer schools for Japanese teachers of English that had begun in 1958,[24] and the appointment of an English-language specialist to the post of regional director, Kyoto.

In marked contrast to their misgivings over the US's virtual monopoly of ELT, Britain was relieved to see the immense resources of its ally acting as a counterweight to the cultural initiatives of the communist powers in Japan. For example, in April 1956 Close had remarked that the US 'brought over the entire Symphony of the Air . . .' in response to the welcome accorded the Russian violinist David Oistrakh.[25] Still, the Soviets laboured hard and by the end of the 1950s almost seemed to be winning through. 1957 was a good year for them, the Bolshoi Ballet achieving 'a striking success', and their successful launch of Sputnik was considered a great achievement by the Japanese. In July 1959 the British ambassador to Japan, Sir Oscar Morland, informed Selwyn Lloyd that it was 'the Soviet Union, with visits from the Moscow Arts Theatre, the Leningrad Symphony Orchestra, the State Circus, Leonid Kogan, the violinist and so on, and not the US, that made the cultural headlines during the past year'.[26] Ultimately, however, the US's dominant position in Japan was secure, its network of cultural centres and its generous investment in scholarships and bursaries (377 awarded in 1958) proving more than a match for Soviet attempts to capture the imagination of the Japanese people.

Britain had neither the resources nor the will to compete with the super-powers, and, in the case of Japan, was falling behind some of the lesser powers by the end of the 1950s, a point made by the British Council's representative (F. J. R. Bottrall) in his 1959–60 annual report:

> . . . our cultural work is far less intensive and extensive than that of the French. The Germans have an Institute and, in addition to large-scale manifestations, they offer more than three times the number of scholarships that we do. Our work in fact does not greatly exceed that of Italy or Austria, which cannot be regarded as a satisfactory state of affairs.

It is easy to understand why Close, Phillips and Bottrall constantly voiced frustration at the constraints within which they had to work. Close repeatedly drew attention to the Japanese 'appetite for foreign cultures' in his reports; Phillips reminded London of 'the postwar race for favour, and as a consequence, trade', and wondered, given the origins of the British Council, why there was no commitment to cultural diplomacy in Japan given 'successful cultural penetration by other nations . . .'. The reasons for Britain's very poor showing in Japan during the 1950s are threefold: first, and most importantly, insufficient funds reflected a 'tight financial policy' on the part of the Treasury; secondly, Britain was ill-disposed to Japan in the area of trade and in any case was unsure of Japan's future economic importance; and thirdly, as has been explained, it was perhaps felt that US cultural programmes in Japan were more than sufficient to keep Japan in the 'free world' camp.[27]

What then was achieved by the British Council in Japan during the 1950s? How effectively were British interests promoted by means of cultural diplomacy during this decade? In their annual reports representatives were required to appraise their performance, first under the heading 'an appraisal of the British Council's work' (section b) and then, from 1957, under the more specific one of 'advantages to British interests' (f).[28] Their comments were invariably disappointing, none more so than the entry for the 1957–8 report which simply read 'nil (advantages)'. The comment for 1959–60 was only a little more promising: 'Nothing to report, except the considerable orders of British books'. In 1954 Close had tried to look on the bright side, highlighting science and medicine as fields in which Britain was sure to have some impact once the Japanese were made aware of British achievements; 'the extent of British progress in the production of isotopes', he observed, 'was a case in point'. Still, his reference to 'material loaned to the Japanese police describing traffic control in London', which apparently had improved the traffic situation in Tokyo, surely indicates how few successes there were to write home about. The following year Close noted successes in the field of medical education, 'where British techniques (we)re now being tried in place of German', and later on in 1961 Mr Bottrall commented that 'apart from increased interest in British science books, the only advantage we can report is the purchase by Japanese organisations of anaesthetic equipment following the lecture tour by Sir Robert Macintosh (December 1959–January 1960)'.[29]

Still, these were very limited returns. The only major success trumpeted by the Council in Japan flowed from Japanese interest in atomic power.[30] Thus, the one significant mention of Japan in a thick Council file entitled 'Commercial effects of British Council work on trade' related to radioactive isotopes, in which connection the representative comments 'I am not sure whether this material is usable, but it does point to a direct tangible result of Council activity in a way that few such cases do'.[31] The following year the British ambassador to Japan stated in his annual review for 1957 that there was every likelihood 'that, if the Japanese could satisfy themselves that a (Calder Hall)... reactor could be made earthquake-proof, they would import one from the United Kingdom' (despite the efforts of the Americans to recommend their own technology).[32] In April 1959 Phillips reported in his handing-over notes that Japanese officials from the Atomic Energy Bureau were attending courses at Harwell,[33] and later on in 1963 the Council's representative (Mr E. W. F. Tomlin) made reference in his annual report to 'the British firm constructing the Atomic Reactor at Tokai mura ...'.[34] However, as Richard Samuels explains, Britain's success in the field of atomic power was a short-lived one:

> Calder Hall came on line in 1966, three years late and 50% over initial budget because of a dozen major design and safety problems ... Even before Calder Hall came on line, the Japanese utilities had bailed out, convinced by American vendors that light water reactors ... were more attractive.[35]

So despite a slow start, the US soon caught up, dealing a body-blow to British competition in atomic technology.

It was the lack of successes to report – apart from the initial attractions of British atomic power – that caused Council representatives in Japan to call for what were called 'cultural manifestations'. These were major exhibitions or performances that were sent overseas with a view to generating interest and positive coverage in the target country's media. As has been made clear, the US and USSR were masters at this game. Britain, however, was not really a contender. Thus, Phillips declared in his report for 1956–7 that 'our failure has lain in our inability to have major impact, in the way that other countries have done':

> No manifestation in music, drama, ballet or the arts in general. No visitor of major importance, no event, no focus for concentration of effort and display. Our efforts have been limited to the routine . . . The Shakespeare Memorial Theatre Company tours six European countries, the English Opera Group three, whilst the City of Birmingham Symphony Orchestra goes to the Netherlands. Nothing comes to Japan.

This was a common complaint throughout the 1950s. In 1959 Bottrall reported the 'outstanding success of the Henry Moore exhibits at the Mainichi Fifth International Art Exhibition' and expressed his delight at the 'unparalleled' reception accorded Somerset Maugham, but he nevertheless concluded that

> [t]here is no doubt that the failure of the British Council to send to Japan any manifestations in the field of music, theatre and ballet caused great disappointment among our supporters and the disappointment was reflected in the press, with a corresponding lowering of British cultural prestige.[36]

Still, the British Council's efforts during the 1950s were not completely fruitless. They ensured that the Japanese were at least made aware of some of Britain's strengths, that they were reminded of what representatives saw as a natural affinity between the two countries. Whereas it would be very difficult to contend that Britain was applying a little cultural diplomacy very skilfully – indeed, the appearance was more of neglect than anything else – it could be argued that a foundation, albeit a very shallow one, was laid for future cultural initiatives. We can assume that cultural diplomats play a 'long game' – when the country in which they work is relatively low on the list of priorities for cultural exchange, as was the case with Japan during the 1950s, they hope for economic or political developments that will reorder priorities in their favour. It was Japan's remarkable rates of economic growth that ensured that Britain's perception of Japan in the 1960s would be very different from her view during the 1950s. Despite Mr Close's direct appeal to the director-general of the British Council, Sir Paul Sinker, in 1956, it was not until 1963 that Sinker visited Japan, this time at the urging of the Foreign Office.

The promise of expansion

In his report on the visit, Sinker declared that '[o]f all the countries I have visited on behalf of the Council, Japan is the only one where, after taking into account the claims of other countries and the inescapable global limitations of finance and manpower, I still felt that our effort is on a totally inadequate scale'. The evidence he provided to support this claim was compelling: expenditure of £40000 a year on Japan, only half of what was spent on Indonesia and less than a third of the sum provided for Iran. Whilst Japanese competed for ten British Council scholarships a year, France offered 60 and Germany and Italy 62 and 65 respectively, not to mention the 'massive US offers'. Moreover, whereas France, Germany and Italy maintained 'centres with regular programmes of activities', the Council was prevented from doing this by its premises.

In trying to explain why 'in response to the opportunities open to us our present scale of activities looks quite incongruous', the director-general argued that Japan had 'fallen between two stools' in the sense that being 'neither "under-developed" nor "European"', it had not benefited from the shift of resources from the latter to the former recommended by the Drogheda Committee. Furthermore, Sinker maintained, the Foreign Office had been reluctant to accord Japan a higher priority, 'both because of the immense scale of American educational and cultural activity and because there ha[d] been no serious threat to Japanese political stability'. And yet this visit by the director-general, ten years after the first representative had been sent to Japan, had been made at the Foreign Office's request, presumably with the intention of inviting recommendations for a fairly large expansion of the Council's activities in Japan.

Sinker proposed a three-stage plan of expansion, beginning with the provision of twice as many scholarships as before (that is to say 20), more funds for 'partly-financed visitorships', more posts for British teachers in Japanese universities (around another six to bring the total to 15), and allowance for three new staff for the Council offices in Tokyo and Kyoto (hopefully to manage more 'manifestations' and book exhibitions). Stage 2 of Sinker's plan was concerned with enhancing the British ELT programme, with an initial emphasis on providing 'English classes based on modern methods for a selected clientele, especially teachers' to be followed by moves into the educational system and TV. Stage 3 focused on extending Council operations in Japan by establishing new centres and libraries at Fukuoka and Sapporo. Sinker estimated the total additional cost of his expansion plans to be £50000 per year, rising to £100000 in three years' time. On consideration of his report and recommendations, the Executive Committee approved their proposed submission to the Foreign Office.

The key to this change of heart regarding Japan was expressed in an 'incidental' comment made in Sinker's report, namely that 'the speed of Japan's economic development is a unique phenomenon, the importance of which cannot be over-emphasized'.[37] For several years Japan's economic stature had been noticeably growing. As early as 1958 the British ambassador to Japan (Sir Daniel Lascelles) had commented on 'Japan's re-emergence as a world power'.[38] However, it seems that the Foreign Office was still wary of Japan despite the latter's keenness to improve relations with Britain. In his annual review of Japan for 1959 Sir Oscar Morland called for closer relations, not least because Japan provided 'an increasingly important market for our exports . . .'. He also stressed the opportunities available for influencing Japan 'through cultural and social contacts', referring to 'the visits of widely-differing representatives of British achievement' (for example, Dame Margot Fonteyn, the archbishop of Canterbury, and a rowing crew from Oxford and Cambridge). As Japan's economic prospects improved, commerce and culture were increasingly mentioned in the same breath, highlighting the degree to which the British Council's fortunes in Japan depended on the state of commercial relations between the two countries.

Morland admitted as much when he stated that '[a]part from the recollection in Britain of Japanese war-time barbarity, the main obstacle to better relations are commercial'. Britain's opposition to Japan's full membership of GATT (General Agreement on Tariffs and Trade) caused great resentment in Japanese circles. Morland was fully cognisant of the reasons why, stating clearly that 'further expansion (of Japan's trade with Britain) may depend to a great extent upon the degree to which we are able to disinvoke Article XXXV of GATT and relax discrimination against Japanese imports'.[39] As one British minister had observed in 1956, the Japanese saw 'the use of waiver as a form of Asiatic discrimination and [we]re . . . prepared to pay almost any price in order to get it withdrawn'.[40]

When Lord Selkirk, the minister in question, visited Japan during the autumn of 1956, he went with low expectations of what could be achieved. He remarked to Selwyn Lloyd that 'ultimately the Japanese will . . . only respect either strength or real marks of friendship', admitting that '[w]e cannot produce the first, and I am doubtful whether public opinion is prepared to consider the second'.[41] The problem of negative public attitudes arose in part from 'serious misconceptions' about Japan, namely that she was 'an unfair competitor who floods the market with . . . cheap goods, and a bad customer who buys goods only to copy them and then undercut their original manufacturers'.[42] In short, as Buckley argues, cordial relations between the two countries were obstructed by economic concerns, 'hardly surprising . . . [g]iven the pressures on both governments to rebuild their economies after the war . . .'.[43] As has been made clear, no real attempt was made to bypass or surmount this economic obstacle by means of vigorous efforts in the sphere of cultural relations. Selkirk's point about 'marks of friendship' raises questions about what could have been achieved if the British Council's representatives in Japan had been granted the resources they needed.

As it was, a cultural agreement between Britain and Japan that 'did little more than formalise existing cultural exchanges' was not signed until December 1960.[44] Given its straightforward provisions, its symbolic importance (at least for the Japanese) and its apparent curative effects on what was a sickly bilateral relationship, the question arises as to why agreement on cultural matters was not reached much earlier, say in the mid-1950s.[45] The answer lies in the close association in British minds between cultural relations and its economic counterpart – only too evident from the short period that elapsed between the ratification of the cultural agreement on 23 June 1961 and the successful conclusion of protracted negotiations for a treaty of commerce on 14 November 1962.

Once there were visible signs that a treaty was on the cards – Oscar Morland suggested a date around the beginning of 1961 – 'the quarantining of Japan'[46] was finally lifted. The British Embassy's annual review of Japan for 1961 reported the great enthusiasm and 'keen interest all over the country' generated by the visit of Princess Alexandra, together with the satisfaction felt in Japanese government circles at the return of 'full friendship' between the two countries.[47] Moreover, there were signs that public attitudes towards Japan were being softened by tourism:

> Partly owing to new air routes and partly to appreciation of Japan as a comfortable and attractive country to visit, Western visitors are pouring into the country, and the new hotels constantly springing up can barely accommodate . . . crowds of tourists and business men.[48]

In his annual report for 1961–2 Mr E. W. F. Tomlin, the British Council's representative in Japan, enthused about 'Japan–British relations . . . on as good a footing as at any time during the present century . . . epitomised by the extremely successful visit in October 1961 of Her Royal Highness Princess Alexandra'. Tomlin was also able to report on two 'outstanding' manifestations – the five-week visit of the Royal Ballet and an exhibition of English medieval pottery from the Guildhall Museum. The backdrop to all this, as he was only too happy to report, was political stability and rising prosperity in Japan.

Perhaps Tomlin was the first overseas representative in Tokyo who could savour his role as Britain's principal cultural diplomat. Just 14 months after taking up his duties (at the end of November 1961), he was receiving the director-general, whose visit quite clearly anticipated a larger Council presence in Japan. In a fascinating twist, Sinker reminded his Japanese hosts that 140 Japanese graduates had benefited from scholarships in Britain since 1952 and expressed a hope that Japan would offer 'more British scholars the opportunity to study in this country', noting that 'now we have only one or two a year'.[49] Now that the Council had acknowledged the merits of cultural diplomacy vis-à-vis Japan, they expected the Japanese government to follow suit, to become an exporter, as well as an importer, of culture and to encourage more visits to Japan.

Finally convinced that cultural diplomacy was 'cost-effective' in Japan, the British government set about doing a more professional job of promoting it. 1964 seems to have been a watershed year, the dividing line between very modest efforts in the field of culture and a more serious commitment to effective presentation of what Britain had to offer. Once again it was commercial interest that was driving this policy of greater cultural impact. In the summary of his review for 1964, Ambassador Rundall coupled good prospects for Anglo-Japanese trade with the need for 'even greater efforts ... [to] be made in future to improve our cultural image in Japan'. The connection was made even more explicit with reference to the British Exhibition, to be held in Japan in September 1965:

It will be important to ensure that the cultural events to accompany the British exhibition ... fully measure up to the major effort we are going to make to expand our trade. They can be of real help in this, and can also play a significant role in promoting Anglo-Japanese relations.

Praising the British Council for its excellent work, the ambassador stated that cultural ties between the two countries had been strengthened by 'the Shakespeare birthday celebrations and the very successful visit of the London Symphony Orchestra', at the same time calling for more to be done 'in the field of cultural manifestations' where the French and the Germans were proving very successful.[50]

Perhaps out of gratitude to its benefactors, the Council's representative in Tokyo seems to have snuggled up to the expatriate business community. Whereas Close had remarked in 1956 that 'The British business community has always tended to feel that the Embassy/Council Group hold themselves rather aloof' and that the two groups did not always have very much in common,[51] Tomlin celebrated the Council's 'good relations with British firms' in August 1962.[52] Their joint efforts were richly rewarded in 1965, described by Rundall as 'a remarkably good year for Anglo-Japanese relations'. The ambassador reported that 775 000 people had attended the British Exhibition in Tokyo 'and for two weeks in September and October Great Britain filled the newspapers, radio and television'.

Much attention had been given to the ten-day visit of Princess Alexandra and her husband, Mr Ogilvy, who, it was stated, 'lit up every important occasion . . .'.[53] Furthermore, around 500 important businessmen visited Japan during the exhibition, some of them for the first time. Their presence attested to the Foreign Office's determination to 'collar' a larger share of 'the most rapidly expanding market in the world'.[54] Whilst the British Exhibition was certainly a success in enlarging the profile of Britain in Japan, there was some regret on the part of Tomlin that the Council had been 'unable to produce the central cultural event which would have proved such an asset'. Indeed it had managed only six 'subsidiary events', including a British new towns and buildings exhibition, a film festival, a watercolour exhibition and the Billingsgate Art Display.[55]

Although the British Exhibition's potential for *cultural* projection was not fully realized by any means, the British Council was making modest advances in Japan during the 1960s, notwithstanding some fallow years. In his first annual report as Japan representative, R. A. H. Duke complained in June 1968 that the 'Tokyo office and library continued to occupy the unsavoury premises taken as a temporary expedient in 1961', and '[o]f major arts manifestations, recommended as a priority after Sir Paul Sinker's visit in 1963, not one took place (though foreign competitors were exceptionally busy in this field)'.[56] The breakthrough came in the autumn of 1969 with 'Tokyo British Week', by which time the Council had moved to modern premises in the new Iwanami Building in central Tokyo. Its programme for British Week, costing around £30 000, was truly impressive, comprising ten concerts by the London Philharmonic Orchestra, 19 performances by London's Festival Ballet, two concerts by Julian Bream, a major exhibition by Henry Moore, special showings of Shakespeare films and the opening of the British Book Display Centre.[57]

Commenting on Duke's report for 1969–70, the Regional Officer for the Far East declared that '[w]ith British Week in September/October 1969 and the opening of Expo-70[58] in mid-March, the year could not be more outstanding, and the British Council played a full part in arranging many of the highly successful cultural contributions'. This was a year of 'firsts', the two most impressive of which were the official visit of a national theatre company (the Royal Shakespeare Company) and the Henry Moore exhibition, 'the first major foreign exhibition to be shown in the newly built Museum of Modern Art, Tokyo'. In May 1970 Ambassador John Pilcher had even gone so far as to say that 'Britain and her culture have been more manifest in Japan during the last twelve months than in all the years since the war'.[59]

Rebranding Britain

The successes of 1969–70 concluded a decade that had witnessed a number of developments that greatly enhanced the image of the British Council in Japan, most notably the expansion plan drawn up by Sir Paul Sinker in 1963, the opening in February 1966 of the new Kyoto Centre and the move of the Tokyo office and library to the Iwanami building at the end of 1968. And yet Sir Fred Warner, Britain's ambassador to Japan, commented in June 1973 that Sir Paul Sinker's judgement of a decade earlier that the Council's effort in Japan was on 'a totally inadequate scale' was still valid. His explanation for this was that Japan was 'a country where one has to run very hard in order to stand still', noting that 'annual budgets for British Council work here have been left trailing behind the march of history'.[60]

However, the increasing success of the Council in Japan in the 1970s and 1980s owed much less to constant levels of public funding than it did to new ways of approaching cultural diplomacy. There was to be more emphasis on contemporary Britain, on British science and technology. As early as 1965, H. P. Croom-Johnson (controller, Overseas B) had noted 'a curiously old-fashioned ring about the activities' outlined in Tomlin's annual report for 1964–5, by which he meant that there was 'a fairly heavy arts bias and relatively little mention of the sciences'.[61]

Likewise, it was noted in August 1969 that Duke's annual report for 1968–9 hardly mentioned science,[62] an area that subsequently assumed a much higher profile with 'the appointment of a former Director of Science Department, London, Mr M. Beatty, to the post of Deputy Representative, Japan . . .' in 1972.[63] By the end of the 1970s 'a marked growth in specialist traffic from Britain to Japan . . . in the sciences' was discernible, a trend presumably strengthened by the introduction of 'a Ministry of Education/British Council scheme for the attachment, for periods of up to one term, of British academic scientists and scholars to Japanese national universities for teaching and joint research'.[64] By the late 1980s several hundred scientists a year were visiting project partners, either in Japan or Britain.[65]

In the crucial area of English-language teaching, a new British Council/NHK programme entitled 'How English Works' was televised from April 1969, a development that represented a real breakthrough in terms of communication. Moreover, language training was no longer targeted just at the academic sector, but now included ties with commercial English schools. As the ambassador, Michael Wilford, explained to Anthony Crosland in September 1976,

the English language is a saleable commodity and (the Council's) business is to provide the Japanese government with advice on teaching methods and to help create the conditions in which other institutions can provide courses on a commercial basis for which the Japanese, in particular the major Japanese companies, can very well afford to pay.[66]

Indeed, by the mid-1980s Japanese learners were paying the British Council for English lessons, a development that had major implications for the health of its finances.

Perhaps most exciting in terms of the British Council's changing role in Japan over recent decades has been its promotion of contemporary art and drama, again explicable in terms of its determination to present Britain as modern, innovative and forward-looking. Thus, to give just a few examples, the Council promoted Henry Moore in 1969, Barbara Hepworth in 1970, a performance group called 'Welfare State International' in 1982, and Gillian Wearing in 1998. As Richard Dorment, writing for *The Daily Telegraph*, recently put it, '[v]isual art is only one part of the vast jigsaw that makes up the council's work, but no other aspect of that work can so vividly project to the world the image of Britain as a modern and dynamic nation'.[67] Allied to this has been a major change in the Council's modus operandi on the arts side in Japan during the last decade – what Mike Barrett (director, 1993–9) describes as 'a change away from being a funding organisation to being a marketing organisation'. As well as being a legacy of Thatcherite spending cuts, this change reflects the development of a highly sophisticated market for British cultural products in Japan.

Conclusion

This chapter raises fundamental questions that lie outside its immediate purview. Perhaps the most important one, evidenced by 'no fewer than twenty-one separate reviews and enquiries' since its establishment in 1934,[68] relates to the value of the British Council vis-à-vis the promotion of national interest and, by extension, the effectiveness of cultural diplomacy as an arm of foreign policy. The problem for the Council has been the long-term nature of its contribution – 'it could never satisfy expectations of speedy returns'.[69] As the Germans understood as early as the 1920s, a long-term investment in cultural diplomacy would pay rich dividends, the essential precondition being that the recipients did not suspect pursuit of short-term advantage.

Japan in the 1950s, therefore, represented an ideal opportunity for the British Council. Strained diplomatic relations ensured that cultural work would be seen in a positive light, as separate from formal diplomacy, and as a genuine attempt to safeguard future relations in the face of temporary setbacks. This is to acknowledge 'the underlying political purpose' of cultural diplomacy, namely that its 'results, often invisible, would ultimately manifest themselves, both directly and indirectly, in various forms of goodwill beneficial to Britain's national interest and prestige'.[70] As it was, Britain wasted the opportunities available for cultural projection in Japan during the 1950s. Its cultural effort was lacklustre and self-defeating in the sense that it seemed to confirm rather than deny rumours about Britain's rapid decline.

It is perhaps surprising that the inertia affecting British cultural diplomacy in 1950s Japan corresponded so closely with a formal diplomacy of neglect and antagonism. After all, according to one of its official publications, the British Council was accorded the long-term aim of 'bringing about a better understanding between Britain and other countries' and in order to do this it was necessary to be 'free from the suspicion that its work was directed to short-term ends, or swayed by transitory political exigencies'. However, in the case of Japan the Council's actions must have provoked just such suspicions – it had a formal association with the British Embassy, largely for financial reasons, and was unable to pursue a long-term policy of cultural penetration due to inadequate resources.

Not fully convinced of the merits of cultural diplomacy and largely indifferent to the importance of Japan, Britain was content – with a few exceptions – to leave the cultural effort to the Americans, whose influence in the area was all-pervasive. For these reasons, no real attempt was made to respond to Ledward's call for 'a carefully and broadly planned policy of cultural infiltration over a long period'. Interestingly, it was the promise of commercial benefits arising from Japan's rapid economic growth that led to the decision to fund an expansion of Council activities. Demonstrating the triumph of 'short-term ends' over long-term perspectives, this approach has since given way to a more mature, sophisticated *dialogue* in cultural matters. This has been occasioned in part by Japan's commitment to its own cultural projection (evidenced by the establishment of the Japan Foundation in 1973), the emergence of a 'critical mass' of cultural activity and interchange by the late 1980s and a surer financial foundation for the Council's operations in Japan. In his recent survey of post-war Britain, entitled *Muddling Through*, Peter Hennessy described the British Council as one of a number of 'glittering intangibles' of British influence – whilst 'glitter' may characterize our cultural show in Japan in the 1990s, it is well to remember that for too long it was difficult for Japanese to appreciate what Britain had to offer in the cultural sphere.

Notes

1. Manuela Aguilar, *Cultural Diplomacy and Foreign Policy: German-American Relations 1955–1968* (New York: Peter Lang, 1996), p. 8.
2. P. M. Taylor, *The Projection of Britain: British Overseas Publicity and Propaganda, 1919–1939* (Cambridge: Cambridge University Press, 1981), pp. 125–6.
3. Ibid., pp. 132–48.

4. Communication dated 12 July 1937 (FO 395/554).
5. Memo from Richard T. D. Ledward, to Tunnard-Moore (Egyptian Dept., FO), dated 2 June 1943, entitled 'Some notes on British cultural policy in Japan, with particular reference to the policy which might be pursued after this war' (PRO BW 2/95).
6. Letter from R. Seymour, dated 13 February 1950; addressed to all Overseas Representatives (PRO BW 1/ 341, file entitled 'Commercial effects of Council activities').
7. Letter from G. H. Shreeve, Deputy Director-General of the British Council; addressed to the Viscount Hinchingbrooke, MP (PRO BW 42/6, 'Criticism of scholarships awarded to Japanese students').
8. Letter from G. H. Shreeve, to Hamilton Kerr, MP, dated 22 January 1951 (BW 42/6).
9. Letter from R. L. Macfarlane, Press Relations Section, Information Department; dated 9 August 1951 (BW 42/6).
10. Taylor, *The Projection of Britain*, p. 173.
11. Report on 'Trends of events in Japan from July 1946 to February 1951' (FO 371/92521).
12. Annual Report, 1952–3. File BW 42/11 contains annual reports, 1952–63.
13. Letter from Close to Sinker, dated 16 February 1956 (BW 42/8).
14. Letter from Controller, Overseas Division 'B', dated 28 November 1955 (BW 42/8).
15. Letter from Close to Sinker, dated 16 February 1956 (BW 42/8). This is the source for the following paragraph unless otherwise stated.
16. Letter dated 20 January 1958; subject: Annual Report Japan, 1956–7 (BW 42/11).
17. Annual Report, 1956–7, dated May 1957.
18. Ibid.
19. Memo to Controller, Overseas 'B', dated 13 August 1953; subject: FO Inspector's report on Japan and Burma (BW 42/8).
20. Statement covering 1 April 1957–31 April 1958 (BW 42/9).
21. Annual report, 1956–7.
22. Comment by Deputy Director-General on Representative's Annual Report, 1957–8 (BW 42/11).
23. Handing-over notes, dated April 1959, written by L. R. Phillips (BW 42/9).
24. Annual Report, 1958–9.
25. Annual Report, 1955–6.
26. British Embassy, Tokyo, 24 July 1959 (FO 924/1269).
27. Annual reports, 1954–5, 1956–7, 1959–60.
28. In the annual reports for 1953–4 and 1954–5, there is also a section 'e' entitled 'particulars of action taken by the Japanese as the direct or indirect result of action by the Council'. In both cases little of substance is specified. In the reports for 1955–6 and 1956–7, this section (e) is completely omitted so that the text skips from (d) to (f).
29. Annual reports.
30. See annual report for 1955–6.
31. Letter from Phillips, dated 21 May 1957 (BW 1/341).
32. FO 371/133577.
33. BW 42/9.
34. Annual report for 1962–3.
35. R. J. Samuels, *The Business of the Japanese State: Energy Markets in Comparative and Historical Perspective* (Ithaca: Cornell University Press, 1987), p. 240.
36. Annual report for 1959–60.

37. Report by the Director-General of his visit to Japan, 25 January–13 February, presented to the Executive Committee on 2 April 1963 (BW 1/362).
38. Despatch no. 69 of 17 June 1958. Mentioned in a letter to Selwyn Lloyd from Sir Oscar Morland, dated 24 July 1959.
39. Annual review for 1959, received 20 January 1960 (FO 371/150561).
40. Letter from Chancellor of the Duchy of Lancaster (Lord Selkirk) to Selwyn Lloyd, dated 24 October 1956 (FO 371/121048).
41. Letter from Chancellor of the Duchy of Lancaster (Lord Selkirk) to Selwyn Lloyd, dated 24 October 1956 (FO 371/121048).
42. 'Anglo-Japanese Motes and Beams', *The Economist*, 20 October 1956, p. 247.
43. R. Buckley, 'From San Francisco to Suez and Beyond: Anglo-Japanese Relations, 1952–1960', in W. I. Cohen and A. Iriye (eds), *The Great Powers in East Asia 1953–1960* (New York: Columbia University Press, 1990), p. 176.
44. Sir Oscar Morland to Lord Home, Japan: annual review for 1960, received 3 January 1961.
45. France signed a cultural agreement with Japan in 1954.
46. R. Buckley, 'From San Francisco to Suez and Beyond', p. 180.
47. Japan: annual review, 1961. Despatched by Oscar Morland to Lord Home on 2 January 1962 (FO 371/164958).
48. Japan: annual review for 1960, received by Lord Home on 3 January 1961 (FO 371/158477).
49. *The Mainichi Daily News*, Tuesday 29 January 1963 (BW 1/362).
50. Japan: annual review for 1964. Sir Francis Rundall to Mr Gordon Walker, received 11 January 1965 (FO 371/181068).
51. Close's notes on Japan for incoming representative, dated 25 June 1956 (BW 42/9).
52. Annual report for 1961–2, dated 9 August 1962.
53. Japan: annual review for 1965. Sir Francis Rundall to Mr Stewart, received 12 January 1966 (FO 371/187076).
54. Comment by C. M. MacLehose, dated 19 January 1965, on annual review for 1964 (FO 371/181068).
55. Annual report for 1965–6. I am very grateful to the British Council for authorizing access to the Japan representative's annual reports (and related documents) for the period 1963 to 1978.
56. Annual report for 1967–8.
57. Annual report for 1969–70.
58. This took place in Osaka.
59. Memo from Regional Officer, SAFE; addressed to Director, SAFE; dated 17 June 1970.
60. Despatch addressed to Sir Alec Douglas-Home, dated 5 June 1973.
61. Comment addressed to Deputy Director-General, dated 10 December 1965.
62. Comments of W. J. Craig (Controller Overseas), dated 12 August 1969.
63. Comments of Regional Officer, SAFE, dated 13 July 1972.
64. Despatch from Ambassador Sir Michael Wilford, addressed to David Owen, and dated 1 August 1978.
65. Conversation with Mike Barrett, the British Council's Director in Japan, 1993–9. I am very grateful to him for giving generously of his time – in London and Tokyo – to outline developments during the 1980s and 1990s.
66. Despatch from Ambassador Wilford, addressed to Anthony Crosland, dated 22 September 1976.

67. *The Daily Telegraph*, 21 February 1998.
68. Simon Jenkins, 'The British Council – a Case for Treatment', *Times Literary Supplement*, 6–12 November 1987, p. 1222.
69. F. Donaldson, *The British Council: the First Fifty Years* (London: Jonathan Cape, 1984), p. 26.
70. Taylor, *The Projection of Britain*, p. 176.

19

Post-war Japan as a Model for British Reform

Kevin McCormick

Introduction

In the 1980s the flow of images and information about Japan surged through Britain in conferences, books, newspapers and television documentaries. Much of the material could be packaged as 'lessons for Britain', offering remedies for Britain's relatively poor economic performance and political discomfort. Programmes and articles ranged from industrial relations to innovation and from education to enterprise. However, champions of 'the Japanese model' did not have the argument all their own way. Some critics contested what purported to be '*the* Japanese model', while others queried its relevance to Britain, and yet others debated both points. More recently, journalists and programme makers, who once documented how Japanese industry had caught up and overtaken their British industrial mentors from the 1960s to the 1980s, have explored what went wrong for Japan in the 1990s. Partly because of Japan's own difficulties and partly because of the more confident mood in Britain, Japan is now less obviously sought out as a source for British reform. Nevertheless, during the 1980s some of the lessons were put into practice, as Japanese ideas and institutions influenced reform in Britain.

While the main focus on the 1980s make this chapter the stuff of contemporary history, British interest in Japan as a source of inspiration for institutional reform in Britain has a surprisingly long history. The efforts of Henry Dyer in establishing the Imperial College of Engineering in Tokyo won the approval of *Nature* and the tart observation that such an institution was needed in Britain.[1] More general admiration for the vision and determination of the Meiji reformers was freely voiced in the 'national efficiency' movement amid concern at the prospect of Britain's decline.[2] The Webbs were particularly enthusiastic.[3] Such British interest seems remarkable given Japanese interest then in catching up with the West and the numbers of foreigners, often British, hired by the Meiji government. However, the view that the respective fortunes of the two economies in the second half of the twentieth century owed much to Meiji far-sightedness and Victorian short-sightedness gained some popularity in the 1980s. Arguably, cultural malaise and institutional inertia inhibited a more effective response to growing economic challenges in Britain, while Japan was laying the foundations for industrial developments which matured after 1945. Japan's post-war recovery and economic successes in the 1960s kindled British interest in Japan. UK interest in foreign experiences was deepened by disappointment with economic performance in the 1970s. It was strengthened by the sharp growth in Japanese direct investment in Britain in the 1980s. Debates about the relevance of Japanese models for the UK no longer seemed hypothetical when Japanese manufacturing companies might apply them and stimulate regeneration in Britain's depressed industrial regions.

After examining the renewed interest in Japan from the 1960s, this essay will concentrate on the debates about Japanese models through the 1980s and 1990s, considering, in particular, discussions of industrial relations, education, training, managers, innovation, social cohesion, and 'transplant' factories. In each area, we find a 'contested history'. Attention will then turn to British perceptions of Japan in the 1990s and doubts about 'the Japanese model'. Finally, the chapter will draw some conclusions on Anglo-Japanese relations and the processes of drawing lessons for institutional reform.

From the 1940s to the 1960s: considering Japan

Despite those Meiji era contacts, British knowledge of Japan seemed quite scant in the 1940s. On his recall to post-war government service, G. C. Allen, one of the few British economists with direct knowledge of Japan, was scathing about both the limits of official knowledge and official attitudes.[4] Ignorance was not confined to the bureaucratic elite. Sadao Oba recalled his surprise in 1945 on being captured as a junior officer in the Imperial Japanese Army in Indonesia and finding that none of the British officers among his captors could speak Japanese. Yet new foundations were being laid. Oba's recollections appear in a book describing a British government initiative to remedy deficiencies with a programme of intensive Japanese studies in London.[5] That generation of students has contributed richly to British understanding of Japan and several reappear prominently in the story of subsequent learning from Japan.[6]

In 1962, the United Kingdom and Japan concluded eight years of negotiation by signing a full commercial treaty, reflecting their strong desire to normalize trade relations. On the British side, there was little sense of the impending challenge from Japanese trade in high-quality and advanced technological products such as automobiles or televisions.[7] British concerns, fuelled by memories of the interwar trade conflicts, were largely motivated by the desire to safeguard traditional industries, such as textiles, pottery and clothing.

In parallel with the treaty negotiations, the two governments supported a mission to Japan by Sir Norman Kipping, president of the Federation of British Industries (FBI). The trip was intended to support trade by dispelling illusions, by providing information and by encouraging British industry to trade with Japan. In his report and press coverage, Kipping emphasized that 'industrially Japan has graduated to first league status'.[8] He supported his comment from plant visits: 'the best in Japan is as good as the best in any country'.[9] The FBI backed the trip with a survey of Japan by the Economist Intelligence Unit.[10] UK press coverage amplified the message of missed trade opportunities.[11] The British Embassy was pleased with Kipping's diplomacy in Japan, but noted that the next difficult part of his mission would be his diplomacy with British industrialists.[12] In the late 1960s, Cortazzi, working as a commercial counsellor (1966–70) in the Tokyo Embassy, still felt that he had to coax much of British industry out of its arrogance and appreciate that it had much to learn from Japanese industry.[13]

Although the embassy's Annual Report for 1962 noted short-term problems in the balance of payments and concern about Japan's commitment to democratic politics, there was continuing confidence about long-term economic development.[14] Even more positive accounts of Japan's economic development were given in reports by an *Economist* magazine staff writer, Norman Macrae, who confessed himself 'goggle-eyed' and urged readers to 'Consider Japan', hailing Japan's example to the developing world in breaking out of the gridlock of poverty.[15]

By mid-decade, Japan was evidently changing from being the prototypical 'newly industrialized country' to being an 'advanced industrial country'. Japan had arrived as a 'developed country', one which could be 'expected to give aid to countries now underdeveloped'.[16] Conversely, the British Embassy was aware of Japanese concern about both the short- and long-run fragility of the British economy.[17] Meanwhile the British ambassador was urging Foreign Office colleagues to support raising Britain's cultural profile in Japan.[18]

Five years after his visit as a staff reporter, Norman Macrae returned to Japan to prepare another series for *The Economist*. He emerged with a set of lessons from a country which had 'become the greatest practical research laboratory of economic growth in our time'.[19] Macrae's lessons were based on 'seven keys to the risen sun', including: 'economic planning' ('the most intelligently dirigiste system in the world today');[20] the 'highly educated society' (where a high proportion remained in education until aged eighteen – 70 per cent in Japan compared to less than 30 per cent in Britain);[21] the 'high levels of investment' (where high levels of saving were being translated into productive investment by fiscal incentives); 'the large scope for productivity increase' in a late industrializer; 'the unorthodox banking and credit system', where heavier reliance on bank rather than equity finance gave banks a more intimate knowledge of companies and industries within their group, and central government more leverage over the economy; 'the pattern of group loyalties' where the readiness of businessmen to listen to and act on 'administrative guidance' from the bureaucracy has been reinforced by the mutual involvement of workers and businessmen in companies; and 'the quality of the bureaucracy' which made 'administrative guidance' worthwhile. Macrae's main interest lay in macroeconomic management, comparing the apparent sophistication of economic planning in Japan with the fumbling efforts of Wilson's Labour government to establish the National Plan in Britain. He heaped praise on the abilities of the Japanese planners, from the minister (the 47-year-old Miyazawa Kiichi) to the civil servants ('some of the most brilliant young men in Japan'), to their techniques ('more scientific and more numerate analyses of desirable trends than in the economic policy of any other country in the world').[22] While Macrae praised Japan's economic planning, he was more sceptical about what he termed the more 'sociological' features of the Japanese economy. For example, he suggested that moving resources into more productive areas was achieved in spite of, rather than because of, the 'lifetime employment system', and he charged that 'group loyalties' often hindered economic advance. If Macrae was sceptical about some of the alleged benefits of the institutional structures of Japan, he was even more sceptical about the likelihood of emulating or imitating them in Britain.

By the end of the 1960s, Japan could boast the second largest economy in the free world. Attention was switching from viewing Japan as a model for the less developed countries to puzzling about Japan's economic development as a model for the industrial countries.[23]

From the 1970s to the 1980s: taking Japan more seriously

At the start of the 1970s, the British media underlined Japan's arrival as an industrial power with Expo '70 in Osaka. Ready parallels were made to Britain's 1851 landmark Great Exhibition at the Crystal Palace.[24] Through the decade, there was growing awareness of the divergent economic experiences in the two countries. Japan appeared to be caught up in a virtuous circle of economic progress, while Britain appeared to be trapped in a vicious circle of economic stagnation.[25] Although Japan's experience of double-digit growth ended with the 1974 oil shock, the subsequent responses to inflationary pressures in the two countries appeared to confirm the more robust character of Japanese institutional arrangements. For example, Japanese pay inflation was brought under control relatively quickly, whereas Britain struggled with inflation and pay disputes until the end of the decade. By the 1980s, it was widely apparent that Japan had become an economic superpower. The British motorcycle industry had collapsed in the face of Honda and Yamaha, while other industrial flagships such as the last remaining British-owned mass volume car manufacturer (BL), and the major British computer manufacturer (ICL), were propped up by Honda's technological support or Fujitsu's ownership respectively.[26]

Nowhere were doubts about the efficacy of British institutions more apparent than in the industrial relations field. Confidence eroded from the 1960s to the 1970s as a variety of models were tried, tested and found wanting. In the 1960s, Britain's characteristic 'voluntarism' (where the state left employers and trade unions to organize the machinery of collective bargaining with relatively little state intervention) was being questioned by the Labour government. Yet the system received a broad vote of confidence from a Royal Commission in 1968 and the Labour government retreated from legal reform. In 1971 a new Conservative government under Edward Heath introduced a comprehensive reform act based on an American model of legally structured industrial relations. However, this system collapsed into disrepute by 1974 and the government fell. A new Labour government overturned the previous legislation and adopted more corporatist solutions in 1974, seeking to engage unions in economic policy with a 'social contract'. Given the priority attached to industrial relations reform in British political debate, Japan attracted considerable attention because its economic success was often attributed to its industrial harmony.

In this context, Ronald Dore's 1973 study of industrial relations in Hitachi and English Electric received wide attention. Using the two large companies as landmarks to map industrial relations in the two countries, he contrasted Britain, where the parties to industrial relations espoused cooperation but often indulged an adversarial style in conducting their relations, with Japan, where the rhetoric, and usually the practice, of industrial relations subordinated sectional interests to broader visions of collective advance at the level of the corporation.[27] While Dore's identification of the central features of Japanese industrial relations – lifetime employment, seniority wages and enterprise unionism – had much in common with the views of other writers, his interpretations of the system's origins and his speculation about future developments had novel and striking aspects. Where earlier writers had attributed these features to feudal hangovers, Dore contended that they stemmed in large part from employer attempts in the 1920s to avoid the class-based antagonisms of Europe. Again, where past writers anticipated the likely convergence of Japan (the follower) with the industrial relations systems of pioneer industrializers, Dore proposed 'reverse convergence', where the follower had the advantages of 'late development effects'. Thus, with the advantage of later technologies (material and social) and some degree of choice, the late developer could become the model, with Japan likely to set the model for Britain. In the policy sphere, Dore was able to draw the attention of the House of Commons Select Committee on Science and Technology to the benefits gained for technical development in Japan from the development of graduate careers in large organizations and from worker participation in the enterprise.[28]

Britain was not alone in looking at the Japanese example. Specialists from OECD countries saw much merit in Japanese industrial relations.[29] G. C. Allen argued that Japan's institutional arrangements were more suited to economic development than those of the UK.[30] Despite caveats against organizational borrowing because history and culture could not be replicated, Allen recalled the Meiji slogan '*Wakon Yosai*' (Japanese soul, western knowledge) and urged that Britain could follow the example of making adaptations from foreign models. Conceding that the working of Japanese institutions were aided by Japanese institutions, Allen's main doubt concerned British readiness to pay the necessary price of institutional adaptation to gain economic success. However, Allen emphasized that reform of British industrial relations institutions was essential.

By the 1980s, the range of comparisons and sources on Japan had greatly expanded. A 1980 BBC television series, *Inside Japan*, was accompanied by a book from Sheffield University's Centre for Japanese Studies. While the focus was on difference and the distinctiveness of Japanese society, there was a sympathetic view of Japanese economy and society.[31] A strong thread through the programmes and the book was Japan's capacity to absorb ideas from outside and adapt them to its own purposes, and the capacity to undertake radical reform. For example, Collick hypothesized that Japan, with its emphasis on consensus-building, had a greater capacity for radical reform than Britain:

> in spite of – or, rather paradoxically, as a result of – the persistence of 'traditional' patterns of social organization, (Japan) is more likely to attempt radical solutions, and to put them into effect, than is the case in supposedly more 'modern' countries like Britain and the United States.[32]

The 1981–2 'Great Japan Exhibition', a celebration of the art of Japan's 'feudal' past in the Edo era between 1600 and 1868, attracted many visitors and extensive media coverage. One explicit purpose was to demonstrate links between Japan's past and present: 'the skill and originality of Edo artists and craftsmen and the cohesion and discipline of Edo society partly explain the phenomenal speed with which Japan's economy has grown since the nineteenth century'.[33] The general aim of dispelling images of Japan as a land of copiers was shared by British and Japanese organizers. They aimed to show that Japan had developed critical skills for later industrial and commercial success in a period of relative isolation. However, Japanese organizers were much less happy about the British proposal to use 'social class' as an organizing theme to understand feudal art. While the Japanese preference for a chronological order partly reflected more familiar practice, it revealed their sensitivity about projections of contemporary Japan too. They were anxious to show a dynamic society on the way to being a 'modern society', without the intrusion of social divisions.[34] British press coverage of the exhibition often linked the exhibition to articles about contemporary Japanese society. For example, some columns put the focus on the educational system and argued that education served as a mirror for the country's style of life and work.[35] The weekend colour supplements of newspapers proved a ready medium in which to combine exhibition coverage and images of contemporary Japan.[36]

Following an initiative at prime ministerial level, the UK–Japan 2000 Group was established in 1985 to provide regular, high-level dialogue between UK and Japan. The forum brought together politicians, civil servants, industrialists and academics to discuss a range of topics of common interest. In 1999, reviewing the previous 15 years, the joint chairmen noted that the group and members had supported cultural and educational exchanges and played important roles in some of the major events from the 'Great Japan Exhibition 1981', 'UK '90', the 'Japan Festival 1991', and 'UK '98'. Moreover, they noted the evolution of UK–Japan 2000 Group meetings from an early preoccupation with bilateral trade and economic issues to an increasing focus on common challenges in a rapidly globalizing world.[37]

A wide range of people and organizations began to report on Japan and assess its relevance for Britain, from newspapers and journalists to research councils and academics. The *Guardian* newspaper sponsored a 'Week in Japan', transporting 17 members of the editorial staff – reporters, specialists, columnists and a photographer – to Tokyo.[38] The Economic and Social Research Council (ESRC) devoted a special issue of its newsletter to the 'Pacific Economies'.[39]

While Japan's economic recovery from the oil shocks of the 1970s had been impressive, whether or not to follow Japan as a model remained contentious. Against official and corporate images of harmonious Japan, John Pilger's critique from the political left pointed to the price of the economic miracle.[40] The Conservative government elected in 1979 rejected the corporatist approaches of the preceding Labour government, particularly in the field of industrial relations. Although Mrs Thatcher's governments increasingly took the 'market' as the touchstone for allocation decisions, reference to Japan could open up ideological currents within the Conservative Party. Nicholas Budgen, a leading marketeer on the right of the party, took issue with Peter Walker's enthusiasm for Japan. Noting Walker's enthusiasm for corporatist approaches, Budgen charged that Walker was too uncritical in his view of Japanese education, bank–government co-operation, and government–industry relations.[41] In pressing Japan on the attention of British and American politicians, Ronald Dore challenged the champions of free-market capitalism with his argument that Japan's search for fairness and community as an organizing principle was an integral part of its economic success.[42] In fact, Japan was being taken seriously across a range of debates on institutional reform in Britain in the 1980s. The following sections deal selectively with some of these debates.

Industrial relations

The 1979 Conservative government's view of industrial relations reform was almost single-mindedly preoccupied with a determined assault on 'union power' for economic and political reasons. Economically, unions were seen as labour monopolists restraining the efficient operation of markets through monopoly control of labour. Politically, Mrs Thatcher resented the 'closed shop' as coercive and an infringement of personal liberties. Moreover, the Conservative electoral defeat in 1974 was attributed to the miners' strike, therefore there was need for redress, with the trade unions put in their place. The assault proceeded in piecemeal fashion, unlike the frontal assault in 1971. However, the signals were clear that a new system of industrial relations was being fashioned and that employers could take the initiative. Inward investors could be advised that employers were not required to recognize a union in Britain – and that many did not.

While the media highlighted 'macho management' in some British companies, an abrasive style to wrest the initiative and assert 'managerial prerogatives', it was not clear whether this was simply short-term shock therapy against unions or the basis for long term union–management relations. In some companies the threat of Japanese competition was used to bring about change, but without any of the employment security present in larger Japanese corporations. The arrival of Japanese companies to operate factories in Britain provided a closer field trial of the relevance of Japanese models for British workplaces.[43]

Under the dramatic heading 'Strike Free', Philip Bassett, labour correspondent of *The Financial Times*, highlighted the role of Japanese investors in shaping new relations between employers, workforces and unions.[44] Four companies – Nissan in automobile assembly, Komatsu in heavy engineering, and Hitachi and Toshiba in electronics – were prominent. Nissan was operating on a 'greenfield site', implying a new site and plant, a new labour force (in the blue-collar sections, even if many mangers were recruited from other UK car plants), and greater scope for new practices. Komatsu, although moving into a factory site vacated by an American rival, was largely recruiting a new labour force. Hitachi and Toshiba were more constrained since they were taking over from failed joint ventures with retreating British partners. Hitachi presented the labour force and unions with its terms for remaining in the UK, including dramatic changes in industrial relations. The central features were: recognition of only one union for representation rather than six existing unions (a 'single union agreement'); an insistence on management initiative in work assignment (implying 'labour flexibility', but with the assurance of company training for re-allocated workers); the establishment of 'a company council' for consultation and negotiation; and a set of procedures in negotiation, including arbitration, which would make strikes highly unlikely in a dispute (the basis for the wrongly named 'no-strike agreement'). Thus a set of interrelated terms – 'single union', 'no strike agreement', 'labour flexibility' and 'company council' – entered journalism and academic research as templates of a new industrial relations being pioneered by Japanese companies. But was it 'made in Japan'?

The term 'Japanization' was adopted for conferences, books and papers.[45] It had various uses, from work organization to industrial relations and from British emulators adopting Japanese methods to Japanese 'transplants', and even to the more general convergence of the whole economic system towards that of Japan. Yet the policies and practices inside more than 200 Japanese factories defy any simple term like 'Japanization'. Usually, companies relied on British personnel managers who have claimed some discretion in designing *hybrid* plants, combining Japanese and British features.[46] The 'company council' of Toshiba owed much to the British managing director's previous experience and links with the participation schemes pioneered at Glacier Metal.[47] The 'no-strike' agreement owed much to a British union's efforts to soothe Japanese managers' fears about British blue-collar workers and their unions – a 'British solution to a British problem'.[48] The ground rules limiting the arbitrator to rule for either one or the other side rather than some intermediate position (sometimes called 'pendulum arbitration') owed more to American then either British or Japanese practice.

The introduction of changes owed much to the British context of recession in the early 1980s and union weaknesses, the result of government assault on and divisions within the union movement. Mindful of rising unemployment and eager to compete for recognition by employers, unions competed vigorously, despite reservations about being pushed into the dangers of surrender in 'beauty contests'. The reaction of the unions can be typified by the responses of three or four unions which were largely responsible for organizing workers where the Japanese employers recognized a union: the EETPU (the Electrical, Electronic, Telecommunications and Plumbing Union), a former craft union advocating 'market unionism' with membership services and concessionary approaches to employers; the GMB, a general union with its roots back into the nineteenth-century among municipal and labouring workers, which tried to secure workers' interests through a mix of collective bargaining and political pressure for workers' rights; and the T&GWU (the Transport and General Workers' Union), another general union with nineteenth century roots among unskilled and semi-skilled workers. This union had created a federal structure to cater for its trade groups, and facilitated a variety of more local workplace and area responses.

The EETPU was very active in courting Japanese companies, even organizing inward investment and recruitment missions to Japan. It became closely linked with the 'single union, no-strike deals', which were widely viewed as the quintessence of 'the new unionism' in the early 1980s. The most celebrated examples were the deals struck with Toshiba and Hitachi which provided models for later deals struck by the EETPU and other unions with both Japanese and British employers. The union's former general secretary claimed that his union was closely involved in retaining the investments of Toshiba and Hitachi within Britain after the joint-venture breakdowns.[49] The central features of the EETPU–Toshiba agreement became a model for other agreements. Subsequently, when the joint venture collapsed at Hitachi's south Wales plant, similar arrangements were made between Hitachi and the EETPU. After the 1981 Toshiba agreement, the EETPU went on to sign 30 further 'single-union' deals by 1993. The Hitachi deal brought the EETPU into conflict with other unions and the Trades Union Congress (TUC) Disputes Committee. The other unions objected that the Hitachi deal took away representation from other unions and their members in a plant where six unions had operated previously. The EETPU claimed that members of other unions approached them and that they did not offend TUC rules on inter-union competition. However, following two further inter-union disputes the EETPU was expelled from the TUC in 1988.

With the EEPTU outside the mainstream of the trade union movement, the AEU, which had roots in craft unionism too, became the closest approximation to a standard-bearer for 'market unionism'. Both unions had lost members and income in the 1980s and there was a logic in their merger talks in the late 1980s. After some false starts, they agreed on a merger in 1992, bringing together the two unions which have been most prominent in signing up 'single-union' agreements with the Japanese companies for their UK sites. The AEU has had mixed feelings about the progress of unionization under some of the agreements. For example at Nissan's Washington site, only 23 per cent of the 2000 workforce were estimated to be union members in 1989 and the AEU considered non-renewal of the agreement.[50] The company responded with renewed encouragement for union membership. Nissan's personnel director confirmed a unionization level of 45 per cent by 1993, against expectations nearer 70 per cent when the agreement was signed. However, he felt that 45 per cent appeared to be a typical level under similar agreements and it compared favourably to the national average of 23 per cent in the private sector.[51]

The GMB particularly resented 'beauty contests' for recognition, arguing that employees, not employers should choose the unions. Therefore they determined a distinctive approach for the future, seeking to add social goals alongside collective bargaining. This reflected the rather different membership and political characteristics of the GMB. Their efforts to secure stronger employee rights were thought to be a drawback in trying to secure recognition at Toyota's new plant in Britain against competition from the AEU.

Where the GMB has tended to remain centralized, the T&GWU began decentralizing activities towards workplace representatives from the 1960s.

This policy gave scope for regional and local activity and two of the T&GWU regional organizations, 6 (Merseyside) and 10 (Humberside), were conspicuous in providing critiques of Japanese work organization and unionism and of attempts to introduce Japanese-style work practices. They criticized simplistic images of Japan, noting that lifetime employment system and enterprise unionism were confined to one-third of the labour force, the creation of the Japanese industrial relations system in bitter struggles in the early post-war years, and the limited export of Japan's employment policies and practices to company overseas transplants.[52] Although the T&GWU had some union membership in Japanese transplants in the UK, their main targets were the British companies who might introduce some Japanese-style policies. Therefore, another aspect of the critique lies in examinations of British company efforts to de-recognize unions or impose a 'single union' recognition agreement, and consequent efforts to change work practices along the lines of 'team working', team briefings, quality circles, and advisory councils. All of these techniques were seen as part of an armoury to probe union strength in the battle for control at the workplace.[53]

Competition between five unions for a single-union deal at Toyota's new UK plant spilt over into bitter and embarrassing arguments at the September 1991 TUC conference. The AEU and the now non-TUC-affiliated EETPU were accused by other unions of colluding in the spread of an 'alien approach to trade union organization'. Ken Gill, the left-wing general secretary of the technical and supervisory union MSF (Manufacturing, Science and Finance) urged a joint union stand against foreign investor pressure for 'company unionism' (company selection of the union), non-representation of white-collar employees, 'no-strike' or compulsory arbitration agreements and imposed single-union deals. The MSF motion was carried, but drew opposition from the AEU and the GMB. The GMB complained that only Japanese inward investors were cited and the AEU general secretary complained of racism. The TUC General Council, alarmed by the 'alien' and 'racist' tags, mounted a campaign of reassurance to inward investors. The MSF denied the racism charge, arguing that the new measures were contrary to the traditional British arrangements and could be properly described as alien.[54]

While a great deal of attention was focused on a few high-profile plants and companies, surveys of Japanese companies in the UK shown a considerable variety of company policies and practices towards trade unions. Oliver and Wilkinson showed a drop in the propensity to recognize a union between their 1987 survey (68 per cent) and 1991 (47 per cent),[55] and a quarter of the companies had neither union nor company representative bodies. Some studies have shown that Japanese managers have used company councils to reach over the heads of British managers to their workforce. In other words, British managers, not British blue-collar workers, were seen as the main problem.[56] Changes of personnel have sometimes changed the use of the new institutions. Recruitment of workers has sometimes re-introduced 'traditional' British trade union practices.[57] The rotation of Japanese managers and the departure of British managers has meant the departure of the pioneers of start-ups and newcomers who reflected new priorities.[58]

Education and training

The British education system has been frequently damned by critics at home and abroad for fostering an anti-industry culture.[59] The comparative education and training of engineers became a focal point in such criticism, leading to new initiatives in higher education.[60]

An alleged tenfold superiority in the number of Japanese engineers served as a powerful, if erroneous, talisman for critics of the British education system. Unfortunately, the tenfold superiority was based, not on the annual output from higher education, but on a comparison of the total numbers enrolled. This led to an obvious exaggeration of Japanese numbers based on four-year courses compared to mainly three-year courses in Britain. The exaggeration was further compounded by several other misleading assumptions about institutions and courses which were included. Comparing the output of engineers per head of population, the Japanese advantage was still impressive, at two-and-a-half times the British total, but a long way from the alarmist tenfold advantage. However, the dubious tenfold enrolment advantage was translated into a tenfold annual output advantage in the TUC critique of British government R&D policy.[61] To demonstrate that exaggeration was not a monopoly of labour, a distinguished captain of British industry joined in. The first chairman of the Engineering Council, Sir Kenneth Corfield, observed that 'between the years 1965 and 1977 Japan doubled the ratio of engineers to its total workforce and by 1978 was turning out ten times as many graduate engineers as Britain'.[62] As head of the Engineering Council, the body appointed by the government to lead lobbying on behalf of engineering, the chairman had the ear of government and influence on policy. The Engineering Council pressed for a shift in the ratios of Science and Engineering students to Arts and Social Studies students from 50:50 to 55:45. Within a year, the government launched the Engineering and Technology Programme to increase engineering student numbers. Since it was launched in a period of severe restraints in other areas of education, it was nicknamed the 'switch programme', although it had little success in changing proportions and led to empty places in polytechnics.

Skirmishes on educational statistics continued through the 1980s, often spliced with qualitative critiques of the British education system. A much-publicized report, *Competence and Competition*, listed shortcomings in British vocational education and training compared to the inputs, systems and outputs in Germany, the United States and Japan.[63] The main thrust of the NEDO/MSC critique lay, not so much in the numerical comparisons, but in the more qualitative comparisons of the broader character of Japanese degree studies, the greater readiness of employers to support training and the Japanese superiority in numbers of intermediate skill ranges. This brief insight into Japan prompted the Manpower Services Commission (MSC) to commission a fuller study to show how Japan's vocational and educational system worked.[64] Much of the subsequent battle on the responsiveness of the educational system to current needs was concentrated on intermediate skills. The main charge led by the engineering lobbies was that Japan was now the leading industrial nation against whom Britain's performance should be judged, not the United States or continental Europe. Moreover, they argued that Britain's major weakness lay in the intermediate skill ranges such as technicians. The Engineering Council chided the Department of Education and Science for complacency and for misunderstanding the role and quality of the *senshu gakko* in supplementing Japan's supply of technicians to support engineers.[65] Prais argued that the main strength of Japan's education was its ability to cater beyond the first quartile of the ability range in order to motivate large numbers of children to high levels of achievement by international comparison.[66] However, Prais also drew attention to an emerging gap in advanced engineering skills in postgraduate numbers at master's degree level.[67]

Beyond vocational education and training, some observers drew on the Japanese educational system to either buttress or criticize British government policy in education. Lynn drew support for Conservative government reforms in introducing a national curriculum and national tests for school pupils, since these features provided targets and incentives in the Japanese system.[68] However, entrance exams and rote learning have often been portrayed as the root of educational problems and reform in Japan. A measured view of the strengths and weaknesses of the Japanese educational system, and efforts to reduce the negative effects of the 'credentialism', the national obsession with exams, was given to a 1991 Japan Festival seminar.[69] Meanwhile, Goodman compared the government styles in educational reform, contrasting the determined bludgeon taken to the educational system by the Thatcher government with the search for consensus sought by the Japanese government's reform commissions.[70]

Managers and management

While the high level of education and qualification among Japanese managers struck visitors to Japan from the 1920s, the relatively low level of education and qualification in Britain only became matters of increasing public concern in the 1960s.[71] In the 1980s, international comparisons included Japan and prompted private reform initiatives supported by government. The 'Handy Report', with significant Japanese reference material, stimulated moves by professional bodies to launch the Management Charter Initiative (MCI).[72] It was bolstered by government support.[73] The aim was to: bring order into the array of business courses; draw up a charter of good management development practice; enrol a growing number of sponsoring charter companies; build networks between local businesses and educational institutions; campaign for the greater popularity of management careers. Two years on, Handy noted that the initiative had much success on these fronts, but the basic problem remained, the relatively low volume of students going into higher education. Britain was still stuck with 14 per cent as the age participation rate compared to 38 per cent in the USA and Japan.[74]

The term 'Japanese Management System', used widely in Japan and elsewhere, usually includes the employment system, reward systems, union organization, *keiretsu* links and bank finance, and so on. Surveying a wide range of literature, the cross-cultural psychologists Smith and Misumi concluded that the Japanese Management System held lessons for the West but that they needed to be translated into a western idiom.[75] They concluded, that it was more likely to be successfully transferred among blue-collar groups in manufacturing operations and where Japanese managers could keep control of key operations. Not only has the concept of the Japanese Management System been wide, Smith and Misumi found that objective assessment has been rare:

> dispassionate analysis of Japanese management is hard to come by. Japanese writers have tended either to stress its uniqueness or to foresee convergence with American practice. Western authors, on the other hand, have preferred either the view that its essentials are readily applicable in the West, or the view that it is a coercive system which would never work in the West.[76]

Reviewing developments in the Japanese Management System in the 1990s, Hasegawa and Hook emphasized the emergence of new institutions – for example, the creation of European regional headquarters less tightly controlled from Japan.[77] In this sense, Japanese corporations might be 'becoming less Japanese'. However, other researchers have suggested that Japanese corporations might be shaping new models for the global corporation. For example, the timing of their overseas R&D developments in an era of globalization might mean that their corporate strategies and practices are more coherent and better integrated than those of western companies moving overseas earlier.[78]

Innovation

The belief that Britain was strong in science, but found the translating of scientific breakthroughs into profitable products and services elusive, animated interests in Japan's evident success in technological development and the respective 'national systems of innovation'. Freeman pointed to the importance of a wide range of social and economic organizational innovations associated with technological innovation, including: MITI; company R&D integrated into production systems; education and training; long-term strategic investments.[79]

Much of the British interest in Anglo-Japanese comparisons focused on the axis of government – industry relations. Discussion of the desirability and feasibility of an 'industry policy' in Britain often seemed polarized between the awareness of the historic role of the Ministry of International Trade and Industry (MITI) in Japan's technological development, and the Conservative government's anathema for anything which smacked of 'industry policy'. Mrs Thatcher had branded such policies as 'corporatist', intended as both description and denunciation. Throughout the debate, the danger was that British observers, anxious to stimulate state action in Britain, overplayed the role of the Japanese state (particularly MITI) and underplayed the role of entrepeneurship in Japan's development and neglected the changing roles of both for the future.

Despite British government sensitivity regarding 'industry policy', the Japanese example served to stimulate the development of a British version of Japan's forum in which scenarios of future scientific and technological developments are shared and disseminated in scientific and industrial networks. From studies of Japanese practice in the early 1980s, the British 'Foresight' programme was developed and continues into the twenty-first century.[80]

Social cohesion

Viewing Japan in its high-growth period, Allen concluded that it had done well in reconciling 'great technical and economic changes with social stability'.[81] A decade later, a leader writer for *The Financial Times* emphasized Japan's low crime rates and safety on the streets, and its relatively egalitarian distribution of income and economic growth. For Prowse, Japan's achievement of 'growth with social harmony' was one of the central lessons that Japan could teach Britain, especially when set against the growing income inequality apparent in Mrs. Thatcher's Britain.[82]

Interest in Japan's social welfare system grew in the West in the 1980s since Japanese welfare provision did not have extensive state involvement. Rose and his colleagues introduced discussion of Japan's 'welfare mix' to look at the different mode of welfare delivery.[83] David Howell, chair of the House of Commons Select Committee on Foreign Affairs, saw reform lessons for Britain's welfare state in East Asia. Under the title 'Easternization', he urged that European countries heed the importance of Asian values which stressed the role of the family in mutual support rather than reliance on the state.[84] However, Mortimer argued that Japanese consumers cannot spend their way out of recession since they maintain savings for the family's welfare needs. Mortimer added that it was good to draw attention to East Asia, but cautioned against the 'Eurosceptic' spin put on the message.[85]

Academic commentaries have been much more circumspect about the relevance of the Japanese welfare model for Britain. Pinker emphasized formal and informal patterns of welfare provision, explaining them in terms of culture, and was cautious about their relevance for other countries.[86] Jones was critical, stating that Japan was not really a 'welfare state' by the standard European definitions.[87] Gould attributed the appeal of Japan's welfare model for the political right in the West to the apparent better accommodation with labour in Japan, compared to the post-war welfare state consensus of Britain and Sweden. However, Gould cautioned that: (1) many needs go unmet in Japan; (2) the Japanese authorities are unlikely to want to increase state involvement; (3) western observers underestimate the problems that Japan will meet in the future.[88] Again, Goodman and White noted the superficial attractions of East Asian welfare for politicians in the West, but they argued that these countries were not really relevant because their systems were designed for their transition from poor countries, whereas the West had gone through this stage and western welfare expectations had become deeply entrenched and were unlikely to be met by East Asian systems.[89]

The theme of Japan's relatively egalitarian distribution of income was picked up in relation to the health experiences of the Japanese population, noting that 'Japanese life expectancy has increased dramatically during the last few decades as its income differences have narrowed'.[90] Drawing on Dore's accounts of Hitachi and English Electric, Wilkinson contrasted both the narrower income differentials and the active public sphere in Japanese life with the moral vacuum created in Britain where income differentials were widening in the 1980s and where the public sphere was being increasingly penetrated and eroded by market values.

Direct investment: from 'greenfield' to 'brownfield' sites

From the 1980s to the 1990s, British governments have boasted of their success in attracting foreign direct investment. Although Japanese investment has been a small proportion of the total, it has been especially welcomed. The high profile given to Japanese investment by government has also been evident in parliamentary inquiries. House of Commons Select Committees have heaped praise on Japanese companies in raising the tail of poor performance in British industry, for example, citing the influence of auto assemblers such as Honda and Nissan and their impact on component suppliers, and challenging the notion that they were only 'screwdriver assembly plants'.[91] The Trade and Industry Committee went even further in arguing that some new practices could not have been introduced without the inward investors, for example, in supply chain improvements and in the empowerment of the workforce.[92] Japanese plants have had high symbolic value. The Washington plant of Nissan has been top of the league in 'workplace tourism', hosting more company visits than any other British plant.

Japanese transplants have occupied two of the top five positions in surveys of 'Britain's Best Factories'.[93]

Not all observers have been so confident about the transfer of industrial 'best practice' through the Japanese transplants in the UK. For example, several studies questioned whether transplant work practices set a model for the 'empowerment' of their workforces.[94] Other observers charged that excessive adulation has been paid to Japanese managers and their production techniques, and that too little attention has been paid to the structural context which had sustained their past success.[95] For example, they argued that Japanese managers' performance is rather ordinary when stripped of their structural supports and they cited Japanese manufacturing after the burst of the 'bubble economy', and in the 'transplants' in Europe. However, some of these judgements might be unduly pessimistic – for example, Japanese transplant profitability seemed much higher in the late, compared to the early, 1990s.[96] Clearly Japanese companies were facing many challenges and much restructuring in the 1990s.

The 1990s: doubts and debates

In the early 1990s, an eight-part documentary series on *Nippon* by Peter Pagnamenta, head of BBC Documentary Films, attempted an even-handed account of Japan and its post-war development.[97] While it did not shy away from some of the dark and seamy sides of Japanese society, it was a striking and sympathetic story of dramatic economic success and Japan's challenge to western economic and political supremacy. From archives and interviews, the Japanese people emerged as remarkable and ingenious in their response to post-war difficulties. Particularly noteworthy and chastening for British audiences were those archival glimpses of British and Japanese workers who met in the 1950s and 1960s when British managers and workers were the industrial mentors in cars, steel and shipbuilding; and their counterpart interviews in the 1980s when the British had much to learn about where they went astray as the Japanese forged ahead. Yet, in January 2000, Peter Pagnamenta Associates returned with a three-part series on 'Bubble Troubles' to document what had gone wrong in Japan in the intervening decade, how that recession glimpsed at the end of the earlier series had proved difficult to shake off and how structural reform had proved difficult to effect.[98] Although rooting Japan's economic problems in the international agreement for yen appreciation in the 1985 Plaza Accord, many of Japan's subsequent current problems seemed self-inflicted – from policy failures, cover-ups or institutional rigidities. A strong subtext was of the wheel coming round, and Japan being urged to adopt Anglo-Saxon models for economic organization.

Compared to Macrae's 1960s high praise, Japanese bureaucracy is often now portrayed as central to the problem, failing in its regulatory duties and permitting the persistence of bad debt and corruption.[99] The community of interests built around company employees, to the relative neglect of share-holders, is cited as a priority for reform.[100] Those who drew lessons from Japan for British industry are likely to be challenged.[101]

The image of 'social cohesion' has been under attack implicitly and explic-itly in many news reports on Japan. 1995 was a particularly bad year. Analyses of the Kobe earthquake drew attention to weaknesses in public ser-vices.[102] Other accounts drew attention to the differential impact of the earthquake damage, and the revealed differences in income and wealth in Japan.[103] The sarin gas attack in Tokyo's subways was another occasion for articles which queried past emphasis on Japan's social cohesion.[104]

Yet against these images of Japan's difficulties in the 1990s, there are still observers who caution that Japan should not abandon some of its past strengths and 'throw out the baby with the bathwater' in adopting Anglo-Saxon models of economic organization. For example, Wolf argued that the true test of an economy should not just be seen in how it performs in good times but in how it does in bad times. Citing the 1997 OECD report on Japan's economy, he noted that, despite all the reported difficulties, Japan has managed to maintain relatively secure jobs for 25–55-year-old men and maintained relatively narrow income differentials between university grad-uates and junior high school graduates.[105] Wolf concluded that Japan has 'managed to distribute the gains from economic activity widely, while shielding those least able to bear the costs of recession'.[106] If Japan can con-tinue to do that in the twenty-first century, then Japan might continue to have lessons for other countries.

Conclusions

British enthusiasm for Japan as a source of inspiration for institutional reform owed much to changing perceptions of the national and interna-tional context of Japanese economic achievements, growing disappoint-ment about British economic performance, doubts about the efficacy of British institutions, and weaknesses in Europe and the USA. Notions of 'Japan as Number One', 'the East Asian Miracle' and 'the Pacific Century' might have been grossly overplayed, just as 'the decline of Britain' may have been too long exaggerated.[107] However, there is much irony in the current fashion in the West for advice to Japan about the virtues of Anglo-Saxon models of capitalism, given the substantial part played by lessons from Japan in reviving American and British manufacturing industry in the 1980s. As British awareness of Japan's economic recovery had grown in the 1960s, images of quality products were augmented by accounts of Japanese insti-tutions from economic planning to schools and factories. By the 1980s, British institutions such as industrial relations and the welfare state, which had enjoyed reverence as distinctively British inventions, were being scrutinized and checked against their Japanese counterparts. Of course, it is altogether too easy to exaggerate a unilinear trend in the recent past. Taking the longer view, we can recall the early admiration for Japan and British self-doubt in the Meiji era and note the six million visitors and favourable press comment for the 1910 'Japan-British Exhibition' in London.[108] However, where Meiji Japan had style and promise for the future, post-war Japan had substance and achievements. Where Japanese workers once arrived in Britain's north-east to learn shipbuilding, they now came to teach car assembly.[109] If their parent companies have started to learn lessons in management from French or American managers, it serves as a reminder that learning from others is a continuous process and that monopolies of virtue should not be too readily lavished on the currently fashionable model.[110]

Learning from Japan came through many channels and in many forms. Academic specialists on Japan have provided an important core of studies of Japanese institutions. That early group identified by Oba has been followed by later cohorts.[111] As Japan's significance in the world economy grew, the specialists were followed by researchers who followed up institutional studies in Britain with comparative study. UK and Japanese government departments have provided important conduits for learning. The UK Department of Trade and Industry has supported engineers' secondments to Japan and seminars for potential suppliers to Japanese inward investors.[112] JETRO, once renowned as a guiding light for Japanese exporters, has become more involved in schemes to support trade with Japan, including staff secondments and improvement seminars. British and Japanese companies have singly and collectively engaged in learning about Japan. While enumerating communication channels in the pubic domain is obviously easier than enumerating those in the private sector, the difficult task in either case is assessing their quality and impact.

While relations between governments are often used as proxy indicators for relations between societies, they are by no means wholly reliable guides. British government enthusiasm for Japanese inward investment has had mixed reactions from UK-based manufacturers and trade unions.[113] Judgements on the contribution of Japanese investment to reforms in British industry are strongly influenced by perspective – for example whether one looks across the economy or particular sectors or regions. In cross-cultural relations the satisfactory portrayal of 'the other' is one of the most intractable issues. For example, a cartoon of geisha set alongside a news report on internet usage among Japanese women invokes a powerful image.[114] The tendency to construct 'Japan' as the 'exotic other' has a long history, a mirror in which westerners can see reflected their own strengths and weaknesses, fears and desires.[115] While the grains of truth in stereotypes might be useful starting points, the danger is that the cartoon obscures the richer human story in the text.[116] While the growth of academic research on Japan has provided useful correctives to many of the overdrawn popular images, Francks felt that they were only modest 'straws in the wind' when compared to the powerful influences on popular attitudes of the exotic images in the media.[117] Although discussions of British media treatment of Japan acknowledge wider coverage, there is disappointment that coverage reflects neither the importance of Japan in the world nor its significance for Britain.[118] One newspaper, *The Financial Times*, is estimated to account for half of the press coverage of Japan.[119] While economic issues are generally thought to be among the better covered areas, discussion of institutional reform soon opens up discussion of the cultural underpinnings of social institutions and their workings.

Some argue that the Anglo-Japanese relationship is 'special' and that it has significant potential in facilitating the strengthening of the Europe-Japan link, widely acknowledged to be the weakest link in the trilateral relations between the three major regional blocks in the global economy (Japan, Europe and the US).[120] Yet the strength of any such link will depend on more than inter-government relations, it will depend also on the health and vigour of the multistranded relationships and mutual learning carried out in the wider society.

Notes

1. W. H. G. Armytage, *The Rise of the Technocrats: a Social History* (London: Routledge & Kegan Paul, 1965).
2. G. R. Searle, *The Quest for National Efficiency: a Study in British Politics and Political Thought, 1899–1914* (Oxford: Basil Blackwell, 1971).
3. C. Holmes, 'Sidney Webb (1859–1947) and Beatrice Webb (1858–1943) and Japan', in H. Cortazzi and G. Daniels (eds), *Britain and Japan 1859–1991: Themes and Personalities* (London: Routledge, 1991).
4. Allen's acquaintance with Japan dated back to his appointment in 1922 as a teacher at the Nagoya Commercial High School. His experiences in British government service are noted in M. M. Gowing, 'George Cyril Allen, 1900–1982', *Proceedings of the British Academy*, vol. 71 (1985), 480–2, and in S. Metzger-Court, 'Japanese Birthday: Taisho II, G. C. Allen (1900–1982) and Japan', in H. Cortazzi and G. Daniels (eds), *Britain and Japan 1859–1991: Themes and Personalities* (London: Routledge and The Japan Society). For a discussion of Allen's impression of interwar Japan, see Jon Pardoe's chapter in this volume.
5. See S. Oba, *The 'Japanese War': London University's WWII Secret Teaching Programme and the Experts Sent to Help Japan*, English edition translated by Anne Kaneko (London: Japan Library, 1995).
6. Brief sketches can be found in Oba, *The 'Japanese' War*. See also Sir Hugh Cortazzi's account of his years in diplomatic service in *Japan and Back and Places Elsewhere: a Memoir* (Folkstone: Global Oriental, 1998); Sir Peter Parker's account of his business involvement and broader Anglo-Japanese relations in *For Starters: a Life in Management* (London: Jonathan Cape, 1989). Ronald Dore's writings range across work organization, education and training, but their relevance for

Britain is most clearly put in *Taking Japan Seriously: a Confucian Perspective on Leading Economic Issues* (London: The Athlone Press, 1987).

7. R. Gray,'The Anglo-Japanese Commercial Treaty: a British Perspective', in I. Nish (ed.), *Britain and Japan: Biographical Portraits Vol. II* (London: Japan Society, 1997).

8. See *A Look at Japan: Report of a Visit Made by Sir Norman Kipping and Mr J. R. M. Whitehorn, October 1961* (London: Federation of British Industries, 1962).

9. Ibid.

10. EIU, *The Japanese Economy: a Survey Prepared for the FBI by the Economist Intelligence Unit (EIU)* (London: Federation of British Industries (FBI), 1962).

11. See, for example, 'Britain "Missing Chances of Japanese Trade"', *Daily Telegraph*, 14 November 1961.

12. See Ambassador Morland note to the Foreign Secretary, The Earl of Home, 8 November 1961: 'Sir Norman now faces the difficult task of encouraging a more informed and sympathetic attitude to Japan on the part of British industry'. PRO FO 371/158533.

13. Cortazzi, *Japan and Back*, p. 113.

14. See 'Annual Review for 1962', PRO FO 371/ 170743.

15. N. Macrae, 'Consider Japan', *The Economist*, 1 September 1962, pp. 787–819.

16. A. Maddison, *Economic Growth in Japan and the USSR* (London: George Allen & Unwin, 1965), p. xx.

17. 'Japan: Annual Report for 1964', PRO FO 371/181068.

18. This call was linked to praise for the efforts of the British Council. See note 17 above and Christopher Aldous' chapter in this volume.

19. N. Macrae, 'The Risen Sun', *The Economist*, 27 May 1967, pp. ix–xxxii.

20. Ibid., p. x.

21. Ibid., p. xii.

22. Ibid., p. xxiii.

23. R. Harris, 'Remnants of Confucianism an aid to industry', *The Times*, 22 May 1969.

24. See, for example, 'Japan: a Special Report', *The Times*, 17 June 1970, pp. i–xii.

25. See K. D. Brown, *Britain and Japan: Comparative Economic and Social History since 1900* (Manchester: Manchester University Press, 1998).

26. For further discussions of the learning from Japanese partners in BL and ICL, see the chapters by G. Owen, 'From Mass Market Manufacturer to Niche Player: Product and Marketing Strategy at British Leyland/Rover from 1968 to 1995', and M. Campbell-Kelly, 'ICL: From National Champion to Fujitsu's Little Helper', in E. Abe and T. Gourvish (eds), *Japanese Success? British Failure: Comparisons in Business Performance Since 1945* (Oxford: Oxford University Press, 1997).

27. R. P. Dore, *British Factory – Japanese Factory* (London: Allen and Unwin, 1973), pp. 358–64.

28. Professor R. P. Dore, 'Minutes of Evidence', Thursday 14 July 1977, The Select Committee on Science and Technology (Japan Sub-Committee) (London: HMSO, 1977).

29. OECD, *The Development of Industrial Relations Systems: Some Implications of Japanese Experience*. Report prepared after a multi-national study group visit, 20th September–4th October, 1975 (Paris: OECD, 1975).

30. C. Nishiyama and G. C. Allen, *The Price of Prosperity: Lessons from Japan*, Hobart Paper no. 58 (London: Institute for Economic Affairs, 1974).

31. See the accompanying book for the series of six films, H. Smith (ed.), *Inside Japan* (London: BBC, 1981).

32. M. Collick, 'A different society', in H Smith, *Inside Japan*, p. 58.

33. N. Wolfers,'The Great Japan Exhibition – a Foreword', in W. Watson (ed.), *The Great Japan Exhibition: Art of the Edo Period 1600–1868* (London: Royal Academy of Arts, 1981).

34. See L. Smith, 'The Great Japan Exhibition at the Royal Academy', *History Today*, October 1981, pp. 34–38, and the newspaper report in M. Walker, 'Inscrutable Plots behind Scrutable Art', *The Guardian*, 9 October 1981.

35. See M. Houser and A. Greville, 'Japan Incorporated', *The Times Educational Supplement*, 23 October 1981.

36. See, for example, the treatment by *The Observer* in 'The Great Japan Show' and 'Inside Japan Today', 18 October 1981.

37. 'The UK–Japan 2000 Group approaches the 21st century'. Chairmen's statement of the 15th Conference of the UK–Japan 2000 Group, Kisarazu, Chiba, 5–7 March 1999.

38. See, for example, R. Gott, 'The History of Isolation that Created the Successful Formula for a Sunrise Nation', *The Guardian*, 3 March 1986.

39. See contributions by Sir Hugh Cortazzi and Ronald Dore on Japan, *ESRC Newsletter*, no. 54, March 1985.

40. J. Pilger, 'Viewpoint 87: Japan – Behind the Mask', broadcast 13 January 1987, ITV.

41. N. Budgen, 'Lessons of Success and Subterfuge: Britain Could Never Copy the Japanese Way to Wealth', *The Guardian*, 2 May 1989.

42. R. Dore, *Taking Japan Seriously* (London: The Athlone Press, 1989).

43. For a fuller discussion of industrial relations in Britain, Japan and Japanese-owned factories in the UK, see B. McCormick and K. McCormick, *Japanese Companies: British Factories* (Aldershot: Avebury, 1996).

44. P. Bassett, *Strike Free: New Industrial Relations in Britain* (London: Macmillan, 1986).

45. See, the special issue of articles on the 'Japanization' of British industry in the *Industrial Relations Journal* (vol. 19, no. 1, 1988) edited by N. Oliver and B. Wilkinson.

46. See Tony Pegg, 'Hitachi two years on', *Personnel Management*, (October 1986), pp. 42–47; P. Wickens, *The Road to Nissan: Flexibility, Quality, Teamwork* (Basingstoke: Macmillan – now Palgrave Macmillan, 1987). The views of the Komatsu (UK) personnel director are given in C. Morton, *Becoming World Class* (Basingstoke: Macmillan – now Palgrave Macmillan, 1994). British managerial perspectives are discussed in M. Trevor, *Toshiba's New British Company: Competitiveness through Innovation in Industry* (London: Policy Studies Institute, 1988).

47. See Trevor, *Toshiba's New British Company*, pp. 47–8.

48. E. Hammond, *Maverick: The Life of a Union Rebel* (London: Weidenfeld & Nicolson, 1992), pp. 119–23.

49. Ibid.

50. K. Harper, 'AEU Threatens to End Single Union Agreement with Nissan', *The Guardian*, 22 March 1989.

51. Wickens, *The Road to Nissan*. p. 282.

52. N. Heaton and L. Linn, *Fighting Back: a Report on the Shop Steward Response to New Management Techniques in TGWU Region 10* (Bradford: Northern College and TGWU Region 10, 1989).

53. CAITS/ MTUCURC, *New Union Strategies: Trade Union Responses to New Management Techniques* (Centre for Alternative Industrial and Technological Strategies

and Merseyside Trade Union community and Unemployed Resource Centre, Liverpool, 1991).

54. K. Gill, 'Accusation of Racism Against Union is "Absurd and Ridiculous"', letter to the editor, *The Financial Times*, 30 September 1991. See the TUC debate in *Report of the 123rd Annual Trades Union Congress* (London: Trades Union Congress, 1991).

55. N. Oliver and B. Wilkinson, *The Japanisation of British Industry* (Oxford: Blackwell, 1992, second edition), p. 268.

56. G. Broad, 'Japan in Britain: the Dynamics of Joint Consultation', *Industrial Relations Journal*, vol. 25, no. 1 (March 1994), pp. 26–39.

57. G. Broad, 'The Managerial Limits to Japanisation: a Manufacturing Case Study', *Human Resources Management Journal*, vol. 4, no. 3 (1994), pp. 41–61.

58. Morton, *Becoming World Class*, p. 46.

59. K. McCormick, *Engineers in Japan and Britain: Education, Training and Employment* (London: Routledge, 2000).

60. For a fuller discussion of the controversy, see McCormick, ibid., pp. 48–54.

61. TUC, *The Future Business: Britain's Research and Development Crisis* (London: Trade Union Congress Publications 1985), p. 12.

62. Sir Kenneth Corfield, 'Getting the Engineers we Need', *Proceedings of the Institution of Mechanical Engineers*, vol. 198B, no. 14 (1984), pp. 243–8.

63. IMS, 'Competence and Competition: Training and Education in the Federal Republic of Germany, the United States and Japan', A report prepared by the Institute of Manpower Studies (IMS) for the National Economic Development Office (NEDO) and the Manpower Services Commission (MSC), 1984.

64. R. P. Dore and M. Sako, *How the Japanese Learn to Work* (London: Routledge, 1989).

65. For the exchanges between the government statisticians and the Engineering Council commissioned studies, see McCormick, *Engineers in Japan*, chapter 2.

66. S. J. Prais, 'Educating for Productivity: Comparisons of Japanese and English Schooling and Vocational Preparation', *National Institute Economic Review*, February 1987, pp. 40–56.

67. S. J. Prais, 'Qualified Manpower in Engineering: Britain and Other Industrially Advanced Countries', *National Institute Economic Review*, no. 127 (February 1988), pp. 76–83.

68. R. Lynn, *Educational Achievement: Lessons for the West* (Basingstoke: Macmillan – now Palgrave Macmillan, 1988).

69. I. Amano, 'The Bright and the Dark Sides of Japanese Education', *RSA Journal* (Journal of the Royal Society of Arts), vol. CXL, no. 5425 (January 1992), pp. 119–28.

70. R. Goodman, 'Who's Looking at Whom? Japanese, South Korean and English Educational Reform in Comparative Perspective', Nissan Occasional Paper Series number 11, 1989. See also M. Howarth, *Britain's Education Reform: a Comparison with Japan* (London: Routledge, 1991).

71. G. C. Allen, *Appointment in Japan* (London: Allen and Unwin, 1995).

72. See C. Handy, *The Making of Managers: a Report on Management Education, Training and Development in the USA, West Germany, France, Japan and the UK* (London: National Economic Development Report (NEDO), 1987); C. Handy, G. Gordon, I. Gow and C. Raddlesome (eds), *Making Managers* (London: Pitman, 1988); I. Gow, 'Japan', in C. Handy, G. Gordon, I. Gow and C. Raddlesome (eds), *Making Managers* (London: Pitman, 1988).

73. M. Richards, 'Baker, Young Back Business Training Reform', *The Times Higher Education Supplement*, 1 May 1987.
74. C. Handy, 'Missing Ingredient; Two Years on from "The Making of Managers", Charles Handy assesses the results', *The Times Higher Education Supplement*, 10 March 1989.
75. P. B. Smith and J. Misumi, 'Japanese Management – a Sun Rising in the West?', in C. L. Cooper and I. Robertson (eds), *International Review of Industrial and Organisational Psychology* (New York: John Wiley and Sons, 1989), pp. 329–69.
76. Ibid., p. 364.
77. H. Hasegawa and G. D. Hook (eds), *Japanese Business Management: Restructuring for Low Growth and Globalisation* (London: Routledge, 1998).
78. See M. Papaanastassiou and R. Pearce, 'The Internationalisation of Research and Development by Japanese Enterprises', *R&D Management*, vol. 24, no. 2 (1994), pp. 155–65, and M. Papaanastassiou and R. Pearce, 'The Research and Development of Japanese Multinational Enterprises in Europe', in F. Sachwald (ed.), *Japanese Firms in Europe* (Luxembourg: Harwood, 1995).
79. See C. Freeman, *Technology and Economic Performance: Lessons from Japan* (London: Frances Pinter and Freeman, 1987), p. 55.
80. The development of the Foresight Programme can be traced from the early studies by John Irvine and Ben Martin in J. Irvine and B. R. Martin, *Foresight in Science: Picking the Winners* (London: Frances Pinter, 1984); B. R. Martin and J. Irvine, *Research Foresight: Priority-Setting in Science* (London: Pinter Publishers, 1989); Office of Science and Technology, *The Future in Focus: a Summary of National Foresight Programmes* (London: Department of Technology, 1998).
81. G. C. Allen, 'Why Japan's Economy has Prospered', *Lloyd's Bank Review*, no. 111 (January 1974), p. 41.
82. M. Prowse, 'What Japan can Teach the West', *The Financial Times*, 26 September 1987. For later research on weakening social cohesion in Japanese neighbourhoods, see C. Aldous and F. Leishman, 'Policing in Post-War Japan: Reform, Reversion and Reinvention'. *International Journal of the Sociology of Law*, vol. 25 (1997) 135–54, and C. Aldous and F. Leishman, 'Police and Community Safety in Japan: Model or Myth?', *Crime Prevention and Community Safety: An International Journal*, vol. 1, no. 1 (1999) pp. 25–39.
83. R. Rose, 'Welfare: the lesson from Japan', *New Society*, 28 June 1989.
84. D. Howell, *Easternisation* (London: Demos, 1995).
85. E. Mortimer, 'Values of the East: the West Could Learn Much by Paying More Attention to Asia', *The Financial Times*, 27 September 1995.
86. R. Pinker, 'Social Welfare in Japan and Britain: a Comparative View. Formal and Informal Aspects of Welfare', in E. Oyen (ed.), *Comparing Welfare States and Their Futures* (Aldershot: Gower, 1986).
87. C. Jones, 'The Pacific Challenge: Confucian Welfare States', in C. Jones (ed.), *New Perspectives on the Welfare State in Europe* (London: Routledge, 1993).
88. A. Gould, *Capitalist Welfare Systems: a Comparison of Japan, Britain and Sweden* (London: Longman 1993), p. 87.
89. G. White and R. Goodman, 'Welfare Orientalism and the Search for an East Asian welfare', in R. Goodman, G. White and H. Kwon (eds), *The East Asian Welfare Model* (London: Routledge, 1998).
90. R. G. Wilkinson, *Unhealthy Societies: the Afflictions of Inequality* (London and New York: Routledge, 1996), p. 130.

91. House of Commons Employment Committee, *The Import and Export of Jobs: The Future for Manufacturing*. Volume 1: Report and Proceedings of the Committee (London: HMSO, 1994).
92. House of Commons Trade and Industry Committee, *Competitiveness of UK Manufacturing Industry*, Second Report, (London: HMSO, 1994).
93. Three of the five had Japanese links: the Nissan and Sony plants were wholly-owned subsidiaries, while ICL was largely Japanese-owned by Fujitsu. See A. Ferguson, 'Britain's Best Factories', *Management Today*, (November 1989), pp. 69–96.
94. Paul Stewart (ed.), *Beyond Japanese Management: the End of Modern Times?* (Ilford, Essex: Frank Cass Publishers, 1997).
95. C. Haslam and K. Williams, with S. Johal and J. Williams, 'A Fallen Idol? Japanese Management in the 1990s' in P. Stewart, *Beyond Japanese Management*, p. 33.
96. JETRO, *The 14th Survey of European Operations of Japanese Companies in the Manufacturing Sector* (Tokyo: JETRO, 1998).
97. A book accompanied the series and drew on many of the film's interviews: W. Horsley and R. Buckley, *Nippon: New Superpower* (London: BBC Books, 1990).
98. Pagnamenta Associates, 'Bubble Trouble' screened on BBC2 10, 17 and 24 January 2000.
99. See, for example: P. Abrahams and G. Tett, 'Japan Reaps What it Sowed: Crisis in the Financial System has its Roots in Flimsy Regulation and Poor Policy-making', *The Financial Times*, 1 December 1997; G. Tett, 'Japan's Mighty Ministry Trembles: Prosecutors raid Tokyo's Most Powerful Economic Policy-making Body', *The Financial Times*, 27 January 1998; M. Nakamoto, 'Japan Sokaiya Scandal Embroils More Companies', *The Financial Times*, 28 October 1997.
100. See P. Abraham, 'Japan's Ray of Hope; Desperately Poor Returns are Forcing the Corporate Sector to Look at Anglo-Saxon Solutions', *The Financial Times*, 6 May 1998.
101. See, for example, J. J. Boulter, 'Evangelists for "Japanese Way" can eat Their Hats', *The Financial Times*, 26 January 1999. Boulter, a manager in the auto component industry, attacked the slavish advocacy of Japan's industrial system for a more fragmented competitive structure in the UK.
102. See, for example, W. Dawkins, 'Faith in the Authorities Fades: William Dawkins Explains why the Japanese were Unprepared for This Week's Earthquake Devastation', *The Financial Times*, 21/22 January 1995, and H. Gourdon, 'Why They Left Her to Weep in the Rubble: the Plight of Kobe's Earthquake Victims was Worsened by the Competence of the Authorities. Hugo Gourdon, Recently Returned from Japan, Explains the Failure', *The Daily Telegraph*, 27 January 1995.
103. K, Rafferty, 'Japan's Poor Bear Brunt of Quake that Ended Middle-class Myth: Kevin Rafferty in Tokyo Examines a Once Hidden Class Divide now Exposed by Nature', *The Guardian*, 26 January 1995.
104. See, for example, W. Dawkins ' "Attack from Within" Leaves Japan Shaken: it Threatens an Ordered Society and Challenges a Cherished Group Ethic', *The Financial Times*, 24 April 1995, and W. Dawkins, 'Trial to Reveal as Much about Japan as Aum', *The Financial Times*, 24 April 1996.
105. M. Wolf, 'Too Great a Sacrifice: Japan Must Reform and Deregulate its Economy, but Without Destroying the Enviable Long-term Security and Trust Enshrined in its Labour Market', *The Financial Times*, 14 January 1997.
106. Ibid.
107. R. Foot and A. Walter, 'Whatever happened to the Pacific Century?', *International Studies Association*, vol. 25, Special Issue, December 1999.

108. A. Hotta-Lister, 'The Japan–British Exhibition of 1910: the Japanese Organisers', in I. Nish (ed.), *Britain and Japan: Biographical Portraits* (Folkstone: Japan Society Publications, 1994).

109. M. Conte-Helm, *Japan and the North East of England: From 1862 to the Present-Day* (London: The Athlone Press, 1989).

110. While the UK plant of Nissan continues to win high praise for its efficiency, Renault has taken a 37 per cent stake in the heavily indebted parent company.

111. Other scholars included Professors Nish and Bownas; see Oba, *The 'Japanese War'*, pp. 137–9.

112. A scheme to send engineers to Japan began in 1982 and was revamped as 'Engineers to Japan' in 1991, administered as by the Royal Academy of Engineering on behalf of the UK Department of Trade and Industry. A 'Learning from Japan – Supply Chain Improvement Seminar' was one of several activities jointly hosted the DTI and JETRO under the 'Action Japan' Campaign' in 1995.

113. Criticism of the impact of Japanese inward investment on employment in existing UK car plants was raised with the House of Commons Select Committee by Ian McAllister (chairman and managing director of Ford UK), see P. Bassett, 'Japanese Rivals Anger Ford', *Financial Times*, 11 March 1993. It was followed by warnings from the president of the Society of Motor Manufacturers and Traders, Geoffrey Whalen (also managing director of Peugeot Talbot UK), see K. Eason, 'Car Chief Warns on Survival', *The Times*, 23 March 1993.

114. See A. Nusbaum, 'Women Lead the Way in Land of Rising Web', *Financial Times*, 11 August 1999.

115. I. Littlewood, *The Idea of Japan: Western Images, Western Myths* (London: Secker & Warburg, 1996). See also the discussion of some similar themes in E. Wilkinson, *Japan versus Europe: a History of Misunderstanding* (Harmondsworth: Penguin Books, 1983), and the revised edition as E. Wilkinson, *Japan versus the West: Image and Reality* (Harmondsworth: Penguin Books, 1990).

116. See C. Hardie, 'This Distasteful Geisha Image is Far From Reality', Letter to the Editor, *Financial Times*, 16 August 1999.

117. P. Francks, 'Alice Through the Looking Glass: we feel threatened by the strength of Japan's economy, but our picture of cut-throat competition is far from reality – a mirror in which we see our own strengths and weaknesses, fears and desires', *The Times Higher Education Supplement*, 20 September 1991.

118. See, for example, D. W. Anthony, 'How Japan is Reported in the British Press', in M. Teeuwen (ed.), *Research Papers in Japanese Studies No. 1* (Cardiff: Cardiff Centre for Japanese Studies, Cardiff Business School, 1996); P. Hammond (ed.), *Images of Japan* (London and Washington: Cassell, 1997); T. Mayes and M. Rowling, 'The Image Makers: British Journalists on Japan', in Hammond (ed.), *Images of Japan*.

119. D. Powers, 'Japan in the Media and Media in Japan', *Proceedings of the Japan Society*, no. 134 (Winter 1999), pp. 5–12.

120. H. Satoh, 'The UK and Japan: a Special Relationship into the 21st Century', Briefing Paper no. 46, Asia-Pacific Programme (London: The Royal Institute of International Affairs, 1998).

Index